VOLUME 641   MAY 2012

THE ANNALS

of The American Academy of Political
and Social Science

Immigration and the Changing Social Fabric of American Cities

Special Editors:

JOHN MacDONALD
University of Pennsylvania

ROBERT J. SAMPSON
Harvard University

Los Angeles | London | New Delhi
Singapore | Washington DC

The American Academy of Political and Social Science

202 S. 36th Street, Annenberg School for Communication, University of Pennsylvania,
Philadelphia, PA 19104-3806; (215) 746-6500; (215) 573-2667 (fax); www.aapss.org

Origin and Purpose. The Academy was organized December 14, 1889, to promote the progress of political and social science, especially through publications and meetings. The Academy does not take sides in controverted questions, but seeks to gather and present reliable information to assist the public in forming an intelligent and accurate judgment.

Meetings. The Academy occasionally holds a meeting in the spring extending over two days.

Publications. THE ANNALS of The American Academy of Political and Social Science is the bimonthly publication of the Academy. Each issue contains articles on some prominent social or political problem, written at the invitation of the editors. These volumes constitute important reference works on the topics with which they deal, and they are extensively cited by authorities throughout the United States and abroad.

Membership. Each member of the Academy receives THE ANNALS and may attend the meetings of the Academy. Membership is open only to individuals. Annual dues: $94.00 for the regular paperbound edition (clothbound, $134.00). Members may also purchase single issues of THE ANNALS for $35 each (clothbound, $48). Student memberships are available for $52.00.

Subscriptions. THE ANNALS of The American Academy of Political and Social Science (ISSN 0002-7162) (J295) is published bimonthly—in January, March, May, July, September, and November—by SAGE Publications, 2455 Teller Road, Thousand Oaks, CA 91320. Periodicals postage paid at Thousand Oaks, California, and at additional mailing offices. POSTMASTER: Send address changes to The Annals of The American Academy of Political and Social Science, c/o SAGE Publications, 2455 Teller Road, Thousand Oaks, CA 91320. Institutions may subscribe to THE ANNALS at the annual rate: $827 (clothbound, $933). Single issues of THE ANNALS may be obtained by individuals who are not members of the Academy for $106 each (clothbound, $155). Single issues of THE ANNALS have proven to be excellent supplementary texts for classroom use. Direct inquiries regarding adoptions to THE ANNALS c/o SAGE Publications (address below).

All correspondence concerning membership in the Academy, dues renewals, inquiries about membership status, and/or purchase of single issues of THE ANNALS should be sent to THE ANNALS c/o SAGE Publications, 2455 Teller Road, Thousand Oaks, CA 91320. Telephone: (800) 818-SAGE (7243) and (805) 499-0721; Fax/Order line: (805) 375-1700; e-mail: journals@sagepub.com. *Please note that orders under $30 must be prepaid.* For all customers outside the Americas, please visit http://www.sagepub.co.uk/customerCare.nav for information.

Printed on acid-free paper

THE ANNALS

Editorial Office: 202 S. 36th Street, Philadelphia, PA 19104-3806
For information about membership* (individuals only) and subscriptions (institutions), address:
SAGE Publications
2455 Teller Road
Thousand Oaks, CA 91320

For SAGE Publications: Allison Leung (Production) and Lori Hart (Marketing)

From India and South Asia, write to:	From Europe, the Middle East, and Africa, write to:
SAGE PUBLICATIONS INDIA Pvt Ltd	SAGE PUBLICATIONS LTD
B-42 Panchsheel Enclave, P.O. Box 4109	1 Oliver's Yard, 55 City Road
New Delhi 110 017	London EC1Y 1SP
INDIA	UNITED KINGDOM

*Please note that members of the Academy receive THE ANNALS with their membership.
International Standard Serial Number ISSN 0002-7162
International Standard Book Number ISBN 978-1-4522-5653-5 (Vol. 641, 2012) paper
International Standard Book Number ISBN 978-1-4522-5-652-8 (Vol. 641, 2012) cloth
Manufactured in the United States of America. First printing, May 2012.

Please visit http://ann.sagepub.com and under the "More about this journal" menu on the right-hand side, click on the Abstracting/Indexing link to view a full list of databases in which this journal is indexed.

Information about membership rates, institutional subscriptions, and back issue prices may be found on the facing page.

Advertising. Current rates and specifications may be obtained by writing to The Annals Advertising and Promotion Manager at the Thousand Oaks office (address above). Acceptance of advertising in this journal in no way implies endorsement of the advertised product or service by SAGE or the journal's affiliated society(ies) or the journal editor(s). No endorsement is intended or implied. SAGE reserves the right to reject any advertising it deems as inappropriate for this journal.

Claims. Claims for undelivered copies must be made no later than six months following month of publication. The publisher will supply replacement issues when losses have been sustained in transit and when the reserve stock will permit.

Change of Address. Six weeks' advance notice must be given when notifying of change of address. Please send the old address label along with the new address to the SAGE office address above to ensure proper identification. Please specify the name of the journal.

THE ANNALS
OF THE AMERICAN ACADEMY OF POLITICAL AND SOCIAL SCIENCE

Volume 641   May 2012

IN THIS ISSUE:

Immigration and the Changing Social Fabric of American Cities

Special Editors: JOHN MacDONALD and ROBERT J. SAMPSON

FORTHCOMING

Bringing Fieldwork Back In: Contemporary Urban Ethnographic Research
Special Editors: ELIJAH ANDERSON, DUKE W. AUSTIN, ESTHER C. KIM,
VANI S. KULKARNI, and DANA ASBURY

Migrant Youth and Children of Migrants in a Globalized World
Special Editors: MARTA TIENDA and ALICIA ADSERA

Keywords: immigration; place; social fabric; demographic changes

The World in a City: Immigration and America's Changing Social Fabric

By
JOHN MacDONALD
and
ROBERT J. SAMPSON

The United States in 2012 faces unprecedented challenges brought on by economic crisis and the unrelenting pace of globalization and technological change. We are perhaps unique as a nation, however, in the changes wrought by continuing population diversification and foreign immigration from countries across the globe. Indeed, the United States is currently one of the most diverse nations on earth, which spells to some observers coming ruin and to others unprecedented renewal. Whichever position one might take, there can be little doubt that immigration has radically changed the nation's composition.

Consider for a moment the magnitude and character of recent change. Foreign immigration to the United States rose sharply in the 1990s, as did its concentration in the immigrant enclaves of our large cities. In fact, the foreign-born population increased by more than 50 percent in just 10 years and neared peak levels

John MacDonald is an associate professor of criminology at the University of Pennsylvania and director of the Jerry Lee Center of Criminology. He works on topics such as interpersonal violence, race and ethnic disparities in criminal justice, and the effectiveness of social policy responses to crime. His recent work appears in the American Journal of Preventive Medicine, Criminology, Journal of the American Statistical Association, American Journal of Public Health, *and* The Economic Journal.

Robert J. Sampson is Henry Ford II Professor of the Social Sciences at Harvard University and director of the Social Sciences Program at the Radcliffe Institute for Advanced Study. He is also president of the American Society of Criminology and the Ernest Burgess Fellow of the American Academy of Political and Social Science. His most recent book, Great American City: Chicago and the Enduring Neighborhood Effect, *was published in January 2012 by the University of Chicago Press.*

DOI: 10.1177/0002716212438939

historically, to over 30 million residents by 2000. Migration from Mexico was especially large, with Latino Americans constituting the largest minority group at 15 percent of the population. Immigrant flows receded somewhat after 9/11 but remained high. Today, there are over 40 million foreign immigrants, representing 13 percent of the total population. Over half of these immigrants are from Latin America (Acosta and Cru 2011). Reaching a demographic "tipping point," minority babies also outnumber white infants, according to new projections from the U.S. Census Bureau (Frey 2011)—whites are thus in line to become the nation's minority in the not-too-distant future. Perhaps unexpectedly, the United States is increasingly diverse not only in its cities but in its suburbs and rural towns as well (Crowley and Lichter 2009; Saenz 2004).

What are the implications of these profound changes in ethnic diversity and immigration for the American twenty-first century? The prognosis is by some accounts dire. Political debates on U.S. immigration policy frequently connect immigrants to a variety of social ills, including crime, lower educational attainment, moral decline, and the lowering of human capital skills. We have been down this road once before, of course, when immigration from Europe reshaped the landscape of American cities in the early twentieth century, prompting widespread fears and predictions of social deterioration. Rather remarkably, then, such concerns are still with us—what has changed is that the targets of concern hail from different parts of the world.

The changing character of immigration combined with the magnitude of recent increases has thus (re)stoked a high-stakes debate about America's future. We enter this debate by presenting a set of original papers on the consequences of immigration for reshaping the nation's social fabric. For more than 100 years, *The Annals* has been devoted to key issues in urban scholarship, with special attention placed on the relationship between immigration and social policy. Within this volume, we build on this long tradition by presenting new research on trends in spatial patterns of immigration that are crucial to understanding how immigration as a social process is transforming the American city and increasingly the hinterland.

The Setting

Social scientists in the early twentieth century focused a considerable amount of attention on how immigration trends affected crime, "pauperism," and other social outcomes. In one of the first papers of its kind, William S. Bennet, congressman from New York and member of the Immigration Commission, authored "Immigrants and Crime" for the 1909 volume of *The Annals* (Vol. 34; Bennet 1909). He argued that the image of immigrants and crime was a result of loose U.S. immigration policy, but that the majority of immigrants arriving through legal means were in fact law-abiding. Carl Kelsey, a professor of sociology at Penn, noted in his later essay on immigration and crime (*The Annals* Vol. 125) that while scholars of the early twentieth century had sought evidence that "later arrivals were more likely to be criminals than were their predecessors" (p. 165), their focus was driven largely by prejudice (Kelsey 1926). He cited evidence that trends in crime rates in New York City from 1830 to 1919 were largely stable, despite a massive wave of immigration in the nineteenth century. Kelsey also noted that immigrants were underrepresented as a share of the population of state prisons.

At about the same time, sociologists of the "Chicago School" of urban sociology began to document how a diverse set of social outcomes varied together across time and space. For example, phenomena as different as crime, infant mortality, tuberculosis, school dropout, and unemployment clustered together in select neighborhoods of cities like Chicago and Philadelphia (for a review, see Sampson 2012). Both ethnographic and quantitative research studies over the first half of the twentieth century continued to reveal consistent connections between the social fabric and physical environment of big-city neighborhoods where immigrants clustered. European immigration, especially from Ireland and Italy, was linked to numerous indicators of population well-being through the process of immigrant settlement into high-poverty and presumably "socially disorganized" neighborhoods (Shaw and McKay 1942/1969). The primary concern ultimately became what happened to second-generation immigrants (the children of immigrants) who were exposed to living in urban neighborhoods that were ethnically diverse, poor, and characterized by vice and crime.

Edwin Sutherland and Thorsten Sellin, prominent sociologists of the first half of the twentieth century, were early proponents of using social science to dispel the myth of the causal connection between immigration and crime. Both of these distinguished sociologists suggested that the correlations between immigrant patterns and crime were largely the result of differential age composition and selection processes that channeled immigrants into neighborhoods with multiple disadvantages. Immigrant youth were more exposed to concentrated poverty, crime, and poor health, they argued, as well as to American cultural norms that were favorable to criminal offending. Sellin referred to the latter as the "culture of conflict," whereas Sutherland discussed this process within the context of his theory of differential association (Sellin 1938; Sutherland 1947). Their common argument was that it was not immigration per se that accounted for social ills but, rather, the conditions in the areas that attracted immigrants on their early entry into American society.

Fast-forwarding to today, we find an eerily similar set of arguments but with different theories and target immigrant groups. The result is that we are witnessing a scenario both similar to and different from early-twentieth-century America. Now, as then, for example, growth in immigration, along with ethnic diversity more generally, is commonly associated in the larger public sphere with increasing crime and social deterioration (Buchanan 2006). The nation's largest cities in the 1920s and 1930s were virtual poster children for the theory of immigration and decay, as they received an influx of European immigrants. But as noted,

Sutherland, Sellin, and others pointed instead to social change rather than the criminal propensity of first-generation immigrants. Similarly, today there is a body of emerging research that challenges the view that immigration, this time largely from Latin America, is linked to increased crime and other social ills. Contemporary research also undermines the oft-stated claim that the second generation is inevitably hobbled in its quest for social mobility and integration into the American mainstream.

There is compelling evidence, for example, that today's immigrant gateway cities in the United States have experienced some of the largest reductions in crime, exactly the opposite of widely voiced predictions. New York, long a leading magnet for immigration, has for the past decade ranked as one of America's safest cities. Crime in Los Angeles dropped considerably in the late 1990s and into the first decade of the 2000s, as it did in other cities with a large Hispanic population such as San Jose, Dallas, and Phoenix. The same can be said for cities along the border, like El Paso and San Diego, which have ranked as low-crime areas for some time. Cities of concentrated immigration are simply some of the safest places around, and many decaying inner-city areas gained population in the 1990s and became more vital in large part through the process of immigrant diffusion. In Chicago, site of the original wave of urban scholarship, crime also dropped in the late 1990s as immigration surged (Sampson 2008). One of the most thriving areas of economic activity in the entire Chicago area, second only to the famed Miracle Mile of Michigan Avenue, is the 26th Street corridor in Little Village. Moreover, there is strong evidence that the second generation is moving into the mainstream in all walks of life even as they retain core aspects of their ethnic heritage (Kasinitz et al. 2008).

These kinds of economic and demographic changes constitute a major social force, and immigrants are not the only potential beneficiaries—native-born blacks, whites, and other traditional groups in the United States have all been exposed (albeit unevenly) to lower crime rates, declines in segregation and concentrated poverty, and increases in the economic and civic health of central cities. For the first time in New York City's history, the income of blacks in Queens has surpassed that of whites, for example, with the surge in the black middle class driven largely by the successes of black immigrants from the West Indies. There are many inner-city neighborhoods rejuvenated by immigration besides Queens and the Lower West Side of Chicago. From Bushwick in Brooklyn, to Miami, to large swaths of south-central Los Angeles and the rural South, to pockets of the north and south sides of Chicago, immigration is reshaping America. It follows that the spatial "externalities" associated with immigration are multiple in character and potentially influence *all* groups in the host society (Sampson 2012).

These patterns suggest that it is time for social scientists to rethink immigration and consider anew the role that immigrants play in patterns of neighborhood population turnover, crime, employment, economic revitalization, and other social outcomes. By doing so in this volume, *The Annals* continues to be on the leading edge of urban scholarship on a timely topic of fundamental importance to current political debates on immigration policy.

About This Volume

Although there is no shortage of research these days on immigration, the editors were motivated to bring together a leading set of scholars to present new research on trends in the spatial forms of immigration that are transforming the American landscape—the effects of "the world in a city," as it were. We aimed for a distinctive analytic focus—as a whole the volume is characterized by a comparative approach, an examination of recent immigration trends, disaggregation by ethnicity or immigrant type wherever possible, a focus on core features of the nation's social fabric (e.g., violence, legitimacy of social institutions, governance, economic well-being), and empirical study going beyond the big cities of traditional concern to a host of smaller cities and towns reaching into far-flung pockets of the country. As a result, the lineup includes papers on both familiar cities such as New York, Los Angles, Chicago, and Miami as well as places as different as San Antonio; Nashville; Boston; Dublin; Hazleton, Pennsylvania; and St. James, Minnesota. While the places studied and features of social fabric may differ, the social processes underlying the spatial forms of immigration are shown to be largely the same.

Before drilling down to specific places, however, we start out the volume with a national and timely focus on key facts about immigration and social policy in the recession's wake. In "Immigration Enforcement Policies, the Economic Recession, and the Size of Local Mexican Immigrant Populations," Emilio A. Parrado discusses the implementation of the federal 287(g) program. This federal program provides incentives for local authorities to participate in immigration control. Parrado examines the effect of the 287(g) program on the geographic dispersion of the Mexican immigration population and the employment prospects for low-skilled native black and white workers. Parrado shows that outside of a few outliers, there is no direct effect of the 287(g) program on the size of the Mexican population or the job prospects of low-skilled white and black workers. Parrado notes that even under the unlikely assumption that all deported undocumented Mexicans would never reenter the United States, it would take almost 30 years to remove this population. Parrado closes by noting that there is a lack of clear economic benefits to native white and black low-skilled workers from the removal of undocumented Mexicans and that particular regions of the country that rely on Mexican immigration to stabilize population loss are harmed through strict immigration enforcement of this kind.

A number of the articles that follow trace the path of immigration in particular cities both large and small. As noted in our introduction, immigration is typically associated in the public imagination with ethnic enclaves in large older cities of the East and Midwest. While this might have been true of twentieth-century immigration, the current scene is fascinating for its differences, with potentially important implications for America's future. Two articles present original data on the phenomenon of global immigration flows into smaller cities, rural towns, and Southern cities.

In "Can Immigration Save Small-Town America? Hispanic Boomtowns and the Uneasy Path to Renewal," Patrick J. Carr, Daniel T. Lichter, and Maria J. Kefalas provide a provocative look at immigration in Hazleton, Pennsylvania, and a matched town of St. James, Minnesota. These authors argue that promoting immigration may be an important source for saving dwindling populations and coincident economic decline in rural communities. At the same time, they note the real challenges that small towns face in incorporating new immigrant residents. The comparative work contrasting two cities with different approaches to immigrant populations highlights the potential strengths of a local stakeholder's approach that takes into account the economic needs of rural American small towns. Their contribution is an important guide to the kinds of social issues that will arise as immigration continues its diffusion from the big gateway cities of traditional scholarship.

Equally provocative, Jamie Winders takes us down to Nashville, Tennessee, to explore "Immigrants in New Cities: Institutional Visibility, Neighborhoods, and Immigration." Winders notes the challenges that arose when the growing, mostly Latino, immigrant population was not directly incorporated into a "new urbanism" plan that provided neighborhood control of local government urban planning and the provision of city services. Winders highlights that an overlooked feature of immigrant incorporation into the social fabric of cities is how cities plan for immigrants within the structures of local government. In the case of Nashville, it appears that the new urbanism plan for the city did not distinctly recognize that immigrants were scattered throughout the city and did not have sufficient representation in any set of neighborhoods to advocate for their own desires for neighborhood planning and city services. Winders concludes that cities moving toward a neighborhood-based governance model will inevitably leave out plans for immigrants if this politically vulnerable group preoccupied with life's struggles is not directly incorporated into city planning and governance.

Winders's article raises the interesting issue of institutional legitimacy in the immigrant experience, with broad implications for governance. This topic is explored in a different way in "The Paradox of Law Enforcement in Immigrant Communities: Does Tough Immigration Enforcement Undermine Public Safety?" by David S. Kirk, Andrew V. Papachristos, Jeffrey Fagan, and Tom R. Tyler. Their article raises important questions about the implications that the enforcement of immigration laws by local police can have for alienating immigrant communities from the criminal justice system. They note that cooperation and compliance with the law is enhanced when local residents believe that laws are enforced fairly. Relying on survey data from New York City residents, this study examines perceived injustices perpetrated by the criminal justice system and the willingness of residents to cooperate with the police in immigrant communities. They find that immigrant communities, compared to nonimmigrant communities, are *more cooperative with the police* and *less cynical of the law*. Kirk and colleagues conclude by questioning the wisdom of enacting "get tough" immigration policies, particularly against noncriminal aliens, and jeopardizing the current heightened cooperation with the police and lack of legal cynicism.

Garth Davies and Jeffrey Fagan take things one step further in their article, "Crime and Policing in Immigrant Neighborhoods: Evidence from New York City." Focusing on the connections between different immigrant concentrations and crime in New York City, Davies and Fagan find that immigrant concentration for the most part is associated with lower crime rates, and at the same time specific immigrant groups experience greater police enforcement than one would expect from simply examining crime rates. Their article contributes to our understanding that immigrant concentration is associated with lower crime rates, and that policing also differs by immigrant clusters. This article raises important questions about whether "zero tolerance" or proactive forms of policing are an appropriate approach to controlling crime in immigrant communities that have crime rates lower than one would expect by simply examining local poverty rates. Taken together, the set of articles by Winders, Kirk and colleagues, and Davies and Fagan raise an important caution about strategies for urban governance in the new wave of immigration.

The next set of articles probe more directly the association, potentially causal, between immigration and crime rates. Because violence is perhaps the leading indicator of a city's viability and prospects for human well-being, it has played a special role in the immigration debate. The articles here extend this debate in new ways.

In "Are Immigrant Youth Less Violent? Specifying the Reasons and Mechanisms," John MacDonald and Jessica Saunders examine the connection between immigrant households and youth violence, drawing on sociological and public health literature. MacDonald and Saunders present a critique of popular culture perspectives on immigrant families and youth violence, showing that crime and violence outcomes are if anything better for youth in immigrant families than one would expect given the social disadvantages that many immigrant households find themselves living in. Their analyses show a persistent lower rate of violence exposure for immigrant youth compared to similarly situated nonimmigrant youth. These differences are not meaningfully understood by traditional sociological mechanisms. The authors focus then on the apparent paradox of why youth living in immigrant households in relative disadvantage have lower violence exposure compared to nonimmigrants living in similar social contexts. The answers, they argue, can be viewed from an examination of the effects that living in poverty and underclass neighborhoods for generations has on nonimmigrants in American cities.

Charis E. Kubrin and Hiromi Ishizawa take a city-level comparative approach to examine how and why patterns of immigration and violence may vary across neighborhoods. In "Why Some Immigrant Neighborhoods Are Safer than Others: Divergent Findings from Los Angeles and Chicago," the authors point to the important role of the larger spatial ecology in which neighborhoods are embedded, in that immigrant enclaves appear to reduce the risk of homicide only when they are situated in specific spatial contexts. When immigrants reside in areas surrounded by high poverty and crime in central Los Angeles, there is no protective effect of immigrant neighborhoods. On the other hand, when immigrant neighborhoods are surrounded by middle-class neighborhoods, as is the case for Chicago and the San Fernando Valley area of Los Angeles, immigrant residential concentration is associated with lower homicide risk. This article shows again the importance of spatial externalities in considering the effects of immigration on the social fabric.

In "Extending Immigration and Crime Studies: National Implications and Local Settings," Ramiro Martinez Jr. and Jacob Stowell revisit the immigration and violence debate with new analyses of homicide in Miami, Florida, and San Antonio, Texas, followed by a national-level analysis. The article starts with these two comparative cases because they mirror the immigration influx, Latino growth, and homicide decline seen throughout the country since 1980. Their findings are also replicated in an analysis of the immigration and crime influx across the nation using U.S. counties in 2000. Comparing different time points, homicide types, and levels of analysis (individual/community/national), and even controlling for Latino regional concentration, they report clear evidence that more immigrants did not mean more homicide. This article highlights the mounting evidence from multiple layers of analyses that immigration is not linked to more violence.

In "Immigrants and Social Distance: Examining the Social Consequences of Immigration for Southern California Neighborhoods over 50 Years," John R. Hipp and Adam Boessen take a different tack by examining the long-term effects of immigration on neighborhood compositional change. Hipp and Boessen note in their 50-year analysis that there are few direct negative consequences of immigrant inflow on neighborhood housing values, home vacancies, or unemployment rates. They instead find no evidence that immigrants reduce the desirability of neighborhoods, at least in terms of home values or unemployment rates. The bottom line in this article counters commonly stated concerns that an influx of immigrants will inevitably lower housing values and employment rates in local neighborhoods. And where these authors find any effect on these outcomes, they are small and very context-dependent.

In "The Limits of Spatial Assimilation for Immigrants' Full Assimilation: Emerging Evidence from African Immigrants in Boston and Dublin," Zoua Vang takes a comparative approach to the question of assimilation and residential integration, in this case revisiting the source of much twentieth-century immigration—Ireland. Vang provides an important contribution for comparative work and methods for measuring residential segregation. This article discusses how differences in migration reasons to the United States and Ireland for immigrants from Africa (primarily economic for the United States versus political for Ireland) and the housing policies in each country shape differences in residential segregation. Ironically, Ireland is more homogeneous in population and yet has less residential segregation of African immigrants. Vang highlights how racial stratification of housing in the United States prevents African immigrants from residential assimilation to the same degree as in Ireland. She argues that the integration in Ireland was made possible by the supply of new housing and private rentals that African immigrants could afford and were permitted to move into. This experience is quite a contrast with that seen in the United States. But at the same time, Vang points out that residential assimilation in Ireland does not translate to economic parity. The comparison of Boston and Dublin provides important insight into the kinds of housing policies that are effective in the incorporation of new immigrant groups.

Finally, Stephanie M. DiPietro and Robert J. Bursik return to the national level for a look at the dangers of aggregating across immigrant groups. In "Studies of the New Immigration: The Dangers of Pan-Ethnic Classifications," they argue that by ignoring country of origin in pan-ethnic classifications, we might mask important differences that emerge on social indicators. DiPietro and Bursik rely on data from the Children of Immigrants Longitudinal Study to illustrate how pan-ethnic classifications in fact mask important within-immigrant variation in fighting behavior among adolescents. This work has important implications for a broad range of research that examines the connections between immigration or immigrants and different social outcomes, since ignoring the context through which different groups migrate and integrate into the United States is critical for understanding how immigration influences the social fabric. DiPietro and Bursik's warning serves as a fitting close to the volume: while immigration as a process yields many commonalities, "immigrants" themselves are not a uniform group and thus experience the manifestations of immigrant incorporation in distinct ways.

Reshaping the City and Beyond

Taken as a whole, the articles in this volume paint a picture of profound change associated with immigration in the twenty-first century. Although poorer than the general U.S. population and facing considerable hardships, there is no consistent evidence that the recent waves of foreign immigration have reshaped the social fabric in somehow un-American or negative ways. If anything, the reverse might be true. If immigration can be said to have brought violence to America, it more likely came when (white) Irish and Scottish immigrants settled in the rural South in the 1700s and 1800s (Sampson 2008). Nisbett and Cohen (1996), for example, present evidence that in areas with little state power to command compliance with the law, the tradition of frontier justice carried over from rural Europe took hold, with a heavy emphasis on retaliation and the use of violence to settle disputes, represented most clearly in the culture of dueling. Yet even here, one could reasonably argue that there was nothing distinct about immigration that brought violence; rather, the lack of state power was to blame. In western U.S. mining and cattle towns in the late 1800s, which similarly lacked state power, the homicide risk was extraordinarily high compared to Canada, Europe, and larger settled cities east of the Mississippi (Roth, Maltz, and Eckberg 2011).

In today's society and possibly always, then, immigration and the increasing cultural diversity that accompanies it apparently generate not the "conflicts of culture" that foster increased violence but more nearly the opposite. Crime and violence are down, cities are growing in population, poor urban neighborhoods are being economically revitalized, and immigrants are renewing small towns on the verge of withering away. The causal role of immigration in these processes is contested and certainly not definitive, but the patterns do sketch the broad outlines of an argument that immigration is either unrelated to or possibly even salubrious for fundamental dimensions of our social fabric.

What we do know for certain is that the process of immigrant diffusion is continuing and that the future will be even more diverse than it is today. It thus behooves policymakers and scholars alike to consider how these changes bear on the nation's social fabric. We believe that the articles presented in this volume provide important insights into this process and can therefore serve as a guidepost for the development of theories and policies for the next phase of immigration's course.

References

Acosta, Yesenia D., and G. Patricia de la Cru. 2011. *The foreign born from Latin America and the Caribbean: 2010*. Washington, DC: U.S. Census Bureau.

Bennet, William S. 1909. Immigrants and crime. *The Annals of the American Academy of Political and Social Science* 34:117–24.

Buchanan, Patrick. 2006. *State of emergency: The third world invasion and conquest of America*. New York, NY: Thomas Dunne Books/St. Martin's.

Crowley, Martha, and Daniel T. Lichter. 2009. Social disorganization in new Latino destinations? *Rural Sociology* 74:573–604.

Frey, William H. 2011. *America reaches its demographic tipping point*. Washington, DC: Brookings Institution.

Kasinitz, Philip, John H. Mollenkopf, Mary C. Waters, and Jennifer Holdaway. 2008. *Inheriting the city: The children of immigrants come of age*. Cambridge, MA: Harvard University Press.

Kelsey, Carl. 1926. Immigration and crime. *The Annals of the American Academy of Political and Social Science* 125:165–74.

Nisbett, Richard E., and Dov Cohen. 1996. *Culture of honor: The psychology of violence in the South*. Boulder, CO: Westview.

Roth, Randolph, Michael D. Maltz, and Douglas L. Eckberg. 2011. Homicide rates in the Old West. *Western Historical Quarterly* 42:173–95.

Saenz, Rogelio. 2004. *Census 2000 Report: Latinos and the changing face of America*. New York, NY, and Washington, DC: Russell Sage Foundation and Population Reference Bureau.

Sampson, Robert J. 2008. Rethinking crime and immigration. *Contexts* 7:28–33.

Sampson, Robert J. 2012. *Great American city: Chicago and the enduring neighborhood effect*. Chicago, IL: University of Chicago Press.

Sellin, Thorsten. 1938. *Culture, conflict and crime*. New York, NY: Social Science Research Council.

Shaw, Clifford R., and Henry D. McKay. 1942/1969. *Juvenile delinquency and urban areas*. Chicago, IL: University of Chicago Press.

Sutherland, Edwin H. 1947. *Principles of criminology*. Philadelphia, PA: Lippincott.

Immigration Enforcement Policies, the Economic Recession, and the Size of Local Mexican Immigrant Populations

By
EMILIO A. PARRADO

This article relies on local area variation in immigration policies, specifically the local implementation of the 287(g) program, and economic conditions to estimate their impact on changes in the size of local Mexican immigrant populations between 2007 and 2009. The author also investigates the impact of the 287(g) program on the employment prospects of low-skilled native black and white workers. The study finds that outside of four influential outliers (Dallas, Los Angeles, Riverside, and Phoenix), there is no evidence that the 287(g) program impacted the size of the Mexican immigrant population. In addition, there is no evidence that immigration enforcement policies mitigated the negative impact of the economic recession on the native population, even in the four outliers where the program was strongly enforced. The author highlights the limited efficacy of immigration enforcement as a way to resolve the issue of the undocumented immigrant population and for altering the employment opportunities of native workers.

Keywords: immigration; immigrants; Mexican population; immigration enforcement policies; deportations

The economic boom of the 1990s and early 2000s coincided with both the rapid growth and dispersion of the foreign-born Mexican population of the United States. Between 2000 and 2007, the foreign-born Mexican population in the United States enjoyed steady and continuous growth from 9.2 to 11.7 million, an increase of more than 27 percent. Between 2007 and 2009, however, this trend reversed; estimates from the American Community Survey indicate that the Mexican foreign-born

Emilio A. Parrado is an associate professor of sociology and director of the Latin American and Latino Studies Center at the University of Pennsylvania. He is the principal investigator of a project studying the connections among gender, migration, and health risks in new immigrant destinations in the United States and sending communities in Latin America. He has published extensively on issues of immigration, immigrant adaptation, and the Hispanic population in the United States.

DOI: 10.1177/0002716211435353

population in 2009 declined by more than 200,000 to 11.5 million. Two salient changes coincide with this reversal. First, starting in December 2007, the collapse of the housing market triggered a severe recession that significantly altered the economic conditions attracting Mexican workers to the United States. Second, stronger immigration enforcement policies associated with growing anti-immigrant sentiment both heightened the costs and danger associated with crossing the U.S.-Mexico border and produced an ever-growing number of deportations. The efficacy of immigration enforcement policies for reducing the size of the foreign-born Mexican population, though, is highly contested, especially since the relative impact of enforcement and changing economic conditions on migration trends is unclear.

This article takes advantage of local area differences in immigration enforcement policies and economic conditions to estimate their unique impact on changes in the size of local Mexican foreign-born populations between 2007 and 2009. In particular, I evaluate the effect of establishing a 287(g) program, which involves local enforcement agencies in immigration control, on the subsequent size of the Mexican immigrant population of local areas. In addition, I also investigate how changing employment opportunities resulting from the economic recession affected the size of the Mexican immigrant population. A central focus of the analysis is on understanding variation in the effectiveness of the 287(g) program and the role of the recession on the size of local immigrant populations. The final part of the article investigates whether participation in the 287(g) program had a positive effect on the native population, specifically whether whites and blacks in areas that enacted the program were less adversely affected by the recession than their counterparts in other areas.

Background: Economic and Policy Changes since 2007

The impact of the immigrant population has always been highly concentrated geographically, though after 1990 the number of local areas experiencing large immigrant inflows grew dramatically. Previous studies have documented the importance of industrial restructuring and larger economic considerations in shaping the distribution of the immigrant population across the country (Parrado and Kandel 2008, 2011), but it remains unclear whether and to what extent policy actions can influence population movements over and above economic considerations.

The economic prosperity of the 1990s and early 2000s ended abruptly in December 2007 with the advent of a global economic recession that began with a housing crisis in the United States. Prior to the recession, economic growth and expanding employment opportunities contributed to declining U.S. unemployment. In the fall of 2000, unemployment levels reached record lows of 3.9 percent; they increased to 6.3 percent in 2003 during a short-term recession and then declined again to 4.4 percent for several months between October 2006 and May 2007. However, the collapse of the U.S. housing market in the fall of 2007 rippled through the world economy and produced dramatically higher unemployment, which reached 10.1 percent by October 2009, more than twice the rate prior to the recession (Fronstin 2010; Sum, Khatiwada, and McLaughlin 2009).

Not surprisingly, the economic boom prior to the recession coincided with large inflows of Mexican immigrant workers. Between 2000 and 2007, the share of the U.S. labor force that was foreign-born increased from 12.5 to 15.6 percent (Newburger and Gryn 2009). While the immigrant contribution to the U.S. labor force is evident across all industries and skill levels, Latin American and Mexican immigration was disproportionately low-skilled. While only 9.5 percent of the native civilian labor force had less than a high school diploma in 2007, 28.6 percent among the foreign-born did. Mexican immigrants represented 62 percent of the workers with less than high school, while an additional 23 percent came from other Latin American countries (Newburger and Gryn 2009).

The overrepresentation of Hispanic immigrants in the low-skilled labor force translates into a particular industrial distribution with direct implications for understanding the impact of the recession on migration flows and its connection with the employment prospects of low-skilled native and immigrant workers. In 2007, the industrial sectors with the largest representation of foreign-born relative to native workers were agriculture, forestry, fishing, and hunting (25.7 percent); followed by accommodation and food services (24.1 percent); and construction (23.4 percent). In general, foreign workers were less likely to be represented in high-skilled industries, representing only 6.9 percent of public administration; 10.1 percent of educational services; 11.7 percent of finance and insurance; and 13.7 percent of professional, scientific, and technical services (Newburger and Gryn 2009).

Thus, the industries in which Hispanic immigrants were concentrated were precisely those that were hit particularly hard by the recession. According to data from the Bureau of Labor Statistics, the construction industry gained 865,000 jobs between December 2001 and 2006 but lost close to 2 million jobs between 2007 and 2009. Accommodation and food services likewise gained close to 1 million jobs between December 2001 and 2006 but lost close to 300,000 jobs between 2007 and 2009. Even employment in the professional and service industry, which tends to employ fewer immigrants, declined by 1.4 million between 2007 and 2009, after increasing by 1.1 million between 2001 and 2006.[1]

It is important to note, though, that there is considerable geographic variation in recession-related job losses. Areas where the pre-recession housing boom was more pronounced likely attracted more foreign-born Mexican migrants due to expanding labor demand in the construction industry. We could expect, therefore, that regional differences in employment conditions will have differential effects on changes in the size of the foreign-born Mexican population, with areas suffering steeper declines in construction and retail services exhibiting greater reductions in their immigrant Mexican population.

While labor market changes may have motivated return migration to Mexico or redistribution within the United States, it is also possible that increased enforcement of immigration laws contributed to the reduction in the foreign-born,

FIGURE 1
Trends in Removals and Returns: 1990–2009

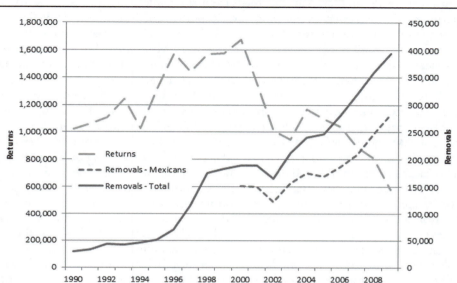

especially Mexican, population. Labeled by proponents as "attrition through enforcement" (Vaughan 2006) and opponents as "the misery strategy" (*New York Times* 2007), the initial immigration enforcement policies as laid out by the Center for Immigration Studies included proposals such as "mandatory workplace verification of immigration status; measures to curb misuse of Social Security and IRS identification numbers; partnerships with state and local law enforcement officials; expanded entry-exit recording under US-VISIT; increased non-criminal removals; and state and local laws to discourage illegal settlement" (Vaughan 2006, 1).

The overall strategy has been variably enforced, but one of the most salient outcomes has been a dramatic increase in the number of deportations/removals[2] and a decline in the number of border apprehensions/returns.[3] Depending on the perspective, the latter change can be differentially attributed to economic conditions or border enforcement. Figure 1 documents these trends. The figure reports immigration statistics from the Department of Homeland Security. The number of returns (border apprehensions), which is usually interpreted as an indication of migration flows, fluctuates over time. Specifically, the number of returns declined during the 2001 recession, increased immediately after in 2004 to 2006, and then declined again to record low levels. More important for our purposes, the number of removals (deportations) shows a dramatic and continuous increase beginning with the passing of the Illegal Immigration Reform and Immigration Responsibility Act (IIRIRA) in 1996. The increase is particularly pronounced after 2002; the number of immigrants removed more than doubled from 165,000 in that year to 393,000 just 7 years later. As many as 67.3 percent of the removals in 2009 had no prior criminal conviction. The vast majority of persons removed (72 percent) were Mexicans, among whom only 34.3 percent had a criminal conviction in 2009. Together, the decline in in-migration flows and increased deportation should logically reduce the overall size of the foreign-born Mexican population in the United States, especially after 2007, in a manner consistent with the attrition through enforcement strategy.

These overall trends, however, mask considerable variation in enforcement policies across local areas. One particular program, the 287(g), has been particularly instrumental in the implementation of the attrition through enforcement strategy (Vaughan and Edwards 2009; Capps et al. 2011). In 1996, IIRIRA amended the Immigration and Nationality Act by the addition of Section 287(g). The amendment authorized the federal government to enter into a written memorandum of agreement (MOA) with state and local law enforcement to participate in immigration control, which until then had fallen under the sole purview of federal immigration agents. At the state level, Florida (2002) and Alabama (2003) were the first to sign on, followed by Arizona (2005). At the local county level, Los Angeles and San Bernardino, California, entered the program in 2005, followed by Orange and Riverside, California, and Mecklenburg, North Carolina, in 2006. Enrollment significantly increased in 2007 with twenty-six new jurisdictions, and again in 2008 with the addition of thirty-four jurisdictions. The program has been tightly linked to the number of deportations; by 2011, 186,000 immigrants had been identified for removal through the program, and 126,000 voluntarily departed.[4]

The program remains highly controversial. Critics argue that it violates human rights, subjects Hispanics to racial profiling, and suffers from a lack of clear goals and oversight (Government Accountability Office [GAO] 2009; Organization of American States [OAS] 2010). Proponents argue it is successful at removing those with standing deportation notices (such as visa over-stayers) who are otherwise not pursued aggressively by immigration authorities (Baker McNeill 2009). Both critics and proponents agree, however, that the program is likely to create an inhospitable environment that will discourage the entry and encourage the exit of immigrants from participating jurisdictions, potentially shifting the distribution of Hispanic immigrants, documented and undocumented alike, within the United States and possibly abroad.

While these policies have garnered significant media attention and controversy, their effects remain unclear. This analysis takes advantage of the variation across U.S. localities in both the impact of the recession and the implementation of the 287(g) program to assess their contribution to changes in the size of local immigrant Mexican population. I first investigate the unique effect of the 287(g) as a policy intervention affecting immigrants. I then elaborate on how differences in employment conditions across local areas also affected the size of the Mexican immigrant population. I pay particular attention to the particular localities that might be important for understanding overall changes at the national level.

Finally, a common rationale motivating the implementation of stronger immigration enforcement policies is the expectation that restrictions on the supply of immigrants will enhance the employment prospects of low-skilled native workers. This might be particularly salient in the context of recessions since low-skilled workers appear to be more strongly affected by economic downturns than their highly skilled counterparts, and are also expected to more directly compete with low-skilled immigrants. Thus, an anticipated outcome of immigration enforcement policies is that the reduction in the supply of foreign workers resulting from the implementation of the 287(g) program should improve the employment position of low-skilled natives. I therefore investigate the extent to which anti-immigrant policies relate to changes in the employment opportunities for low-skilled native workers.

Data, Analytic Strategy, and Model Specification

The data for the analysis come from the 2005–2009 American Community Survey (ACS). I restrict the sample to the male population between the ages of 20 and 45 to capture the prime working and mobility years. The primary geographic unit of analysis is the metropolitan area. In cases where individuals are not residing in a metro area, the geographic unit becomes the consistent Public Use Microdata Area (PUMA). I limit the analysis to places with at least an estimated 2,500 foreign-born Mexican residents in 2005 to reduce estimation variability. The end product is panel data of 161 metropolitan and consistent PUMAs, spanning 2005–2009, with estimates of population size and employment conditions aggregated for the local area. Thus, there are observations before and after the implementation of the 287(g) program and the initiation of the economic recession.

The analysis focuses on changes in the size of the Mexican foreign-born population at two time points: 2007 and 2009. In addition, I investigate changes in the unemployment rate of low-skilled white and black native workers at those two time points. The temporal and spatial variation in the panel data design is particularly well suited for difference-in-difference (DID) methods to evaluate the effect of the 287(g) program and the recession on outcomes. DID methods have become widespread in the area of policy and program evaluation. They are a type of fixed effects estimation that relies on aggregate data. The basic approach is to compare outcomes before and after a policy intervention in a treatment group and a control group. The method has been applied in a wide variety of areas, including studies on the effect of minimum wage policies on employment (Card and Krueger 1994), the impact of competition in the retail market and gas prices (Hastings 1994), and how immigrant inflows shape the employment and wages of natives (Card 1992).

In this case, signing an MOA to participate in the 287(g) program is treated as a policy intervention that affects the conditions of immigrants and natives in the localities where it is introduced. The DID approach compares the difference in outcomes before and after the introduction of the 287(g) program in the localities affected by the policy, that is, the treatment group, to the same difference for unaffected areas, that is, the control group. Average changes over time in the localities without the 287(g) program are then subtracted from average changes over time in localities with the program. This double difference or difference-in-difference removes the effect that could result from permanent differences between the two groups as well as the effect of changes over time in the intervention group unrelated to the treatment, thus substantially reducing the omitted variable problems in cross-sectional analyses.[5]

The DID approach is particularly appropriate when the assignment into the treatment group is close to random, enhancing the comparability between treatment and control groups (Meyer 1995). Recent developments, however, have highlighted that the simple two-period two-group comparison can be improved by expanding the design to multiple groups as well as investigating the role of preintervention conditions and changes other than the policy intervention in affecting the comparability of groups. Such extensions can further check and refine hypotheses and allow for alternative sources of variation to be ruled out. I explore such extensions in this analysis by extending the two-group comparison and modeling change in a regression framework.

I use ordinary least squared (OLS) regression to estimate DID. The regression formulation provides a convenient way to obtain estimates and standard errors. In addition, it facilitates investigating additional comparison groups, pretreatment conditions, and changes other than the policy interventions on outcomes.[6] Since I focus on average changes over two periods, the initial approach follows a simple first difference specification. An alternative approach to policy evaluation introduces lagged dependent variables as covariates into the model. This strategy assumes that the causal effect of the program intervention is conditional not only on the permanent characteristics of the local areas but also on the lagged outcome under consideration, which makes the treatment and control groups comparable in terms of initial conditions.[7] There is considerable debate in the literature about the choice between first difference relative to lagged dependent variable specification. I report results from both approaches to assess their differences and add robustness to the results.

Variable specification

The focus of the analysis is on changes to two main outcomes: the size of the Mexican foreign-born population and the unemployment rate among the low-skilled native population between 2007 and 2009. The intervention group (P_i) includes twenty metropolitan and consolidated PUMA areas that implemented the 287(g) program before 2008. It is important to note that P_i need not be constrained to two groups. As will be seen in the analysis, I investigate the particular role of specific localities in affecting the overall changes in the foreign-born

TABLE 1
Metropolitan Areas and Counties with 287(g) Agreements Prior to 2009

Los Angeles–Long Beach, CA	2005
Riverside–San Bernardino, CA	2005
Charlotte–Gastonia–Rock Hill, NC-SC	2006
Atlanta, GA	2007
Colorado Springs, CO	2007
Fayetteville-Springdale, AR	2007
Greensboro–Winston Salem–High Point, NC	2007
Naples, FL	2007
Nashville, TN	2007
Phoenix, AZ	2007
Tulsa, OK	2007
Washington, DC/MD/VA	2007
Beaufort County, SC	2008
Dallas–Fort Worth, TX	2008
Houston-Brazoria, TX	2008
Las Vegas, NV	2008
Raleigh-Durham, NC	2008
Salt Lake City–Ogden, UT	2008
Tucson, AZ	2008
Yavapai County, AZ	2008

Mexican population. Table 1 lists the areas included in the intervention group together with the year in which they signed their agreements with the federal government. Interestingly, no area outside the South or Southwest signed a 287(g) agreement, aside from Monmouth County, New Jersey (part of the New York metropolitan area), and the City of Danbury in Fairfield County, Connecticut, which signed on in 2009.[8]

One of the advantages of the regression specification is that it allows for the inclusion of controls for the role of other time-varying trends different from the policy groups in affecting the size of the Mexican immigrant population or native unemployment. Specifically, it allows me to investigate the role of other employment changes associated with the recession as well as prior population changes that might have resulted in the application of the 287(g) program on changes in outcomes. These simultaneous and prior changes confound the evaluation of the 287(g) program.

The models include the following set of controls. Since the introduction of the 287(g) program might have been influenced by population changes, especially rapid immigrant in-flows, I include as a covariate the rate of change of the Mexican immigrant population in each particular locale between 2005 and 2007, prior to the recession and policy changes.

The effect of the recession is measured by including changes in employment conditions affecting both low- and high-skilled native workers. Specifically,

I include as predictors changes in the size of the native population employed in agriculture, construction, and retail, which are the main industries concentrating Mexican immigrants. In addition, I include measures of changes in the employment opportunities for highly skilled native workers, since they reflect the effect of the recession on the wider, non-immigrant-niche economy. Specifically, I include changes in the size of the native college-educated labor force employed in finance, professional, and public administration industries, as well as a measure of the unemployment rate among college-educated natives.

The final part of the article evaluates the impact of the recession and immigration policy on the change in the unemployment rate of native whites and blacks with a high school education or less. The models include the same industrial and employment conditions as predictors, but since the dependent variable is a change in rate, independent predictors are defined as changes in the percentage of the labor force employed in particular industries. Finally, to reduce variability in the estimators, I further restrict the analysis of unemployment change to areas with at least 2,500 low-skilled black and white individuals in 2005. The overlap in the size of the Mexican foreign-born and low-skilled native population restriction results in 89 and 156 geographic areas for the final analysis of blacks and whites, respectively.

Variation in the Decline of the Mexican Foreign-Born Population across Local Areas

The overall pattern of decline in the size of the Mexican immigrant population aged 20 to 45 from 2007 to 2009 masks considerable variation across local areas. Descriptive results plotting the distribution of the dependent variable show that the majority of local areas witnessed a modest decline in Mexican immigrant populations, with the average being a drop of 1,615 men between 2007 and 2009. Positive change is evidenced only in 32 percent of cases. The highest gains occurred in Miami-Hialeah, Florida, where the number of foreign-born Mexicans increased by 4,446 during the period. However, the description also shows four clear outliers that experienced dramatic declines in their Mexican foreign-born population, specifically Los Angeles–Long Beach, California (–40,701); Riverside–San Bernardino, California (–34,776); Phoenix, Arizona (–26,991); and Dallas–Fort Worth, Texas (–14,964). All these areas implemented 287(g) programs during the period. Without these outliers, the distribution is very close to normal. As will be seen below, these outliers are critical to evaluating the effect of the 287(g) on the size of the Mexican immigrant population.

To further investigate the role of the 287(g) intervention, Figure 2 traces the average size of the foreign-born Mexican population, separating the local areas by whether they implemented the 287(g) program. The two-group comparison shows that for both groups, the immigrant Mexican population grew in the years leading up to 2007 and fell afterward. The decline, however, was particularly

FIGURE 2
Size of the Mexican Male Immigrant Population According to 287(g) Status of Local
Areas: 2005–2009

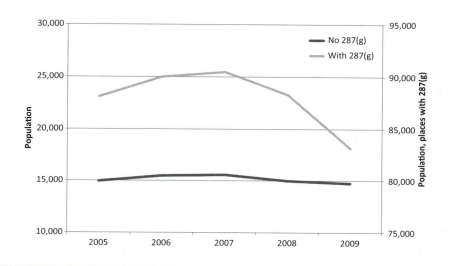

dramatic in the group with the 287(g). Between 2007 and 2009, the Mexican immigrant population declined by more than 7,000 in areas with the 287(g) program, on average, compared to declines of less than 1,000 in areas without it.

Since the treatment and control groups differ in the size of their initial immigrant populations, and since larger starting populations imply greater potential for declines, I next expand the two-group typology to account for initial population size in two ways. First, I distinguish within policy groups between areas with more or fewer than 50,000 Mexican foreign-born residents in 2005, which results in a four-group typology. Second, I expand the four-group classification by separating out outliers identified in the description of the dependent variable, all of which were 287(g) implementers with large initial Mexican immigrant populations. This results in five distinct groups: small initial population / no 287(g) ($n = 134$); small initial population / with 287(g) ($n = 13$); large initial population / no 287(g) ($n = 7$); large initial population / with 287(g) but not outlier ($n = 3$); and large initial population / with 287(g) but outlier ($n = 4$). The expansion directly investigates the comparability between groups as highlighted in recent developments in the literature on program evaluation.

Table 2 reports the DID estimates of the average decline in the Mexican foreign-born population between 2007 and 2009 according to the two-, four-, and five-group typology. Confirming the pattern shown in Figure 2, the most

TABLE 2
Difference-in-Difference Estimates of the Average Change in Mexican Male Immigrant Population by 287(g) Status: 2007–2009

	Two-Group		Four-Group			
			Size Mexican Foreign-Born in 2005			
			< 50,000		≥ 50,000	
			287(g)			
	No (1)	Yes (2)	No (3)	Yes (4)	No (5)	Yes (6)
Average FB Mexican population in						
2007	15,557	90,465	10,570	15,740	111,026	229,241
2009	14,748	83,168	9,909	14,369	107,383	210,938
Change (2009–2007)	−810	−7,298	−661	−1,371	−3,644	−18,303
Difference-in-difference estimates						
Reference group: (1)		−6,488				
Reference group: (3)				−710	−2,982	−17,642

			Five-group				
						Outlier	
			(3)	(4)	(5)	No (7)	Yes (8)
Average FB Mexican population in							
2007			10,570	15,740	111,026	119,972	311,192
2009			9,909	14,369	107,383	116,409	281,834
Change (2009–2007)			−661	−1,371	−3,644	−3,563	−29,358
Difference-in-difference estimates							
Reference group: (3)				−710	−2,982	−2,902	−28,697
Reference group: (5)						80	−25,714
Reference group: (7)							−25,795
N (local areas)	141	20	134	13	7	3	4

basic two-group comparison shows that the Mexican immigrant population in areas with the 287(g) program declined by an additional 6,488 relative to areas without the program. However, estimates vary considerably when I separate the groups by initial size of the immigrant population. The four-group typology shows that among areas with small initial immigrant populations, those with the 287(g) program (group 4) exhibit a slightly greater (–710) average reduction in their Mexican immigrant populations than areas without the program (group 3).

Comparing larger immigrant areas with small areas without the program (group 3) shows that between 2007 and 2009, the Mexican foreign-born population in large areas without the 287(g) (group 5) declined by 2,982. There are seven areas in this category: Chicago, Illinois; Denver-Boulder, Colorado; Fresno, California; New York–Northeastern New Jersey; San Diego, California; San Francisco, California; and San Jose, California. These areas tend to be referred to among immigration opponents as "sanctuary" cities since they do not openly enforce immigration controls. Results from the four-group typology also show that the decline was considerably more pronounced in large areas with the 287(g) program (group 6). As compared to small areas without the program, the DID estimator shows a decline of 17,642 in large areas with the policy intervention.

However, interesting results are obtained when I separate the outliers from other large immigrant areas with the 287(g) program in the bottom panel of Table 2. Three areas fall under the large initial population with 287(g) but not outlier (group 7): Atlanta, Georgia; Houston, Texas; and Las Vegas, Nevada. Among these areas, the DID estimator shows their Mexican foreign-born population declining by 2,902 relative to small areas without the program (group 3), which is almost identical to the –2,982 DID estimator obtained for large areas without the 287g program (group 5). In fact, if one takes areas with large Mexican populations and no 287g program (group 5) as the reference group, the DID estimate for nonoutliers (group 7) is in fact positive, 80.

Most of the decline in the Mexican foreign-born population related to the 287(g) program is accounted for by the four outliers (group 8). The DID calculations show that for this group, the Mexican immigrant population declined by 28,697 and declined by 25,714 relative to small and large areas without the 287(g) program. Even compared to other large areas with the program, the decline in these four outliers was 25,795 higher. The salience of these four outliers (Los Angeles, Riverside, Phoenix, and Dallas) in explaining trends in the size of the Mexican foreign-born population is a recurrent finding in the study.

One possibility is that the impact of the collapse of the housing market was more pronounced in these four outliers than in the rest of the metropolitan areas with large Mexican immigrant populations. To investigate the issue, Table 3 lists changes in the size of the foreign-born Mexican population in the fourteen areas with more than 50,000 foreign-born Mexican men in 2005 together with an indicator of participation in the 287(g) program and absolute changes in the number of native workers employed in the construction industry. The highlighted rows indicate the outlying areas in terms of foreign-born change.

Results document considerable lack of correspondence between changes in the size of the foreign-born Mexican population and construction employment. The metropolitan area with the largest losses in construction is Chicago (–29,972); however, it lost only 4,433 Mexican immigrant men between 2007 and 2009. At

TABLE 3
Change in Mexican Male Immigrant Population and Construction Employment in Large
Metropolitan Areas: 2007–2009

| | | Absolute Change 2007–2009 | |
	287(g) program	Mexican Immigrant Population	Construction Employment (Native Workers)
Atlanta, GA	Yes	−1,788	−25,227
Chicago, IL	No	−4,433	−29,972
Dallas–Fort Worth, TX	**Yes**	**−14,964**	**−4,283**
Denver-Boulder, CO	No	−3,715	−7,782
Fresno, CA	No	−6,254	−4,066
Houston-Brazoria, TX	Yes	−1,572	−2,293
Las Vegas, NV	Yes	−7,330	−3,162
Los Angeles–Long Beach, CA	**Yes**	**−40,701**	**−12,678**
New York– Northeastern NJ	No	−357	−16,416
Phoenix, AZ	**Yes**	**−26,991**	**−8,698**
Riverside–San Bernardino, CA	**Yes**	**−34,776**	**−15,946**
San Diego, CA	No	−9,113	−3,070
San Francisco– Oakland–Vallejo, CA	No	597	−5,782
San Jose, CA	No	−2,231	−5,382

Outliers are indicated in bold.

the other extreme, Los Angeles–Long Beach lost considerably more Mexican immigrants (–40,701) than construction jobs for natives (–12,678). A similar pattern is evident for the neighboring Riverside–San Bernardino metropolitan area. The difference is particularly dramatic as compared to New York, which lost a similar number of construction jobs but only 357 Mexican immigrants.

Dramatic disparities are also evident for the comparison between Phoenix and Denver-Boulder. Both metropolitan areas lost close to 8,000 jobs in the construction industry. However, Phoenix saw its Mexican immigrant population decline by almost 27,000 compared to only 3,715 in Denver. San Francisco and Dallas–Fort Worth also present contrasting images. Both metropolitan areas lost close to 5,000 jobs in construction, but the decline in the Mexican foreign-born population was 14,964 in Dallas, compared to a 597 increase in San Francisco. Overall, results document that the outliers are not unusual in terms of the impact of the recession on construction employment and that the change in the size of the Mexican immigrant population does not perfectly correlate with economic conditions, issues that will be explored more systematically in the multivariate analyses.

Regression Results: First Difference and Lagged Dependent Variable Models

The next set of analyses model group differences in changes in the size of the foreign-born Mexican population, controlling for prior population conditions and changes in employment opportunities associated with the recession. Table 4 reports results from OLS first difference and lagged dependent variable models predicting changes in the size of the local foreign-born Mexican population. Following the descriptive findings, the top panel reports results from the two-group specification, and the bottom panel reports results obtained from the expansion to five groups.

The model in column 1, which does not include covariates, reproduces the DID estimates reported in Table 2. Adding the changes in employment conditions associated with the recession as predictors in column 2 reduces the overall effect of the 287(g) program by 29 percent, from –6,488 to –4,630. The lagged dependent variable results in column 3 show that even after conditioning the estimates on the prior size of the immigrant population, areas that implemented the 287(g) program reduced their Mexican foreign-born populations by 1,870. In the lagged dependent variable specification, which relates changes in size of the Mexican immigrant population to the prior size of the group in addition to policy changes, the effect completely disappears after controlling for changes in employment conditions associated with the recession (column 4).

Results for the five-group specification reported in the bottom panel of Table 4 adds further precision to the role of policy and the economy in affecting changes in the foreign-born Mexican population. As with the two-group case, column 1 reproduces the DID results reported in Table 2. Small areas with the 287(g) program are no different from small areas without it, but all other area types show significantly larger losses, with the largest deficit by far registered among the large 287(g) outliers, as would be expected. After accounting for socioeconomic conditions, large areas without the policy intervention reduce their immigrant population by 3,196 (column 2). The effect is actually higher among large areas with the 287(g) that are not outliers in the change distribution. This group saw its immigrant Mexican population decline by 2,290. Again, the four outliers experienced a ten-times-larger decline in their Mexican immigrant populations (–27,030) than either of the other large area groups.

Results from the lagged dependent variable specification show that controlling for prior size of the Mexican population eliminates the effect of the 287(g) policies for all except the four-outlier group. Accounting for the negative effect

TABLE 4
OLS Estimates from Fixed Effects and Lagged Dependent Variable Models Predicting Change in Mexican Male Immigrant Population

Two-Group Specification							
	Fixed Effects Models				Lagged Dependent Variable Models		
	(1)		(2)		(3)		(4)	
Intercept	−809.5**	(398.4)	3,495.6**	(1,176.1)	149.5	(279.3)	3,154.5**	(838.1)
Implemented 287(g)	−6,488.0**	(1,130.4)	−4,630.9**	(952.4)	−1,870.1**	(838.0)	−1,156.0	(735.4)
Size of Mexican immigrant population in 2007 (000s)					0.9**	(0.0)	0.9**	(0.0)
Changes in # of native workers employed in (industry) (000s):								
Agriculture			11.1	(238.9)			−177.4	(170.8)
Construction			285.5**	(83.7)			257.4**	(59.6)
Retail			−273.5**	(89.0)			−128.9**	(64.5)
Changes in # of college ed. natives (000s):								
Employed in professional industry			786.0**	(101.8)			320.2**	(81.9)
Unemployed			−1,166.9**	(234.3)			519.7**	(216.4)
Growth rate of Mexican population 2005–07			−2,799.0**	(1,055.2)			−2,548.2**	(751.8)
R-squared	.2		.5		.6		.7	

Five-Group Specification							
	Fixed Effects Models				Lagged Dependent Variable Models		
	(1)		(2)		(3)		(4)	
Intercept	−661.5**	(224.6)	2,646.0**	(731.1)	−388.0	(221.9)	2,735.3**	(685.5)
Group (reference: small + no 287(g))								
Small + 287(g)	−709.9	(755.3)	−1,170.3	(700.9)	−576.1	(716.2)	−830.0	(661.0)
Large + no 287(g)	−2,982.2**	(1,008.1)	−3,196.8**	(1,084.5)	−383.3	(1,127.1)	−1,569.8	(1,074.5)
Large + 287(g) + not outlier	−2,901.8**	(1,517.8)	−2,290.4**	(1,416.3)	−71.5	(1,578.8)	270.8	(1,436.3)
Large + 287(g) + outlier	−28,697.0**	(1,319.3)	−27,030.0**	(1,539.7)	−20,919.0**	(2,184.7)	−18,962.0**	(2,251.7)
Size of Mexican immigrant population in 2007 (000s)					1.0**	(0.0)	1.0**	(0.0)
Changes in # of native workers employed in (industry) (000s):								
Agriculture			−38.1	(148.2)			−112.0	(139.8)
Construction			135.0**	(52.9)			170.9**	(50.2)
Retail			103.0	(60.4)			67.2	(57.2)
Changes in # of college ed. natives (000s):								
Employed in professional industry			285.3**	(72.0)			211.0**	(69.4)
Unemployed			−385.6**	(157.2)			121.7	(183.1)
Growth rate of Mexican population 2005–07			−2,684.8**	(654.4)			−2,589.5**	(613.6)
R-squared	.8		.8		.8		.8	
N = 161								

**p <.05

associated with prior population size, the Mexican foreign-born population declined by 20,919 among the group that had large initial immigrant populations and 287(g) but were not outliers (column 3). Accounting for other socioeconomic changes reduces the effect of the group by 25 percent to 18,962 (column 4). Thus, even relating changes in the size of the foreign-born Mexican population to prior conditions in addition to policy does not eliminate the effect of the outliers.

The role of socioeconomic changes in affecting the size of the immigrant Mexican population is consistent across specifications. The main factor reducing the decline is changes in construction employment. Each additional native worker employed in construction reduces the decline in the Mexican foreign-born population by 0.15 to 0.28 persons (columns 2 and 4), depending on specification. Interestingly, results show that the size of the Mexican immigrant population is also affected by changes in employment conditions among natives in highly skilled industries. Specifically, places with larger expansions of the college-educated native population employed in professional industries lost fewer Mexican immigrants than areas that did not gain highly skilled natives. At the same time, more pronounced growth in the unemployment of college-educated natives was associated with larger drops in the Mexican immigrant population (–385 in the bottom panel of column 2). These effects support perspectives that stress the role of labor demand processes, even stemming from changes in employment conditions among the high-skilled native population, in affecting the size of immigrant groups.

Changes in the Unemployment Rate of the Low-Skilled Native Black and White Populations

I next explore the possibility that immigrant enforcement measures may enhance native employment prospects by examining changes in the unemployment rate of low-skilled black and white workers between 2007 and 2009. Estimates from the ACS show the unemployment rate for native black and white men with a high school education or less increased from 17.6 to 26.8 percent and from 8.0 to 14.4 percent between 2007 and 2009, respectively. As with the changes in the size of the immigrant Mexican population, we can expect considerable variation across geographic areas in changes in the unemployment rate.

Table 5 reports results from OLS models predicting change in the unemployment rate of black and white low-skilled native workers from 2007 to 2009 across local areas. The change models follow the specification applied in models predicting change in the foreign-born Mexican population. Since the dependent variable is change in rates, the explanatory covariates are measured as percentage of the labor force, not absolute values. As before, I report both first difference and lagged dependent variable estimates.

In all cases, results show no effect of the five-area typology on the changes in the unemployment rate of low-skilled native black and white men. One might have expected that given the strong effect of the four area outliers in reducing the local size of the foreign-born Mexican population, the strong enforcement of 287(g) policies would have facilitated the expansion or at least buffered the

TABLE 5

OLS Estimates from Fixed Effects and Lagged Dependent Variable Models Predicting Change in the Low-Skilled Black and White Men Unemployment Rate

	Black Men				White Men			
Fixed effects models								
Intercept	11.36°°	(1.19)	15.84°°	(4.63)	6.89°°	(0.43)	9.19°°	(1.60)
Group (reference: small + no 287(g))								
Small + 287(g)	−1.93	(3.91)	−1.44	(3.89)	−0.32	(1.42)	−0.46	(1.38)
Large + no 287(g)	−1.44	(4.20)	−1.68	(4.22)	0.24	(1.89)	0.65	(1.83)
Large + 287(g) + not outlier	−2.93	(5.82)	−2.92	(5.68)	0.80	(2.84)	1.11	(2.73)
Large + 287(g) + outlier	−3.23	(5.07)	−3.09	(4.95)	−0.50	(2.47)	−0.03	(2.37)
Change in % of native labor force employed in:								
Agriculture			0.06	(0.74)			0.30°	(0.18)
Construction			−0.93°°	(0.41)			−0.26°°	(0.12)
Retail			−0.51	(0.44)			−0.03	(0.12)
Change in % of college-educated natives:								
Employed in professional industry			−0.57	(0.59)			0.02	(0.15)
Unemployed			0.86	(1.74)			−0.48	(0.49)
Growth rate of Mexican population 2005–07			−5.85°	(3.82)			−2.68°°	(1.36)
R-squared	.01		.15		.01		.12	
Lagged dependent variable models								
Intercept	18.94°°	(2.34)	21.18°°	(4.44)	8.90°°	(1.00)	11.08°°	(1.72)
Group (reference: small + no 287(g))								
Small + 287(g)	−3.96	(3.69)	−4.29	(3.63)	−0.51	(1.40)	−0.72	(1.36)
Large + no 287(g)	−0.53	(3.92)	−1.00	(3.87)	0.36	(1.87)	0.75	(1.79)
Large + 287(g) + not outlier	−4.18	(5.44)	−4.75	(5.22)	0.36	(2.81)	0.62	(2.68)
Large + 287(g) + outlier	−3.12	(4.73)	−2.67	(4.54)	−0.31	(2.44)	0.13	(2.32)
Unemployment rate in 2007 (000s)	0.62°°	(0.11)	0.57°°	(0.11)	0.74°°	(0.12)	0.69°°	(0.12)
Change in % of native labor force employed in:								
Agriculture			0.17	(0.67)			0.37°°	(0.18)
Construction			−1.13°°	(0.38)			−0.25°°	(0.11)
Retail			−0.56	(0.40)			0.03	(0.12)
Change in % of college-educated natives:								
Employed in professional industry			−0.18	(0.54)			0.02	(0.15)
Unemployed			0.94	(1.60)			−0.33	(0.49)
Growth rate of Mexican population 2005–07			−3.56	(3.54)			−2.41°°	(1.34)
R-square	.15		.29		.03		.16	
N		89				156		

°°p <.05

deterioration of employment opportunities for low-skilled native workers. However, there is no evidence of such an effect. Similar lack of effects is obtained when estimating the models using the simpler two- or four-group typology.

Similarly, the rate of growth of the Mexican immigrant population between 2005 and 2007 also shows no effect on the change in the native unemployment rate resulting from the recession. The main predictor of the impact of the recession on natives is the trend in construction employment. Areas that enjoyed smaller declines (or gains) in construction employment saw smaller increases in native unemployment than areas in which construction contracted more sharply. Since conditions in the local construction industry also affected the size of the Mexican immigrant population, this suggests that the employment prospects of both native and foreign workers are connected. Rather than evidence of competition, this supports a view of foreign and native workers as complements directly affected by the decline in construction employment resulting from the recession.

Conclusion

Estimates from the ACS document a considerable decline in the size of the U.S. Mexican immigrant population since 2007. This is perhaps not surprising given the dramatic increase in immigration control at the federal level, resulting in far more deportations and lower in-migration flows. However, there is considerable variation across areas within the United States in changes in the size of the immigrant Mexican population. Two processes are potentially salient in encouraging immigrants to relocate either within the United States or abroad: the enactment of local immigration control provisions and the variable impact of the economic recession across local areas. In this analysis, I evaluated the relative impact of more stringent immigration enforcement policies—namely, the 287(g) program—and employment change associated with the 2007 recession on the size of local Mexican immigrant populations between 2007 and 2009. In addition, I investigated the extent to which immigration policies and economic conditions affected the unemployment rate of non-Hispanic black and white low-skilled natives.

In investigating the effect of the 287(g) program on changes in the immigrant Mexican population, several conclusions are evident. Overall, the 287(g) is not particularly effective at reducing the local Mexican population. The lack of effect is particularly evident once the initial size of the immigrant population is taken into account. Among areas with small Mexican immigrant populations, 287(g) implementation was not associated with larger reductions in immigrant populations over time. And among areas with large immigrant concentrations, 287(g) programs were associated with significant declines in Mexican immigrant populations in only four localities, namely, Los Angeles, Riverside, Phoenix, and Dallas. These areas experienced a dramatically larger reduction of their Mexican immigrant population than other communities of similar size that also implemented the 287(g) program, such as Atlanta, Houston, and Las Vegas. Interestingly, among this last set of areas, the reduction in the Mexican immigrant population was actually smaller than that experienced by other large communities that as of 2008 had not implemented the program, such as Chicago, Denver, Fresno, New York, San Diego, San Francisco, and San Jose. Thus, aside from four outliers, there is no evidence that 287(g) implementation reduced Mexican immigrant populations at the local level.

The economic recession, on the other hand, was highly effective in reducing the size and growth of the Mexican immigrant population. Deteriorating employment opportunities, particularly in the construction industry but also in high-skilled sectors, had a pronounced effect on the Mexican immigrant population of local areas. However, variation in employment opportunities across local areas does not account for the outlier status of Phoenix, Los Angeles, Riverside, and Dallas. Accounting for the employment trajectories of these locales reduces the effect of the 287(g) program on Mexican immigrant populations by only 6 percent. This reinforces the interpretation that what distinguishes these outliers from the rest of the United States is the particular form of 287(g) implementation and not the economic impact of the recession.

The final part of the article evaluated the proposition that removing immigrants would result in better employment prospects for native low-skilled workers. The analysis found no effect of the 287(g) program on changes in the unemployment rate of low-skilled black and white workers. Even among the four outliers, I found no evidence that accelerated reduction of the foreign-born improved economic opportunities for natives. The key determinant of native unemployment was, not surprisingly, local economic conditions. Changes in employment in the construction industry, not the presence or absence of immigrants, explained the lion's share of local variation in native unemployment for both blacks and whites. The fact that both the size of the immigrant population and native employment are sensitive to conditions in the construction industry undermines the argument that immigrant competition fuels low-skill native unemployment.

These findings have numerous policy implications. Overall, they indicate that merely implementing a program like the 287(g) alone is not sufficient to secure attrition in the Mexican foreign-born population. Rather, the experience of the outliers suggests that the policies are successful only if they are enforced with extreme vigor. Indeed, the outlier communities have often received extensive media coverage at the local, national, and even international level for the severity of their program implementation. In Phoenix, Maricopa County Sheriff Joe Arpaio, who promotes himself as America's toughest sheriff, is well known for his outspoken stance against immigration and frequent high-profile raids used to round up suspected undocumented immigrants. His publicity stunts include parading Mexican men awaiting deportation in front of TV cameras dressed in pink underwear and pink handcuffs that are available online for purchase (*New York Times* 2009). His practices have been the focus of several Justice Department investigations for alleged civil rights violations and have been sharply criticized for diverting resources away from basic law enforcement, even by respected conservative groups such as the Goldwater Institute (Bolick 2008). In spite of the many controversies, they still became a model for Arizona's controversial anti-immigrant legislation known as SB1070 (which was also closely shaped by the private prison industry[9]).

Likewise, the sheriff of Los Angeles County, Lee Baca, is another vocal advocate of a get-tough approach to immigration. Baca has opposed many other sheriffs in the state (such as those of Yolo, Sacramento, San Francisco, and Santa Clara counties) and even the local Los Angeles City Council who advocate limiting local participation in deportation programs (*Los Angeles Times* 2011) and instead has worked to expand the use of his police for immigration enforcement. He is currently facing an FBI investigation for inmate abuse and has publicly argued that immigrants are not entitled to the basic civil rights protections guaranteed to American citizens (CBS Los Angeles 2011).

Another implication is that even when applied with draconian measures, the attrition through enforcement strategy is not very effective at eliminating the undocumented worker problem. For instance, if all fourteen metropolitan areas with large Mexican immigrant populations in 2005 were to become as effective at reducing their immigrant populations as the four 287(g) outliers in this analysis, we could expect an average of 190,000 (27,000 × 14/2) fewer Mexican male immigrants in these areas annually. If one made the highly unlikely assumptions that all immigrants who left these areas returned to Mexico, voluntarily or through deportations, *and* that undocumented migration into the United States would cease, it would still take almost *30 years* to remove all of the estimated 5 million undocumented Mexican men currently estimated to reside in the United States. Thus, even under this highly unlikely, "best-case" scenario, it would still take an inordinate amount of time (not to mention resources) to eliminate the undocumented population in the United States.

Given the lack of obvious economic benefits to natives from such policies, even in their most severe applications, it is particularly sobering that the current drift of our immigration policy continues to be toward "attrition through enforcement." Examples at the state level include the Arizona SB1070 legislation and the recently enacted Alabama anti-immigration law that went so far as to require public schools to verify the legal status of their pupils, leading to a large-scale withdrawal of Hispanic children from local schools. At the federal level, the Obama administration initiated the Secure Communities program in 2008, a program that builds on the 287(g) experience and relies on partnership among federal, state, and local law enforcement agencies to identify deportable aliens. A main objective is to eliminate the "sanctuary" areas that have resisted pressures to participate in immigration enforcement. However, the Northeast and Midwest, which have struggled since the 1970s with anemic population growth, have received an important boost in recent years from immigrants, who have contributed to demographic vitality, neighborhood revitalization, and small business formation throughout the region. This analysis shows that while slow, the extreme application of these programs does in fact reduce the local immigrant population. It is not surprising, then, that states such as New York, Illinois, and Massachusetts have tried (so far unsuccessfully) to withdraw from the Secure Communities program. For these areas, enforcing immigration laws might go against their demographic interests.

Notes

1. http://www.bls.gov/data/#employment (accessed 22 March 2011).

2. Removals are the compulsory and confirmed movement of an inadmissible or deportable alien out of the United States based on an order of removal. An alien who is removed has administrative or criminal consequences placed on subsequent reentry owing to the fact of the removal (U.S. Department of Homeland Security, *Yearbook of Immigration Statistics—2009*, available at http://www.dhs.gov/files/statistics/publications/YrBk09En.shtm).

3. Returns are the confirmed movement of an inadmissible or deportable alien out of the United States not based on an order of removal (see ibid.). Most of the voluntary returns are of Mexican nationals who have been apprehended by the U.S. Border Patrol and are returned to Mexico.

4. For a detailed description of the program, see Capps et al. (2011).

5. Formally, $\delta = (\overline{Y}_{C\text{-}2009} - \overline{Y}_{C\text{-}2007}) - (\overline{Y}_{T\text{-}2009} - \overline{Y}_{T\text{-}2007})$, where δ is the DID causal effect of interest and eq \o(Y,¯) is the average outcome in control (C) and treatment (T) groups in years 2009 and 2007.

6. Specifically, this implies estimating $Y_{i2009} - Y_{i2007} = \beta + \delta P_i + \lambda X_i + \varepsilon_i$, where Y_{it} is the outcome in 2007 and 2009 in local area i; P_i is a dummy variable policy group indicator that is equal to 1 if the area implemented a 287(g) program and 0 otherwise; X_i is a vector of local area controls that include conditions before and changes between the two periods; δ is the causal effect of the policy intervention as specified in (1); and λ are parameters to be estimated

7. Specifically, this implies estimating $Y_{i2009} = \beta + \delta P_i + \lambda X_i + Y_{i2007} + \varepsilon_i$, where Y_{i2007} controls for the value of the outcome in 2007.

8. Ideally, all the policy changes should have taken place after 2007. Only three areas implemented the changes before the period under consideration. In those situations, these estimates also reflect the prior effect of the policy.

9. See http://www.npr.org/templates/story/story.php?storyId=130833741; also http://www.cipamericas.org/archives/3304.

References

Baker McNeill, Jena. 2009. *Section 287(g): State and local immigration enforcement efforts are working.* Washington, DC: Heritage Foundation.

Bolick, Clint. 2008. Mission unaccomplished: The misplaced priorities of the Maricopa County Sheriff's Office. Policy Report #229. Phoenix, AZ: Goldwater Institute.

Capps, Randy, Marc R. Rosenblum, Cristina Rodriguez, and Muzaffar Chishti. 2011. *Delegation and divergence: A study of 287(g) state and local immigration enforcement.* Washington, DC: Migration Policy Institute.

Card, David. 1992. Using regional variation in wages to measure the effects of the federal minimum wage. *Industrial and Labor Relations Review* 46 (1): 22–37.

Card, David, and Alan B. Krueger. 1994. Minimum wages and employment: A case study of the fast-food industry in New Jersey and Pennsylvania. *American Economic Review* 84 (4): 772–93.

CBS Los Angeles. 2011. Sheriff Baca questions civil rights of illegal immigrants. Available from http://losangeles.cbslocal.com/2011/05/13/sheriff-baca-questions-civil-rights-of-illegal-immigrants/.

Fronstin, Paul. 2010. *The impact of the recession on employment-based health coverage.* Issue Brief 342. Washington, DC: Employee Benefit Research Institute.

Government Accountability Office (GAO). 2009. *Immigration enforcement: Better controls needed over program authorizing state and local enforcement of federal immigration laws.* Washington, DC: GAO.

Hastings, Justin. 1994. Vertical relationships and competition in retail gasoline markets: Empirical evidence from contract changes in Southern California. *American Economic Review* 94 (1): 317–28.

Los Angeles Times. 2011. L.A. is urged to support limiting local participation in deportation program. Available from http://articles.latimes.com/2011/may/26/local/la-me-0526-secure-communities-20110526.

Meyer, Bruce. 1995. Natural and quasi-experiments in economics. *Journal of Business & Economic Statistics* 13 (2): 151–61.

Newburger, Eric, and Thomas Gryn. 2009. *The foreign-born labor force in the United States: 2007.* American Community Survey Reports, ACS-10. Washington, DC: U.S. Census Bureau.

New York Times. 9 August 2007. The misery strategy.

New York Times. 2009. Arpaio's America. Available from http://www.nytimes.com/2009/02/06/opinion/06fri2.html?scp=3&sq=arpaio&st=cse.

Organization of American States (OAS). 2010. *Report on immigration in the United States: Detention and due process.* Washington, DC: OAS.

Parrado, Emilio A., and William Kandel. 2008. New Hispanic migrant destinations: A tale of two industries. In *New faces in new places: The changing geography of American immigration*, ed. Douglas S. Massey, 99–123. New York, NY: Russell Sage Foundation.

Parrado, Emilio A., and William Kandel. 2011. Industrial change, Hispanic immigration, and the internal migration of low-skilled native workers in the United States, 1995–2000. *Social Science Research* 40 (2): 626–40.

Sum, Andrew, Ishwar Khatiwada, and Joseph McLaughlin. 2009. *The economic recession of 2007-2009: Comparative perspective on its duration and the severity of its labor market impact.* Boston, MA: Center for Labor Market Studies, Northeastern University.

Vaughan, Jessica. 2006. *Attrition through enforcement: A cost-effective strategy to shrink the illegal population.* Backgrounder. Washington, DC: Center for Immigration Studies.

Vaughan, Jessica M., and James R. Edwards Jr. 2009. *The 287g program: Protecting home towns and homeland.* Backgrounder. Washington, DC: Center for Immigration Studies.

Can Immigration Save Small-Town America? Hispanic Boomtowns and the Uneasy Path to Renewal

By
PATRICK J. CARR,
DANIEL T. LICHTER,
and
MARIA J. KEFALAS

In the often polarized discussions over immigration, the point is sometimes missed that immigration often brings immediate and tangible benefits. Nowhere is this truer than in the hollowing-out parts of America. Many nonmetropolitan counties in America have seen net out-migration for decades. While young people have always left small towns, the loss of this group comes at a time when opportunities for those who stay have been severely reduced. One trend that runs counter to the decline of many nonmetro areas is the influx of immigrants, the majority of Hispanic origin, during the 1990s and 2000s. The authors argue that if immigration is "done right," it can provide a lifeline to many places that are hollowing out. In this article, the authors outline the complex nature of immigration in rural America and offer two case studies of small towns, one where immigration became a lightning rod for controversy and division and one where the process has occurred with little divisiveness and a great deal of success. The authors conclude with some policy suggestions as to how to better accommodate immigration in rural America.

Keywords: immigration; rural; small towns; social change; policy

Patrick J. Carr is an associate professor of sociology at Rutgers University–New Brunswick and is an associate member of the MacArthur Foundation's Research Network on Transitions to Adulthood. He is the author of Clean Streets: Controlling Crime, Maintaining Order and Building Community Activism *(NYU Press 2005) and coauthor, with Maria Kefalas, of* Hollowing Out the Middle *(Beacon 2009). His current research focuses on the Stop Snitching movement and the transition to adulthood for vulnerable populations.*

Daniel T. Lichter is the Ferris Family Professor in the Department of Policy Analysis and Management, a professor of sociology, and director of the Cornell Population Center at Cornell University. Much of his recent empirical work focuses on immigration and changing ethnoracial boundaries in rural America. His 2011 paper titled "Rural America in an Urban Society: Changing Spatial and Social Boundaries" was published in the Annual Review of Sociology.

Maria J. Kefalas is a professor in the Department of Sociology at Saint Joseph's University. She is the author of numerous books and articles on topics including urban/rural communities, culture, youth, and the family, including Working-Class Heroes *(University of California Press 2003);* Promises I Can Keep, *with Kathryn Edin (University of California Press 2005); and* Hollowing Out the Middle *(Beacon 2009). She serves as an associate member of the MacArthur Foundation's Research Network on Transitions to Adulthood.*

DOI: 10.1177/0002716211433445

In the vexed and often polarized discussions over immigration and the more notable flashpoints in the recent debate, such as the strict anti–illegal immigration law (State Bill 1070) that was passed in Arizona in early 2010, the point is sometimes missed that immigration often brings immediate and tangible benefits. Nowhere is this truer than in the hollowing-out parts of America. Many nonmetro small towns in the heartland, northern Plains states, and elsewhere in rural America from Maine to the Delta and Appalachia to the Dakotas have seen net out-migration over the past three decades (Johnson 2011; McGranahan, Cromartie, and Wojin 2010). Any demographic and economic effects have been exacerbated by who is leaving, namely, young adults of reproductive age and the most educated and talented (Carr and Kefalas 2009; Domina 2006). While young people have always left small towns, the exodus comes at a time when opportunities for those who stay have been severely reduced by consolidation in agriculture and the globalization of manufacturing. The "Great Recession" of the late 2000s has not helped matters. The net result is that the jobs remaining in nonmetro America are fewer and often pay less than they did even a decade ago. Real median household income in nonmetro America decreased between 2000 and 2009, from $40,999 to $40,135 in 2009 dollars (U.S. Department of Agriculture [USDA] 2011a).

In this article, we argue that promoting new immigration may be an important source of population growth and economic dynamism in many distressed rural communities. Specifically, we describe how in-migration—especially of Hispanic immigrants—has transformed American small-town community life and slowed incipient population decline. We describe the new opportunities and challenges faced by small towns in incorporating new residents who may not share the same ethnic heritage, cultural values, or skin color. And we contrast two communities— Hazleton, Pennsylvania, and St. James, Minnesota—that have responded much differently to rapid demographic change, an approach also taken by Vitiello (2008). We conclude with lessons learned and some modest policy recommendations drawn from the ongoing social and demographic upheavals brought by rural immigration.

Immigration in Rural America: A Life Preserver or an Albatross?

With the restructuring of nonmetro America, many places are declining slowly and inexorably, with the most visible final vestige of hollowing out being the closing of a local school (Lyson 2002). The demographic shifts that mark this process are not limited to population loss. With the out-migration of the young and educated, those remaining in nonmetro America are older, less educated, and more likely to work in manual professions. The loss of population also means a declining tax base, less support for local and small businesses, more retirees in need of health care, and less incentive for young professionals to locate in these areas.

For instance, almost half of nonmetro counties in Iowa have at least two medically underserved areas, the net result being that many living there have to travel great distances to see a primary care physician or a dentist (Rural Policy Research Institute 2006).

One way of looking at this phenomenon is to see it as part of an inevitable boom-and-bust cycle, which typified frontier or gold-rush towns in the nineteenth century. Boom towns sometimes go bust even today (Broadway and Stull 2006). But we would argue that the problem is simply too widespread and debilitating to be just another cycle, and the transformation has been slow-moving, unlike the rapid flowering and denouement of towns like Bodie, California (Hendrix 1992). Both literally and figuratively, many small towns, especially in the Midwest, have been on their death beds for decades. And the end is near for some places where deaths far exceed births (Johnson 2011).

Unlike the travails of big cities, the decline of nonmetro America has received scant national media attention, perhaps because its incidence is so spatially diffuse and less visible. Big-city newspaper editors and journalists are mostly outsiders to rural America; they have little firsthand experience or real understanding of life in America's small and chronically depressed rural communities. However, for those living through it, the issue and what to do about incipient community decline has become a daily obsession. Small towns, counties, and even states that feel the effects of persistent out-migration have tried a raft of policy measures designed to stem brain drain and entice people to stay in or relocate to nonmetro America. Ideas as diverse as free land programs in Kansas, student loan forgiveness programs in West Virginia and Maine, and programs such as the Cool Cities Initiative in Michigan and "Come Back to Iowa, Please" have all been instituted as antidotes to out-migration. However, the jury is still out as to whether many of these have the intended effect of stemming population loss and/or retaining educated young adults.

The overwhelming demographic story of the past century in America is one of ongoing urbanization—growth in the nation's cities and suburbs at the expense of small towns and the farm population. To some observers, America has lost something important in the process. One trend that runs counter to rural decline is the new influx of immigrants, the majority of Hispanic origin, during the 1990s and 2000s. Johnson and Lichter (2008) report that rural Hispanics accounted for nearly 26 percent of nonmetro population growth over the 1990s and 45 percent between 2000 and 2006, while representing just 5.4 percent of the nonmetro population. Much of the growth was concentrated in rural Hispanic "boom towns" that have sprung from the relocation of America's slaughterhouses and meatpacking plants to the hinterland (Johnson and Lichter 2008; Kandel and Parrado 2005).

Early results from the 2010 decennial census shows that Hispanics accounted for the most of the growth in nonmetro areas over the 2000s. Nonmetro areas overall grew modestly over the past decade, from 48.4 to 50.4 million people. As shown in Table 1, the nonmetro Hispanic population alone grew from 2.6 million

TABLE 1
Racial and Ethnic Distribution of the U.S. Population, by Metro Status and Year

	2000		2010	
Race/ethnicity	Total population	Percentage of total population	Total population	Percentage of total population
Nonmetro areas				
White	39,765,577	82.2	40,142,918	79.6
Minorities	8,586,502	17.8	10,284,857	20.4
Black	4,088,836	8.5	4,182,761	8.3
Native American	904,193	1.9	968,881	1.9
Asian	344,552	0.7	456,723	0.9
Mixed race	562,856	1.2	805,090	1.6
Hispanic	2,604,811	5.4	3,767,645	7.5
Metro areas				
White	154,787,197	66.4	156,674,634	60.7
Minorities	78,282,630	33.6	101,643,129	39.3
Black	29,859,001	12.8	33,503,087	13.0
Native American	1,164,690	0.5	1,278,217	0.5
Asian	9,778,617	4.2	14,008,401	5.4
Mixed race	4,039,290	1.7	5,161,391	2.0
Hispanic	32,701,007	14.0	46,709,949	18.1

Source: 2000 and 2010 U.S. Census: Summary File 1.
Note: Hispanics may be of any race.

to 3.8 million over the same period. Although Hispanics represented only 7.5 percent of the total nonmetro population in 2010, they nevertheless accounted for the majority of population growth. This demographic pattern was played out across America's heartland over the 2000s.

In the agricultural state of Iowa, for example, population growth increased only modestly over the past decade—a little over 120,000 people. Iowa's population growth was driven entirely by Hispanics, a population that increased by 84 percent, or just over 150,000 persons, over the decade. Hispanic growth was concentrated mainly in small towns such as Marshalltown, West Liberty, Perry, and Storm Lake. In Denison, Iowa, Hispanics now account for a little over one-third of the population. With the comparatively higher birth rates of the in-migrants, the 13-year decline in school enrollment in the state also has been arrested. Rebecca Jackson, who works for the state-funded agency that oversees immigrant job placement in Denison agribusiness, said in a recent National Public Radio interview that immigrants are "keeping our schools open while other school districts are having to consolidate" (Dade 2011).

In terms of raw numbers, then, the rural immigrant influx has helped stabilize population loss in several economically hard-hit places. Johnson and Lichter (2008), in fact, showed that 221 nonmetropolitan counties would have experienced absolute population decline between 2000 and 2005 in the absence of Hispanic growth. Moreover, the new settlement of families with school-age children provides the added bonus of shoring up flagging school enrollments. With these positive developments also come some difficulties.

Much of the reason that immigrants move to rural America is to work in agriculture and agribusiness, as the Denison example mentioned above attests. For example, the meat-processing industry has targeted Hispanic workers to meet its labor needs (Kandel 2006; Kandel and Parrado 2005). Kandel (2006) notes that between 1980 and 2000, the Hispanic share of meat-processing workers tripled from 10 to 30 percent, and this share has continued to rise. At the same time, broader changes in the food-processing industry, including the development of distribution channels, permitted the meatpacking industry, for example, to locate plants closer to raw materials and where labor was cheap, abundant, and not unionized. As large conglomerates (e.g., ConAgra and IBP) began to dominate food processing—by the late 1990s, the top four firms accounted for 50 percent of all poultry and pork and 80 percent of beef production—the drive to increase profits led to decreased wages and more dangerous working conditions (*NOW on PBS* 2006). Though the Occupational Safety and Health Administration (OSHA) has strict guidelines for worker safety, the industry remains one of the most dangerous in America, with an average of 12.6 injuries or illnesses per 100 full-time workers in 2005 (Bureau of Labor Statistics 2005). Wages in this industry were once comparable to those in manufacturing. For instance, in 1960, the average meatpacker actually made slightly more than his manufacturing counterpart, but this has changed dramatically in recent times. Adjusting for inflation, the average hourly wage in meatpacking has decreased from $17.41 an hour in 1976 to $11.42 an hour in 2009 (Bureau of Labor Statistics 2009).

The overall transformation of the food-processing industry, which includes a move away from cities to nonmetro areas, the consolidation of manufacturing, and mechanization and de-skilling of the jobs, has profoundly impacted rural areas and the makeup of workers. In particular, immigrant workers have responded to the demand from food-processing companies for cheap labor. Most immigrants today are from Mexico and Latin America, but they also include Asians and Africans in some communities. Many have arrived directly from abroad rather than from traditional urban gateways and have little familiarity with local customs, the English language, or America's political and social institutions. These immigration trends have implications for the well-being and future of nonmetropolitan America.

First, in terms of the raw economic impact, a sudden rise in population injects life into what are, in many cases, moribund local economies. Immigrants add to the tax base, spend their money locally, and inject cash into housing markets, and local goods, and services. In North Carolina, for example, the Hispanic population contributed more than $9 billion annually to the state's economy through its purchases and taxes (Kasarda and Johnson 2006). The costs in higher taxes and public services, such as health care and education, were far less than the taxes paid. A study in Oregon focused on the economic impacts of eliminating unauthorized immigrants, finding a reduction of state and local tax revenues of between $400 and $656 million per year (Jaeger 2008). Under the circumstances, it is hardly surprising that local political and business elites are often more receptive than local workers to new Hispanic arrivals (Fennelly 2008).

Second, as we mentioned above, immigrants to nonmetro areas tend to be young and of childbearing age with school-age children. Unlike in the past (e.g., seasonal farm workers), many new arrivals increasingly are likely to be married and have families looking to settle (Farmer and Moon 2009). Indeed, fertility rates among Hispanics, especially new immigrants, are well in excess of those of native-born whites (Parrado 2011), and ethnic differentials are greatest in new destinations (Lichter et al. forthcoming). High Hispanic fertility is often an unappreciated second-order effect of new rural in-migration of Hispanic immigrants. The demographic implications are further magnified by below-replacement fertility among non-Hispanic whites. In rural places with chronic declines in school enrollment, immigrants have bolstered numbers and helped keep schools viable, but they also have raised new educational and fiscal challenges (e.g., English as a Second Language).

Third, alongside boons for local economies and school enrollments come demands on resources that, in many cases, are unforeseen by host communities. Immigrants tend to be younger and more economically disadvantaged than native-born residents and can consequently place demands on local services, such as health, education, and public assistance (Crowley and Lichter 2009; Kandel 2006). For example, in Worthington, Minnesota, home of the Swift meatpacking company, poverty rates among Hispanics exceeded 50 percent in the late 2000s. Nationally, the nonmetro Hispanic poverty rate in 2010 was nearly 30 percent, a figure exceeding the rate in metro areas (USDA 2011b). Rapid changes in the ethnoracial composition of local school districts also may raise new ethnic hostilities if the costs are borne disproportionately by aging white taxpayers on fixed incomes who are unaccustomed to ethnically diverse neighbors (Poterba 1997). The generation gap now has a racial component in many new Hispanic destinations.

Fourth, immigration in many small towns has unfolded rapidly and unexpectedly, and the speed at which the nonnative population settles can have a destabilizing effect. This is most apparent where there is little effort to integrate the nonnative population into local institutions (Grey 2006). So, for instance, immigrants are residentially and socially segregated (Lichter et al. 2010). Because of their willingness to work hard for low pay and under poor working conditions, local manual and low-skill workers in some cases blame immigrants for lowering wages in local industry, which further fuels resentment toward outsiders (Jensen 2006; Marrow 2009). Local residents also sometimes believe—usually incorrectly—that immigrants bring trouble. But so far, there is little evidence that immigration is associated with higher crime rates in areas of Hispanic settlement (Crowley and Lichter 2009; Sampson 2008).

Clearly there are both new opportunities and ongoing challenges posed by the unprecedented influx of immigrants to nonmetro America. If immigration is "done right," it can provide an economic lifeline to many distressed places that are hollowing out because of chronic out-migration of young people. Below, we outline the complex nature of immigration in rural America by sketching how the issue has played out in the state of Iowa. We then offer two case studies of small towns. In one community, immigration became a lightning rod for controversy and division. Rapid in-migration of Hispanics in the other town brought much less divisiveness and a great deal of success. We conclude with some policy suggestions as to how to better facilitate immigration in rural America.

A New Ellis Island? Iowa's Back-and-Forth Immigration Stance

The state of Iowa provides an interesting test case for examining how a heartland state has dealt with the often politically charged issue of immigration. Rural areas of Iowa, in common with their counterparts elsewhere in the Midwest, have been hollowing out for the past three decades (Carr and Kefalas 2009). While the overall population level of the state has been stable and even increasing slightly, the fact is that the urban centers around Des Moines, Cedar Rapids, and Iowa City have provided the bulk of this growth. Nonmetropolitan areas have seen declines, especially in the proportion of young people. Iowa's population grew between 2000 and 2010 by just under 3 percent; all of this increase was accounted for by the growth in the Hispanic population, which increased 83 percent to 151,544 persons. The only thing keeping Iowa from losing overall population is the increase in Hispanics settling there. Indeed, immigration masks the underlying trends of nonmetro population aging among the native-born and continued out-migration of the young and educated from small towns and rural areas. Both of these trends have been in evidence for at least three decades, and they overlie other important transformations in the socioeconomic landscape of the state.

During the same time period, rural areas in Iowa increasingly saw the growth of large food and meat-processing plants, as that industry moved closer to the source of its raw materials to cut costs and increase productivity. The sudden demand for low-skilled labor among these agribusiness employers attracted immigrants to towns such as Postville, West Liberty, and Storm Lake (Grey 1996; Grey, Devlin, and Goldsmith 2009). The new ethnic diversification of many areas that were predominantly populated by whites has been eye-opening (Johnson and Lichter 2010). Grey, Devlin, and Goldsmith (2009, 3) note the example of Conesville, Iowa, which is located in the eastern part of the state and whose population of 424 is over one-half Latino.

Indeed, it is not just Hispanic immigrants and migrants who have diversified Iowa. Des Moines, for example, is host to the second largest concentration of

Sudanese refugees in the nation behind Omaha, Nebraska. Elsewhere in the state, there are concentrations of Lao, Bosnian, Somali, and Iraqi immigrants.

The main draw for immigrants is job opportunities in food processing and, to a lesser extent, construction and hospitality. The influx of workers meets a well-documented labor shortage in the state (Leland 2008), though not in all areas of need. For instance, Iowa Workforce Development estimates that the state will create upward of 172,000 jobs between now and 2018, an increase of about 10 percent, and because the population is aging and not increasing at the same rate, labor demand will have to be met by attracting workers and/or retaining college graduates in the state. Many of the jobs that will be created, in industries such as health care and technology broadly conceived, will require at least some postsecondary education; for many immigrants these jobs will be out of reach, at least initially.

As the state tried to plan for the labor shortages in the 1990s and through the early 2000s, immigration was increasingly touted as the single best hope for meeting demand for low-skilled jobs. Employers and town officials in some cases aggressively recruited immigrants to work in food processing and other industries. Then–Marshalltown mayor Floyd Harthun famously went to Villachuato, Mexico to recruit workers after he found that many newcomers to the town were from that region. Other communities such as Perry have seen their population grow by almost a third in the 2000s because of sustained immigration, much of it to meet demand for workers at the Tyson Foods plant there; the town is currently 31 percent Hispanic. In Perry, 12 percent of the male workforce is employed by the food-processing industry, and the town has experienced an economic revitalization that has invigorated the local housing market and downtown business district (Schneider 2010).

The shot in the arm that immigration was providing for places like Perry, Marshalltown, and Storm Lake obscured some of the more divisive implications of this rapid change. This is best underscored by the political reaction to immigration personified by then-governor Tom Vilsack. As immigrants flocked to fill jobs that natives could not or would not take, Governor Vilsack welcomed the influx and made encouraging immigration a legislative priority. Upon entering office in 1998, he appointed a Strategic Planning Council to make Iowa "the Ellis Island of the Midwest." Vilsack also touted plans to make Iowa an "immigrant enterprise zone," but as opposition to immigration in the state started to grow, he later cooled in his efforts to promote immigration. A measure of his rethinking on the issue came in February 2002, when the Republican-led state legislature passed legislation to make English the state's official language, which Vilsack then signed into law. Indeed, the early 2000s saw immigration become one of the most divisive issues in the state, with pro- and anti-immigration groups proliferating and engaging in a war of words on the airwaves. In 2002, a group of Catholic nuns based in the Mississippi Valley and working under the banner Sisters United News (SUN) ran a billboard campaign in eight cities that had experienced an increase in immigration featuring a picture of an extended Hispanic immigrant family, dressed in their Sunday best with the tagline "Welcome the Immigrant *You* Once Were!—Catholic Sisters of this area." The campaign garnered attention beyond Iowa and was influential in the 2007 formation of the national group Welcoming America, which now operates in twelve states.

But in spite of the best efforts of SUN and other activists, the immigration question has become more vexed in Iowa. In 2004, a group called the Coalition for the Future of the American Worker began running an anti-immigration ad in Iowa that featured a fist repeatedly punching an inflatable dummy with the narration stating that greedy corporations and politicians are beating up on Iowa workers and favoring immigrants. The ad was based on a study of meatpacking in Storm Lake (Stull, Broadway, and Griffith 1995) that showed how IBP Processors had taken over the local plant and cut wages in part by attracting immigrants to come and work there for a little under $6 an hour. While based on research, the ad implied that immigrants were the source of all that ailed Iowa workers. The ad was roundly condemned by organized labor in the state and was eventually taken off the air, but the polarizing sentiment behind it has lingered since, and the massive Immigration and Customs Enforcement (ICE) raids at the Swift & Company processors in Marshalltown in December 2006 (Perkins, Brasher, and Alex 2006) and at Agriprocessors Inc. in Postville (Hsu 2008; Grey, Devlin, and Goldsmith 2009) in May 2008 have fanned the flames of this controversial issue. The fallout from the raid in Postville has garnered national and scholarly attention (see, for instance, Camayd-Freixas 2008; *New York Times* 2008; Peterson 2009) and has led to at least one documentary (*AbUSed in America*) being made about its aftermath.

As test cases go, the Iowa experience of the past two decades shows the problems and promise of immigration for small towns in America. On the plus side, there is little doubt that immigration has arrested population decline in nonmetro counties and has stabilized many small towns economically, as well as slowed or ended declining school enrollments. However, Iowa has also been host to divisive rhetoric, anti-immigrant legislation, and interdiction efforts that were clearly meant to be the model of things to come with respect to the treatment of undocumented workers. Still, Iowa's Hispanic population continues to grow rapidly.

To better flesh out the dynamics of what happens on the ground in a small town, we turn to two case studies of places that have seen a pronounced, growth in nonnative populations in the past few decades: Hazleton, Pennsylvania, and St. James, Minnesota.

Immigration Enforcement: Hazleton, Pennsylvania

The town of Hazleton is located in Luzerne County in the midsection of eastern Pennsylvania and was traditionally a coal and manufacturing town. With a 2010 population of 25,340, Hazleton is one of the many former industrial towns that have suffered the downdraft of deindustrialization and the rise of global markets. Though it is located relatively close to several major metropolitan centers, it faces stiff competition for employers who have perhaps better options when it comes to setting up shop. As fortunes had just about reached a nadir in the town around the turn of the twenty-first century, Hispanic immigrants began settling there. Hispanics accounted for less than 1 percent of the Hazleton population in 1990, and this figure increased to 4.9 percent in 2000. However, the pace of settlement increased dramatically during the 2000s, when Hazleton reversed a seven-decade decline in population. The community added 2,011 inhabitants—mostly Hispanics—who now make up 37.3 percent of Hazleton's population. Hazleton is well on its way to be becoming a majority-minority community. Immigrants and migrants moved to Hazleton for many reasons: the relatively low cost of living and cheaper housing, compared to larger metropolitan areas; the availability of entry-level jobs, mostly in the service sector; and perhaps because of chain migration.

The rapid growth of Hispanics in Hazleton in the two decades since 1990 has provoked an often vocal response, where some native Hazletonians have pushed back against the influx of newcomers. At the time, CNN's Lou Dobbs, in his nightly news hour, used Hazleton as a case in point to describe the putative immigrant threat to America and the need for shutting down the borders and saving jobs for real Americans. The pushback began in mid-2000s when then–Hazleton mayor and current congressman for Pennsylvania's Eleventh District Louis Barletta Jr. proposed an ordinance to the City Council that he called the Illegal Immigration Relief Act. It imposed a $1,000-a-day fine for any landlord renting to an illegal immigrant and suspended for five years the business license of anyone hiring an illegal immigrant (Powell and Garcia 2006). The ordinance itself originated with Kris Kobach, who was then a law professor at the University of Missouri–Kansas City and is now secretary of state for Kansas. Kobach was, in the words of someone familiar with the Hazleton case, "looking for a test case"; and so the law itself was "not organic in origin, but written by an out-of-towner, shopped by an out-of-towner, and embraced by a mayor who saw this as his signature issue." A similar law was also being debated at the time in Escondido, California. In a July 2006 meeting, the Hazleton City Council voted four to one to pass the act into law. Barletta, who arrived at that meeting sporting a bulletproof vest under his jacket, had long maintained that "illegal" immigrants had flooded the town and driven up crime rates. In fact, violent crime rates had declined in Hazleton between 2000 and 2003. For instance, reported rapes, robberies, homicides, and assaults declined between 2000 and 2003,[1] as did the number of arrests, which went down 16 percent over the same period (Federal Bureau of Investigation 2000, 2001, 2002, 2003).

Perhaps what became more important in Hazleton was not the amount of crime, but what Innes (2004) calls signal crimes, where certain incidents serve as warnings to people about the perceived or actual risk to their safety. As current mayor and then–council president Joseph Yannuzzi recalled in an interview with us on September 6, 2011, before the ordinance was crafted there had been what he described as a "cold-blooded murder" in Hazleton where Derek Kichline was gunned down by two assailants on May 10, 2006. Two men, both undocumented Dominican nationals, were arrested and charged with the killing, but were later released and deported because of a lack of forensic evidence and inconsistent eyewitness testimony. This incident, along with a shooting at a local park, cohered as signal crimes that symptomized, for some, the dangers of an unlawful immigrant population. At the time, Mayor Lou Barletta said that residents were afraid to sit on their stoops and that illegal immigrants made up a disproportionate share of all arrests (Young 2007). Mayor Yannuzzi said that though the ordinance created a great deal of controversy, there was, in his opinion, widespread support for it in the town, and that even a "small proportion of the Latino community felt that they were being blamed and they wanted [undocumented aliens] gone." We asked the mayor whether, if he had it to do over again, he would choose the same path of action, and he replied that he "would basically do the same thing. I thought it was right and I felt strongly about it." He adds, though, that he "would be better prepared for the limelight, [which] caught me off guard."

Soon after the Illegal Immigration Relief Act was passed, which incidentally became a model of sorts for other municipalities around the nation, a lawsuit filed by the Puerto Rican Legal Defense and Education Fund challenged the new ordinance on constitutional grounds, namely, that the city cannot infringe upon the federal government's right to regulate immigration.

The legal challenge to the act was eventually led by the American Civil Liberties Union (ACLU), and the suit, *Lozano v. The City of Hazleton*, was heard by the Third Circuit Court of Appeals in Philadelphia in 2008. The resulting judgment of the Third Circuit was to strike down the law on the grounds that it infringed on the federal government's exclusive right to regulate immigration. The City of Hazleton appealed to the U.S. Supreme Court and, based on a May 2011 ruling in the case of *U.S. Chamber of Commerce v. Whiting*, the court in June 2011 opted to vacate the Third Circuit ruling and issue a writ of *certiorari* directing the lower court to reconsider the case. In the *Whiting* ruling, the Supreme Court voted to affirm the ruling of lower courts that the Legal Arizona Workers Act, which mandates the use of the E-Verify system to judge the legal status of workers and has penalties and licensing restrictions for employers who employ illegal immigrants, does not preempt federal law. The *Whiting* ruling opened the door for states and municipalities to issue laws that impose sanctions against illegal immigrants and those businesses that employ or rent housing to them. Up until now, the legal fees for Hazleton have been paid for by donations from outside the town. At the time of writing, the city has used up the fund of just shy of $500,000 and faces the prospect of having to pay legal fees for the next court hearing. Joseph Yannuzzi reflects that he would just like to "get it over with" and move on.

Though the legal future of the Illegal Immigration Relief Act is uncertain, the deep divisions that the issue has opened up in the town itself seem, if not set in stone, certain to have hardened over the past six years. One of the ironic wrinkles in the Hazleton story is the targeting of Puerto Ricans as illegal immigrants, when, in fact, they are U.S. citizens. In alluding to this widespread misconception, Amanda Bergson-Shilcock of the Pennsylvania Welcome Center pointed out in an interview with us on August 26, 2011, that despite the fact that there are approximately 300,000 Puerto Ricans in Pennsylvania, some are routinely detained on immigration waivers and are processed for deportation. Bergson-Shilcock says that this is symptomatic of a wider misconception that can extend to government officials and that underscores some of the complexities of the debate.

Whatever the legal ramifications of the Hazleton ordinance, the town and its immigration stance became a national cause célèbre at the time and propelled then-mayor Barletta into the thick of the larger debate around immigration. However, even proponents of the ordinance are quick to point out that migration/immigration has brought some tangible benefits to Hazleton. Mayor Yannuzzi told us that "Latinos revitalized the city of Hazleton," and in particular, they "turned one section of town around." Boarded-up storefronts and the vacant apartments above them have been replaced by a bustling shopping area—and people. Even the fact that the local schools are "busting at the seams" is not all bad, according to the mayor. It is, after all, preferable to having to close schools because of a lack of students.

Looking to the future in Hazleton, Yannuzzi says that in 10 years things will have progressed socially to the point where newcomers "will be blending in socially and people [will be] accepting them." In particular, he says that when young people intermingle, for example, by playing on the same sports teams, the acrimony between the groups will die out. Familiarity breeds understanding and acceptance, but it takes time and patience (see Putnam 2007).

Despite the optimistic note of Mayor Yannuzzi, the fact remains that immigration has been a divisive issue in Hazleton. The first real response to newcomers, immigrants and migrants alike, was to create legislation designed to exclude rather than to integrate, and, in so doing, blur the distinction between undocumented immigrants, legal immigrants, and Hispanic U.S. citizens. It is also unclear whether anti-immigrant sentiment has slowed the growth of the Hispanic population, including unauthorized immigrants, or whether Hispanic in-migration has slowed, reversed course, or been diverted to other areas. Nationally, the late 2000s "Great Recession" has been associated with both declines in new Hispanic immigration and return migration to Mexico or elsewhere (Rendall, Brownell, and Kups 2011).

This would seem to suggest that many new immigrants may be either "frozen" in place (including places like Hazleton) or "trapped" in the United States. The militarization of the border may keep some unauthorized immigrants out, but it also keeps others in. That is, the difficulties—financial and otherwise—of returning to the United States create large disincentives to leaving the United States in the first place. Massey and Akresh (2006), in fact, have shown that most Mexican immigrants often do not intend to become citizens. Rather, they "seek to maximize earnings in the short term while retaining little commitment to any particular society or national labor market over the longer term" (p. 954). Current U.S. immigration policy may effectively trap uncommitted immigrants and reduce the circular migration between the United States and Mexico that characterized the past (Massey and Singer 1995).

Hazleton is an important case mostly because it reflects the temperature of the immigration issue as it has played out in many small towns over the past decade, but it is not the only pathway available. Specifically, the experience of St. James, Minnesota provides a contrast to that of Hazleton.

Integration: St. James, Minnesota

St. James is a small town of 4,685 people in south-central Minnesota. It is the county seat of Matonwan County, a largely rural part of the state about 120 miles southwest of Minneapolis-St. Paul. Mankato is its closest "city"—roughly thirty miles away. As with Hazleton, St. James has become a destination point of Hispanic immigration and migration, though the timing and scale of the change illustrates a slightly different pattern. Currently, as measured by the 2010 census, slightly less than one-quarter of the population is Hispanic, and this has been stable since 2000. In St. James, the main influx of immigrants occurred during the 1990s. Hispanics had a toehold in the community in 1990, but they represented only 7.6 percent of the total population. Initially, immigrants were attracted to St. James by opportunities in manufacturing there, specifically in meat processing and machine-tool works. Now, more than half of the children in grades 8 and below are of Hispanic origin, and this has been crucial in maintaining enrollment levels in the system.

The modern history of immigration in St. James started in the 1970s and 1980s, when Tony Downs Foods, a plant that processes spent hens, had a labor shortage and the company went to south Texas to recruit workers. At first, they recruited only single men, nearly all of them Hispanics, who were housed in a large disused building on the edge of St. James that had been refitted to become a residential development. However, this approach proved to be fraught with problems; specifically, warehousing young single men in an isolated part of town led to trouble. In the words of Sue Harris, whom we interviewed on August 31, 2011, and who has worked in the education department of the county for 30 years teaching and coordinating preschool and adult programming, these were "not pleasant circumstances."

Soon after, Tony Downs Foods decided to change its labor recruitment strategy to encourage more families to relocate to St. James. This had a positive initial impact on the town, although many teething issues remained, not least of which was ensuring that families could access services they needed. So in the mid-1990s the town convened a large group of local stakeholders under the moniker "Spirit of St. James" to put together a strategic plan for the area. Though the initial group was made up entirely of native whites, there was a spin-off group that tried to gauge the experiences of newcomers. The testimonies gathered from this exercise catalogued a host of contentious issues. New arrivals, for example, reported that they often felt like they were being watched everywhere, but especially in stores. Many were uncomfortable and felt that they were "not welcome" in St. James. As this information filtered back to the main planning group, it proved to be "very eye-opening for everyone," while prompting a rich discussion about what to do next.

The next step saw several local stakeholders come together and form the Family Services Collaborative. The Collaborative brought together social and school stakeholders to help families access services. As Sue Harris explains, "So many families can't access services, and in many cases the children are the interpreters for the parents, and the schools can be quickly overwhelmed." The Collaborative oversaw efforts at expanding English as a Second Language (ESL) programs at the local schools, translating documents and information pamphlets into Spanish, and putting a migrant support program into place for those who are transitory residents.

The work of the Collaborative has been continued by several initiatives since, including a program called Horizons, which provides integration training. Another one, called Unity-Unidad, was formed by local groups, including the police, to foster closer relations between native and nonnative communities. Despite the many efforts at integration, there was, and still is, some resistance to newcomers, according to Sue Harris. But community conflict and ethnic hostilities have decreased over the years. The early strategic planning instilled a spirit of mutual understanding and accommodation, helping the process of community integration. The local Hispanic population is stable and newcomers are staying, replacing the highly transitory population that characterized the past. Providing tangible evidence of positive community change are the recent Hispanic homecoming kings and queens at the local high school.

In contrast to Hazleton, the St. James municipal and county governments have not tried to pass any ordinances that would seek to prosecute employers or landlords for hiring or renting to undocumented people. Instead, the approach has been one that has sought to integrate immigrants. The institutions that have led the way on this are the schools, the churches, and social-service providers in the county. For instance, when there was going to be an Immigration and Customs Enforcement (ICE) raid on the town in October 2008, school officials were notified in advance of the operation and put an emergency plan in place to ensure that teachers stayed behind after hours and schools remained open in case the parents of school-going children had been detained (Chang 2008).

The lack of outright acrimony over the immigrant population in St. James is in stark contrast with Hazleton. There are several possible explanations for the difference in experience. One possible reason is the scale of the change. Immigrants make up a smaller portion of the overall population in St. James than they do in Hazleton, and the population change in the Minnesota town has been more gradual, as opposed to the rapid and convulsive change in Hazleton. However, because St. James is a much smaller place than Hazleton, it could be argued that newcomers are even more visible in a town of 4,600 people than they are in one of 25,000.

A second possible explanation is that the social and political climate is different in each place. At the local level politics in Hazleton have cohered around old industrial fault lines and the ethnic whites who populated the steel and manufacturing industries in their heyday, whereas in St. James there was no such tradition or established political order. Also, state politics and policies may have a formative effect on local anti-immigrant sentiments. For instance, a report commissioned and published by the Minneapolis Foundation (Otteson, Owen, and Meyerson 2010, 1) recognizes that because "immigration can be a polarizing topic, the main purpose of this report is to provide a clear, balanced and fact-based overview of what is known, and what is not known, about the economic, cultural and social impact of recent immigrants to Minnesota." More interesting was the finding that after exhaustive efforts interviewing scores of key informants on the issue of immigration in the state, the researchers could not find anyone who "expressed the need for greater enforcement of current immigration laws, or increased limitations and requirements . . . [which suggests] significant concern among certain individuals that the expression of anti-immigration views may not only be unpopular but even unacceptable among certain leaders, policymakers and academics throughout Minnesota's communities" (Otteson, Owen, and Meyerson 2010, 35). The difference in tone around the issue in Minnesota as opposed to Pennsylvania is striking, as the laws and ordinances that focus on enforcement of existing laws and additional sanctions in the case of the latter state attest.

Furthermore, the approach in Minnesota more generally has focused on integrating the host and nonnative communities, a symmetrical rather than asymmetrical process. For instance, many communities have established "diversity coalitions," which have several iterations, but the unifying theme is the promotion of improved relations between foreign-born and U.S. residents. Downs-Schwei and Fennelly (2007) find that there are several initiatives under the banner of diversity coalitions ranging from community festivals to civic engagement campaigns. However, what is still lacking—and needed—are effective efforts to educate the native U.S. white population, without which successful integration will be difficult to achieve. But as Sue Harris points out, the perspective of many rural Minnesotans is that the past history of sustained population loss makes the goal of keeping current residents essential to the community's long-term viability. She acknowledges that St. James would lose half of its population if one of the meat-processing or engineering plants were to close. Single-industry small towns are vulnerable in this way, and St. James is no exception.

For now, St. James is beating the odds. The downtown, which had been empty, is thriving, mainly with Hispanic-owned businesses, and school enrollment is robust. While the journey to full integration of native and nonnative populations in St. James is far from over, the signs are more positive than negative. However, Sue Harris strikes a note of caution when she says that despite the almost two decades of planning, she feels that St. James could be "one election away from things changing." Harris cites the experience of the central Minnesota town of Willmar as evidence of what can happen when a new mayor with a different orientation—a less receptive one—to the immigration issue is elected (Espinoza 2010).

What Can We Learn from the Case Studies? Policy Implications for Immigration and Small Towns

The evidence seems clear: immigration has the potential to arrest long-standing population and economic declines in small towns in rural America, but only if it is done right. There are scores of examples of Hazletons who have gone down the road of draconian and divisive measures. Indeed, the growth of local anti-immigration ordinances has skyrocketed in recent years (Hopkins 2010). There are many fewer examples like St. James where a conscious effort was made to encourage integration and build bridges between the native and nonnative communities. This is easier said than done for several reasons.

First, immigration policy is being made, remade, and interpreted at the national, state, and increasingly at the local level. It is an altogether murky picture as to what law, ordinance, or court decision takes precedence, and the upshot is that the policy is in flux, while enforcement seems also to vary depending on the political trade winds. What is needed is clarity and vision as to what immigration policy is at every level of U.S. society. With regard to the hollowing out of rural areas, a policy of depending solely on interdiction ignores how detrimental mass criminalization and deportation can be, as was evident in the case of Postville (Grey, Devlin, and Goldsmith 2009).

Second, there is a need to synthesize and publicize the growing body of scholarly work on the net impacts of immigration on small towns (e.g., Crowley and Lichter 2009; Kandel et al. 2011). The Hazleton case study brings to life how the supposed positive impact of immigration can be contested. The town has seen long-term depopulation arrested, but those who have resisted newcomers have argued that the net economic impact of Hazleton's new residents has been negative because of the increased expenditures in education and social services. Although prejudice is often immune to facts, community leaders and stakeholders desperately need clarity on the actual impact of migrants and immigrants to a local and regional economy, in the short, medium, and long terms. For instance, several contradictory trends can be simultaneously present as some have argued (Otteson, Owen, and Myerson 2010). So more workers, home owners, and retail sales can increase the local tax base but also expand the need for more government assistance and local funding for students with limited English proficiency. What can often be missed in isolating one statistic is what each trend might mean in the long term, as an economy stabilizes and expands and the need for transfer payments or school subsidies diminishes.

In many places immigration has been divisive, and much can be attributed to misinformation, but often what is needed in the discourse about the issue goes much further than providing facts. Amanda Bergson-Shilcock says that, in her experience at hundreds of community meetings on the issue, for many people who actively resist immigration the facts of the economic benefits of arresting depopulation do not matter. In such a context, she says that experts coming in and spouting off facts is often perceived as telling natives that "your emotions don't count." Paternalism does not usually work. It is crucial then for a dialogue to start from a place where people understand that for many natives the changes assailing their communities are "viewed as a loss" (see also Gans 1963; Kefalas 2003; Suttles 1968). Key in this process is that change must come from within the community and cannot be imposed from without, and it cannot be fast-paced; it should be gradual. St. James has been successful precisely because the change came from within the community—local leaders decided that they would make every effort to include newcomers and plan for a future that reflected the changing demographic reality there.

In terms of policy changes that should be on the table, we should begin to tackle immigration reform, especially with respect to the longtime undocumented workers who are raising families here. Passage of the so-called "Dream Act" may be one place to start; Hispanic-origin children who came to this country illegally with their parents are stuck in a legal netherworld. For instance, in St. James, one young woman who was homecoming queen and who will graduate in May 2012 near the top of her class has no Social Security number and thus cannot take her place at a local university. But we should also address some of the changes that will be needed in terms of agricultural policy and labor laws that can ensure that pay is fair and working conditions in agri-processing are safe for all workers. Perhaps the organizing experience of the United Farm Workers Union in California offers hope and caution in this regard (Pawel 2009). Cesar Chavez and many talented individuals did succeed in organizing migrant labor, but the movement that initiated these changes splintered. A smart guest worker program might prevent exploitation by employers while also ensuring that workers pay taxes and receive the public services that they are due. One recent by-product of the criminalizing of the undocumented is the onion farmers in Georgia, who do not now have the labor they need to harvest their crops (National Public Radio, 23 May 2010); crops are left rotting in the fields for lack of field workers, who have left for more receptive states (such as North Carolina). So we have a ludicrous situation where we need these workers in agriculture or in food processing or manufacturing but the wider debate has created a policy chimera where one state or municipality goes one way, while its neighbors go another. The law passed in Alabama in October 2011 has had an immediate displacement effect (Robertson 2011), with residents fleeing to Tennessee, Illinois, or Arkansas.

From the foregoing, there are several implications about the future of nonmetro America. First, the long-standing declines in population and jobs can be turned around through immigration, as the experiences of many small towns can attest. Second, the response of local stakeholders and local leaders to demographic change can have a profound impact on the community; that is, whether to respond with diffidence or to do so with inclusiveness. Third, the immigration policy landscape and enforcement climate is so muddled that a comprehensive overhaul at all levels of government is needed as a matter of urgency. The immigration debate is often held hostage to divisive politics that too often ignore the on-the-ground realities. It is time that the debate is informed by what is really happening locally, while also acknowledging the viewpoints of natives who sometimes feel that their way of life is under threat. These are lofty goals, and we are aware that a seismic shift is needed to move the issue forward. But failure to address them will mean that the new rural immigration will remain a vexed, contentious, and intractable issue for the foreseeable future.

Note

1. There are no available and sanctioned Uniform Crime Reports for the years 2004 through 2007 for Hazleton, so it is difficult to say exactly what went on in the years immediately before and after the Illegal Immigrant Relief Act. The rate for violent crime does increase in the years 2008 and 2009, when there were 81 reported violent crimes, which equates to a rate of just under 400 per 100,000 inhabitants. This rate is still below state and national levels.

References

Broadway, Michael J., and Donald D. Stull. 2006. Meat processing and Garden City, KS: Boom and bust. *Journal of Rural Studies* 22:55–66.

Bureau of Labor Statistics. 2005. *Workplace injuries and illnesses*. Washington, DC: U.S. Department of Labor.

Bureau of Labor Statistics. 2009. *Occupational employment and wages, May 2009: Slaughterers and meat packers*. Washington, DC: U.S. Department of Labor.

Camayd-Freixas, Erik. 2008. Interpreting after the largest ICE raid in US history: A personal account. Manuscript. Available from http://graphics8.nytimes.com/images/2008/07/14/opinion/14ed-camayd.pdf.

Carr, Patrick J., and Maria J. Kefalas. 2009. *Hollowing out the middle: The rural brain drain and what it means for America*. Boston, MA: Beacon.

Chang, Bea. 23 October 2008. Immigration raids in Madelia, St. James. Associated Press. Available from http://www.kare11.com/news/news_article.aspx?storyid=527614.

Crowley, Martha, and Daniel T. Lichter. 2009. Social disorganization in new Latino destinations? *Rural Sociology* 74:573–604.

Dade, Corey. 2011. Hispanic clout trails population growth, for now. NPR News. Available from http://www.npr.org/2011/03/25/134856635/hispanic-clout-trails-population-growth-for-now.

Domina, Thurston. 2006. What clean break? Education and nonmetropolitan migration patterns, 1989–2004. *Rural Sociology* 71:373–98.

Downs-Schwei, Tamar, and Katherine Fennelly. 2007. Diversity coalitions in rural communities. *CURA Reporter*. 37 (Winter): 13–22.

Espinoza, Ambar. 21 December 2010. New mayor brings back interest in contested immigration program in Willmar. Minnesota Public Radio. Available from http://minnesota.publicradio.org/display/web/2010/12/21/willmar-immigration-proposal/.

Farmer, Frank L., and Zola K. Moon. 2009. An empirical examination of characteristics of Mexican migrants to metropolitan and nonmetropolitan areas of the United States. *Rural Sociology* 74:220–40.

Federal Bureau of Investigation. 2000. *Uniform crime report*. Washington, DC: U.S. Department of Justice.

Federal Bureau of Investigation. 2001. *Uniform crime report*. Washington, DC: U.S. Department of Justice.

Federal Bureau of Investigation. 2002. *Uniform crime report*. Washington, DC: U.S. Department of Justice.

Federal Bureau of Investigation. 2003. *Uniform crime report.* Washington, DC: U.S. Department of Justice.

Fennelly, Katherine. 2008. Prejudice toward immigrants in the Midwest. In *New faces in new places: The changing geography of American immigration,* ed. Douglas Massey, 151–78. New York, NY: Russell Sage Foundation.

Gans, Herbert. 1963. *The urban villagers: Group and class in the life of Italian Americans.* New York, NY: Free Press.

Grey, Mark. 1996. Meat-packing and the migration of refugee and immigrant labor to Storm Lake, Iowa. *Changing Face* 2(3). Available from http://migration.ucdavis.edu/cf/comments.php?id=154_0_2_0.

Grey, Mark. 2006. *New Americans, new Iowans: Welcoming immigrant and refugee newcomers.* Cedar Falls: Iowa Center for Immigrant Leadership and Integration, University of Northern Iowa.

Grey, Mark, Michele Devlin, and Aaron Goldsmith. 2009. *Postville, USA: Surviving diversity in small-town America.* Boston, MA: Gemmamedia.

Hendrix, Kathleen. 2 July 1992. Boom or bust? Can the ghost town of Bodie survive another gold rush? Mining companies say yes; opponents say no. *Los Angeles Times,* E3.

Hopkins, Daniel J. 2010. Politicized places: Explaining where and when immigrants provoke local opposition. *American Political Science Review* 104:40–60.

Hsu, Spencer S. 18 May 2008. Immigration raid jars a small town: Critics say employers should be targeted. *Washington Post,* A6.

Innes, Martin. 2004. Signal crime and signal disorders: Notes on deviance as communicative action. *British Journal of Sociology* 55 (3): 335–55.

Jaeger, William K. 2008. *Potential economic impacts in Oregon of implementing proposed Department of Homeland Security "no match" immigration rules.* Wilsonville, OR: Coalition for a Working Oregon.

Jensen, Leif. 2006. *Immigrant settlements in rural America: Problems, prospects, and policies.* Durham: University of New Hampshire, Carsey Institute.

Johnson, Kenneth M. 2011. The continuing incidence of natural decrease in American counties. *Rural Sociology* 76:74–100.

Johnson, Kenneth M., and Daniel T. Lichter. 2008. Natural increase: A new source of population growth in emerging Hispanic destinations. *Population and Development Review* 34:327–46.

Johnson, Kenneth M., and Daniel T. Lichter. 2010. Growing diversity among America's children and youth: Spatial and temporal dimensions. *Population and Development Review* 36:151–76.

Kandel, William. June 2006. Meat-processing firms attract Hispanic workers to rural America. *Amber Waves.* 4 (3): 10–15.

Kandel, William, Jamila Henderson, Heather Koball, and Randy Capps. 2011. Moving up in rural America: Economic attainment of nonmetro Latino immigrants. *Rural Sociology* 76:101–28.

Kandel, William, and Emilio Parrado. 2005. Restructuring of the US meat-processing industry and new Hispanic migrant destinations. *Population and Development Review* 31 (3): 447–71.

Kasarda, John D., and James H. Johnson. 2006. *The impact of the Hispanic population on the state of North Carolina.* Chapel Hill: Kenan Center, University of North Carolina at Chapel Hill.

Kefalas, Maria J. 2003. *Working-class heroes: Protecting home, community and nation in a Chicago neighborhood.* Berkeley: University of California Press.

Leland, John. 21 May 2008. As Iowa job surplus grows, workers call the shots. *New York Times,* A5.

Lichter, Daniel T., Kenneth M. Johnson, Richard Turner, and Allison Churilla. Forthcoming. Hispanic assimilation and fertility in new destinations. *International Migration Review.*

Lichter, Daniel T., Domenico Parisi, Michael C. Taquino, and Steven Michael Grice. 2010. Residential segregation in new Hispanic destinations: Cities, suburbs, and rural communities compared. *Social Science Research* 38:215–30.

Lyson, Thomas A. 2002. What does a school mean to a community? Assessing the social and economic benefits of rural villages in New York. *Journal of Research in Rural Education* 17:131–37.

Marrow, Helen B. 2009. New immigrant destinations and the American color line. *Ethnic and Racial Studies* 32:1037–57.

Massey, Douglas S., and Ilana Redstone Akresh. 2006. Immigrant intentions and mobility in a global economy: The attitudes and behaviors of recently arrived U.S. immigrants. *Social Science Quarterly* 87:954–71.

Massey, Douglas S., and Audrey Singer. 1995. New estimates of undocumented Mexican migration and the probability of apprehension. *Demography* 32:203–13.

McGranahan, David, John Cromartie, and Timothy Wojan. 2010. The two faces of rural population loss through outmigration. *Amber Waves* 8 (4): 38–45.

New York Times. 13 July 2008. Editorial: The shame of Postville. A24.

NOW on PBS. 15 December 2006. Meatpacking in the U.S.: Still a jungle out there? Public Broadcasting Service.

Otteson, Christa, Greg Owen, and Jessica Myerson. 2010. *A new age of immigrants: Making immigration work for Minnesota*. St. Paul, MN: The Minneapolis Foundation.

Parrado, Emilio A. 2011. How high is Hispanic/Mexican fertility in the United States? Immigration and tempo considerations. *Demography* 48:1059–80.

Pawel, Miriam. 2009. *The union of their dreams: Power, hope, and struggle in Cesar Chavez's farm worker movement*. New York, NY: Bloomsbury.

Perkins, Jerry, Phillip Brasher, and Tom Alex. 12 December 2006. Feds raid Marshalltown plant; busloads of workers arrested. *Des Moines Register*, A1.

Peterson, Cassie. 2009. An Iowa immigration raid leads to unprecedented criminal consequences: Why ICE should rethink the Postville model. *Iowa Law Review* 95:323–46.

Poterba, James M. 1997. Demographic structure and the political economy of public education. *Journal of Policy Analysis and Management* 16:48–66.

Powell, Michael, and Michelle Garcia. 22 August 2006. Pa. city puts illegal immigrants on notice: "They must leave" Mayor of Hazleton says after signing tough new law. *Washington Post*.

Putnam, Robert D. 2007. *E pluribus unum*: Diversity and community in the twenty-first century. *Scandinavian Political Studies* 30:137–74.

Rendall, Michael S., Peter Brownell, and Sarah Kups. 2011. Declining return migration from the United States to Mexico in the late-2000s recession: A research note. *Demography* 48:1049–58.

Robertson, Campbell. 4 October 2011. After ruling, Hispanics flee an Alabama town. *New York Times*, A1.

Rural Policy Research Institute. 2006. *Demographic and economic profile: Iowa*. Columbia: University of Missouri Press.

Sampson, Robert J. 2008. Rethinking crime and immigration. *Contexts* 7 (1): 28–33.

Schneider, Keith. 13 April 2010. Rebuilding a town, one piece at a time. *New York Times*, B6.

Stull, Donald D., Michael J. Broadway, and David Griffith, eds. 1995. *Any way you cut it: Meat processing and small town America*. Lawrence: University Press of Kansas.

Suttles, Gerald D. 1968. *The social order of the slum: Ethnicity and territory in the inner-city*. Chicago, IL: University of Chicago Press.

U.S. Department of Agriculture. 2011a. *Rural income, poverty, and welfare*. Available at http://www.ers.usda.gov/Briefing/IncomePovertyWelfare/Overview.htm.

U.S. Department of Agriculture. 2011b. *Rural income, poverty, and welfare: Poverty demographics*. Available from http://www.ers.usda.gov/Briefing/IncomePovertyWelfare/PovertyDemographics.htm.

Vitiello, Domenic. October 2008. The metropolitics of immigration: A tale of two Philadelphia suburbs. Presented at Metropolis International Conference, Bonn, Germany.

Young, Mary. 17 October 2007. Mayor Lou Barletta of Hazleton at immigration firestorm's center. *Reading Eagle*, 1.

Seeing Immigrants: Institutional Visibility and Immigrant Incorporation in New Immigrant Destinations

By
JAMIE WINDERS

Since the 1990s, immigrant settlement has expanded beyond gateway cities and transformed the social fabric of a growing number of American cities. In the process, it has raised new questions for urban and migration scholars. This article argues that immigration to new destinations provides an opportunity to sharpen understandings of the relationship between immigration and the urban by exploring it under new conditions. Through a discussion of immigrant settlement in Nashville, Tennessee, it identifies an overlooked precursor to immigrant incorporation—how cities see, or do not see, immigrants within the structure of local government. If immigrants are not institutionally visible to government or nongovernmental organizations, immigrant abilities to make claims to or on the city as urban residents are diminished. Through the combination of trends toward neighborhood-based urban governance and neoliberal streamlining across American cities, immigrants can become institutionally hard to find and, thus, plan for in the city.

Keywords: immigrant incorporation; new immigrant destinations; urban politics; neighborhood empowerment; Southern cities; neoliberalism

Since the late 1990s, immigration has transformed the social fabric of a growing number of American cities, as the geography of

Jamie Winders is an associate professor of geography in the Maxwell School at Syracuse University. Her research addresses immigration, urban transformation, and racial and cultural politics, especially in the U.S. South. She is completing a book on Latino migration to Nashville and its impacts on schools and neighborhoods.

NOTE: Portions of this article were developed while I was a visiting scholar at the Russell Sage Foundation. The support Russell Sage has given this research from its inception, along with the feedback from Russell Sage scholars, has been truly invaluable. I also thank Sandra Sanchez, who provided much-needed assistance on this project as it was conducted, and Barbara Ellen Smith, who helped me work through some of the ideas presented here. Finally, I thank Rob Sampson and John MacDonald for inviting me to be part of this special issue, as well as other authors for feedback on earlier versions of this article.

DOI: 10.1177/0002716211432281

immigration has expanded beyond immigrant gateways and into cities up and down the urban hierarchy (e.g., Brettell and Nibbs 2011; H. Smith and Furuseth 2006; Zúñiga and Hernández-León 2005; Fink 2003; Odem and Lacy 2009; McClain et al. 2006; Striffler 2007; Wang and Li 2007; Winders 2006, 2008). This new geography of immigrant, especially Latino, settlement challenges both what we know of and how we think about immigration and American cities, as it forces us to consider both topics from new perspectives. Immigrants are moving directly to American suburbs, bypassing the central city and destabilizing the spatial frameworks scholars and policymakers have used to evaluate neighborhood change, immigrant assimilation, race relations, and so on. Immigrants are also moving to new places, both skipping and leaving gateways such as Los Angeles in favor of locations in the U.S. South and elsewhere (Lichter and Johnson 2009). Further complicating these patterns, Doug Massey and his coauthors (2010) have documented a link between nontraditional destinations in the South and nontraditional sending communities in Mexico, thus pointing to new geographies of migration not only in the United States but also in sending countries. In short, more American cities are being drawn onto the map of immigration, and the task of thinking through immigration's impact on the social fabric of U.S. cities is becoming more complicated.

As immigrant settlement has expanded across urban America (and rural America; see Cuadros 2006; Kandel and Parrado 2005; Marrow 2009; McConnell and Miraftab 2009), the politics of immigration have heated up as well (e.g., Winders 2007; Sziarto and Leitner 2010; Varsanyi 2011). With immigrant workers becoming mixed-status families with children in local schools, homes in local neighborhoods, and cultural institutions across local landscapes, responses to immigrants, especially undocumented immigrants, have become increasingly shrill, particularly in new destinations (B. Smith and Winders 2008). Southern states such as Alabama have drafted, and partially enacted, some of the nation's most restrictive legislation concerning immigration, and small towns from Pennsylvania to Tennessee have become epicenters in national immigration debates. Add to this mix the Great Recession, which has made immigrant economic survival precarious in many places, and not only the map but also the politics of immigration's impacts on the social fabric of American cities have become increasingly complex.

This article considers the relationship between the changing map of immigrant, especially Latino, settlement and understandings of American urban dynamics more broadly. Geographic shifts in where Latino immigrants are settling, demographic shifts in what immigrant communities look like, and political shifts in how immigrants are received have transformed the relationship between immigration and urban America and destabilized the frameworks through which both topics are examined. This immigration to new destinations provides an opportunity to sharpen understandings of key concepts such as immigrant incorporation and immigrant urban politics by exploring them under new conditions. Through a discussion of institutional awareness of and responses to Latino immigrants in a new Southern destination, I argue that drawing new immigrant destinations onto the maps of urban America reconfigures how we see and understand immigration's impacts on and interactions with the social fabric of American cities.

The basis of this article is an ethnographic study of immigration, urban transformation, and racial politics in Nashville, Tennessee. Nashville is similar to other new urban destinations in that into the mid-2000s, it had a strong economy; booming service and construction industries in need of cheap, flexible labor; and Latino population growth amid growing native black and white populations. Initially, Latino migrants came to Nashville from elsewhere in the United States but over time, more and more immigrants came directly from various parts of Latin America. Drawn, and sometimes recruited, by Nashville's construction, hospitality, and wider service economies, Latino immigrants to Nashville are primarily Mexican but also include smaller numbers of Central and South Americans, creating complex class and nationality politics within "the Hispanic community" (Winders 2008). In Nashville, Latino immigrants have settled in the southeastern quadrant, transforming historically white, working-class neighborhoods and racially mixed newer apartment complexes into the city's "Little Mexico" and international districts.

This larger project examined the political, social, and spatial dynamics between Latino immigrants and long-term white and black residents in southeast Nashville neighborhoods and public schools with growing immigrant populations. It compared dynamics in these two institutions with broader discourses on immigration, community change, race relations, and urban transformation circulating throughout Nashville. This article draws on a portion of that wider study—a series of interviews with key actors across Nashville's governmental and nonprofit organizations on how Latino migration impacted their work and missions, as well as a review of relevant government documents, policies, and publications. These interviews and document analyses focused on how Nashville's local government saw, and did not see, Latino immigrants in the context of its wider view of the city, and with what consequences for immigrant incorporation in the Music City.

This article contributes to the growing body of work on immigrant incorporation in new destinations, especially the claim that immigrant incorporation may proceed differently in these sites (e.g., Erwin 2003; Waters and Jiménez 2005; Marrow 2009; O'Neil and Tienda 2010). As this scholarship suggests, local institutions from government agencies to churches function as "jumping-off" points (Cabell 2007) for immigrants seeking a place in new destinations, especially in the absence of immigrant political incorporation and formal political participation (Odem 2004; Bullock and Hood 2006). In the most extensive study to date of immigrant incorporation in a new destination, Helen Marrow (2009) shows that in rural North Carolina, immigrant *bureaucratic* incorporation has preceded and outpaced immigrant *political* incorporation because of both Latino immigrants' limited formal political participation and elected officials' reluctance to see Latino immigrants as legitimate political constituents. Marrow suggests that in new destinations, immigrant incorporation is driven by government and nongovernment agencies and institutions, rather than by coethnic political officials or leaders. This bureaucratic immigrant incorporation, she shows, proceeds unevenly across institutions from schools to law enforcement to health care, because of the different public missions these institutions have vis-à-vis immigrants and because of federal mandates that limit how and to whom their services are distributed. As a result, in new destinations, some institutions reach out to immigrants, and some ignore them.

As this article will demonstrate, the unevenness of immigrant incorporation in new destinations is produced not only through the politics of inclusion or exclusion embedded in the missions of different institutions but also through the visibility or invisibility of immigrants themselves within those institutions. Examining how local government sees, and does not see, immigrants in new destinations, it suggests, can refine understandings of immigrant incorporation more broadly by demonstrating that such incorporation is predicated on immigrants' *institutional visibility* as urban residents or constituents. In cities such as Nashville, that visibility has been partial at best, with consequences for how immigrants subsequently can make political claims in and on the city. Examining immigrant incorporation in the context of a local government still struggling to see immigrants as part of the urban social fabric can show how efforts to create a more responsive local government can inadvertently exclude immigrants if they are not institutionally visible.

In Nashville in the 2000s, two trends seen across American cities helped produce this limited immigrant visibility: a focus on neighborhood- or community-based governance and neoliberal transformations in the structure of local government. Together, these changes made it hard for Nashville to see and, thus, respond to *immigrants as urban residents*, even as *immigration as a political issue* became increasingly visible across the city. On one hand, the turn to neighborhood-based governance offered Latino immigrants few opportunities to represent themselves or be represented as urban residents and positioned them instead as problems in local neighborhoods. On the other, neoliberal streamlining of local government in the mid-2000s eliminated a clear institutional place for immigrant issues in Nashville by integrating immigrant services into other social-service departments. Through these two processes, as *immigration* became politically visible across Nashville, *immigrant residents* became institutionally invisible to and within it.

Planning for Diversity

On an early evening in July 2007, my research assistant and I wandered into a Draft Concept Plan Meeting organized by Metro Nashville's Planning Department. Held in the heart of southeast Nashville, this meeting was part of a visioning exercise designed to create a new land use plan for the area. At this gathering and others like it, Metro urban planners asked residents to brainstorm about what they wanted their neighborhoods to look like, compiling across meetings a collective sense of what attendees thought their neighborhoods could be and translating those aspirations into neighborhood design plans. Finding a seat along the edge of the room, close to but not at the tables set up for participants, I made the first entry in my field notes: *"all white attendees."* This observation would be noted again at the meeting's conclusion—this time, by attendees themselves—as it would be at similar meetings across southeast Nashville. It would also become a leitmotif of Nashville's institutional interactions with immigrants.

To begin the session, the lead planner reminded people in the room that "the neighborhood spoke" at these sessions, mapping the idea of "neighborhood" onto the people at the meeting and linking their involvement to the neighborhood's ability to be represented. At this session, as at others, conversations bounced between urban planners' calls for the "diversity" necessary to transform the area into a functioning urban community and long-term residents' hopes for the "small-town" feel that would re-create the neighborhood they nostalgically recalled. Planners stressed that this combination of diversity and quaintness was attainable, with the right planning approach. Mixed-used development, they explained, would give the area defined centers and make its main road more than a thoroughfare out of the city. To do so, however, residents had to "declare your neighborhood" and mark its limits, the facilitator reiterated.

The remainder of the meeting debated that "declared" neighborhood, with planners stressing that it was "up to the neighborhood" to drive changes. "You all are the watchdogs" who could pressure council representatives. "You, as a community, are watching over" the neighborhood, the planners explained. Throughout this discussion, participants periodically marked the demographic trend I recorded in my field notes. As one participant quipped, "I'm just gonna say it. There are no Hispanics here." It was true that there were no Latino/as present at the session, aside from my Puerto Rican research assistant. To say that Latino/as were absent in the content of the meeting, however, was not true, as a Latino *presence* was central to the session in all sorts of ways. When facilitators turned to a proposed corridor to link a local park and a community center that served Latino immigrants, for example, a particularly vocal attendee opined that the community center was no longer a *neighborhood* center and "not what it once was," obliquely referencing tensions surrounding its immigrant outreach and directly noting its failure to merit identification as a neighborhood node. An absent Latino presence was also central to how the meeting itself was organized. When organizers explained toward the end that budget limitations did not allow them to send out multiple announcements or announcements in multiple languages, an attendee lamented that despite its hard work, the "core group committed to the *neighborhood . . .* doesn't represent the demographics of the *community*." Through this immigrant absence, the distance between the *neighborhood* represented by and reproduced through a core group of active residents and the *community* constituted by an increasingly diverse residential population came to the fore in a meeting whose legitimacy was premised on their connection.

The remainder of this article examines what that immigrant presence looked like to government and nongovernment institutions across Nashville and how the invisibility of Latino immigrants as city *residents* impacted their efforts to find a place in the city. Coming on the coattails of smaller refugee populations (Winders 2006) and in the midst of overall population growth (Kocchar, Suro, and Tafoya 2005),

Latino/as arriving in Nashville encountered a city unprepared for their presence. This situation, of course, is well documented across new destinations (e.g., Atiles and Bohon 2002; Odem 2004; Wainer 2004; Rich and Miranda 2005; Cabell 2007), almost none of which anticipated or were institutionally prepared for an immigrant influx. The discussion here, however, sharpens understandings of these patterns by focusing not only on instances of immigrant exclusion or oversight by ill-prepared cities but also on broader ways of seeing and not seeing Latino immigrants as part of urban dynamics and issues themselves. As it shows, immigrant institutional visibility is an unacknowledged precursor to immigrant incorporation and, as such, merits attention from migration and urban scholars as well as policymakers.

The impact of immigrant institutional invisibility is particularly clear in the context of neighborhoods, where the politics of immigrant settlement are often intense. In Nashville, however, Latino immigrants *as residents* occupied a paradoxical space as politically central to but institutionally marginal within official and grassroots efforts to manage neighborhoods. Because Latino immigrants were unevenly drawn into efforts to address Nashville neighborhoods, when Nashville's local government did see immigrants as residents, it did so in ways that minimized opportunities for immigrant integration and further marginalized immigrants within the social fabric of the Music City. Immigrant institutional visibility, however, must also be situated vis-à-vis overall neoliberal transformations in Nashville's government. Wider changes in the structure of Nashville's local government, for example, made it difficult for government institutions to see immigrants and, thus, for immigrants to be seen by them as relevant constituents. Immigrant invisibility in Nashville, then, was driven by the way that the city engaged its neighborhoods and their governance *and* the way that local government parceled out immigrant issues across Metro departments. Through both sets of practices, the visibility of Latino immigrants in Nashville was institutionally attenuated, and immigrant Nashville became hard to see and, thus, plan for from an institutional perspective.

Planning to See Immigrants

The growth of Nashville's Latino communities and the emergence of Latino social, political, and business organizations in the late 1990s and early 2000s transformed the Music City into a multiethnic city and, in the process, reworked the structure and daily practice of its governance. Institutions across the city began to notice an immigrant presence and to understand immigration as a phenomenon that potentially changed their missions and daily activities. At the same time, immigrant *settlement* in Nashville received little public attention. Latino immigrants moved into neighborhoods that were marginal to and within Nashville's political and social systems, and immigrants' residential impacts did not spread across the city. As *immigration* became a political and social debate across Nashville in the 2000s, *immigrant settlement* remained a localized phenomenon impacting parts of the city. The space between these two geographies sat at the heart of how Nashville saw Latino immigrants at the turn of the twenty-first century. In part because Latino immigrants in Nashville were initially seen as workers and in part because they settled in neighborhoods that were not visible across the city, Latino/as in the Music City, especially for the early years of this migration, were not seen, or planned for, as urban *residents*.[1]

For some Nashville institutions, awareness of Latino migration was filtered through understandings of the city's refugee communities, portions of which date to the arrival of Cubans in the 1960s and Southeast Asians in the 1970s (Winders 2006). Thus, when Latino immigrants began to settle in Nashville, government and nonprofit agencies across the city initially interpreted a Latino presence through their experiences with a smaller, more diverse refugee population, smoothing ethnic, cultural, religious, and linguistic differences among Nashville's foreign-born into an international community that could be discussed and addressed collectively (e.g., Ray and Morse 2004). Both governmental and non-governmental institutions soon realized, however, especially with the jolt of the 9/11 attacks, that refugees and Latino immigrants were not institutionally inter-changeable and faced different cultural and political issues. As a result, programs designed to work with refugees often found themselves unable to address Nashville's growing Latino, especially undocumented, population. Even though an early refugee presence made Nashville institutions more sensitive to the idea of immigrants in the city, Latino immigrants coming to Nashville still entered through gaps in the city's institutional frameworks, especially in relation to its neighborhoods.

Neighborhood activism in Nashville has a long history; but neighborhoods assumed an even greater role in local government in the early 2000s through two processes: on one hand, the neoliberal devolution of responsibility seen across American cities (Martin 2003; Herbert 2005; Ellis 2006), and on the other, spe-cific transformations to Nashville governance. The bulk of both sets of changes began in 1999, when Bill Purcell was elected Nashville's mayor on a platform of neighborhood empowerment that offered "a neighborhood-based approach to addressing the [city's] problems and opportunities" (Jones 2000, 5). Shortly after taking office, Purcell made two decisions that transformed the governance of Nashville neighborhoods. Since these changes took place just as Nashville's immigrant population was establishing itself residentially in the city, they had a direct impact on where immigrants fit into the management of Nashville's neighborhoods.

First, in 2000, Purcell hired a new lead urban planner who brought Nashville a framework of new urbanism, a planning approach that has received critical atten-tion and public praise since the early 1990s. Sampling idealized notions of com-munity and marketing a nostalgic past, new urbanism taps a reservoir of collective longing for how things were to produce new community landscapes removed from, and defined against, both the urban and the suburban (Till 1993). With a focus on mixed land use and human-scale development, it works to "reform the sprawling pattern of suburban growth" while creating a "strong sense of community" (Mendez 2005, 34) that residents can, quite literally, purchase. For this reason, and especially through studies of high-profile experiments such as Disney's Celebration, scholars have debated the politics of new urbanism's spatial determinism, as well as its reliance on market dynamics to generate a residential mix that hearkens back to an envisioned, if not actual, golden era of neighborhoods.

More recently, new urbanism has moved from new developments to urban heartlands, as cities have embraced it as a planning paradigm (Kenny and Zimmerman 2003; Mendez 2005). In Nashville, new urbanism, in combination with Purcell's focus on residents' participation in planning decisions, reconfigured Nashville's planning practices in the early 2000s, sending planners into neighborhoods and making the neighborhood the new planning unit. Under this model, urban planners envisioned Nashville as a mosaic of human-scale neighborhoods with streetscapes, limited traffic, and strong visual corridors. Although a focus on downtown development remained, especially in urban design and public arts campaigns, the Metro Planning Department from 2000 onward increasingly worked with and solicited input from local residents and neighborhood associations. In the process, neighborhood associations became the official venue through which the city saw its neighborhoods *and* the institutional link through which local government interacted with residents.

In addition to instituting a new focus on neighborhoods for urban planning, Purcell formed a Mayor's Office of Neighborhoods (MON) to link his office, other Metro departments, and Nashville neighborhoods.[2] Designed to "give our constituents a voice in government," in the words of its executive director in 2006, MON provided information and technical assistance to "help organize neighborhoods around their issues" and, equally important, to organize residents into formal neighborhood associations. In one of its earliest acts, for example, MON created a Neighborhood Training Institute designed "to build capacity and assist in the establishment and development of neighborhood associations" (*How to Be a Better Neighbor* 2006, 19). Sponsoring Mayor's Nights Out, Neighborhood Nights Out against Crime, and the Neighborhood Response Team, MON worked to keep neighborhoods and Metro government on the same page. Through MON's efforts, Metro government came to see the city through an institutional map in which residential Nashville—and, thus, city residents—was represented by neighborhood associations that covered the entire city.

This effort to blanket Nashville with neighborhood associations was largely successful. When MON began in 1999, approximately 125 neighborhood groups were identifiable across Nashville. By 2006, that number reached closer to 600, and neighborhood empowerment *through neighborhood associations* had become a mantra across the city. MON, however, also elevated neighborhood associations' importance as the institutionally recognized representative of Nashville residents *and* the institutionally encouraged way for residents to see their neighborhood and its place in local government (e.g., *Future of Neighborhoods 2006*). The turn to neighborhood empowerment in Nashville, however, was not always smooth.

Across the city, "expectations were way down because participation was way down," as one neighborhood association president put it; convincing residents to get involved was a challenge, as is often the case in neighborhood activism (Martin 2003; Herbert 2005). Under Purcell's administration, however, neighborhood associations had a new motivation to come *and stay* together to take advantage of grants, services, and other opportunities available to them. To access those services, local residents had to commit to active participation in neighborhood associations, thus creating a strong link between local *governance* of the neighborhood and local *government* of the city cultivated through neighborhood associations.

In southeast Nashville, maintaining that link was not easy. Even with increased incentives for neighborhoods to organize, the relationship between the cohesion necessary to create an association and the growing ethnic and racial diversity in neighborhoods was often tense (Martin 2003). As one nonprofit director in southeast Nashville described the process, groups "are really trying to work together but when it trickles down to the average Joe coming from whatever country, then I think there is still a lot of segregation." Nonetheless, in Nashville, cohesive neighborhood participation, no matter the composition of residents, was cast as a duty for and expectation of local residents who wanted either visibility to or action from Metro government. Intent on empowering neighborhoods, Nashville followed wider trends in urban governance in the early 2000s and "recast [local participation] as a moral duty of active citizenship" (Grundy and Boudreau 2008, 348). Under this model, as Luke Desforges and his coauthors (2005, 441) suggest, "active citizens are judged to have succeeded or failed . . . as a place-based community, with repercussions for the further treatment of that locality by the state." In Nashville, active citizenship through neighborhood associations became both the way the city saw and engaged its residential spaces *and* the necessary attribute for residents wishing to be acknowledged by local government. As residents worked to make themselves, their neighborhoods, and their local issues visible to Nashville government, however, immigrants in those same spaces became hard to find.

Finding Immigrant Nashville

Part of Latino immigrants' limited institutional visibility in Nashville is bound up in the geography of immigrant settlement itself. Within Nashville, immigrants are residentially concentrated in southeast Nashville neighborhoods, which, since as early as the 1920s, have been white, working-class communities with strong local identities and a tight-knit group of residents. In the early 2000s, these areas began experiencing turnover, as residents aged and houses became available for purchase or rent, often by new Latino residents.[3] As a result, these neighborhoods soon saw marked change, from owner-occupied to rented, from English to Spanish, from elderly white residents to young Latino families. Because this transformation remained incomplete throughout the 2000s, both groups soon occupied the same residential, if not social, spaces and lived side by side.

How did Nashville's neighborhood-empowerment movement proceed amid these demographic changes in southeast Nashville? Although Latino immigrants were discussed by neighborhood associations in southeast Nashville, most associations did not involve Latino immigrants and, instead, were led by and composed of white, often older, residents. Some neighborhood associations made attempts to involve Latino immigrants, and some immigrant organizations had outreach programs in southeast Nashville neighborhoods. Latino immigrants, however, were an absent presence in most neighborhood associations in the 2000s, influencing what associations addressed but having little say in how they did so. As the former MON executive director explained, neighborhood organizations in southeast Nashville "don't have the participation of the immigrant population. . . . People are making decisions for those groups. They [immigrants] are not participating, but they are being discussed."

The reasons for this immigrant absence included language barriers, cultural mistrust, and the general challenges of social activism in urban neighborhoods (Herbert 2005). It was also produced, however, through the gap between Nashville's social geographies of immigrant settlement and the institutional structure of neighborhood governance. Because Latino residents lived *across* southeast Nashville neighborhoods, they were not visible as an ethnic enclave in any one neighborhood; nor were they concentrated, or established, enough to form their own neighborhood association. Instead, immigrant settlement took the form of a heterolocalist community (Zelinsky and Barrett 1998), with immigrant social networks, consumption spaces, and workplaces stretched throughout southeast Nashville and beyond. Equally important, Nashville's network of immigrant or ethnic organizations worked with immigrants living anywhere in the city and, thus, did not address neighborhood issues per se. As a result, MON and other neighborhood-focused groups viewed immigrant organizations as institutionally separate from their own missions and worked on the assumption that immigrant communities, stretched as they were across neighborhoods, had their own organizations to address their concerns as immigrants, not neighborhood residents. As an official at MON explained, "most immigrant populations . . . have their own resources, so they don't need us." Other agencies, she noted, "give them [immigrants] the information and work with them through the system," which was seen as separate from MON's own work. In this way, Latino immigrants in Nashville sat in the space between geographically defined *neighborhoods* that were central to local government and ethnically defined *communities* that were central to Nashville's immigrant organizations. Because immigrant organizations did not address neighborhood issues and because neighborhood organizations assumed immigrants had their own "system," immigrants were not visible *as residents* who could contribute to Purcell's neighborhood-based approach to addressing Nashville's issues.

How, then, did Metro government eventually find immigrants within Nashville neighborhoods? A primary way was through the emergence of immigrants in complaints to Metro departments tasked with regulating residential spaces. This was especially true for zoning changes and codes violations—two aspects of neighborhood politics intimately linked to immigrant settlement in new destinations (McConnell and Miraftab 2009; Brettell and Nibbs 2011). Various scholars have noted that in new destinations, Latino residents often revitalize declining business districts (e.g., Wortham, Mortimer, and Allard 2009), and Nashville is no different. As its immigrant population grew, southeast Nashville's business districts, which had struggled since the late 1970s, began to thrive again. In a short time, southeast Nashville roads were lined with Mexican groceries, clothing stores, Western Unions, and car dealerships, which seemed to emerge "overnight," according to many. The form of this rejuvenation was often contested by long-term residents, who saw car lots as a commercial "intrusion" against which neighborhood associations had to "hold our boundaries," as one member explained at a 2006 meeting on zoning change requests.

In the 2000s, under Nashville's model of neighborhood empowerment, the ability to hold neighborhood boundaries lay in the hands of neighborhood associations, which partially vetted zoning proposals for the Metro Planning Department and often responded to such requests through an image of the neighborhood as it was remembered by long-term residents. Neighborhood associations, however, were empowered not only to make decisions about zoning requests but also to monitor residential spaces for codes violations, another topic tightly linked to immigrant settlement and cultural change. For long-term residents in southeast Nashville, codes enforcement was a tense topic, as questions of cultural and ethnic diversity among neighbors became inseparable from the changing material conditions of neighborhoods. Where (and how many) vehicles were parked at dwellings, how many residents lived in one house, and whose responsibility it was to maintain rental units became points of contention and surveillance for neighborhood associations (Erwin 2003). As these associations addressed factors from the visibility of Latino day laborers to language barriers between new and old residents, not only the composition but also the politics of neighborhoods and their governance became increasingly complex, and the process of democratizing decision-making through neighborhood empowerment rubbed up against the politics of ethnic diversification through immigration.

The Metro Department of Codes and Building Safety (hereafter, the Codes Department) became a key interface in this encounter between neighborhood empowerment and neighborhood diversity. It also became a key way that Latino immigrants as residents became institutionally visible to the city. As the codes director explained, throughout the 2000s, his department increasingly had contact with Latino immigrants, often at the urging of long-term residents, over codes violations. Through its work with residential structures and spaces, the Codes Department institutionally mediated contact between long-term residents and immigrants, who lived side by side but did not themselves interact, by intervening in how Latino immigrants used and occupied neighborhood spaces. In response to my question about how Latino migration had affected southeast Nashville's neighborhood relations, for example, a codes official exclaimed, "I don't think they are interacting. I got a call yesterday. A neighbor has a problem with his neighbor. They call me! They use me as their conduit."

Amid demands for involvement from the Codes Department in the process of immigrant settlement, the department adopted a new approach to neighborhood monitoring through its N.O.T.I.C.E. (Neighborhoods Organized to Initiate Codes Enforcement) initiative. This neighborhood audit program, begun in 2002, trained local residents in neighborhood associations to detect, document, and report codes violations in their neighborhood (*How to Be a Better Neighbor* 2006). As the name suggests, N.O.T.I.C.E. enabled the Codes Department to become more involved in neighborhood management without additional personnel. From the perspective of neighborhood associations, it was a way to make Metro government "accountable" and "responsible" to the neighborhood, in the words of one president. N.O.T.I.C.E., however, also asked neighborhood associations to assume increased responsibility for their own streets and to step in where the state stepped back. In this way, the program made local residents equally accountable to Metro government and made sure, as the same association president stressed, "that the residents are keeping up their end of the job" to monitor neighborhoods at little cost to local government.

Neoliberalizing Immigrant Nashville

These shifts toward increased local involvement in and responsibility for Nashville neighborhoods were part of well-documented neoliberal redistributions of responsibility from urban governments to nonstate actors across U.S. cities (Jones 2000; Martin 2003; Herbert 2005). In Nashville, such transformations took off in the 2000s, when key Metro departments began to seek, in the words of one official, "a vantage point of 5,000 feet to help connect things and to give assistance and push when it was needed." As a longtime Metro employee described the change, in the early 2000s, "a lot of folks in the community and groups—nonprofits, government agencies—[were] doing things . . . , but none of them were really coordinated." In response, many governmental and nongovernmental institutions that previously provided direct services to different urban constituencies were redefined as clearinghouses that offered bird's-eye views of Nashville's network of service provision but provided few direct services themselves. Although this reconfiguration was not explicitly related to immigrant settlement, it impacted immigrant visibility across Nashville, as service providers came to see and respond to Latino immigrants in new ways.

This transition and its impacts on immigrant institutional visibility are evident in a number of nonprofit organizations working with immigrants across Nashville but are perhaps clearest in the context of local government and the provision of social services, the topic of a number of studies of new destinations. Natalia Deeb-Sossa and Jennifer Bickham Mendez (2008, 617), for example, suggest that in new destinations, the administration of social services represents "a key site for the construction and enforcement of social membership" for Latino immigrants (see also Cabell 2007). As they note, social service providers often decide who is and is not seen as deserving of support and, thus, who merits social inclusion in the wider community. In the realm of social service provision in new destinations, several scholars also suggest that Latino/as are often "othered" and framed as "undeserving" of aid or community resources, if in uneven ways across institutions (Cabell 2007; Marrow 2009). Such attitudes toward immigrants, however, are themselves contingent on immigrants' first being institutionally visible to such organizations as a constituency that they *might* serve. In Nashville, this initial step was missing in many institutions addressing social services in the late 2000s.

Up to 2005, Metro government had a clear institutional place for foreign-born residents in Nashville through the Metro Refugee Services Program (MRSP), the only refugee services program in the United States run through local government. The location of refugee services within Metro government, rather than solely within nongovernmental agencies, linked refugee communities to local government in a way that elevated their visibility across Nashville and changed the nature of local conversations about diversity (Winders 2006). In 2005, however, at the recommendation of a performance audit of Metro Social Services (MSS), MRSP was discontinued, refugee services were returned to state government,[4] and refugee service provision was handed off to voluntary agencies like Catholic Charities.

The motivations behind this change in how Metro government distributed social services to the foreign-born population were multiple.[5] On a basic level, MRSP formed prior to the arrival of Latino immigrants and in the context of a different, much smaller foreign-born population. Thus, when Latino immigrants began to settle in Nashville, an institutional mismatch arose between a Metro department designed to address the needs of a relatively small refugee population and a larger Latino population, many of whom were undocumented. This new demand, coupled with a post-9/11 decrease in federal funding for refugee resettlement (Singer and Wilson 2006), led to MSS's interest in working less with refugees and immigrants directly, and then only with legal ones, and more with providing technical assistance to agencies working with immigrants or refugees outside local government.

In place of MRSP, MSS created an Immigrant Services Coordinator who was responsible for both immigrants and refugees in Nashville and whose work shifted "from direct service delivery, case support and coordination for individual and/or refugee families" to "overall service planning and coordination."[6] Tapping both neoliberal discourses of individual responsibility and assimilationist language of immigrant adjustment, this new system, according to those working with it, helped "immigrants and refugees *develop a kind of independence* . . . so that they can *integrate rather than . . . go just to one office that always deals with that [one immigrant] issue.*" In the words of a key official involved in MSS's redesign, "we are trying to . . . support the infrastructure that allows them [immigrants] to navigate the system," bringing immigrants into Metro government by eliminating a specific program to deal with them. Under this new infrastructure, institutional opportunities to direct immigrants to available services outside local government expanded but institutional opportunities to provide basic services to immigrants contracted across Metro government.

Wrapped up with this change in what services MSS offered immigrants and how they did so was a redefinition of how MSS understood Nashville's foreign-born population itself. Through the creation of the Immigrant Services Coordinator, MSS shifted from working with refugees in their own program to working with immigrants and refugees across its programs, integrating immigrants into the city's social service infrastructure by dis-integrating components of immigrant services across Metro departments. Under MSS's new design and new focus on "issues rather than ethnicity," refugees, legal immigrants, and undocumented immigrants were rolled into "immigrant." The Immigrant Services Coordinator was, then, expected to make internal differences among immigrants visible to Metro departments and to make immigrant needs visible as part of Nashville's wider landscape of social need. At the same time, Metro departments themselves were expected to address immigrants as a component of the broader project of "representing everybody." In this way, as immigrant needs became part of a wider mission of service provision across Metro government, a clear institutional place for immigrants was eliminated in Metro government, and their institutional visibility as urban constituents was markedly attenuated.

Two clear exceptions to immigrants' attenuated institutional presence merit mention: Nashville's wider politics of immigration and the realm of policing. At the same time that the institutional presence of immigrants, especially Latino immigrants, was diminishing in local government, the figure of the immigrant, especially the undocumented immigrant, was coming into sharp focus for state and local political actors in Nashville, as in other new destinations (Winders 2007; Coleman 2009). By 2005, a campaign to "de-magnetize Tennessee" for undocumented immigrants was becoming the "de-magnetize America" movement and Tennessee was well on its way to outlawing opportunities for undocumented residents to obtain driver's licenses. State and local elected officials in Nashville were crafting legislation to restrict undocumented immigrants' access to state services, affordable housing, and other facets of daily life. In 2006, immigrants took to the streets of downtown Nashville to make their presence known and call for immigration reform, as they did across the country. This visibility backfired in some ways and became a catalyst for wider efforts to exclude immigrants from Nashville's social fabric. By 2008, such efforts culminated in an unsuccessful ordinance to make Nashville "English only."

Of all these maneuvers, Davidson County's entrance into the 287(g) program in 2007 had the most profound impact on how immigrants were seen by the city (see Parrado this volume; Marrow 2009). Part of the 1996 Illegal Immigration Reform and Immigrant Responsibility Act, the 287(g) program enables "state, county, and city police to arrest and detain aliens for federal authorities as well as investigate immigration cases for prosecution in the courts" (Coleman 2009, 907). Post-9/11, counties and states across the United States, but especially in the South, touted the 287(g) program as a way to address undocumented immigration and public safety simultaneously (for a critique of this idea, see Nguyen and Gill 2010) by allowing local law enforcement to act as border patrol. As Nashville's local government struggled to see Latino immigrants as residents in the city, the Davidson County Sheriff's Department began to see immigrants through the eyes, and with the legal power, of the federal state. By late 2010, local police had detained 7,887 immigrants and deported 68 percent of them.[7] Of those deported, nearly 80 percent were stopped for misdemeanors or traffic violations.[8] Throughout the late 2000s, then, local police in Nashville had no problem finding immigrants in the city. The same could not be said, however, for other institutions, which consistently missed immigrants across the city.

Missing Immigrant Nashville

The transformations in local government described above are important reminders that in new destinations, planning for immigrant populations takes place amid wider reconfigurations in how social services are managed and how government and nongovernmental institutions understand their roles in changing demographics. By the mid-2000s, such institutional changes in Nashville had solidified into a system in which many Metro departments serving Latino immigrants no longer did so directly and in which Latino immigrants were missing from many big-picture assessments of the city. In conversations about Nashville's future in planning offices and design centers, for example, Latino immigrants were often absent—a sentiment conveyed most poignantly by an urban designer who remarked that this study of the impacts of Latino migration on Nashville was "a few years too early." When immigrants *did* become visible in Nashville's urban future, they did so in familiar ways. As a director of an urban-design center explained in 2006,

> The changing of Nashville is a big thing. In the last five years, as we started to build stuff, the media started to write about the fact that there were *people who weren't from this country who were part of the construction process* and that if we didn't have them, we wouldn't be building anything at all.

Perhaps in the next two or three years, the director noted, the center would get "some Hispanic neighborhoods . . . , organizations coming in and saying, 'how could you help us? We want to do this.'" For now, though, Latino immigrants, from the perspective of urban design and Nashville's urban future, remained workers, not residents, building Nashville's urban landscape but not forming part of its social fabric.[9]

What explains this immigrant institutional invisibility across much of Nashville? In new destinations, research has documented the uneven geography of Latino reception (e.g., Marrow 2009; Rich and Miranda 2005; Nelson and Hiemstra

2008), as well as uneven patterns of Latino access to resources at both the state and local levels (Ray and Morse 2004). Collectively, these works suggest that unevenness in how immigrants are received and what resources they can access has consequences for how immigrant communities themselves are addressed by new receiving communities. This uneven picture of immigrant incorporation in new destinations, however, is also produced through *immigrant visibility or invisibility as urban constituents or community members*. Meredith Cabell (2007, 24) argues that in new destinations, "governmental institutions are struggling to determine what their role should be in the integration" of immigrants. That struggle to sort out how and whether local institutions will integrate immigrants in new destinations is itself predicated on how those institutions do and do not see immigrants *within* and in relation to the overall urban constituency. If such institutions do not see immigrants as constituents whom they might serve or work with, immigrant incorporation or political participation will be limited. Simply put, it is hard for institutions to incorporate a group that they institutionally cannot see.

Another factor in understanding immigrant invisibility in new destinations is the geography of immigrant settlement. Because in Nashville, as in most new destinations, Latino immigrants moved into some, not all, parts of the city, and because there were, at least through the mid-2000s, few flashpoints associated with Latino migration in Nashville, Latino settlement became a situation with a restricted geography (and, thus, visibility) and, according to key actors in the city, no wider resolution. With steady growth but concentrated settlement, Latino migration to Nashville simply grew day by day. As an official with the Metro Human Relations Commission explained, in contrast to Nashville's Muslim community, which experienced high-profile cases that were ultimately resolved, "with the Latino community, I don't think there has been a case like that that has been resolved."

Resolving Immigrant Nashville

[Latino immigrants] are so family oriented . . . that they are the perfect candidates for. . . finding themselves in things that feel like neighborhoods, as opposed to high rises. And so I think that as long as there are places that are affordable, *they would be the next . . . generation of people who are in neighborhoods, wherever they can afford to be. I don't know what happens once they have really become entrenched in part of the community* and hit that next economic level. *I don't know what they do in terms of organizing or rebuilding or improving their neighborhoods.* (Southeast Nashville political representative)

In one of the final interviews in this study, I sat down with a political representative in southeast Nashville. Representing an array of neighborhoods, this representative had watched his district change, especially since 2000, when its immigrant population began to grow. As the Latino population grew, he found himself caught between dealing with long-standing issues that the area faced and understanding the new dynamics that Latino settlement generated. He did so, however, without a "go-to guy" for Latino residents in his area. Although he acknowledged that Latino immigrants were the next generation in his neighborhoods, he did not know what happened when they became "entrenched in part of the community." This representative, like elected officials in other new destinations (Marrow 2009), had yet to "throw out a hand of acceptance" to immigrants in his area in part because they had yet to come into view for him as a recognized part of the community. Having "nobody from that side of the aisle at the table" was problematic, but how to bring immigrant Nashville into focus was not clear.

Within Nashville, figuring out how to see and place immigrants in the city has been an ongoing process. As this article has shown, immigrants in the 2000s were not only invisible to many of the institutions that governed Nashville neighborhoods and administered social services but were also institutionally unclear to decision-makers charged with seeing and responding to the city as a whole. Much scholarship has shown that local government plays a role in immigrant incorporation into the social fabric of American cities. The field of Latino studies, for example, has examined what Raymond Rocco (1997, 122) describes as Latino/as' "right to have access to major institutions" as "'legitimate' members of a community." In sociology, Dina Okamoto and Kim Ebert (2010) argue that institutional openings play important roles in immigrant political claims, especially for groups that traditionally have not had access to political power and in new destinations where that access has been even more limited. What this study of immigrant institutional visibility in a new destination adds to these understandings, however, is a clearer sense of the unintended consequences of wider urban transformations—neighborhood-based governance and neoliberal institutional streamlining, in this case—on immigrant incorporation. In Nashville in the 2000s, immigrant claims to community membership and political visibility were limited not only because of active efforts to socially exclude immigrants in the city or immigrant reticence to actively participate in the city's political system. Such claims were also inhibited by *the institutional structure of Nashville government itself*—a structure in which Latino immigrants were often invisible.

This immigrant institutional invisibility was produced in multiple ways. Latino immigrants *as residents* were institutionally invisible to Metro government because they were not present in neighborhood associations and, thus, not seen by Metro departments that relied on Nashville's system of community-based governance to evaluate the city and its residents. Even as Nashville tried to be more locally responsive to the needs and desires of its residents, it did so through an institutional structure—neighborhood associations—that defined neighborhoods as geographically discrete and, thus, excluded immigrant residents who lived *across* southeast Nashville neighborhoods. Latino immigrants *as recipients of social services* were institutionally invisible to Metro government because they were spread across departments, none of which focused specifically on immigrants but all of which dealt with portions of immigrant needs. As Nashville tried to make its provision of social services more efficient, it inadvertently made immigrants fall out of the institutional picture of social need in the city. Finally, Latino immigrants were institutionally invisible *as urban constituents* in visions of Nashville's future because they were not seen to have impacted Nashville's urban landscapes as a whole. Present as a necessary labor force but not seen as an established part of the Nashville community, Latino immigrants occupied a paradoxical place in the city's present and future. Through the ways that Latino immigrants were geographically located in and institutionally seen by the city, they remained hard to find across Nashville institutions and, thus, hard to address as urban constituents.

How specific this immigrant institutional invisibility is to new destinations such as Nashville remains unclear in the absence of comparative studies across new and traditional urban destinations. What is clear, however, is that cities such as Nashville face the challenges and complexities of immigrant incorporation in the context not only of urban social relations and dynamics but also of how local governments are structured to reflect and address a changing population. A first—and, to date, largely unacknowledged—step in the process of immigrant incorporation is how cities, and the institutions that compose them, see and do not see immigrants as local residents. This question of immigrant institutional visibility must be addressed in studies of immigrant incorporation, especially in new destinations, if we are to understand how and why immigrants are and are not integrated into and themselves transform the social fabric of American cities beyond gateways such as Los Angeles.

At the same time, the question of how immigrants are and are not visible to local government and other institutions must also be addressed in efforts to work with immigrant populations in U.S. cities. As this article has shown, attempts to empower local neighborhoods across American cities must acknowledge and institutionally account for the fact that "neighborhood" and "community" are not equivalent terms and do not necessarily work through the same residential geographies. In Nashville, recognition of this fact might lead local government to work not only with neighborhood associations but also with immigrant organizations involved across the city and its neighborhoods. In doing so, local government would have to expand how it sees its neighborhoods and how it institutionally responds to the different ways and geographies through which Nashville residents understand and practice "neighborhood" and "community." As this study showed, the political, institutional, and cultural impacts of Latino settlement on cities such as Nashville are still coming into view for politicians, government officials, grassroots leaders, and long-term residents. A first step in understanding these impacts, and local responses to them, is drawing new destinations more fully onto the map of urban America and institutionally adjusting to the new demographic realities across American cities.

Notes

1. As I discuss more fully in the wider project, public schools are exceptions to this trend.

2. When Karl Dean became mayor in 2008, he continued MON.

3. Prior to the arrival of Latino residents, many of these neighborhoods were also home to Nashville's refugee populations (Winders 2006).

4. Minutes from Metro Social Services Board of Commissioners Meeting, 26 January 2005. Available from http://www.nashville.gov/sservices/minutes/050126.asp (accessed 21 July 2009).

5. Minutes from Metro Social Services Board of Commissioners Meeting, 26 January 2005. Available from http://www.nashville.gov/sservices/minutes/050126.asp (acessed 21 July 2009).

6. "Issue Brief: Immigrant Community Assessment," *Metropolitan Social Services* 1, iss. 3 (14 October 2005). Available from http://www.nashville.gov/sservices/docs/ImmigrantIssueBrief.pdf (accessed 21 July 2009).

7. Chris Echegaray, "Immigration Proposal Won't Affect Davidson Jailers," *The Tennessean*, 11 September 2010.

8. Brian Haas, "Davidson County's Rate of Deporting Immigrants for Minor Offenses Is Among Highest," *The Tennessean*, 4 February 2011.

9. Although through the mid-2000s public discourse surrounding Latino migration to Nashville tightly linked the presence of Latino immigrants and the value of their labor, that framing did not translate into interest in Latino labor from the perspective of Nashville's economic development. Metro offices responsible for economic and community development explained in 2006 that they had not felt the "full effects" of Latino migration. Although companies interested in Nashville were "aware" of its Latino labor force, Latino labor was not a recruitment tool for Metro government, which instead sought to highlight higher-paying jobs and higher-skill workers.

References

Atiles, Jorge and Stephanie Bohon. 2002. *The needs of Georgia's new Latinos: A policy agenda for the decade ahead*. Public Policy Research Series. Carl Vinson Institute of Government. Athens: University of Georgia.

Brettell, Caroline, and Faith Nibbs. 2011. Immigrant suburban settlement and the "threat" to middle class status and identity: The case of Farmers Branch, Texas. *International Migration* 49 (1): 1–30.

Bullock, Charles, and M. Hood. 2006. A mile-wide gap: The evolution of Hispanic political emergence in the Deep South. *Social Science Quarterly* 87 (5): 1118–35.

Cabell, Meredith. 2007. Mexican immigrant integration in the U.S. Southeast: Institutional approaches to immigration integration in Owensboro, Kentucky. Working Paper 153, Center for Comparative Immigration Studies, University of California, San Diego.

Coleman, Mathew. 2009. What counts as the politics and practice of security, and where? Devolution and immigrant insecurity after 9/11. *Annals of the Association of American Geographers* 99 (5): 904–13.

Cuadros, Paul. 2006. *A home on the field: How one championship soccer team inspires hope for the revival of small town America*. New York, NY: Harper.

Deeb-Sossa, Natalia, and Jennifer Bickham Mendez. 2008. Enforcing the borders in the Nuevo South: Gender and migration in Williamsburg, Virginia, and the Research Triangle, North Carolina. *Gender & Society* 22 (5): 613–38.

Desforges, Luke, Rhys Jones, and Mike Woods. 2005. New geographies of citizenship. *Citizenship Studies* 9 (5): 439–51.

Ellis, Mark. 2006. Unsettling immigrant geographies: US immigration and the politics of scale. *Tijdschrift voor Economische en Sociale Geografie* 97 (1): 49–58.

Erwin, Deborah. 2003. An ethnographic description of Latino immigration in rural Arkansas: Intergroup relations and utilization of healthcare services. *Southern Rural Sociology* 19 (1): 46–72.

Fink, Leon. 2003. *The Maya of Morganton: Work and community in the Nuevo New South*. Chapel Hill: University of North Carolina Press.

Grundy, John, and Julie-Anne Boudreau. 2008. "Living with culture": Creative citizenship practices in Toronto. *Citizenship Studies* 12 (4): 347–63.

Herbert, Steve. 2005. The trapdoor of community. *Annals of the Association of American Geographers* 95 (4): 850–65.

How to be a better neighbor. 2006. Nashville, TN: Metropolitan Government of Nashville and Davidson County, Department of Codes Administration.

Jones, Grant. 2000. *Developing a neighborhood-focused agenda: Tools for cities getting started*. Baltimore, MD: Annie E. Casey Foundation.

Kandel, William, and Emilio Parrado. 2005. Restructuring of the US meat processing industry and new Hispanic migrant destinations. *Population and Development Review* 31 (3): 447–71.

Kenny, Judith, and Jeffrey Zimmerman. 2003. Constructing the "genuine American city": Neo-traditionalism, new urbanism and neo-liberalism in the remaking of downtown Milwaukee. *Cultural Geographies* 11:74–98.

Kocchar, Rakesh, Roberto Suro, and Sonya Tafoya. 2005. *The New South: The context and consequences of rapid population growth*. Washington, DC: Pew Hispanic Center.

Lichter, Daniel, and Kenneth Johnson. 2009. Immigrant gateways and Hispanic migration to new destinations. *International Migration Review* 43 (3): 496–518.

Marrow, Helen. 2009. Immigrant bureaucratic incorporation: The dual roles of professional missions and government policies. *American Sociological Review* 74:756–76.

Martin, Deborah. 2003. Enacting neighborhood. *Urban Geography* 24 (5): 361–85.

Massey, Douglas, Jacob Rugh, and Karen Pren. 2010. The geography of undocumented Mexican migration. *Mexican Studies* 26 (1): 129–52.

McClain, Paula, Niambi Carter, Victoria DeFrancesco, Monique Lyle, Shayla Nunnally, Thomas Scotto, Alan Kendrick, Jeffrey Grynaviski, Gerald Lackey, and Kendra Cotton. 2006. Racial distancing in a Southern city: Latino immigrants' views of black Americans. *Journal of Politics* 68 (3): 571–84.

McConnell, Eileen Diaz, and Faranak Miraftab. 2009. Sundown towns to "Little Mexico": Old-timers and newcomers in an American small town. *Rural Sociology* 74 (4): 605–29.

Mendez, Michael. 2005. Latino new urbanism: Building on cultural preferences. *Opolis: An International Journal of Suburban and Metropolitan Studies* 1 (1): 33–48.

Nelson, Lise, and Nancy Hiemstra. 2008. Latino immigrants and the renegotiation of place and belonging in small town America. *Social and Cultural Geography* 9 (3): 319–42.

Nguyen, Mai Thi, and Hannah Gill. 2010. *The 287(g) program: The costs and consequences of local immigration enforcement in North Carolina communities*. Chapel Hill, NC: The Latino Migration Project, Institute for the Study of the Americas and the Center for Global Initiatives, University of North Carolina at Chapel Hill.

Odem, Mary. 2004. Our Lady of Guadalupe in the New South: Latino immigrants and the politics of integration in the Catholic Church. *Journal of American Ethnic History* 24 (1): 26–57.

Odem, Mary, and Elaine Lacy, eds. 2009. *Latino immigrants and the transformation of the U.S. South*. Athens: University of Georgia Press.

Okamoto, Dina, and Kim Ebert. 2010. Beyond the ballot: Immigrant collective action in gateways and new destinations in the United States. *Social Problems* 57 (4): 529–58.

O'Neil, Kevin, and Marta Tienda. 2010. A tale of two counties: Natives' opinions toward immigration in North Carolina. *International Migration Review* 44 (3): 728–61.

Ray, Brian, and Ann Morse. 2004. *Building the new American community: Newcomer integration and inclusion experiences in non-traditional gateway cities*. Sponsored by the Office of Refugee Resettlement. Washington, DC: Migration Policy Institute.

Rich, Brian, and Marta Miranda. 2005. The sociopolitical dynamics of Mexican immigration in Lexington, Kentucky, 1997 to 2002: An ambivalent community responds. In *New destinations: Mexican immigration in the United States*, eds. Víctor Zúñiga and Rubén Hernández-León, 187–219. New York, NY: Russell Sage Foundation.

Rocco, Raymond. 1997. Citizenship, culture, and community: Restructuring in Southeast Los Angeles. In *Latino cultural citizenship: Claiming identity, space, and rights*, eds. William Flores and Rina Benmayor,

97–123. Boston, MA: Beacon.

Singer, Audrey, and Jill Wilson. 2006. *From "there" to "here": Refugee resettlement in metropolitan America*. Washington, DC: Metropolitan Policy Program, Brookings Institution.

Smith, Barbara Ellen, and Jamie Winders. 2008. "We're here to stay": Economic restructuring, Latino migration, and place-making in the U.S. South. *Transactions of the Institute of British Geographers* 33:60–72.

Smith, Heather, and Owen Furuseth, eds. 2006. *Latinos in the New South: Transformations of place*. Aldershot, UK: Ashgate.

Striffler, Steve. 2007. Neither here nor there: Mexican immigrant workers and the search for home. *American Ethnologist* 34 (4): 674–88.

Sziarto, Kristin, and Helga Leitner. 2010. Immigrants riding for justice: Space-time and emotions in the constructions of a counterpublic. *Political Geography* 39:381–91.

The future of neighborhoods: A vision for the future of Nashville and Davidson County, Tennessee. 2006. Nashville, TN: Neighborhood Resource Center for the Neighborhoods of Nashville.

Till, Karen. 1993. Neotraditional towns and urban villages: The cultural production of a geography of "otherness." *Environment and Planning D: Society and Space* 11:709–32.

Varsanyi, Monica. 2011. Neoliberalism and nativism: Local anti-immigrant policy activism and an emerging politics of scale. *International Journal of Urban and Regional Research* 35 (2): 295–311.

Wainer, Andrew. 2004. *The new Latino South and the challenge to public education: Strategies for educators and policymakers in emerging immigrant communities*. Los Angeles, CA: Tomás Rivera Policy Institute.

Wang, Qingfang, and Wei Li. 2007. Entrepreneurship, ethnicity and local contexts: Hispanic entrepreneurs in three U.S. Southern metropolitan areas. *GeoJournal* 68:167–82.

Waters, Mary, and Tomás Jiménez. 2005. Assessing immigrant assimilation: New empirical and theoretical challenges. *Annual Review of Sociology* 31:105–25.

Winders, Jamie. 2006. "New Americans" in a "New South" city? Immigrant and refugee politics in the Music City. *Social and Cultural Geography* 7 (3): 421–35.

Winders, Jamie. 2007. Bringing back the (b)order: Post-9/11 politics of immigration, borders, and belonging in the contemporary U.S. South. *Antipode* 39 (5): 920–42.

Winders, Jamie. 2008. An "incomplete" picture? Race, Latino migration, and urban politics in Nashville, Tennessee. *Urban Geography* 29 (3): 246–63.

Wortham, Stanton, Katherine Mortimer, and Elaine Allard. 2009. Mexicans as model minorities in the new Latino diaspora. *Anthropology and Education Quarterly* 40 (4): 388–404.

Zelinsky, Wilbur, and Lee Barrett. 1998. Heterolocalism: An alternative model of the sociospatial behaviour of immigrant ethnic communities. *International Journal of Population Geography* 4:281–98.

Zúñiga, Víctor, and Rubén Hernández-León, eds. 2005. *New destinations of Mexican immigration in the United States*. New York, NY: Russell Sage Foundation.

The Paradox of Law Enforcement in Immigrant Communities: Does Tough Immigration Enforcement Undermine Public Safety?

By
DAVID S. KIRK,
ANDREW V. PAPACHRISTOS,
JEFFREY FAGAN,
and
TOM R. TYLER

Frustrated by federal inaction on immigration reform, several U.S. states in recent years have proposed or enacted laws designed to stem the flow of illegal immigrants into the United States and to facilitate their removal. An underappreciated implication of these laws is the potential alienation of immigrant communities—even law-abiding, cooperative individuals—from the criminal justice system. The ability of the criminal justice system to detect and sanction criminal behavior is dependent upon the cooperation of the general public, including acts such as the reporting of crime and identifying suspects. Cooperation is enhanced when local residents believe that laws are enforced fairly. In contrast, research reveals that cynicism of the police and the legal system undermines individuals' willingness to cooperate with the police and engage in the collective actions necessary to socially control crime. By implication, recent trends toward strict local enforcement of immigration laws may actually undercut public safety by creating a cynicism of the law in immigrant communities. Using data from a 2002 survey of New York City residents, this study explores the implications of perceived injustices perpetrated by the criminal justice system for resident willingness to cooperate with the police in immigrant communities.

Keywords: immigration; legal cynicism; legitimacy; cooperation; procedural justice

Since the tragic 9/11 terrorist attacks, the number of yearly deportations of illegal aliens has more than doubled in the United States, rising from 165,000 deportations in 2002 to nearly 400,000 in 2009 (U.S. Department of Homeland Security [DHS] 2010). A vast majority of this increase can be attributed to the growing number of *noncriminal* aliens now being deported. In fact, 67 percent of deportations in 2009 were of noncriminal immigrants. Not surprisingly, then, fears of deportation are prevalent in immigrant communities, especially given recent political shifts in many states toward increased enactment and enforcement of immigration laws. For instance, in a 2009 evaluation of the federal 287(g) program, which expands the authority of local and state

DOI: 10.1177/0002716211431818

law enforcement officials to enforce civil immigration violations—the U.S. Government Accountability Office (GAO) reported evidence of considerable fear among community residents that police would deport individuals because of incidents as minor as a traffic violation (GAO 2009). Similar concerns were recently expressed by community stakeholders and interested parties in public hearings conducted by a federal task force assigned to review the U.S. Immigration and Customs Enforcement's (ICE) Secure Communities program, which facilitates the sharing of fingerprint information between the Federal Bureau of Investigation and ICE (Homeland Security Advisory Council 2011).

In spite of the growing use of deportation as an enforcement tool, numerous states over the past several years have grown frustrated with federal inaction on immigration reform and have proposed or enacted their own measures to stem the flow of illegal immigrants into the United States and to facilitate their removal. For example, Arizona Senate Bill 1070 (SB 1070), passed in April 2010, set an early precedent. This law mandates local law enforcement to detain individuals suspected of being in the U.S. illegally. Alabama, Georgia, Indiana, South Carolina, and Utah all have recently passed copycat bills, and several other states are eyeing similar measures. Not to be outdone, an even newer wave of proposed reforms in Arizona and other states aims to sanction illegal immigration by withdrawing the citizenship of U.S.-born children if their parents are illegal immigrants.

As the next presidential election nears and rhetoric on immigration intensifies, it is an opportune time to assess the potential unintended consequences of increasing the enactment and enforcement of punitive immigration laws. The criminal justice system depends on the cooperation of the general public to detect and sanction criminal behavior (Skogan and Frydl 2004). Cooperation is enhanced when local residents believe that laws are enforced fairly and when law enforcement officers pursue "procedural justice" in their everyday contacts with residents (Fagan and Meares 2008; Tyler and Fagan 2008; Tyler 2010). Yet increased and harsh enforcement of laws may undermine the ability of the police to control crime by reducing the willingness of immigrants to report crimes and cooperate

David S. Kirk is an associate professor of sociology and a faculty research associate of the Population Research Center at the University of Texas at Austin. His research explores the effects of neighborhood context and residential mobility on behavior. His recent research has appeared in American Journal of Sociology, American Sociological Review, *and* Criminology.

Andrew V. Papachristos is a Robert Wood Johnson Health & Society Scholar at Harvard University and an associate professor of sociology at Yale University. His research focuses on social networks, neighborhood social organization, and interpersonal violence.

Jeffrey Fagan is the Isidor and Seville Sulzbacher Professor of Law at Columbia University. His research examines policing, capital punishment, the legitimacy of the criminal law, and juvenile crime and punishment. He serves on the editorial boards of several journals on criminology and law. He is a fellow of the American Society of Criminology.

Tom R. Tyler is a professor of law and psychology at Yale Law School. His research and teaching focus on social psychology and the psychology of procedural justice—the fairness of group rules and processes, and the motivations that lead people to cooperate when they are within groups.

with the police in criminal investigations. Recent studies show that cynicism of the police and the legal system not only leads to an increased likelihood of neighborhood crime and violence but also undermines individuals' willingness to cooperate with the police and engage in the collective actions necessary to socially control crime (Sampson, Morenoff, and Raudenbush 2005; Tyler and Fagan 2008; Kirk and Matsuda 2011; Kirk and Papachristos 2011; Sampson 2011; Papachristos, Meares, and Fagan forthcoming). Thus, while strict immigration laws are often touted politically as ways to ensure public safety, the enactment and enforcement of harsh immigration laws may actually undercut public safety by creating a cynicism of the law in immigrant communities.

This study examines the extent to which a cynicism of the law characterizes immigrant communities in the United States and, more important, the extent to which the actions of law enforcement influence resident cynicism. We pay particular attention to the consequences of cynicism of the law in immigrant communities, focusing on the willingness of residents to report crimes and assist the police in locating individuals suspected of committing crimes.

Background

Immigrants in the United States have a complex, if not tenuous, relationship with the law. On one hand, many immigrants come to the United States for the protections of the very laws that make this country great: freedom of speech, religion, and assembly; the right to due process; and other rights guaranteed by the Constitution and upheld by our legal institutions. Immigrants are generally a self-selected group whose motivations for relocation to the United States suggest that their social and political values are compatible with the moral underpinnings of American laws. Not surprisingly, then, first-generation immigrants tend to be less criminally inclined than native-born blacks, Hispanics, and whites, a research finding that has been replicated time and again in studies over the past one hundred years (U.S. Immigration Commission 1911; Wickersham Commission 1931; Sampson, Morenoff, and Raudenbush 2005; Morenoff and Astor 2006).

On the other hand, immigrants have reason to be wary of American legal institutions, and especially the police. Both the civil and criminal legal systems in the United States often treat immigrants more harshly than native-born citizens, even though immigrants are generally less crime-prone and more attentive to civil legal obligations. From the Naturalization Act of 1790 and the 1882 Chinese Exclusion Act to the Patriot Act, immigrants face greater intrusions on their privacy and considerably higher penalties and legal consequences for their actions, at times without the due process granted to native-born citizens. Several court cases, from *Korematsu v. U.S.* (1942) to *Martinez-Fuerte v. U.S.* (1973) and *U.S. v. Brignoni-Ponce* (1975), have sanctioned statutory barriers to full equality for immigrants.

As noted, the latest movement in immigration reform has been dominated at the state level due to the perceived inaction at the federal level. Arizona SB 1070 has been a trailblazer for subsequent laws. It specifies, among other provisions, that law enforcement must make efforts to determine the immigration status of individuals during an arrest or lawful stop if they have reasonable suspicion that the individual is an illegal alien. In July 2010, one day before the law was to take effect, a federal district court judge struck down key provisions of the bill, with the ruling subsequently appealed by the State of Arizona. In April 2011, the U.S. Court of Appeals for the Ninth Circuit rejected the appeal and let stand the lower court's decision. In August 2011, Arizona Governor Jan Brewer appealed to the U.S. Supreme Court, asking for the Court to overturn the decision of the lower court.

The potential consequences of the passage and enforcement of immigration laws such as Arizona SB 1070 are as of yet unknown. At a minimum, the assignment of immigration enforcement to local police may overburden law enforcement agencies already struggling to enforce criminal statutes in the wake of economic crises and declining tax revenues.[1] This expansion of the mission of local law enforcement may have complications that its proponents may not have anticipated. One potentially significant by-product of such enforcement is the changing of attitudes toward the law, legal authority, and especially the police in immigrant communities.

A robust body of research shows that the cooperation of the general public to detect and sanction criminal behavior is critical to effective law enforcement (Skogan and Frydl 2004; Tyler 2010). Other studies show that cooperation as well as compliance with the law is enhanced when local residents believe that laws are enforced fairly and when law enforcement officers pursue procedural justice in their everyday contacts with citizens (Sunshine and Tyler 2003; Fagan and Meares 2008; Tyler and Fagan 2008; Tyler 2010). This connection between procedural justice and cooperation and compliance has been found among adults but also among children and adolescents, thereby revealing that procedural justice and the resulting process of legal socialization are core components of child development (Fagan and Tyler 2005; Fagan and Piquero 2007). Procedural justice in turn promotes shared perceptions that the law and legal actors are legitimate, leading to shared obligations to both cooperate with legal actors and to abide by legal codes. For instance, Tyler, Schulhofer, and Huq (2010) find that Muslim-American residents of New York are more likely to cooperate with the police when they view the police as a legitimate and just authority.

Whereas belief in the fairness of the law and legal procedures increases cooperation with police and legal authorities, the converse might also be true: unduly harsh laws and legal procedures may produce cynicism of the law and legal institutions. This may be increasingly true in immigrant communities, which face heightened scrutiny and an intensified police gaze. In these communities, harsh policing and legal efforts may be viewed as unjust and thereby undermine the ability of the police to control crime by reducing the willingness of immigrants to report crimes and cooperate with the police in criminal investigations. Thus, a *paradox* arises: harsh legal sanctions against immigrants are often framed as a means to keep communities "safe," yet they may in fact have the opposite effect by decreasing cooperation with police. In fact, recent studies show that cynicism of the police and the legal system not only leads to an increased likelihood of neighborhood crime and violence but also undermines individuals' willingness to cooperate with the police and to engage in the collective actions necessary to socially control crime (Sampson, Morenoff, and Raudenbush 2005; Tyler and Fagan 2008; Kirk and Matsuda 2011; Kirk and Papachristos 2011; Sampson 2012; Papachristos, Meares, and Fagan forthcoming).

Legitimacy and legal cynicism work in tandem to either strengthen or corrode the relationships of citizens to the law.[2] Legitimacy is the property that a rule or an authority has when others feel obligated to voluntarily defer to that rule or authority. In other words, a legitimate authority is an authority regarded by people as entitled to have its decisions and rules accepted and followed by others (see, e.g., French and Raven 1959). The roots of the modern discussion of legitimacy are usually traced to Weber's (1968) writing on authority and to Beetham's (1991) dynamic theory on the political economic conditions under which citizens consent to authority. Legitimacy, therefore, is a quality possessed by an authority, a law, or an institution that leads others to feel obligated to obey its decisions and directives.

The legitimacy of authority is a product of the *means* by which that authority is utilized. Individuals are more willing to accept decisions of law enforcement if they think the police are acting in a just manner (Tyler 1990). In fact, evidence suggests that assessments of whether a law or legal actor is considered "just" is more strongly linked to perceptions of police legitimacy than are evaluations of their effectiveness in controlling crime. There are several elements to individuals' assessment of procedural justice. First, views of justice will be enhanced when individuals are allowed to provide input into the justice process, particularly in investigations that involve themselves. Similarly, if individuals are treated with respect and dignity by legal officials, they are more likely to judge the police as a just institution. Finally, if law enforcement authorities are trustworthy and act in a fair and neutral manner, individuals are more likely to conceive of the police as just and ultimately as a legitimate authority. In short, the police and other agents of the justice system can facilitate cooperation with the law and compliance with it by conducting their operations in ways that the public deems fair and just (Tyler 1990).

Legal cynicism occurs when people perceive the law, and the police in particular, as illegitimate, unresponsive, and ill-equipped to ensure public safety (Kirk and Papachristos 2011). This cynicism often is the product of societal structural conditions (such as concentrated poverty) and resident interactions with the justice system, but also unfair treatment by legal actors (Sampson and Bartusch 1998; Fagan and Piquero 2007; Tyler and Fagan 2008; Kirk and Papachristos 2011). In socially and economically disadvantaged neighborhoods, people come to perceive that the dominant societal institutions (of which the police and the justice system are emblematic) will offer them little in the way of security, either

FIGURE 1
A Conceptual Model of Legal Cynicism and Its Consequences

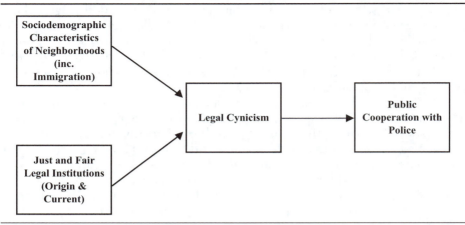

economic or personal. In particular, harassing behavior by the police and insufficient or ineffective crime control breeds cynicism (Fagan and Meares 2008; Tyler and Fagan 2008). Through interaction among neighborhood residents, cynicism of the law can become embedded into the culture of a community. In this way, legal cynicism represents a quality of *neighborhoods*, and not simply the views of a particular individual (Sampson and Bartusch 1998; Kirk and Papachristos 2011). In turn, crime may flourish in neighborhoods characterized by a culture of cynicism, yet because of legal cynicism, these crimes may go unreported and therefore unsolved.

These perspectives on justice, legitimacy, and legal cynicism are especially salient for immigrants, who may face greater exposure to and contact with the police. Not only does one's status as an immigrant demark him or her for more focused legal attention, but immigrants also tend to settle in areas within cities that experience high levels of ecological risk factors known to predict crime and other social problems. In other words, immigrants may become more susceptible to legal cynicism because of their *individual* status as well as their *ecological* position within a city. One implication of legal cynicism is that intensive local enforcement of immigration laws, and order-maintenance policing strategies more generally, could potentially undermine the ability of the police to control crime in neighborhoods with high concentrations of immigrants because of reduced public cooperation. If enforcement of immigration laws weakens perceptions of fairness and legitimacy, and thereby prompts a cynicism of the law, then the very public safety that police practices are designed to protect may evaporate.

In the analysis that follows, we examine the relationship between immigration, procedural justice, legal cynicism, and public cooperation with the law. The conceptual model in Figure 1 provides a visual snapshot of the discussion above and guides our ensuing analysis. We assess the extent to which a cynicism of the law characterizes immigrant communities and seek to determine whether the prevalence of just and fair police practices prevents the development and spread of legal cynicism. Importantly, in our model there is a *dualism to justice*. Perceptions of fairness, particularly for foreign-born populations, reflect characteristics of the justice system in the United States but also in sending societies. Yet the direction of this "halo effect" is not altogether clear. On one hand, having been born within and experienced a repressive society and government may have a lasting negative effect on an immigrant's general perception of authority institutions (Tyler, Schulhofer, and Huq 2010). Indeed, experience with oppressive regimes in countries of origin may be one of the "push" factors driving immigration, yet one which continues to influence perceptions of authority among immigrant communities even after they are well established in the United States. On the other hand, perceptions of injustices in origin countries may lead immigrants to have positive views about the U.S. justice system because the United States is perceived to be a relatively more equitable and just society. This may be true even if immigrants are denied the full rights and protections enjoyed by citizens of the United States. After analyzing the determinants of legal cynicism, we then explore the extent of public cooperation with the law in immigrant communities and the extent to which a cynicism of the law undermines this cooperation.

Sources of Data

Data utilized in this study come from the 2000 U.S. Census, the World Bank's World Governance Indicators project, and a 2002 survey of New York City residents (see Sunshine and Tyler 2003). For the survey, a total of 1,653 respondents were drawn via a stratified random sample of residential telephone numbers in the City. Interviews were conducted in English or Spanish, per the language preference of the respondent. Interviews were conducted with the adult in the household with the most recent birthday. The response rate for the survey was 64 percent of eligible respondents. Survey questions included, among others, items about police legitimacy, legal cynicism, and willingness to cooperate with the police to fight crime.

Our units of analysis are neighborhoods consisting of several census tracts each. Our units were drawn from New York City neighborhood boundaries defined by Kenneth Jackson and John Manbeck (1998) based on interviews with local residents and a physical examination of the neighborhoods.[3] These boundaries form "natural" areas within the city with a community history and identity among residents (see Figure 2 for a map of the 2000 distribution of foreign-born population across these neighborhoods in the five New York boroughs). We geocoded the location of the 1,653 respondents and then assigned them to their respective neighborhoods. Our survey sample is spread across 227 neighborhoods (out of 295 total in New York City), with 79 of those neighborhoods containing 8 or more survey respondents. We drop neighborhoods with fewer than 8 respondents from our analysis.[4]

FIGURE 2
Proportion of Foreign-Born Population in New York City Neighborhoods, 2000 Census

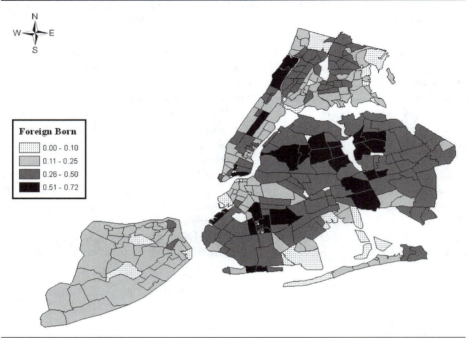

Variables

The variables we use in our analyses can be categorized into four broad classes: immigration measures, neighborhood structural characteristics, neighborhood disorder, and perceptions of the criminal justice system.

We measure immigration by three different dimensions, all derived from U.S. Census data. First, *Immigrant Concentration* represents a combined measure of the percentage of foreign-born residents in the neighborhood and linguistic isolation. The latter is an indicator of the percentage of households in which no person age 14 or older speaks English very well. In analyses, we use measures for the years 1990 and 2000, as well as a measure of the residual change from 1990 to 2000.[5] We created our *Immigrant Concentration* scale via principal components analysis. Specifically, we pooled data from both years into the same dataset (i.e., each neighborhood had two observations). By doing so, the factor loadings for each of the census items do not vary across the two time points, thus ensuring comparability across time. Second, we include a measure of *Recent Immigrants*, which represents the percent of foreign-born population in a neighborhood in the year 2000 who had arrived in the United States within the previous five years.

Third, we construct a measure of *Language Diversity* in a neighborhood in a similar manner as in Graif and Sampson (2009). It measures the diversity of languages spoken among residents of a neighborhood, per 2000 Census data, and is computed as one minus the Herfindahl index.[6] The index is a product of both the total number of languages spoken in a neighborhood and the evenness in the proportion of residents who speak each language. Conceptually, there is overlap in our measures of immigrant concentration and language diversity, such that a neighborhood with much language diversity is likely to have a concentration of foreign-born residents. However, there are also relatively homogeneous immigrant communities with most residents from the same sending country or region. In such cases, concentration would be high, but diversity would be low. Measuring both immigrant concentration and language diversity allows us to assess these different dynamics of immigration. The most common of the fifty-eight reported languages spoken in New York City are English, Spanish, Italian, Chinese, Russian, Polish, German, Korean, and Hebrew. Among the most linguistically diverse neighborhoods in New York City are Borough Park and Kensington in Brooklyn and Flushing, East Flushing, and Queensboro Hill in Queens. In sum, these three measures capture the spatial concentration of immigrants in New York as well as the diversity of immigration status and the sending countries.

Neighborhood structural data come from the 2000 U.S. Census. Consistent with prior work on neighborhoods and crime, we utilize three measures of neighborhood structure: *Concentrated Poverty*, *Residential Instability*, and *Population Density*. *Concentrated Poverty* is a scale of economic disadvantage in a given neighborhood created via principal components analysis, based on the following indicators: the percentage of families below the poverty line, of families receiving public assistance, of unemployed individuals in the civilian labor force, of individuals not in the labor force, of female-headed families with children, of neighborhood population between the ages of 5 and 15, of nonwhite population, and of income inequality (as measured by the Gini coefficient). *Residential Stability* is similarly created with principal components analysis, based on the following census items: the percentage of residents 5 years old and older who lived in the same house 5 years earlier and of homes that are owner-occupied. *Population Density* measures the number of residents per square mile.

Neighborhood Disorder measures the extent of physical and social disorder in a neighborhood, constructed via principal components analysis from responses from the aforementioned survey of New York residents. Respondents were asked how often they see the following objects and occurrences in their neighborhood: (1) garbage in the streets or on the sidewalk; (2) empty beer bottles; (3) graffiti; (4) gangs hanging out; (5) people drinking beer, wine, or liquor on the street; and (6) people buying or selling drugs on the street. We include this measure in our analyses to account for instrumental reasons for why neighborhood residents may be cynical of the law and therefore unwilling to cooperate with the law. Legal cynicism may be a product of the effectiveness of the police in eliminating disorderly conditions, in addition to or instead of procedural justice.

We include four different measures of perceptions of the criminal justice system. Two of these measures, *Origin Rule of Law* and *Procedural Justice*, contain information about the fairness of the legal system. The former represents perceptions of fairness in immigrants' origin country, whereas the latter represents perceptions of the U.S. criminal justice system, specifically related to the police operating in the respondent's neighborhood. Per Figure 1, we argue that these dimensions of fairness directly or indirectly predict our other two measures, *Legal Cynicism* and *Public Cooperation with the Police*.

To construct a measure of rule of law in origin countries of immigrants, we draw upon 2000 data from the World Bank's World Governance Indicators (WGI) project (www.govindicators.org). The WGI produces aggregate country-level indicators of several dimensions of governance, culled from a variety of existing data sources. Data sources include the Gallup World Poll (GWP), the World Economic Forum's Global Competitiveness Report (GCS), and the Economist Intelligence Unit's Risk-Wire & Democracy Index (EIU). The rule of law indicator measures "perceptions of the extent to which agents [individuals and organizations] have confidence in and abide by the rules of society, and in particular the quality of contract enforcement, property rights, the police, and the courts, as well as the likelihood of crime and violence" (Kaufmann, Kraay, and Mastruzzi 2010, 4). Example indicators include public confidence in the police and justice system (from the GWP), the independence of the judiciary from political influences (from the GCS), and fairness and speediness of the judicial process (from the EIU). We developed a neighborhood-level measure that is the weighted average of origin-country *Rule of Law* characteristics among the foreign-born population in the neighborhood. Simply, the greater the representation of a given country among the foreign-born population in a neighborhood (as determined by 2000 U.S. Census data), the more the *Rule of Law* variable will represent the views of the legal system in that origin country.

Procedural Justice, *Legal Cynicism*, and *Public Cooperation with the Police* were all constructed with principal components analysis from data from the survey of New York residents. *Procedural Justice* measures the extent to which residents regard that the police in their neighborhood act in a fair, respectful, and equitable manner. Respondents were asked the frequency with which the police engaged in the following behavior: (1) "Use fair procedures to decide how to handle the problems they deal with" and (2) "Treat people in fair ways." Respondents were also asked the extent to which they agree with the following statements about police behavior: the police (3) "Consider the views of the people involved when deciding what to do," (4) "Take account of the needs and concerns of the people they deal with," (5) "Treat people with dignity and respect," (6) "Respect people's rights," (7) "Usually accurately understand and apply the law," (8) "Make their decisions based upon facts, not their personal biases or opinions," (9) "Try to get the facts in a situation before deciding how to act," (10) "Give honest explanations for their actions to the people they deal with," and (11) "Apply the rules consistently to different people."

To measure *Legal Cynicism*, we combine four items from our survey.[7] Respondents of the survey were asked the extent to which they agree to the following: (1) "Sometimes you have to bend the law for things to come out right," (2) "The law represents the values of the people in power, rather than the values of people like you," (3) "People in power use the law to try to control people like you," and (4) "The law does not protect your interests."

Willingness of residents to cooperate with the police to fight crime and solve existing crimes (i.e., *Public Cooperation with Police*) is measured from three items designed to ask respondents how likely they would be to: (1) "Call the police to report a crime occurring in your neighborhood," (2) "Help the police to find someone suspected of committing a crime by providing them with information," and (3) "Report dangerous or suspicious activities in your neighborhood to the police."

Cynicism of the Law in Immigrant Communities

Table 1 presents results of our statistical analysis of legal cynicism.[8] Findings from model 1 reveal that residents of impoverished neighborhoods are much more likely to be cynical of the law than residents of more affluent areas. Net of other neighborhood characteristics, the extent of disorderly conditions in a neighborhood appears to have little influence on cynical perceptions of the law. Results from model 1 also importantly demonstrate a negative relationship between immigrant concentration and legal cynicism: *neighborhoods characterized by a high concentration of foreign-born residents are less likely to be cynical of the law than in neighborhoods with lesser concentrations*. One interpretation of this finding is that acculturation begets a greater cynicism of societal institutions, particularly the law. In preliminary analysis, we also included an interaction term between concentrated poverty and immigrant concentration to determine if the relationship between immigration and legal cynicism is dependent upon the level of neighborhood poverty. However, we found no significant interaction effect. Overall, the *R*-squared statistic reveals that we have explained 51 percent of the variation in legal cynicism across neighborhoods with the predictors included in model 1.

To unpack the reasons for the negative relationship between concentrated immigration and legal cynicism, we examine the role of language diversity, recent immigration, and the extent of change in the neighborhood proportion of foreign-born residents. Model 2 shows that the extent of ethnic diversity in a neighborhood is unrelated to legal cynicism.[9] Similarly, in model 3 we can see that the extent to which the foreign-born population is dominated by recent arrivals (within the past five years) is unrelated to legal cynicism. Interestingly, in model 4 we find that legal cynicism is a product of the proportional size of the foreign-born population in a neighborhood and the extent to which that population has grown over time (1990 to 2000). Immigrant neighborhoods generally have less

TABLE 1
The Relationship between Immigration and Legal Cynicism

	Model 1		Model 2		Model 3		Model 4	
	Coefficient	(Robust SE)	Coefficient	(Robust SE)	Coefficient	(Robust SE)	Coefficient	(Robust SE)
Intercept	.089	(.072)	.160	(.174)	.206	(.164)	.074	(.072)
Concentrated poverty	.267	(.042)***	.261	(.043)***	.258	(.043)***	.273	(.042)***
Residential stability	.070	(.058)	.062	(.060)	.043	(.068)	.074	(.057)
Population density	−.008	(.013)	−.011	(.014)	−.008	(.014)	−.012	(.014)
Neighborhood disorder	.025	(.107)	.024	(.108)	.037	(.110)	.013	(.105)
Immigrant concentration, 2000	−.068	(.025)**	−.054	(.039)	−.059	(.030)*		
Language diversity			−.133	(.308)				
Recent immigrants					−.006	(.008)		
Immigrant concentration, 1990							−.061	(.030)*
Resid. change imm. conc., 1990 to 2000							−.172	(.102)*
R-squared	.51		.51		.51		.51	

$^*p < .05.$ $^{**}p < .01.$ $^{***}p < .001$ (one-tailed test).

TABLE 2
The Duality of Justice as a Predictor of Legal Cynicism

	Model 5		Model 6	
	Coefficient	(Robust *SE*)	Coefficient	(Robust *SE*)
Intercept	.062	(.067)	.024	(.074)
Concentrated poverty	.215	(.045)***	.141	(.059)**
Residential stability	.060	(.055)	.014	(.052)
Population density	−.010	(.013)	−.011	(.014)
Neighborhood disorder	−.033	(.110)	−.013	(.111)
Immigrant concentration, 1990	−.042	(.029)	−.087	(.035)**
Resid. change imm. conc., 1990 to 2000	−.064	(.112)	−.133	(.113)
Procedural justice	−.287	(.112)**	−.247	(.116)*
Origin rule of law			−.359	(.153)**
R-squared		.56		.58

*$p < .05$. **$p < .01$. ***$p < .001$ (one-tailed test).

cynicism of the law than in neighborhoods populated predominantly by native-born groups, and cynicism is even lower in neighborhoods where the relative size of the immigrant population is growing. That said, while statistically significant, adding a measure of the growth in the proportion of the immigrant population does not add to the amount of variability in legal cynicism that we have explained (i.e., 51 percent, just as in model 1).

Table 2 considers how perceptions of justice influence legal cynicism. Model 5 shows, as expected, that legal cynicism varies inversely with perceptions of procedural justice. Neighborhood residents tend to be less cynical of the law when legal procedures are deemed to be fair and just. Yet fair practice by the police in the United States is not the only measure of justice with bearing on residents' perceptions of legal cynicism. In model 6, we see that the fairness of and confidence in the law in countries of birth (i.e., *Origin Rule of Law*) has a strong negative effect on legal cynicism. If a neighborhood is populated by immigrants from countries with a fair justice system and a legitimate rule of law, then residents will generally not be cynical toward the law. Standardized effects presented in Figure 3—which we use to compare the relative importance of different explanatory factors—reveal that only concentrated poverty has a stronger effect on legal cynicism than rule of law, which is followed closely by procedural justice and immigrant concentration.

In summary, our evidence from the largest and most ethnically diverse urban area in the country reveals that cynical views of the law among neighborhood residents are the product of not only perceptions of the police in the United States, but also origin countries. There is, in a sense, a duality to justice: the

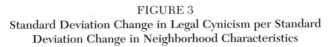

FIGURE 3
Standard Deviation Change in Legal Cynicism per Standard
Deviation Change in Neighborhood Characteristics

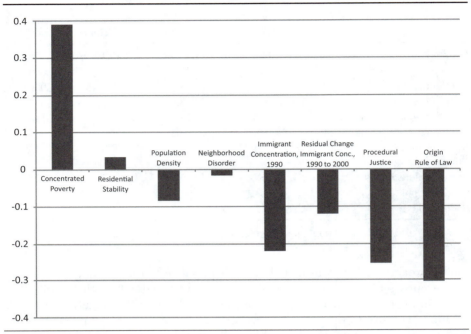

immediate institutional and social context is highly relevant for legal cynicism, yet so are prior contexts, in this case the rule of law in countries of origin for immigrant populations.[10] Nevertheless, controlling for this dual nature of justice, we still find a strong, negative relationship between immigration and legal cynicism. In general, immigrant communities in New York City have less cynicism than areas heavily populated by native groups.

Fostering Cooperation with the Police

We next investigate the relationship between immigration, legal cynicism, and public cooperation with the law. Model 1 of Table 3 reveals that the extent of resident cooperation with police in a neighborhood varies negatively with the level of concentrated poverty yet positively with residential stability. With respect to the latter, residential stability can signify resident investment in the neighborhood, including the development and maintenance of neighborly social ties (Bursik and Grasmick 1993). Cooperating with the police to control crime, then, is a corollary outcome of this investment process.

TABLE 3
The Relationship between Immigration and Public Cooperation with the Police

	Model 1		Model 2		Model 3	
	Coefficient	(Robust SE)	Coefficient	(Robust SE)	Coefficient	(Robust SE)
Intercept	.014	(.090)	.029	(.091)	.297	(.180)
Concentrated poverty	−.187	(.049)***	−.142	(.057)**	−.163	(.055)**
Residential stability	.141	(.059)**	.153	(.059)**	.123	(.065)*
Population density	.003	(.014)	.002	(.015)	−.007	(.017)
Neighborhood disorder	.082	(.115)	.086	(.116)	.085	(.111)
Immigrant concentration, 2000	.082	(.036)*	.071	(.036)*	.124	(.042)**
Legal cynicism			−.167	(.099)*	−.178	(.099)*
Language diversity					−.501	(.258)*
R-squared	.38		.40		.42	

*$p < .05$. **$p < .01$. ***$p < .001$ (one-tailed test).

Findings show a positive relationship between immigrant concentration and public cooperation with the police. Recall that the former is measured by the combination of the percentage of foreign-born residents in a neighborhood and linguistic isolation (i.e., the percent of households in which no person age 14 or older speaks English very well). Thus, the greater the percentage of foreign-born residents in a neighborhood as well as of linguistic isolation, the more likely that residents will cooperate with the police to report crimes and assist the police with solving crimes. Somewhat surprisingly, then, even in immigrant neighborhoods where language may be a barrier to communicating with the police, cooperation with the police is rather prevalent. Contrary to some political portrayals of immigrants as being less cooperative with authorities, our findings clearly indicate that residents of immigrant neighborhoods are actually *more* cooperative with the police than are residents of native-born neighborhoods.

Results in model 2 indicate that legal cynicism and public cooperation with the police are negatively related and that legal cynicism partially mediates the relationship between immigrant concentration and public cooperation. Hence, one reason why immigrant communities are generally more cooperative with the police than other types of neighborhoods is because such neighborhood communities are less cynical about the law.

To investigate the relationship between immigration, cynicism, and cooperation with the police while distinguishing between homogeneous and heterogeneous immigrant communities, we next add the measure of language diversity to the model. In contrast to our linguistic isolation measure, this variable represents the total number of languages spoken in a neighborhood as well as the evenness in the proportion of residents who speak each language. We find a negative relationship between language diversity and cooperation with the police, net of the effect of immigrant concentration/linguistic isolation. Ethnic heterogeneity appears to impede communication and interaction among neighborhood residents, thereby undermining processes of informal social control. When neighbors do not know each other or do not communicate with or trust each other, then they are less likely to intervene on behalf of a common good or to collectively solve problems (see Kornhauser 1978; Shaw and McKay 1942). Take, for instance, the following scenario: in a diverse neighborhood that lacks trusting relations between ethnic groups, a resident may fear retaliation or retribution if he or she helps the police solve a crime committed by a member of another group. Because of a lack of trust and shared understanding among neighborhood residents, individuals may be unwilling to expose themselves to potential risks by cooperating with the police, even if they generally hold favorable views of the police and the law. On the other hand, immigrant enclaves characterized by a relatively homogeneous ethnic settlement have particularly high levels of cooperation with the police. Remarkably, this is true even in mostly non-English-speaking communities where one might assume that language barriers would deter residents from calling the police.

In summary, cooperation with the police is significantly *more likely* in neighborhoods with concentrations of immigrants, particularly in neighborhoods with a relatively homogeneous immigrant community. Yet because cynicism of the law is such a powerful predictor of cooperation with the police, the cooperative, amiable relations found in many immigrant communities between police and residents can easily erode if the perceived fairness and legitimacy of the U.S. justice system decay. Immigration enforcement, particularly those laws and initiatives that would inevitably cast a wide net, may alienate the very communities in the United States that most reliably work with the police to protect public safety.

Discussion

The results of this study shed new light on the way the law is perceived in immigrant communities. Our study finds that immigrant communities, even more so than neighborhoods populated predominantly by native-born citizens, are *less* cynical of the law and *more* cooperative with legal authority. To these findings, we again note that a host of social science studies reveal that immigrants, on average, do not commit as many crimes as native-born groups (see, e.g., Sampson, Morenoff, and Raudenbush 2005; Morenoff and Astor 2006). Moreover, neighborhoods characterized by a concentration of immigrants do not have elevated levels of community violence; rather, immigration appears to produce a protective effect against violence (e.g., Butcher and Piehl 1998; Hagan and Palloni 1998; Lee, Martinez, and Rosenfeld 2001; Davies and Fagan this volume). This growing body of social science research, then, calls into question the rationale of enacting "get tough" immigration policies, particularly against noncriminal aliens. Present-day proposals of immigration reform will not likely benefit public safety. Rather, draconian immigration laws such as Arizona SB 1070 and Alabama House Bill 56 will likely undermine the very public safety that they were purportedly designed to protect.

An underlying context surrounding political debates on immigration is the question of whether public safety—an undeniable common good—is best secured through the use, show, or threat of force or sanction. Generally, there are two strategies available for obtaining obedience to laws: forced compliance and normative compliance. Forced compliance refers to the use of sanctions and punishments as an incentive (or disincentive) for behavior. Forced compliance is the foundation of nearly all deterrence-based criminal policies, increasing the costs, certainty, and severity of sanctions is supposed to ensure the obedience of individuals to the law (see Zimring and Hawkins 1973; Nagin 1998). In contrast, normative compliance fosters obedience to the law based on the belief that those making the law have a right to do so and, by extension, that the laws they create are in some way "just" (Tyler 1990). When individuals perceive that the law is unjust and illegitimate, they are more likely to become cynical of the intent and utility of the law and are more likely to disobey it.

Our study, as well as other research on legitimacy (Tyler 1990), stresses the Durkheimian idea that societies can and do regulate themselves more efficiently by fostering normative compliance with the law. Namely, individuals are less likely to break laws when they believe the laws are morally just and that the procedures and authorities charged with enforcing the laws are fair. While no society could do without some amount of forced compliance, the legitimacy perspective suggests that the common good is better served when compliance is developed normatively rather than at the edge of a sword.

We motivated our study by noting the trend in increasing deportations of illegal aliens in the post-9/11 era, particularly of noncriminal aliens. Indeed, over much of the past three years, the Obama administration has displayed more aggressive enforcement of immigration laws than the preceding administration. A risk of such harsh enforcement is that immigrants will become alienated from the law, thereby undermining their willingness to cooperate with the law and even comply with the law. In a possible reverse of course, on August 18, 2011, the Obama administration announced that it would suspend deportation hearings against illegal immigrants who pose minimal risk to public safety and national security (Pear 2011). Under this new policy, the DHS has been conducting case-by-case reviews of some 300,000 deportation filings to ensure that illegal immigrants with criminal convictions are the focus of deportation instead of individuals who pose a minimal risk to safety and security. This shift in policy should impact public safety, but not in the way that immigration foes may think. The Obama administration seemingly swapped a policy of forced compliance for one of normative compliance. To be sure, the administration still intends to deport criminal aliens. Yet by redirecting enforcement away from lawful immigrants, this new strategy should enhance public safety by preventing the government from destroying the support for the law that is found in so many immigrant communities.

Notes

1. In fact, in some small jurisdictions—including Alto, Texas; Wells, Texas; and Half Moon Bay, California—local police departments have been completely disbanded or furloughed in recent months because cities simply could no longer afford to maintain a police force given the economic downturn. Many other police departments have cut positions, yet are now being called upon to engage in immigration enforcement.

2. Legitimacy and cynicism are not necessarily two sides of the same coin, and while sharing some predicates, such as evaluations of procedural justice, they also reflect other ex ante views of police and of law that are modifiers of how citizens perceive and value law. See Tyler and Fagan (2008) and Fagan and Piquero (2007) for examples of the complex relationship between legitimacy and legal cynicism.

3. We thank Amanda Geller for assistance with data preparation and the construction of our units of analysis.

4. We selected eight respondents as our cutoff point to retain at least 25 percent of the New York City neighborhoods in our sample. Nevertheless, we also conducted our analysis using ten respondents as the cutoff—resulting in fifty-three neighborhoods—with comparable statistical inferences.

5. This is computed by regressing the 2000 value of immigrant concentration on the 1990 value and outputting the unstandardized residual.

6. Language diversity is computed as follows:

$$L_t = 1 - \left(\sum s_r^2 \right)_t,$$

where t references the neighborhood, r refers to the languages in the neighborhood, and s_r represents the proportion of the neighborhood population that speaks a given language at home.

7. We utilize an operationalization of "legal cynicism" that differs to some degree from measurements employed in previous research on legal cynicism, but nevertheless measures cynical perceptions of the legitimacy and equitability of the law. Sampson and Bartusch (1998), Fagan and Tyler (2005), and Fagan and Piquero (2007) use measures that tap a broader construct which combines cynicism of the law with moral cynicism and anomie, whereas Kirk and Papachristos (2011) more narrowly focus on perceptions of the "legal" system and the police in particular. The measure we use here similarly provides a narrow focus on legal cynicism, but does not focus specifically on perceptions of the police.

8. All models in Tables 1, 2, and 3 were estimated via a least squares regression with robust standard errors. Robust standard errors are useful for accounting for heteroskedasticity and yield a more conservative test of statistical significance than otherwise.

9. Many of our variables are significantly correlated, including immigrant concentration and language diversity. Including highly correlated, redundant variables in a statistical model can potentially inflate the standard errors of our regression parameters. We assessed this potential condition, which is termed multicollinearity, by calculating variance inflation factors (VIF) for all independent variables in all of our models. A high VIF indicates that a given variable is highly correlated with the other independent variables in the model. For all models presented in Tables 1, 2, and 3, VIF values all fell well below the generally accepted threshold of 10, indicating that multicollinearity does not adversely affect the precision of our parameter estimates (Kennedy 1998). Concentrated poverty and residential stability had the highest VIFs, yet with values still below 5 in all models.

10. In additional analyses, we also include an interaction term between the two measures of justice to assess whether there might be an accentuating or compensatory relationship between the two, yet we find no evidence of an interactive effect.

References

Beetham, David. 1991. *The legitimation of power*. London: MacMillan Education.

Bursik, Robert J. Jr., and Harold G. Grasmick. 1993. *Neighborhoods and crime: The dimensions of effective community control*. New York, NY: Lexington Books.

Butcher, Kristin F., and Anne M. Piehl. 1998. Cross-city evidence on the relationship between immigration and crime. *Journal of Policy Analysis and Management* 17:457–93.

Davies, Garth, and Jeffrey Fagan. 2012. Crime and policing in immigrant neighborhoods: Evidence from New York City. *The Annals of the American Academy of Political and Social Science* (this volume).

Fagan, Jeffrey, and Tracey Meares. 2008. Punishment, deterrence and social control: The paradox of punishment in minority communities. *Ohio State Journal of Criminal Law* 6:173–229.

Fagan, Jeffrey, and Alexis Piquero. 2007. Rational choice and developmental influences on recidivism among adolescent felony offenders. *Journal of Empirical Legal Studies* 4:715–48.

Fagan, Jeffrey, and Tom T. Tyler. 2005. Legal socialization of children and adolescents. *Social Justice Research* 18:217–42.

French, John R. P., and Bertram Raven. 1959. The bases of social power. In *Studies in social power*, ed. Dorwin Cartwright. Ann Arbor: University of Michigan Press.

Graif, Corina, and Robert J. Sampson. 2009. Spatial heterogeneity in the effects of immigration and diversity on neighborhood homicide rates. *Homicide Studies* 13:242–60.

Hagan, John, and Alberto Palloni. 1998. Immigration and crime in the United States. In *The immigration debate: Studies on the economic, demographic, and fiscal effects of immigration*, eds. James P. Smith and Barry Edmonston. Washington, DC: National Academy Press.

Homeland Security Advisory Council. 2011. *Task Force on Secure Communities: Findings and recommendations*. Washington, DC: Department of Homeland Security. Available from http://www.dhs.gov/xlibrary/assets/hsac-task-force-on-secure-communities-findings-and-recommendations-report.pdf.

Jackson, Kenneth L., and John Manbeck. 1998. *The neighborhoods of Brooklyn*. New Haven, CT: Yale University Press.

Kaufmann, Daniel, Aart Kraay, and Massimo Mastruzzi. 2010. The worldwide governance indicators: Methodology and analytical issues. World Bank Policy Research Working Paper No. 5430. Available from http://ssrn.com/abstract=1682130.

Kennedy, Peter. 1998. *A guide to econometrics*. 4th ed. Cambridge, MA: MIT Press.

Kirk, David S., and Mauri Matsuda. 2011. Legal cynicism, collective efficacy, and the ecology of arrest. *Criminology* 49:443–72.

Kirk, David S., and Andrew V. Papachristos. 2011. Cultural mechanisms and the presence of neighborhood violence. *American Journal of Sociology* 116:1190–233.

Kornhauser, Ruth. 1978. *Social sources of delinquency*. Chicago, IL: University of Chicago Press.

Lee, Matthew T., Ramiro Martinez Jr., and Richard Rosenfeld. 2001. Does immigration increase homicide? Negative evidence from three border cities. *Sociological Quarterly* 42:559–80.

Morenoff, Jeffrey D., and Avraham Astor. 2006. Immigrant assimilation and crime: Generational differences in youth violence in Chicago. In *Immigration and crime: Race, ethnicity, and violence*, eds. Ramiro Martinez Jr. and Abel Valenzuela Jr. New York, NY: New York University Press.

Nagin, Daniel S. 1998. Criminal deterrence research at the outset of the twenty-first century. In *Crime and justice: An annual review of research*, vol. 23, ed. Michael Tonry. Chicago, IL: University of Chicago Press.

Papachristos, Andrew V., Tracey L. Meares, and Jeffrey Fagan. Forthcoming. Why do criminals obey the law? The influence of legitimacy and social networks on active gun offenders. *Journal of Criminal Law and Criminology*.

Pear, Robert. 18 August 2011. Fewer youths to be deported in new policy. *New York Times*. Available from http://www.nytimes.com/2011/08/19/us/19immig.html.

Sampson, Robert J. 2012. *Great American city: Chicago and the enduring neighborhood effect*. Chicago, IL: University of Chicago Press.

Sampson, Robert J., and Dawn Jeglum Bartusch. 1998. Legal cynicism and (subcultural) tolerance of deviance: The neighborhood context of racial differences. *Law & Society Review* 32:777–804.

Sampson, Robert J., Jeffrey D. Morenoff, and Stephen Raudenbush. 2005. Social anatomy of racial and ethnic disparities in violence. *American Journal of Public Health* 95:224–32.

Shaw, Clifford R., and Henry D. McKay. 1942. *Juvenile delinquency and urban areas*. Chicago, IL: University of Chicago Press.

Skogan, Wesley, and Kathleen Frydl. 2004. *Fairness and effectiveness in policing: The evidence*. Washington, DC: National Academy Press.

Sunshine, Jason, and Tom R. Tyler. 2003. The role of procedural justice and legitimacy in shaping public support for policing. *Law and Society Review* 37:555–89.

Tyler, Tom R. 1990. *Why people obey the law*. New Haven, CT: Yale University Press.

Tyler, Tom R. 2010. *Why people cooperate*. Princeton, NJ: Princeton University Press.

Tyler, Tom R., and Jeffrey Fagan. 2008. Legitimacy, compliance and cooperation: Procedural justice and citizen ties to the law. *Ohio State Journal of Criminal Law* 6:231–75.

Tyler, Tom R., Stephen Schulhofer, and Aziz Huq. 2010. Legitimacy and deterrence effects in counterterrorism policing: A study of Muslim Americans. *Law and Society Review* 44:365–401.

U.S. Department of Homeland Security (DHS). 2010. *Yearbook of immigration statistics: 2009*. Washington, DC: DHS, Office of Immigration Statistics. Available from http://www.dhs.gov/xlibrary/assets/statistics/yearbook/2009/ois_yb_2009.pdf.

U.S. Government Accountability Office (GAO). 2009. *Immigration enforcement: Better controls needed over program authorizing state and local enforcement of federal immigration laws*. GAO-09-109. Report to Congressional Requesters. Washington, DC: GAO. Available from http://www.gao.gov/products/GAO-09-109.

U.S. Immigration Commission. 1911. *Immigration and crime*. Vol. 36. Washington, DC: Government Printing Office.

Weber, Max. 1968. *Economy and society*. Edited by G. Roth and C. Wittich. New York, NY: Bedminster Press.

Wickersham Commission. 1931. *National Commission on Law Observance and Enforcement: Report on crime and the foreign born*. No. 10. Washington, DC: Government Printing Office.

Zimring, Franklin E., and Gordon J. Hawkins. 1973. *Deterrence: The legal threat in crime control*. Chicago, IL: University of Chicago Press.

Crime and Enforcement in Immigrant Neighborhoods: Evidence from New York City

By
GARTH DAVIES
and
JEFFREY FAGAN

Immigration and crime have received much popular and political attention in the past decade and have been a focus of episodic social attention for much of the history of the United States. Recent policy and legal discourse suggests that the stigmatic link between immigrants and crime has endured, even in the face of evidence to the contrary. This study addresses the relationship between immigration and crime in urban settings, focusing on areal units where immigrants tend to cluster spatially as well as socially. The authors ask whether immigration creates risks or benefits for neighborhoods in terms of lower crime rates. The question is animated in part by a durable claim in criminology that areas with large immigrant populations are burdened by elevated levels of social disorder and crime. In contrast, more recent theory and research suggest that "immigrant neighborhoods" may simply be differentially organized and function in a manner that reduces the incidence of crime. Accordingly, this research investigates whether immigrants are associated with differences in area crime rates. In addition, the authors ask whether there are differences in the effects of immigration on neighborhood crime rates by the racial and ethnic makeup of the foreign-born populations. Finally, the authors examine the effects of immigration on patterns of enforcement.

Keywords: immigration; ethnicity; law enforcement; generalized propensity scores

Garth Davies is an associate professor at Simon Fraser University. His current work examines the intersections of immigration, segregation, crime, and policing. He is also interested in alternative techniques for analyzing neighborhood effects.

Jeffrey Fagan is the Isidor and Seville Sulzbacher Professor of Law and director of the Center for Crime, Community and Law at Columbia Law School. He also is a senior research scholar at Yale Law School. His recent scholarship examines policing, the legitimacy of the criminal law, capital punishment, and juvenile crime and punishment. He is a fellow of the American Society of Criminology.

NOTE: The authors wish to express their sincerest appreciation to Amanda Geller for her excellent assistance with data wrangling and to Rob Sampson and John MacDonald for improving our article with their comments and insights.

DOI: 10.1177/0002716212438938

Historically, immigration has been associated with crime and other social ills in popular and political culture (Hagan and Palloni 1999; McDonald 2009). Waves of immigration in the nineteenth and twentieth centuries brought with them moral panics on drugs and alcohol, gangs, delinquency, organized crime, wage suppression, and drains on public resources (Hagan, Levi, and Dinovitzer 2008; Sampson 2008). More recently, the presumed link to crime has provided a significant rationale for a variety of punitive responses to immigration. In Arizona, the 2010 killing of Robert Krentz made tangible generalized anxiety about immigrant crime (Archibold 2010). Although no suspect was identified, speculation that the killer was an illegal alien helped secure the passage of Arizona's draconian (anti)immigration bill. The specter of immigrant crime similarly aided in generating public support for "copycat" legislation in Georgia and Alabama. Even laws that ostensibly were more about the economics of immigration, such as California's Proposition 187, nonetheless were buttressed by allusions not just to the potential for financial burdens on labor markets, education, and health care from illegal immigration, but also to criminal activity among some illegal immigrants.

Thus, as part of the broader debate about immigration, the putative connection between immigration and crime is of considerable political and practical import. The presumptive connection has motivated new efforts to link local law enforcement with immigration enforcement (Varsanyi et al. forthcoming). The new intersection of criminal enforcement with immigration has led some scholars to label illegal immigration as "crimigration," a linguistic and conceptual move to broaden the mandate of local police to systematically and routinely engage in immigration enforcement (Sklansky forthcoming).

Still, despite the recent involvement of local police in immigration enforcement, research and theoretical interest in immigration in criminology has been episodic (Hagan, Levi, and Dinovitzer 2008). In the early twentieth century, immigration figured prominently in theories of neighborhood and crime, particularly *social disorganization* (Shaw and McKay 1943; Bursik 1988; Bursik and Grasmick 1993; Sampson 2008). Often arriving in poverty, many immigrants, principally from Southern and Eastern Europe, were forced to settle in the poorest areas of the city. Subsequently, immigrants were scapegoated for the problems attendant with these urban slums. Studies of street gangs in the 1920s in Chicago depicted gang conflict as a function of ethnic and racial conflicts among first- and second-generation immigrant youth (e.g., Thrasher 1927). The early juvenile courts in Chicago and other urban areas targeted the children of immigrants for a paternalistic form of social control (Tanenhaus 2004; Platt 1969; Sealander 2003). Shaw and McKay's (1943) critical insight was that rates of delinquency remained pretty stable among Chicago's neighborhoods between 1900 and 1933, despite dramatic changes in the composition of these neighborhoods. In other words, crime rates were not contingent upon the racial and ethnic makeup of an area; rather, crime was related to neighborhood conditions, specifically poverty, anonymity, and heterogeneity. In this way, the legacy of social disorganization in relation to immigrants is somewhat mixed. On one hand, the theory offers a strong refutation of the notion that immigrants are inherently criminal. On the other hand, the theory does predict higher crime rates in areas inhabited by newly arrived immigrants.

Interest in immigration among criminologists has ebbed and flowed with immigration itself. Between the 1920s and 1965, restrictions on the number of immigrants entering the United States pushed immigration to the background. When the 1965 amendments to the Immigration and Nationality Act ended quotas based on nationality, immigration rates leaped dramatically, and the stigmatic link between immigration and crime again became part of the political and popular discourse on immigration. Still, interest in immigration among criminologists has revived only in the past decade, as theories of neighborhoods (Sampson, Morenoff, and Gannon-Rowley 2002) and social networks (Kasinitz, Mollenkopf, and Waters 2009) began to incorporate the unique contexts of immigration. Much of this more recent research has challenged stereotypical assertions and suggested that the connection between immigration and crime is more myth than reality: immigrants are not more "crime-prone" than native-born Americans, and, on balance, immigration does not increase neighborhood crime rates (Butcher and Piehl 1998). In fact, emerging evidence indicates that immigration may improve neighborhood conditions and reduce levels of crime.

Nonetheless, research on the immigration-crime nexus continues to be a work in progress, and a number of important issues remain. Among the most important of these concerns is the disaggregation of immigration. As noted above, *total* immigration does not appear to promote higher crime rates. But this population is hardly homogeneous. Immigrants are drawn from a wide range of diverse countries, cultures, and racial and ethnic groups. Nowhere is this more evident than in New York City (NYC) (Kasinitz, Mollenkopf, and Waters 2009). For this reason, this study examines patterns of crime among racial and ethnic subgroups in NYC and the effects of New York's Order Maintenance Policing strategy (Fagan et al. 2010; Zimring 2011) in immigrant neighborhoods.

Perspectives on Immigration, Crime, and Enforcement

As in the past, the specter of elevated crime rates among immigrants has animated or reinforced specific law enforcement tactics that seek to counter unique forms of criminal activity or organizations among immigrants (Rumbaut and Ewing 2007). Programs such as the federal Secure Communities Program (U.S. Immigration and Customs Enforcement [ICE] 2009; Homeland Security Advisory Council 2011) up the ante in this debate by attempting to establish a link between "ordinary" crime, immigration violations, and national security threats (Hagan, Levi, and Dinovitzer 2008; Varsanyi et al. forthcoming; Sklansky forthcoming). Some gang violence suppression initiatives also focus on the nexus of immigration and street gangs, and these links become even more contentious when immigration is linked to violence from drug trafficking (Stuntz 2002), as in the Robert Krentz case in Arizona.

These efforts are predicated on assumptions that immigrants commit more crimes and that urban neighborhoods of immigrant concentration are important targets for enhanced law enforcement. Whether immigration contributes to or attenuates neighborhood crime rates is a contentious debate (see, e.g., Butcher and Piehl 1998, 2007). The sociological and criminological literature offers grounds to both support and reject these claims. Below we briefly sketch out the evidence on these competing perspectives on the effects of immigration, and we follow that with empirical tests from NYC, a place that has been an important immigration reception context throughout the history of the United States (Kasinitz, Mollenkopf, and Waters 2009; Portes and Rumbaut 2006).

The bad: Why might immigration increase neighborhood crime rates?

The presumptive association between immigration and crime does not reflect only simple nativism and prejudice. Immigration was, from the start, built into theories of crime in neighborhoods. Social disorganization theory was formulated by Shaw and McKay (1943) in response to the disruptions fostered by successive waves of immigration into Chicago. It was, in other words, largely a theory about the effects of immigration and political economy, and the basic argument linking immigration with crime endured even as the terms of the debate changed (Bursik and Grasmick 1993).

For example, the key construct linking social disorganization and crime is informal social control (or lack thereof). Neighborhoods can accomplish collective goals, including crime control, through mechanisms of informal social control, such as local institutions, social networks, and shared expectations regarding behavioral regulation (Sampson, Raudenbush, and Earls 1997). One version of the immigration link to crime focuses on the compromising effects of immigrant concentration on local efforts at informal social control. Often arriving with few financial resources and limited job prospects, immigrants tend to be sorted or self-selected into already disadvantaged areas (Sampson 2008). Immigrants have little attachment to these neighborhoods upon their arrival, and they leave for better social and material conditions as soon as possible, only to be succeeded by other immigrant groups (Shaw and McKay 1943). The population turnover caused by the influx and outflow of immigrants destabilizes these areas. The resulting racial and ethnic heterogeneity hampers interpersonal communication, renders trust more elusive, and, at the extremes, leads to territorial conflict and ethnic rivalry. In short, the rapid social change brought on by widespread immigration serves to undermine local institutions and networks and weakens the foundations of informal social control.

The demographics of immigration may also increase crime rates, net of any individual criminal tendencies of newly arrived immigrants or their second-generation children. In general though hardly uniformly, immigrants tend to be young, male, relatively poor, and uneducated (Portes and Rumbaut 2006). In other words, immigrants tend to share a demographic profile consistent with groups that already commit a disproportionate share of crime. So immigration may increase crime levels simply by increasing the pool of more likely offenders. At the same time, immigration may also elevate crime by reinforcing existing disadvantage in high-risk neighborhoods. With low incomes and limited skills, immigrant populations can sustain the lower socioeconomic status of these areas. Over time, this status may become entrenched. In extreme circumstances, neighborhoods may reach a tipping point, with spiraling levels of crime and violence.

Opportunity structures may also be implicated in immigrant crime patterns. Often residing in distressed neighborhoods and lacking job skills, connections, and social capital, immigrants are confronted by blocked economic opportunities. One potential response to attenuated access to capital and legal markets is for immigrants to "innovate" (Merton 1938) by resorting to crime as an alternative avenue for advancement. The probability of innovative crime is enhanced by greater access to illegitimate opportunity structures, which are more prevalent in disadvantaged areas (Cloward and Ohlin 1960).

Finally, immigrants may increase crime not as offenders, but as victims. Immigrant populations are at greater risk of victimization for several reasons. Immigrants tend to reside, at least initially, in high-crime areas. Alba, Logan, and Bellair (1994) found that Hispanics who were born outside the United States, had immigrated only recently, or were less linguistically assimilated lived in areas with higher crime rates than did other groups. Increasingly, research has paid particular attention to particular types of immigrant victimization, such as hate crimes (Hendricks et al. 2007) and sexual violence against women (Decker, Raj, and Silverman 2007). But immigrants are also vulnerable to a wide range of exploitations, including unscrupulous landlords, bankers, financiers, and employers (Chiswick and Miller 2008). Language barriers and cultural mistrust of the police may make immigrants reluctant to report crime and otherwise interact with authorities, making immigrants more open to predation.

The good: Why might immigration reduce crime?

Running through the traditional theoretical perspectives are a series of assumptions about the process of immigration (see, e.g., Lewis 1966; Portes and Sensenbrenner 1993). The simplistic image of socially isolated immigrants with little education and limited employment potential being funneled into disadvantaged neighborhoods is becoming anachronistic. The post-1965 wave of immigration has been marked by greater diversity in education, job skills, and access to employment networks (Wadsworth 2010). These changes to immigrants' profiles have forced a reconceptualization of the connection between immigration and crime. Rather than serving to increase crime rates, there are a number of ways in which immigration might instead be a protective factor that reduces crime.

One reason that immigration might mitigate crime is what Wadsworth (2010) has referred to as the "healthy immigrant thesis." Immigration is not a random process, and immigrants do not represent a random sample from their countries of origin. They are among the most highly motivated individuals, with the lowest propensities toward criminal behavior. After immigrants have arrived, they have greater stakes in conformity and are much less likely to jeopardize their achievements by participating in crime. It is also possible that immigrants have different frameworks for evaluating their neighborhood environments and work conditions. The "disadvantaged" neighborhoods and "low-skilled" jobs immigrants might encounter in the United States are still improvements compared to conditions in their countries of origins.

Similarly, there may be aspects of culture that serve to protect immigrants from crime. Immigrant communities foster closer social ties and networks, provide social support, promote cultural preservation, and aid in the maintenance of traditional norms and values. It has been suggested that immigrants may place greater emphasis on marriage and intact families (Ousey and Kurbrin 2009). More recent immigrants also benefit from the existing coethnic networks, enclaves that can provide assistance as immigrants navigate the new circumstances. The growth and concentration of ethnic enclaves may also offer economic opportunities that were previously unavailable to immigrants. Ethnically organized or segmented economies often provide jobs in businesses established by earlier immigrants (Portes and Zhou 1992), affording opportunities perhaps inaccessible in the broader labor market. Niche employment may also improve the prospects of some immigrants who might otherwise find it difficult to find work (Kasinitz, Mollenkopf, and Waters 2009). Some groups may be particularly entrepreneurial.

At the same time, widespread immigration can provide advantages that extend beyond the confines of enclaves, by repopulating moribund neighborhoods, rejuvenating local economies, and encouraging local development. More generally, the potential boon of immigration is captured by the "immigrant revitalization" perspective. Martinez (2006) has posited that the influx of immigrants fosters "new forms of social organization and adaptive social structures" that may mediate the deleterious consequences of residing in disadvantaged areas. In addition to reinvigorating economies and nurturing familial ties and social networks, large-scale immigration can expand and strengthen community institutions (Velez 2009). Immigrant revitalization does not represent a complete rebuttal of social disorganization but, rather, suggests that in some circumstances, instability is decoupled from the inhibition of social control and, thus, does not necessarily function as a precursor to crime (Martinez, Stowell, and Lee 2010).

The evidence thus far

Although immigration and crime have long been conflated, both on theoretical grounds and in the popular imagination, there is strikingly little evidence to support this nexus. There is a smattering of supporting examples (see, e.g., Taft 1933; Hagan and Palloni 1999), but these analyses are more anecdotal than systematic. Most early research on immigration and crime is beset with methodological shortcomings (Tonry 1997). In a detailed review of more contemporary aggregate-level studies, Ousey and Kubrin (2009) found that the supposition that immigration contributes to crime rates was unwarranted. With few exceptions, immigration either (1) was not associated with measures of crime and violence or (2) actually reduced violence levels.

These "neutral" or "protective" effects of immigration have been shown across a number of research settings and levels (see Sampson [2008] for a review). For example, Butcher and Piehl (1998) concluded that, after controlling for demographic characteristics, immigration had no effect on either crime rates or changes in crime rates in a sample of 43 metropolitan areas. Analogous results were presented by Martinez (2008) in a study of 111 cities with at least 5,000 Latinos. Immigration was positively associated with total homicide rate and negatively associated with Latino homicide rates, but neither relationship was significant. Using a random sample of 150 Metropolitan Statistical Areas and Primary Metropolitan Statistical Areas (MSAs and PMSAs), Reid et al. (2005) found recent immigration had a significant negative effect on homicide rates, but otherwise showed no effect for robbery, burglary, or larceny rates. In a longitudinal study of 159 cities between 1980 and 2000, immigration had a mildly significant negative influence on violent crime rates (Ousey and Kubrin 2009).

Cities are an important unit of macro-level analysis, but it is possible that their size masks important variation between neighborhoods. A series of census tract-level studies by Martinez and colleagues have generally confirmed the results from the cities. For example, recent immigration did not affect Latino homicide rates in Miami or San Diego neighborhoods or black homicide rates in El Paso (Lee, Martinez, and Rosenfeld 2001). Recent immigration was negatively, and significantly, related to Latino homicide in El Paso and black homicide in Miami. Only for black homicide rates in San Diego was immigration a significant positive predictor. Similar results were produced when homicide was disaggregated by motivational types (Nielsen, Lee, and Martinez 2005). When more nuanced measures of immigration were used, ethnic-specific models showed no association between immigration and violent crime rates in Houston and mostly significant negative effects for San Diego (Stowell and Martinez 2007, 2009). Finally, in a longitudinal study of San Diego neighborhoods between 1980 and 2000, neighborhoods with higher proportions of immigrants had lower levels of total, Latino, and non-Latino white victimization (Martinez, Stowell, and Lee 2010).

Taken together, these studies, utilizing a variety of crime types, measures of immigration, research designs, and units of analysis, offer a preponderance of evidence demonstrating that "immigration reduces crime." Lee and Martinez (2009) have characterized this proposal as an "emerging scholarly consensus," and several authors have begun to explain the precipitous crime decline of the 1990s as a function of rising immigration (Sampson 2008; MacDonald, Hipp, and Gill 2008; Stowell et al. 2009; Wadsworth 2010). At a minimum, the findings of contemporary research call into question previous theoretical perspectives supposing a positive correlation between immigration and crime. Nonetheless, research on the immigration-crime nexus continues to be a work in progress, and a number of important issues remain. One such issue concerns the disaggregation of racial and ethnic effects. Much of the current wave of research has focused on Latino immigrants. Few if any studies have extended their comparisons to include African, West Indian, and Asian populations. The present study analyzes criminogenic effects across this wider spectrum of groups.

Enforcement

Interest in the overlap of policing and immigration has been expressed on a number of fronts (Stuntz 2002; Hagan, Levi, and Dinovitzer 2008; Sklansky forthcoming; Epp, Maynard-Moody, and Heider-Markel forthcoming). At present, special attention is being paid to the issue of illegal immigration, the security of U.S. borders, and the broader "war on terrorism." Once a primarily federal issue, these concerns are increasingly playing out on more local stages (Harris 2006). September 11, 2001, led to a sea change, as the Department of Justice began utilizing local police to supplement immigration enforcement (Gladstein 2005), blurring the lines between immigration offenses under federal law and criminal offenses under state statutes. This, in turn, has altered substantially and problematized the relationship between immigrant communities and local agencies. Most notably, the shift in emphasis has proved difficult to reconcile with the dictates of "community policing" (Tyler, Schulhofer, and Huq 2010). Tyler and colleagues (2010) show, in a survey of Muslim Americans in NYC, that the trust and legitimacy required for effective community policing is elusive when many residents fear that contact with the police could lead to deportation. In fact, the degradation of police-community relations has been most acute in immigrant communities (Jones and Supinski 2010).

A second line of inquiry has involved an expansion of the literature on public perceptions of the police to include immigrant populations. Race and ethnicity have long been central to understanding disparate levels of support for and satisfaction with the police, but only recently has immigrant status been incorporated into this literature. Some of the findings regarding immigrant attitudes are consistent with previous opinion surveys. For example, quantity of police contacts was negatively related to rating of the police for Chinese immigrants in NYC, while quality of interaction was a key determinant of satisfaction with the police (Chu, Song, and Dombrink 2005). However, evaluations of the police may also reflect considerations unique to immigrants, such as their former experiences with and perceptions of the criminal justice systems of the countries from which they emigrated (Davis and Henderson 2003). The specific information about the police conveyed through social networks of family, friends, acquaintances, neighbors, and coworkers similarly plays a pivotal role in the development of sentiments toward the police (Menjívar and Bejarano 2004).

As the scale of immigration has grown, the challenges inherent in policing immigrants and immigrant communities have also begun to garner more consideration.

Perhaps the most prominent obstacle confronting police-immigrant relations is language. The inability to communicate effectively and efficiently is a source of considerable delay and frustration for officers. Moreover, many immigrants arrive from countries where violence, corruption, and incompetence are endemic to the police (Mears 2001; Skogan 2009). The fear of the police that may be imported from these originating countries can pose another significant barrier to communication. As well, newcomers often lack knowledge pertaining to the criminal justice system, which complicates relationship-building with the police. In certain circumstances, the specific nature of police-immigrant contacts may be a point of contention. Culver (2004) noted that the sizable number of interactions involving traffic and false identification offenses in one small Midwestern community resulted in disproportionately negative contacts between the police and the Hispanic community.

Law enforcement has always been an important corollary to crime, but the correlation between the two has never been perfect. There are a host of factors that can influence patterns of enforcement independent of crime. Of particular interest here are the contextual effects of neighborhoods on policing. In contrast to the issue of crime, the contingent relationship with law enforcement continues to be largely absent from the criminological treatment of immigration. To be more precise, the aggregate-level impact of immigration levels on rates of enforcement has not, as yet, received sufficient attention. This research is a first step in trying to understand patterns of enforcement in immigrant neighborhoods.

Research Questions

As the quintessential "gateway" city, NYC provides a crucial platform for exploring the effects of immigration on local crime and enforcement. The sheer scale and variety of immigration in NYC allows for analyses to be disaggregated by racial/ethnic groups. The rich immigrant history facilitates a number of conceptually important comparisons, including those involving "newer" immigrants and native coethnics. And as with other large U.S. cities, patterns of immigration, crime, and enforcement continue to evolve. The period of time under consideration here, from 1990 to 2000, saw a notable increase in the diversity of NYC's immigrant population. In light of these ongoing changes, this study updates and reconsiders a series of questions relating to NYC neighborhoods.

First, where do immigrants settle in NYC? The choice of residential locations is not random. Rather, immigrants self-select into neighborhoods. Immigrants have traditionally settled in disadvantaged areas characterized by high levels of poverty, racial heterogeneity, mobility, and crime. If settlement patterns have changed, past theoretical explanations of immigration and crime need to be revisited. This study investigates the social, economic, and crime conditions that affect the self-selection process for immigrants. The nonrandom nature of residential location has an important methodological dimension as well. Criminological evaluations have not sufficiently addressed the potential for *selection bias* resulting from self-selection. That is, prior work has not accounted for the propensity of newly arriving groups to select specific areas for settlement where people look like them and have similar resources. This study uses a generalized propensity score (GPS) approach to control for selection bias in the analysis of immigration and crime.

Second, do local crime rates vary by level of immigration? Most current research indicates that immigration either is unrelated to, or mitigates, neighborhood crime. This study utilizes a larger number of more diverse neighborhoods, and a wider variety of crimes, than have previous efforts. In addition to assessing the broad effects of immigration on crime, this study also examines whether local crime rates vary by race- and ethnic-specific immigrant groups.

Third, is there a relationship between immigration and patterns of police enforcement? Prior research has not examined how immigration may influence neighborhood patterns of enforcement of "regular" crime. It is important to evaluate enforcement in addition to crime, given what is known about the complex dynamics of policing in relation to neighborhood and race more generally. Finally, as with crime, this study also disaggregates effects by various immigrant groups.

Methods

The concentration of foreign-born population is used to estimate the effects of immigration on crime and enforcement in NYC neighborhoods from 2004 to 2008. We begin by estimating the selection of immigrants into a neighborhood by adjusting immigration rates by their correlation with observed characteristics of the neighborhoods, including social structure, political economy, and crime. We estimate the selection of immigrant groups into neighborhoods for four racial and ethnic groups, and also for specific varieties of crime and enforcement. We use generalized propensity score (GPS) analysis (Hirano and Imbens 2004; Feng et al. 2011) to estimate the probability (p) of a proportion of immigrants residing in a neighborhood conditional on the observed characteristics of each neighborhood. Like the standard propensity score approach, GPS aims to establish the effect of a "treatment" (in this case, level of immigration) with observational data where the treatment is not randomly assigned. But while propensity scores attempt to control for differences between treatment groups when the treatment is binary, GPS allows for continuous treatments (Imai and van Dyk 2004). The GPS approach begins by estimating a propensity score (the variables used to model immigration are illustrated in Table 1). GPS assumes that the disturbances for the estimation model are normally distributed and tests this assumption using the Kolmogorov-Smirnov equality-of-distributions test. Finally, the balance on the covariates is evaluated at specified intervals of the treatment variable (Bia and Mattei 2008).

Once the normality of disturbances and balancing properties have been confirmed, the GPS is used to identify the effects of immigration on crime and enforcement using a dose-response model. The dose-response model takes the form of a regression equation

$$Y = T + \text{GPS},$$

Where

Y = outcome,

T = treatment, and

GPS = generalized propensity score.

That is, the dose-response model estimates the marginal effects of increases in the levels of concentration of immigrants in a neighborhood (the "treatment") on the outcomes of interest. Similar to the use of propensity scores to estimate the nonrandom selection of individuals into neighborhoods (MacDonald, this volume), this technique allows us to include both immigrant concentration and the control variables in models of both crime and enforcement. This estimation strategy produces an unbiased test of the effect of immigrant concentration on crime.

Data

Immigration. Immigration here refers to foreign-born individuals. Immigration data were obtained from decennial census data on tracts in NYC in 2000. Race- and ethnic-specific data were taken from STF4 census files. "Newer" immigrants are those individuals who arrived in the United States between 1995 and 2000. We include immigrants from Caribbean and African nations among "black" immigrants, despite potential differences in the countries of origin in each of these populations. One reason to combine these groups is the potential reactivity of police officers to Afrocentric features that are shared among this population as well as native-born African Americans (Eberhardt et al. 2006). We also include Latino immigrants who self-identify in the census as both "black" and "Hispanic origin" among blacks.

Neighborhood social structure. Data estimating the socioeconomic and demographic characteristics of neighborhoods were obtained from the 1990 and 2000 decennial census. Housing price sale data were obtained from an archive of real estate transactions maintained by the Department of Finance in NYC. Transactions were recorded by address and were geocoded and assigned to census tracts.

Crime. Homicide and assault rates between 1990 and 2000 were computed from the records provided by the New York City Department of Health and Mental Hygiene. Homicide data were obtained from Vital Statistics records. Assault data were obtained from emergency room and hospital admissions for intentional injuries. These data were geocoded and assigned to census block groups and tracts. Detailed data on crime incidents from 2004 to 2008 were obtained from the Oniform records system of the New York City Police Department (NYPD), which is the method for compiling crime complaints.[1] Each record included spatial coordinates (i.e., latitude and longitude) of the

TABLE 1
Modal Neighborhood Comparisons for Foreign-Born Populations

Variables	Foreign-Born Black		Foreign-Born Latino		Foreign-Born Asian		Foreign-Born White	
	Mean	SD	Mean	SD	Mean	SD	Mean	SD
Foreign-born 2000 (%)	29.56	13.31	37.20	16.21	48.47	11.50	3.49	14.89
Foreign-born 1990 (%)	22.08	12.79	28.87	14.51	36.04	12.30	25.20	12.23
Black (%)	54.87	23.94	22.44	22.28	5.77	8.16	5.61	9.75
Latino (%)	27.69	19.21	34.52	16.09	22.33	17.10	17.21	15.20
Asian (%)	4.37	7.23	11.76	13.69	2.58	3.44	12.59	12.24
White (%)	8.12	13.37	25.03	22.81	44.34	23.21	61.15	22.41
Poverty (%)	27.67	12.69	24.81	13.47	16.60	9.07	13.01	1.74
Public assistance (%)	12.99	7.75	1.12	7.90	4.78	3.47	3.26	3.75
Gini index	.44	.07	.42	.06	.38	.07	.33	.08
Less than high school (%)	34.20	11.53	33.96	11.95	27.17	11.64	19.01	12.60
Unemployment (%)	14.83	7.54	11.84	7.50	7.29	3.22	6.20	4.15
Not in labor force (%)	45.09	7.42	45.04	9.01	42.81	6.89	38.52	1.81
Female-headed households (%)	17.74	8.81	13.13	9.33	5.79	3.71	4.70	4.36
Supervision ratio	.64	.18	.58	.20	.47	.13	.41	.23
White isolation index	.10	.14	.27	.24	.46	.23	.63	.21
Residential mobility (% < 5 years)	62.36	7.83	6.59	7.76	6.37	7.86	59.83	11.87
Housing vacancy rate (%)	7.93	5.38	5.48	3.87	3.81	2.48	4.78	3.23
Renters (%)	71.11	23.10	73.31	19.58	61.28	2.65	58.18	24.70
Population (logged)	8.09	0.56	8.17	0.52	8.21	0.42	8.14	0.64
Average housing price	29.92	9.10	34.96	19.55	48.29	133.48	62.79	116.13
Average homicide rate	2.95	1.79	1.82	1.60	0.80	0.65	0.64	0.73
Average assault rate	18.09	1.35	12.44	11.89	5.32	3.97	5.92	8.16

crime location, as well as details on the specific offense (New York State Penal Law section). Crime rates were averaged over the five-year period to provide stability and were logged to minimize the influence of outliers.

Enforcement. Detailed data on arrests were obtained from the Online Booking System (OLBS) of the NYPD. Records include both offense and arrest location, as well as details on the specific Penal Law section.

Data on street stops were also obtained from the NYPD for the years 2004 to 2008. Records include the specific location of the stop, the suspected crime, the rationale for and outcome of the stop, and demographic characteristics of the person stopped.

Arrests and street stops were combined to create an overall index of enforcement.[2] Rates of enforcement were created by using crimes as a denominator. Thus, enforcement rate is a measure of enforcement per crime. Enforcement rates were averaged over the five-year period and logged.

Results

Where do immigrants settle?

Comparisons of modal neighborhood characteristics for each race- or ethnicity-specific population group are shown in Table 1.[3] In the main, each group tends to sort into tracts where people look like them and have similar resources. The proclivity is most pronounced among white immigrants, who reside in largely white (61 percent) neighborhoods. Black immigrants similarly settle in predominantly black (55 percent) areas. While Latino immigrants also live where Latinos comprise the majority of residents, the distribution of race/ethnic groups is more even. Latino immigrants are much more likely than black immigrants to reside near whites and Asians. In contrast to other groups, Asian immigrants are living not in Asian neighborhoods, but in primarily white locations. It is possible that Asian immigrants have greater financial resources and are less constrained in terms of choice of residential neighborhood.

Black immigrants tend to settle in places where social and economic disadvantage are greatest. Relative to the other groups, modal black immigrant neighborhoods have the highest rates of poverty, public assistance, unemployment, and female-headed households. These areas also have lower access to wealth, as indicated by housing prices. A similar pattern is found in relation to violent crime. In addition to socioeconomic distress, black immigrants reside in areas with much higher levels of homicide and assault. At the other end of the spectrum, white and Asian immigrants face much less danger in their neighborhoods. Similar to immigrants of African descent, Latino immigrants also tend to live in disadvantaged neighborhoods, but these places are less economically isolated than the places where black immigrants settle. Whites tend to avoid socioeconomic or structural disadvantage and enjoy greater access to wealth in the neighborhoods where they settle. Areas occupied by Asian immigrants are less well-off than those of whites but nonetheless are more like white neighborhoods than are those occupied by other groups.

The results of the GPS models confirm these descriptive statistics. Table 2 shows the factors that predict the concentration of the total and race/ethnic-specific foreign-born population in 2000. As the goal of the propensity score approach is to improve estimates of immigration by using a large number of relevant variables, the coefficients presented in Table 2 should be interpreted cautiously. However, the results nonetheless reveal some interesting patterns. The large effect for immigrant concentration at the outset of the 1990 to 2000 decade is not surprising and suggests that immigrant neighborhoods remain stable as reception contexts for new arrivals in NYC. The effect size for the 1990 baseline dwarfs the strength of the other factors. Beyond the stability of immigrant concentration, the effects of wealth and safety are predictors of where immigrants settle. The results in Table 2 for total immigration reflect the skew toward wealth or less disadvantage for white immigrants: immigrant concentration is higher in neighborhoods with fewer indicia of disadvantage and in places that are safer.

Immigration and crime

Next, GPS regressions of total and recent immigration on crime were estimated. Figure 1 shows the results of the full models, which include controls for GPS score for immigration at 2000. Race- and ethnic-specific immigration breakdowns are presented in Figure 2.[4] Immigration is a protective factor for both total crime and three specific categories of crime. Total immigration shows a significant (lower than −2) effect for all crime categories. The preventive effects of immigration are less pronounced for recent immigrants, as significant negative coefficients are found only for total and drug crime rates.

Immigration effects vary by the specific crime and racial/ethnic group. Figure 2 shows that white immigration, mostly from Russia and other Eastern European countries, has strong insulating effects. Since white immigrants tend to settle in areas with low crime rates and greater access to economic wealth and resources, the strong negative parameter suggests that white immigration exerts a protective effect beyond other factors that also reduce crime risks.

Total and violent crime rates are lower when concentrations of foreign-born persons of African descent are higher. This is particularly important given the racial components of the distribution of crime across NYC neighborhoods. We assume that these are largely Caribbean immigrants, although immigration from the African continent has increased in the past decade.

The effects of Latino and Asian immigration on crime are more modest. The direction of the effects is negative, but they do not reach significance in any of the models. It is possible that this attenuated influence of immigration reflects the heterogeneity of residential settlement that is characteristic of these groups. Many Latino immigrants, for example, settle in diverse areas of the city, including both low-crime places (northwest Queens) and high-crime areas (Sunset Park in Brooklyn). The overall average effect may mask some important micro-effects.

Immigration and enforcement

The relationship between immigration and enforcement is illustrated in Figure 3. The effects of immigration on enforcement are quite different from its protective effects on crime. Enforcement for total, violent, and property crimes is substantially higher in places with greater proportions of immigrants. This effect is especially pronounced for newer immigrants, those who have been in the

TABLE 2
Generalized Propensity Score Models—Foreign-Born 2000, Overall and by Race

	Overall		Black		Latino		Asian		White	
	Est.	SE	Est.	SE	Est.	SE	Est.	SE	Est.	SE
Foreign-born 1990	.139***	.003	−.005	.015	.009	.033	2.122***	.205	.198***	.018
Poverty	−.042***	.006	−.087*	.035	−.175*	.075	1.164*	.474	−.144***	.042
Public assistance	−.014**	.005	−.253***	.030	.340***	.064	1.457***	.404	.136***	.036
Gini index	.051***	.005	.214***	.029	−.183**	.062	.758	.392	.285***	.035
% less than high school	.034***	.005	−.403***	.024	.656***	.052	.327	.328	−.143***	.029
% unemployment	−.011**	.004	.016***	.021	−.039	.045	−.500	.284	−.024	.025
% labor force nonparticipation	.003	.004	−.091***	.020	.063	.042	.820**	.267	.163***	.024
% female-headed households	−.009	.005	.383***	.027	−.198***	.058	−4.638***	.367	−.249***	.033
Supervision ratio (pop 25–50/5–15)	−.014***	.003	.104***	.019	−.036	.042	−1.101***	.264	−.075**	.024
White isolation index	−.030***	.004	−.561***	.022	−.322***	.047	−1.666***	.295	1.175***	.026
Residential mobility	−.027***	.003	.155***	.016	−.296***	.034	−2.002***	.212	−.132***	.019
Housing vacancy	−.015***	.003	.023	.015	−.158***	.031	−.598**	.198	−.081	.018
% renters	−.021***	.004	−.086***	.023	.332***	.050	−1.986***	.317	.035	.028
Population (logged)	−.006*	.003	.096***	.015	.440***	.032	2.637***	.201	.053*	.018
Mean housing sale price	.000	.002	.001	.012	−.078**	.026	−.045	.166	−.017	.015
Homicide rate per 100,000	−.007	.004	.137***	.020	−.160***	.043	−1.349***	.274	−.110***	.024
Assault rate per 100,000	.003	.003	−.002	.017	−.055	.037	−.107	.233	−.033	.021
Log likelihood	−1,811.890		−1,459.010		−2,984.620		−6,622.130		−1,845.390	
Wald chi-square	5,806.540***		4,002.670***		1,783.070***		1,233.480***		10,036.320***	

*$p < .05$. **$p < .01$. ***$p < .001$.

FIGURE 1
Effects of Immigrant Concentration on Crime by Type of Crime (Z-Score)

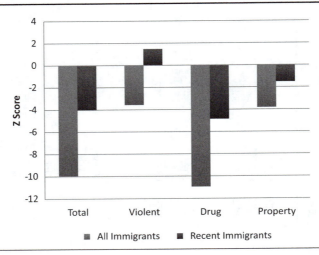

FIGURE 2
Effects of Immigrant Concentration on Crime by Ethnicity (Z-Score)

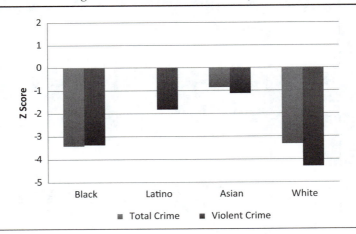

country for fewer than five years. Although crime is on balance lower in neighborhoods with higher immigrant concentrations, the ratio of stops and arrests to crime is higher in these same places. The police response per crime seems to be more aggressive and legally formal in immigrant neighborhoods, despite the lower crime rates in these neighborhoods. The reasons for this disparity

FIGURE 3
Effects of Immigrant Concentration on Enforcement by Type of Crime (Z-Score)

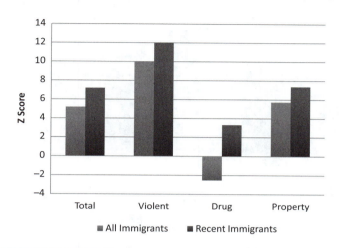

are neither obvious nor unambiguous. For example, one effect of the higher enforcement rates in immigrant neighborhoods may be lower crime overall, a trend we observed in Figures 1 and 2. But the higher crime rates in black neighborhoods generally are not observed here: immigration exerts a protective effect on crime for black and white immigrants, yet both groups are policed less intensively compared to Latino or Asian neighborhoods. Still, the effect of enforcement on crime is difficult to statistically identify and remains ambiguous absent a more complete empirical understanding of the simultaneous relationships between police stops, race or ethnicity, immigration, and crime.

The disaggregation of race- and ethnic-specific effects presented in Figure 4 further complicates the enforcement narrative. No particular group is driving the overall results from Figure 3; that is, the higher rates of enforcement activity are not concentrated among immigrants of particular races/ethnicities. Latino and Asian locales experience higher enforcement ratios, but the magnitude of the association fails to reach significance. Enforcement is lower in neighborhoods with higher concentrations of white immigrants, after controlling for crime, but again the effect is negligible. Only for African immigrant neighborhoods is there a significant relationship to enforcement, and here the effect is negative: enforcement in black immigrant neighborhoods is far lower than in other immigrant enclaves. This finding is quite unexpected given that policing has tended to be a central feature of areas populated by native-born African Americans (Fagan and Davies 2000; Fagan et al. 2010; Geller and Fagan 2010).

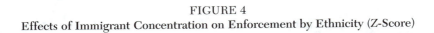

FIGURE 4
Effects of Immigrant Concentration on Enforcement by Ethnicity (Z-Score)

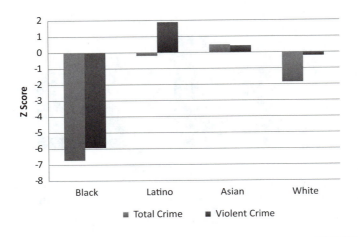

Figure 5 shows the extent of differences in enforcement patterns across foreign-born versus native-born black neighborhoods in NYC. For other racial/ethnic groups, the rates of enforcement between native- and foreign-born enclaves tend to be similar. Interestingly, for both Latinos and Asians, enforcement rates for most types of crime are marginally higher in native-born areas. It is only in white immigrant neighborhoods that immigrants see a greater concentration of enforcement. But for all groups, the differences are not striking, as the ratios of enforcement rates generally cluster around a value of 1.[5] Conversely, the ratios in African areas are markedly higher. For overall crime, the rate of enforcement is more than twice (2.34) as large in native-born neighborhoods; the ratio is higher still for drug offenses. Simply stated, largely native-born black areas experience a much greater concentration of enforcement than do places where foreign-born blacks live.

Discussion

Consistent with much contemporary research, this study confirms that immigration exerts a protective effect on crime, controlling for the characteristics of neighborhoods that tend to attract immigrants. In New York and other cities (Sampson 2008; Martinez et al., this volume), there is no evidence that crime rates are higher in places with higher immigration rates. On the contrary, immigration often functions as a prophylactic against crime. But the results here also demonstrate that all immigrants are not alike; immigration experiences vary

FIGURE 5
Ratio of Enforcement in Native-Born to Foreign-Born Enclaves, by Type of Enforcement
(2004–2008)

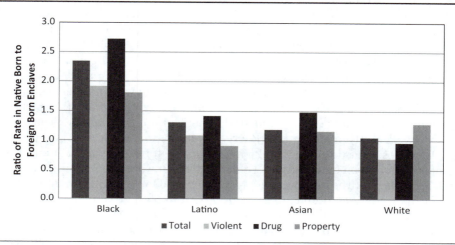

SOURCE: U.S. Census Bureau, STF-3A; New York City Police Department, Stop and Frisk Archive, Online Booking System.

across racial and ethnic groups. To a considerable extent, these pathways are influenced by broader patterns of race relations in the United States. White immigrants have leveraged their relative advantage to reside in areas characterized by higher socioeconomic status and lower crime, while black immigrants, likely facing some of the same discriminatory forces as native-born blacks, have settled in more deprived, more dangerous areas. In other words, when disaggregated by race, the distributions of relevant characteristics in immigrant neighborhoods closely resemble those evident in native-born neighborhoods.

Race, however, does not tell the whole story. We find support for the notion that "culture matters" (Kasinitz et al. 2008). It is true, for example, that white immigrants such as Russian Jews are less encumbered by invidious discrimination in housing and employment. But compared to other groups, Russian Jews also tend to be more urban and better educated and have family structures (low levels of single-parent households and high levels of intergenerational living) that are more amenable to upward mobility (Orleck 2001; Kasinitz et al. 2008). They may also arrive here with more capital and entry into networks of well-assimilated predecessors. At odds with outmoded expectations of social disorganization and crime, these comparative advantages help explain why crime and violence are less prevalent in white immigrant communities.

A more ambiguous but no less telling example of cultural effects involves Haitians and Jamaicans, "West Indian" groups that together account for much of the black immigration to NYC. Haitians and Jamaicans both are doubly stigmatized. Phenotypically black, both groups are often identified simply as "black" by whites and experience discrimination and residential segregation similar to native-born blacks. But owing to differences in cultures and languages, both are distinguished within the black population as immigrants (Stafford 1987; Foner 1987, 2007). Still, this "minorities within a minority" status has not increased crime and violence in black immigrant neighborhoods. Instead, there are several aspects of West Indian life that appear to reduce crime: families are frequently multigenerational, parental employment rates are high, and the community has a high level of home ownership (Kasinitz et al. 2008). Moreover, as English speakers, Jamaicans in particular are able to find employment in service industries. These advantages seem to translate into distinctly different treatment of immigrants of African descent compared to native-born African Americans.

The two largest Latino groups, Puerto Ricans and Dominicans,[6] face greater disadvantages than do other immigrant groups in terms of language and economic position upon entry into the United States. However, the interpretation of social class is relative. Ethnographic research with Dominican garment workers in NYC indicates that, despite their hardships, most of these women judged their social status to be "middle class." Pessar (1987) suggests that immigrants' ability to secure prestigious consumer goods that were not necessarily available to the middle class in the Dominican Republic provided the trappings of a middle-class life in the United States. To the extent that immigrants have tangibly improved their station, they have vested interests in their stable, if relatively poor, neighborhoods where isolation is both spatial and social, compounding their economic and other structural disadvantages.

Latino immigrants from South America, including Colombians, Ecuadorans, and Peruvians, while encountering similar barriers related to language, nonetheless tend to have higher levels of education and two-parent families and settle in less-distressed neighborhoods. The net effect of Latino immigration on total crime is negligible; it is negatively associated with violence, but the magnitude of the effect is not statistically significant.[7] The distinct social worlds of the various Latino subgroups highlight the need for research that further disaggregates ethnicity by sending country. This may be possible in the future, as the sizes of these subgroups grow.

The findings for Asian immigration are similarly ambiguous, and similarly illustrate the need for further refinement in the categorization of groups. Although they are growing quickly, Asians are the smallest of the race/ethnic groups. This is reflected in unique residential patterns. There are, for example, no solid Korean immigrant enclaves. There are "medium"-sized settlements of Koreans in Koreatown (Manhattan) and Sunnyside (Queens), but no Korean analogs to Dominicans in Washington Heights (Manhattan), Puerto Ricans in Spanish Harlem (Manhattan), West Indians in Jamaica (Queens), or Russians in Brighton Beach (Brooklyn). This is not merely a function of the size of the Korean population; as with the other groups, culture plays a role. The most recent Korean immigrants are urban, well educated, and middle to upper-middle class. Utilizing a model of small business entrepreneurship, Korean immigrants have taken advantage of opportunities in commercial districts in minority neighborhoods presented by the outflow of "old immigrant" shopkeepers (Kim 1987). This strategy has yielded tremendous economic benefit, but it has also left Koreans dispersed throughout the city. In lieu of geographic proximity, Koreans have embraced modern institutions, including business associations and especially the Protestant Church, as substitutes for ethnic neighborhoods.

There is no mistaking the center of immigrant life for NYC's Chinese population, as Manhattan's Chinatown has continued to swell with the influx of settlers. Perhaps more than other groups, there is a distinct "old" versus "new" dichotomy at play in relation to Chinese immigration. It was once dominated by "sojourners" from Kwangtung Province, but many of the post-1965 arrivals originally hailed from North China, Shanghai, Hong Kong, Fukien, and Taiwan (Wong 1987). More recent arrivals differ from earlier Chinese immigrants in a myriad of ways, but essentially, the newer immigrants consider themselves to be more urban, literate, and modern than their predecessors. In addition, Cantonese has replaced the Toysan dialect as the primary means of communication, further adding to intergenerational difficulties. The superior social and economic resources of the current wave of Chinese immigrants may well herald lower rates of crime as they become a larger proportion of the population.

In short, the results presented here support the emerging consensus that immigration does not lead to higher rates of crime, and in some instances protects against crime. The story of immigration and crime in NYC comprises many chapters that reflect the unique experiences of different racial and ethnic groups. Each of the groups has added to the revitalization of the city in its own unique way, through repopulation, participation in niche economies, and entrepreneurial spirit. The nature of immigration has changed. At the very least, today's newcomers are better positioned to leverage established ethnic networks for employment opportunities and social support. Writing about the second generation of post-1965 immigrants, Kasinitz et al. (2008, 63) assert that "the parents have developed *cultural understandings* and *strategic repertoires*" for responding to the opportunities and challenges of immigrant life. These understandings and repertoires helped to maintain relatively low crime rates in immigrant neighborhoods.

Despite reduced crime, however, immigrant areas experience disproportionately higher levels of enforcement. The present study does not allow for definitive explanations, but several are possible. First, immigrant neighborhoods tend to be geographically adjacent to traditionally high-crime neighborhoods. Elevated enforcement practices in these immigrant areas may reflect a spillover effect, where the crime risks associated with proximate neighborhoods are also attributed to immigrant neighborhoods. Second, it is possible that the police are reacting to the immigrant status of the neighborhood. Extending the idea of neighborhood racial stigma (Sampson and Raudenbush 2004), the police may see and interpret disorder and crime risk differently in neighborhoods marked by higher concentrations of immigrants. Immigration, like race, may be imbued with social meaning that leads to greater exercise of coercive authority.

As with crime, the results of this study also underscore the importance of disaggregating the relationship between immigration and enforcement. Of particular interest is the significant negative association for black immigrants. We can only speculate about the reasons for this finding. Reduced enforcement in black immigrant neighborhoods may be indicative of underpolicing (Kane 2005). These areas, which are particularly socially isolated (even in relation to other immigrant neighborhoods) and have limited political capital, may experience a form of "malign neglect" in the form of attenuated police resources. Future research should further investigate the nature of this relationship, and whether it is unique to NYC.

The policy implications of this study are complicated, not unexpectedly given the complexity of the associations between immigration, crime, and enforcement. The results presented here add further voice to the growing chorus cautioning against the politically simplistic and expedient scapegoating of immigrants. The stereotypical but erroneous linkage between immigration and crime is increasingly unsustainable, especially to the extent that it may be implicated in unduly high levels of enforcement. There are dangers in this disparity for the second and later generations of immigrants, who experience more intrusive policing regimes than native-born New Yorkers yet are not as involved in crime. The potential alienation of immigrant communities—even law-abiding, cooperative individuals—from the criminal justice system can compromise safety through the loss of legitimacy and the withdrawal of citizens from cooperation with the police (Kirk et al., this volume). Cooperation with the police is an essential component of the production of security (Tyler and Fagan 2008), whereby citizens undertake both individual and collective actions to control crime. Cooperation and security are closely tied for all racial groups, whether immigrants or native-born. Cooperation implies collaboration with the police, and trust in the police is a predicate for such actions. Differential policing of immigrant neighborhoods when crime rates suggest otherwise corrodes trust and creates risks for crime, both now and in the future as immigrants take their place in American society.

Notes

1. The Omniform record collects the two hundred pieces of information for each crime complaint that are entered into the Compstat system used by the NYPD for crime analysis.

2. Since the arrest rates pursuant to street stops are less than 5 percent, there is little overlap in these two measures. See Fagan et al. (2010).

3. For each population group, census tracts with no immigrant population for that group were excluded. The remaining tracts were divided into three quantiles. Tracts in the second, or middle, quantile were categorized as modal neighborhoods.

4. Race- and ethnic-specific models also include the interaction of percentage foreign-born with the GPS score.

5. A ratio of 1 indicates that the enforcement rate in native-born enclaves is equal to the enforcement rate in foreign-born enclaves.

6. Although geographically West Indian, Dominicans are ethnically Latino.

7. It is important to note that there is substantial heterogeneity in Latino populations across cities.

The finding here may reflect New York City's specific composition, and the effect of Latino population may vary from other cities with different compositions.

References

Alba, Richard D., John R. Logan, and Paul E. Bellair. 1994. Living with crime: The implications of racial/ethnic differences in suburban location. *Social Forces* 73 (2): 395–434.

Archibold, Randal. 5 April 2010. Ranchers alarmed by killing near border. *New York Times*, A9.

Bia, Michela, and Alessandra Mattei. 2008. A Stata package for the estimation of dose-response function through adjustment for the generalized propensity score. *The Stata Journal* 8:354–73.

Bursik, Robert. J. 1988. Social disorganization and theories of crime and delinquency: Problems and prospects. *Criminology* 26:519–52.

Bursik, Robert J., and Harold Grasmick. 1993. *Neighborhoods and crime: The dimensions of effective community control.* Boston, MA: Lexington Books.

Butcher, Kristin F., and Anne M. Piehl. 1998. Cross-city evidence on the relationship between immigration and crime. *Journal of Policy Analysis and Management* 17 (3): 457–93.

Butcher, Kristin F., and Anne M. Piehl. 2007. Why are immigrants' incarceration rates so low? Evidence on selective immigration, deterrence, and deportation. NBER Working Paper No. 13229, National Bureau of Economic Research, Cambridge, MA.

Chiswick, Barry R., and Paul W. Miller. 2008. Modeling immigrants' language skills. *Research in Labor Economics* 27:75–128.

Chu, Doris, John H. Song, and John Dombrink. 2005. Chinese immigrants' perceptions of the police in New York City. *International Criminal Justice Review* 15 (2): 101–14.

Cloward, Richard, and Lloyd Ohlin. 1960. *Delinquency and opportunity.* New York, NY: Free Press.

Culver, Leigh. 2004. The impact of new immigration patterns on the provision of police services in midwestern communities. *Journal of Criminal Justice* 32:329–44.

Davis, Robert C., and Nicole J. Henderson. 2003. Willingness to report crimes: The role of ethnic group membership and community efficacy. *Crime & Delinquency* 49 (4): 564–80.

Decker, Michele R., Anita Raj, and Jay G. Silverman. 2007. Sexual violence against adolescent girls. *Violence Against Women* 13 (5): 498–513.

Eberhardt, Jennifer, Paul Davies, Valerie Purdie-Vaughns, and Sheri Lynn Johnson. 2006. Looking deathworthy: Perceived stereotypicality of black defendants predicts capital-sentencing outcomes. *Psychological Science* 17:383–86.

Epp, Charles, Steven Maynard-Moody, and Donald Heider-Markel. Forthcoming. *Pulled over: Racial framing of police stops.* Chicago, IL: University of Chicago Press.

Fagan, Jeffrey, and Garth Davies. 2000. Street stops and broken windows: *Terry,* race and disorder in New York City. *Fordham Urban Law Journal* 28:457–504.

Fagan, Jeffrey, Amanda Geller, Garth Davies, and Valerie West. 2010. Street stops and broken windows revisited: Race and order maintenance policing in a safe and changing city. In *Exploring race, ethnicity and policing: Essential readings,* eds. Stephen K. Rice and Michael D. White. New York, NY: New York University Press.

Feng, Ping, Xiao-Hua Zhou, Qing-Ming Zou, Ming-Yu Fan, and Xiao-Song Li. 24 February 2011. Generalized propensity score for estimating the average treatment effect of multiple treatments. *Statistics in Medicine.* doi:10.1002/sim.4168

Foner, Nancy. 1987. The Jamaicans: Race and ethnicity among migrants in New York City. In *New immigrants in New York,* ed. Nancy Foner. New York, NY: Columbia University Press.

Foner, Nancy. 2007. How exceptional is New York? Migration and multiculturalism in the empire city. *Ethnic and Racial Studies* 30 (6): 999–1023.

Geller, Amanda B., and Jeffrey Fagan. 2010. Pot as pretext: Marijuana, race and the new disorder in New York City street policing. *Journal of Empirical Legal Studies* 7:59–97.

Gladstein, Hannah. 2005. *Blurring the lines: A profile of state and local police enforcement of immigration law using the National Crime Information Center database, 2002–2004.* Washington, DC: Migration Policy Institute.

Hagan, John, Ron Levi, and Ronit Dinovitzer. 2008. The symbolic violence of the crime-immigration nexus: Migrant mythologies in the Americas. *Criminology & Public Policy* 7:95–112.

Hagan, John, and Alberto Palloni. 1998. Immigration and crime in the United States. In *The immigration debate: Studies on the economic, demographic, and fiscal effects of immigration*, eds. James P. Smith and Barry Edmonston. Washington, DC: National Academy Press.

Hagan, John, and Alberto Palloni. 1999. Sociological criminology and the mythology of Hispanic immigration and crime. *Social Problems* 46 (4): 617–32.

Harris, David A. 2006. The war on terror, local police, and immigration enforcement: A curious tale of police power in post-9/11 America. BE Press Legal Series, Working Paper 1382. Available from http://law.bepress.com/expresso/eps/1382.

Hendricks, Nicole J., Christopher Ortiz, Naomi Sugie, and Joel Miller. 2007. Beyond the numbers: Hate crimes and cultural trauma within Arab American immigrant communities. *International Review of Victimology* 14 (1): 95–113.

Hirano, Keisuke, and Guido W. Imbens. 2004. The propensity score with continuous treatments. In *Applied Bayesian modeling and causal inference from incomplete-data perspectives*, eds. Andrew Gelman and Xiao-Li Meng. Chichester, UK: John Wiley.

Homeland Security Advisory Council. 2011. *Task Force on Secure Communities: Findings and recommendations*. Washington, DC: Department of Homeland Security. Available from http://www.dhs.gov/xlibrary/assets/hsac-task-force-on-secure-communities-findings-and-recommendations-report.pdf.

Imai, Kosuke, and David A. van Dyk. 2004. Causal inference with generalized treatment regimes: Generalizing the propensity score. *Journal of the American Statistical Association* 99:854–66.

Jones, Chapin, and Stanley B. Supinski. 2010. Policing and community relations in the homeland security era. *Journal of Homeland Security and Emergency Management*. Available from http://www.bepress.com/jhsem/vol7/iss1/43.

Kane, Robert J. 2005. Compromised police legitimacy as a predictor of violent crime in structurally disadvantaged communities. *Criminology* 43 (2): 469–98.

Kasinitz, Philip, John H. Mollenkopf, and Mary C. Waters. 2009. *Becoming New Yorkers: The children of immigrants come of age*. New York, NY: Russell Sage Foundation.

Kasinitz, Philip, John H. Mollenkopf, Mary C. Waters, and Jennifer Holdaway. 2008. *Inheriting the city: The children of immigrants come of age*. Cambridge, MA: Harvard University Press.

Kim, Illsoo. 1987. The Koreans: Small business in an urban frontier. In *New immigrants in New York*, ed. Nancy Foner. New York, NY: Columbia University Press.

Lee, Matthew T., and Ramiro Martinez Jr. 2009. Immigration reduces crime: An emerging scholarly consensus. In *Immigration, crime and justice*, ed. W. F. McDonald. Bingley: UK: Emerald Group Publishing Limited.

Lee, Matthew T., Ramiro Martinez Jr., and Richard Rosenfeld. 2001. Does immigration increase homicide? Negative evidence from three border cities. *Sociological Quarterly* 42 (4): 559–80.

Lewis, Oscar. 1966. *La Vida: A Puerto Rican family in the culture of poverty—San Juan and New York*. New York, NY: Random House.

MacDonald, John M., John R. Hipp, and Charlotte Gill. 2008. Neighborhood effects of immigrant succession on crime: Did immigrants cause the crime drop in Los Angeles? Paper presented at the annual Workshop on Crime and Population Dynamics, 2–3 June, Baltimore, MD.

Martinez, Ramiro, Jr. 2006. Coming to America: The impact of the new immigration on crime. In *Immigration and crime: Race, ethnicity, and violence*, eds. Ramiro Martinez Jr. and Abel Valenzuela. New York, NY: New York University Press.

Martinez, Ramiro, Jr. 2008. The impact of immigration policy on criminological research *Criminology & Public Policy* 7 (1): 53–58.

Martinez, Ramiro, Jr., Jacob I. Stowell, and Matthew T. Lee. 2010. Immigration and crime in an era of transformation: A longitudinal analysis of homicides in San Diego neighborhoods, 1980–2000. *Criminology* 48 (3): 797–829.

McDonald, William F. 2009. New takes on an old problematic: An introduction to the immigration, crime, and justice nexus. In *Immigration, crime and justice*, ed. W. F. McDonald. Bingley: UK: Emerald Group Publishing Limited.

Mears, Daniel P. 2001. The immigration-crime nexus: Toward an analytic framework for assessing and guiding theory, research and policy. *Sociological Perspectives* 44 (11): 1–19.

Menjívar, Cecilia, and Cynthia Bejarano. 2004. Latino immigrants' perceptions of crime and police authorities in the United States: A case study from the Phoenix metropolitan area. *Ethnic and Racial Studies* 27:120–48.

Merton, Robert K. 1938. Social structure and anomie. *American Sociological Review* 3:672–82.

Nielsen, Amie L., Matthew T. Lee, and Ramiro Martinez Jr. 2005. Integrating race, place and motive in social disorganization theory: Lessons from a comparison of black and Latino homicide types in two immigrant destination cities. *Criminology* 43 (3): 837–72.

Orleck, Annelise. 2001. Soviet Jews: The city's newest immigrants transform New York Jewish life. In *New immigrants in New York*, rev. edition, ed. Nancy Foner. New York, NY: Columbia University Press.

Ousey, Graham C., and Charis E. Kubrin. 2009. Exploring the connection between immigration and violent crime rates in U.S. cities, 1980–2000. *Social Problems* 56 (3): 447–73.

Pessar, Patricia. 1987. The Dominicans: Women in the household and the garment industry. In *New immigrants in New York*, ed. Nancy Foner. New York, NY: Columbia University Press.

Platt, Anthony. 1969. *The child savers: The invention of delinquency*. Chicago, IL: University of Chicago Press.

Portes, Alejandro, and Rubén Rumbaut. 2006. *Immigrant America: A portrait*. 3rd ed. Berkeley: University of California Press.

Portes, Alejandro, and Julia Sensenbrenner. 1993. Embeddedness and immigration: Notes on the social determinants of economic action. *American Journal of Sociology* 98 (6): 1320–50.

Portes, Alejandro, and Min Zhou. 1992. Gaining the upper hand: Economic mobility among immigrant and domestic minorities. *Ethnic and Racial Studies* 15:491–522.

Reid, Lesley W., Harald E. Weiss, Robert M. Adelman, and Charles Jaret. 2005. The immigration–crime relationship: Evidence across US metropolitan areas. *Social Science Research* 34 (4): 757–80.

Rumbaut, Rubén G., and Walter A. Ewing. 2007. *The myth of immigrant criminality and the paradox of assimilation: Incarceration rates among native and foreign-born men*. Washington, DC: Immigration Policy Center, American Immigration Law Foundation.

Sampson, Robert J. 2008. Rethinking crime and immigration. *Contexts* 7 (1): 28–33.

Sampson, Robert J., Jeffrey D. Morenoff, and Thomas Gannon-Rowley. 2002. Assessing neighborhood effects: Social processes and new directions in research. *Annual Review of Sociology* 28:443–78.

Sampson, Robert J., and Steven W. Raudenbush. 2004. Seeing disorder: Neighborhood stigma and the social construction of "broken windows." *Social Psychology Quarterly* 67:319–42.

Sampson, Robert J., Stephen W. Raudenbush, and Felton Earls. 1997. Neighborhoods and violent crime: A multilevel study of collective efficacy. *Science* 15:918–24.

Sealander, Judith. 2003. *The failed century of the child: Governing America's young in the twentieth century*. New York, NY: Cambridge University Press.

Shaw, Clifford, and Henry D. McKay. 1943. *Juvenile delinquency in urban areas*. Chicago, IL: University of Chicago Press.

Sklansky, David. Forthcoming. Crime, immigration and ad hoc instrumentalism. *New Criminal Law Review*.

Skogan, Wesley G. 2009. Policing immigrant communities in the United States. In *Immigration, crime and justice*, ed. W. F. McDonald. Bingley: UK: Emerald Group Publishing Limited.

Stafford, Susan B. 1987. The Haitians: The cultural meaning of race and ethnicity. In *New immigrants in New York*, ed. Nancy Foner. New York, NY: Columbia University Press.

Stowell, Jacob I., and Ramiro Martinez Jr. 2007. Displaced, dispossessed, or lawless? Examining the link between ethnicity, immigration, and violence. *Aggression and Violent Behavior* 12 (5): 564–81.

Stowell, Jacob I., and Ramiro Martinez Jr. 2009. Incorporating ethnic-specific measures of immigration in the study of lethal violence. *Homicide Studies* 13 (3): 315–24.

Stowell, Jacob I., Steven F. Messner, Kelly F. McGeever, and Lawrence E. Raffalovich. 2009. Immigration and the recent violent crime drop in the United States: A pooled, cross-sectional time-series analysis of metropolitan areas. *Criminology* 47 (3): 889–928.

Stuntz, William J. 2002. Local policing after the terror. *Yale Law Journal* 111:2137–94.

Taft, Donald R. 1933. Does immigration increase crime? *Social Forces* 12 (1): 69–77.

Tanenhaus, David. 2004. *Juvenile justice in the making*. Chicago, IL: University of Chicago Press.

Thrasher, Frederick. 1927. *The gang: A study of 1,313 gangs in Chicago*. Chicago, IL: University of Chicago Press.

Tonry, Michael. 1997. Ethnicity, crime, and immigration. In *Ethnicity, crime, and immigration: Comparative and cross-national perspectives*, ed. Michael Tonry. Chicago, IL: University of Chicago Press.

Tyler, Tom R., and Jeffrey Fagan. 2008. Legitimacy and cooperation: Why do people help the police fight crime in their communities? *Ohio State Journal of Criminal Law* 6 (1): 231–75.

Tyler, Tom R., Stephen Schulhofer, and Aziz Huq. 2010. Legitimacy and deterrence effects in counterterrorism policing: A study of Muslim Americans. *Law & Society Review* 44:365-402.

U.S. Immigration and Customs Enforcement (ICE). 2009. *Secure communities: A comprehensive plan to identify and remove criminal aliens (strategic plan)*. Available from http://www.ice.gov/doclib/foia/secure_communities/securecommunitiesstrategicplan09.pdf.

Varsanyi, Monica, Paul Lewis, Marie Provine, and Scott Decker. Forthcoming. A multilayered jurisdictional patchwork: The reemergence of immigration federalism in the United States. *Law and Policy*.

Velez, Maria B. 2009. Contextualizing the immigration and crime effect: An analysis of homicide in Chicago neighborhoods. *Homicide Studies* 13 (3): 325–35.

Wadsworth, Tim. 2010. Is immigration responsible for the crime drop? An assessment of the influence of immigration on changes in violent crime between 1990 and 2000. *Social Science Quarterly* 91 (2): 531–53.

Wong, Bernard. 1987. The Chinese: New immigrants in New York City's Chinatown. In *New immigrants in New York*, ed. Nancy Foner. New York, NY: Columbia University Press.

Zimring, Franklin E. 2011. *The city that became safe*. New York, NY: Oxford University Press.

Are Immigrant Youth Less Violent? Specifying the Reasons and Mechanisms

By
JOHN MacDONALD
and
JESSICA SAUNDERS

In this article, the authors present an overview of the relationship between immigrant households and crime and violence, drawing on sociological and public health literature. They present a critique of popular culture perspectives on immigrant families and youth violence, showing that crime and violence outcomes are if anything better for youth in immigrant families than one would expect given the social disadvantages that many immigrant households find themselves living in. They examine the extent to which exposure to violence among immigrant youth is comparably lower than among nonimmigrants living in similar social contexts and the extent to which social control and social learning frameworks can account for the apparent lower prevalence of violence exposure among immigrant youth. Their analyses show a persistent lower rate of violence exposure for immigrant youth compared to similarly situated nonimmigrant youth—and that these differences are not meaningfully understood by observed social control or social learning mechanisms. The authors focus then on the apparent paradox of why youth living in immigrant households in relative disadvantage have lower violence exposure compared to nonimmigrants living in similar social contexts. The answers, they argue, can be viewed from an examination of the effects that living in poverty and underclass neighborhoods for generations has on nonimmigrants in American cities.

Keywords: immigration; crime; youth violence; Hispanic paradox

NOTE: Earlier drafts of this article were presented at the 2009 American Society of Criminology meeting, Philadelphia, Pennsylvania. Terry Fain at RAND provided programming assistance. The authors thank David Kirk, Jeffrey Morenoff, and Robert Sampson for their helpful suggestions on an earlier draft. All errors and omissions are those of the authors. Support for this project was made possible in part by funding from the Centers for Disease Control and Prevention: 1U49CE000773 to the RAND Corporation. The points of view are those of the authors only.

DOI: 10.1177/0002716211432279

In this article, we examine traditional sociological explanations for the relationship between immigration and criminal behavior. Despite more than a century of social science research suggesting that immigrant youth are at no greater risk for crime and violence (Hart 1896), there persisted a strong institutional bias in the social sciences and popular culture that immigrants and the children on immigrants were at greater risk for a variety of poor life outcomes, including the participation and exposure to crime and violence. This institutionalized bias was due to the focus on studying the immigrant experience and the children of immigrants, as numerous case studies and empirical analyses showed that immigrant households were at relative social disadvantage in most U.S. cities in terms of neighborhood and economic resources, family socialization, and the exposure to delinquent peers (Sellin 1938; Shaw and McKay 1942). The tradition of research in the social sciences during the twentieth century established that immigrants often settle into densely populated neighborhoods in U.S. cities that for environmental reasons are more prone to crime, violence, and early mortality—from homicide as well as all other causes of death. While this perspective still dominates public policy discourse on the role of immigrants and the social circumstances of city neighborhoods, less attention has been placed in recent years on the role that the immigrant household itself has in explaining violence given equivalent social circumstances.

In the sections that follow, we argue that it is time to reconsider the connection between immigrant status and criminal behaviors committed or experienced by youth as victims. There appears to be a lack of reasonably articulated sociological theories that can account for the current state of research showing a lack of an immigrant-crime/victimization connection, or even a trend between increasing immigration and reductions in rates of crime and violence. In the second section, we provide some descriptive theories that explain why immigrant status may place individuals at reduced risk for criminal offending and violent victimization net the effects of traditional predictors of these outcomes. This section is followed by an empirical examination of the connections between immigrant household status and violent victimization outcomes among youth in almost two hundred Los Angeles neighborhoods. We examine the extent to which immigrant household status is a signal for a reduced likelihood of violent victimization, even after taking into account individual-, peer-, family-, school-, and neighborhood-related processes. We examine whether traditional sociological perspectives of social control and social learning can explain the connection between immigrant

John MacDonald is an associate professor of criminology at the University of Pennsylvania and director of the Jerry Lee Center of Criminology. He works on a wide variety of research topics that include the study of interpersonal violence, race and ethnic disparities in criminal justice, and the effectiveness of social policy responses to crime.

Jessica Saunders is a behavioral scientist at the RAND Corporation. Her research interests include policing, immigration and crime, developmental criminology, evaluation research, and quantitative methods.

household status and violent victimization, through the mediators of deviant attitudes and delinquent peer association, family and school bonds, and the level of reported informal social controls exerted in neighborhoods. In the final section, we discuss the implications of our findings for development of sociological theories and public policy discourse on the role of immigrant households in producing crime and violence among adolescents.

To put it simply, this study along with a mounting body of empirical research suggests that immigrant households are an important resource for reducing violence in disadvantaged neighborhoods. But the fact that the experiences of children living in immigrant households are so different from those of children of native-born parents living in similar conditions of social disadvantage suggests that immigration is a transitory social process and that it is not an ontogenic explanation for the etiology of crime and violence.

Background

Despite positions taken by many policymakers and some public perception, there is little contemporary social science research indicating that immigrants cause crime (Sampson 2008). A number of studies published in the past decade have found that immigrants have equivalent likelihoods of offending when they are compared to similarly situated nonimmigrants, or that immigrant status is associated with less crime and violence (Hagan and Palloni 1999; Morenoff and Astor 2006; Sampson, Morenoff, and Raudenbush 2005; Zhou and Bankston 2006). Other research has found that aggregate rates of crime and violence at the neighborhood level are lower in areas of concentrated immigration than one would expect from household measures of poverty (Lee, Martinez, and Rosenfeld 2001; Martinez, Stowell, and Lee 2010; Schreck, McGloin, and Kirk 2009).

Yet there remains a long tradition of sociology that suggests immigrant status is associated with lower parental supervision, cultural conflict, and other individual mechanisms that foster crime and violence (Thrasher 1927; Sellin 1938). Ironically, the initial American-produced research in sociology on crime and immigration argued there was little to no association between the two (Hart 1896). The rich set of theories of place and crime that developed at the University of Chicago in the 1930s suggested that the influx of immigrants into neighborhoods erodes group-level processes of informal social controls for residents and fosters an increased likelihood of unsupervised youth, a propensity for gang formation, and all forms of criminal behavior in exposed communities (Shaw and McKay 1942). While much of the American sociology of crime during the pre–World War II period focused on the relationship among immigration, neighborhood change, and crime, this literature did not remain a central feature of sociological theorizing on crime (cf. Kirk and Laub 2010).

While individual and group-level associations between immigrants and crime patterns may have been true during the early part of the twentieth century, the recent body of empirical research suggests that immigrants have the same or better than expected crime and violence outcomes compared to nonimmigrants

(Butcher and Piehl 1998) and that poor neighborhoods fare better when they become more heavily settled by immigrants. Desmond and Kubrin (2009) find that youth residing in neighborhoods with greater immigrant concentration generally have lower average levels of violence and that these effects are stronger for Hispanics, Asians, and adolescents born outside the United States. MacDonald, Hipp, and Gill (2009) examined whether increases in the concentration of immigrants in Los Angeles neighborhoods during the 1990s led to changes in neighborhood crime counts. They found that neighborhoods undergoing a greater rise in immigrant concentration had greater than expected reductions in total crime and violence, net of the effects of neighborhood measures of social disadvantage.

This more recent body of empirical work has not resulted in any fundamental shifts in theorizing how, if at all, immigrants lead to reductions in crime and violence. But there are theories from other branches of sociology on immigrant assimilation that provide clear guidance on these relationships (Alba and Nee 2003). We think it is time to reconsider the theoretical connection between immigrant households and prevalence of crime and violence.

The social context of immigration and crime: An overview

Historically, there has been an overriding belief in popular culture about the connection between immigration and crime. Every major wave of immigration has coincided with discussions of the "less than desirable" attributes of new arrivals and their lack of human capital. Sociologists in the early 1900s pondered the relationship between immigrant status and crime (Bennet 1909), and it was a topic of great policy interest. The 1931 report by the National Committee on Law Observation and Enforcement, popularly called the Wickersham Commission, observed no evidence linking immigration to increased crime patterns (Tonry 1997). Despite the Wickersham Commission's observations, decades of research by social scientists has focused on the immigrant experience and the role of immigration in patterns of neighborhood social structure, crime, and violence.

There was criticism of the Wickersham Commission among sociologists for its "pro-alien" bias in ignoring the facts that there is systematic underreporting of crimes in neighborhoods inhabited primarily by immigrants, that immigration may produce problems for children of immigrants, and that this second generation was conflated with native population in the commission's analysis of arrest and conviction data (Taft 1933). Sociological explanations for their findings suggested that immigrant status itself had little relationship to criminal behavior. Rather, immigrants on average settled into disadvantaged areas that exposed their children to higher rates of offending and victimization. This second generation of immigrants was exposed to economic disadvantage, a culture of conflict, and underclass norms that were more favorable to violations of the law in the presence of relative economic disadvantage (Taft 1933; Sellin 1938).

The most popular explanation for the link between immigration and crime became the social disorganization theory of Shaw and McKay, rooted in the classic school of human ecology advanced at the University of Chicago. Shaw and McKay (1931) noted in the Wickersham report that the children of "foreign and Negro" persons were a "disproportionate percentage of the delinquents in the juvenile court" (pp. 80–81). Shaw and McKay's (1942) work articulated that the link between immigration and crime was the result of the basic ecological model of residential mobility. They argued that immigrants relocate from foreign countries to urban neighborhoods with low levels of economic resources and greater anonymity, which reduces shared parental monitoring of youth and allows for the formation of play groups that evolve into gangs (Thrasher 1927). Immigrant youth, then, are involved in more crime and violence because they live in these crime-prone environments that erode familial and residential social controls (see also Taft 1933).

More recent lines of empirical research on the immigration-crime nexus suggest that we need to reconsider the sociological processes that link immigrant settlements to individual- and neighborhood-level crime rates, including a reformulated interpretation of social disorganization theory (cf. Morenoff and Astor 2006; Martinez, Stowell, and Lee 2010). Recent demographic trends show that children whose parents are born outside the United States are the fastest growing segment of the population (Schmidley 2001). The growing immigrant household segment of the U.S. population, as in the past, is more likely than the general population to live below the poverty line. Traditional sociological theories of crime predict that immigrants will be more involved in crime and violent victimization because they experience these higher levels of poverty, lower education attainment, and related human capital formation; are more likely to live in urban poverty centers with lower levels of informal social control; and have to adjust to new sets of cultural norms (Sellin 1938; Shaw and McKay 1942).

Contemporary empirical studies have shown that immigrants are less likely than native-born counterparts to be engaged in criminal behavior, which is seemingly antithetical to the traditional sociological theories. Morenoff and Astor (2006), for example, found that first-generation immigrants in Chicago had lower violence rates than either second- or third-generation comparison groups, adjusting for individual-level differences and neighborhood-level associations. Beside the differences between the violence rates between the generations of immigrants, they found that some contextual contributors may actually work in the opposite direction for immigrants. For instance, first-generation immigrants were less likely to engage in violence as neighborhood disadvantage increased; this relationship worked in the opposite direction for third-generation immigrants, and there was no relationship in the second immigrant generation, suggesting that neighborhood effects are at least partially contingent on immigration generation status.[1]

Sellin's (1938) culture of conflict thesis argued that the process of assimilation explained a disproportionate involvement of lower-class immigrant youth in crime, not their actual country of origin. Assimilation and acculturation into American society may be associated with a higher propensity for being involved with crime and victimization, such that by the second or third generation, the risk of these outcomes becomes equivalent to that of natives or those of similar social status. These findings are consistent with Thrasher's (1927) early observation of youth gangs in Chicago, in which he argued that immigrant youth joined gangs as part of their assimilation into neighborhood play groups. Yet the more recent body of empirical research in sociology suggests that immigrant status may actually reduce one's risk for criminal offending or violent victimization, once one compares similarly situated individuals. But the exact theoretical mechanisms remain underdeveloped.

There is a similar body of research on immigration in the field of public health, commonly referred to as the "Hispanic paradox," which finds that immigrants of Hispanic ethnicity have much better health outcomes than would be expected based on their socioeconomic status, interrupted social support system, and education levels (Palloni and Arias 2004; Scribner 1996). Morales et al. (2002), for example, found that Hispanic immigrants with higher scores on a measure of acculturation were more likely to experience negative health effects. A number of other studies have speculated on the root causes whereby immigrants who are less culturally assimilated and living in social disadvantage appear to have better than expected health outcomes (LeClere, Rodgers, and Peters 1997; Abraido-Lanza et al. 1999).

Three separate processes have been offered to explain this relationship, including data artifacts, self-selection or the "healthy immigrant" effect, and social buffering effects. The argument for data artifacts is logical, as there are a number of ways in which missing data can artificially create the appearance of Hispanic immigrants' having better than expected health outcomes, such as those with the worst health outcomes failing to be detected in public records or observational studies. This argument is similar to Taft's (1933) suggestion that immigrants are underrepresented in official crime statistics because of underreporting of crime in heavily immigrant enclaves. However, as the better than expected outcomes appear across multiple life domains that rely on different data sources, this explanation appears to be less than satisfactory.

There is more compelling evidence that self-selection effects are at least partially responsible for lower mortality rates among immigrants than one would expect given their social class positions. Immigrants have lower mortality rates compared to those in their countries of origin, suggesting that healthier immigrants self-select into the United States in search of work and improved life opportunities. Additionally, it is possible that immigrants who suffer from especially acute health problems are more likely to return to their native countries for medical care and treatment. While this explanation may contribute to lower mortality rates, the pattern of positive outcomes emerges from adolescence to adulthood— well before mortality and health become a pressing concern. Several tests of the selective migration hypothesis have failed to uncover clear support for the "healthy immigrant" effect (e.g., Abraido-Lanza et al. 1999; Palloni and Arias 2004).

Some scholars have suggested that there must be a cultural effect, whereby the family structures and social networks of recent migrants produce healthier lifestyle behaviors. Cultural norms among immigrants may prevent certain risk behaviors, such as smoking and drug use, or increase protective factors, such as family cohesion and social support. Immigrant enclaves may provide a buffer to external risk factors associated with poor living conditions in American cities by providing immigrants with a greater density of positive social networks and social support (Portes 1995). Support for the cultural effect has gained increasing traction, as the greater than expected benefits in health outcomes appear to decrease with length of residence in the United States and other indicators of assimilation (Singh and Siahpush 2002; Finch and Vega 2003).

Could it be that the same processes that result in the "Hispanic paradox" for health outcomes also explain disparities in crime and violent victimization outcomes? While a substantive body of research has examined the link between immigrant status and participation in crime and homicide victimization, less research has examined the effect of immigrant status on negative health outcomes for youth related to violent victimization. It has been, widely assumed that immigrants, and undocumented immigrants in particular, make particularly attractive crime victims because they may be less likely to report their victimization to the police (Davis and Erez 1998). But there is little evidence that immigrants have higher victimization rates than similarly situated nonimmigrants (Davis and Erez 1998; Silverman, Decker, and Raj 2007).

Theoretical Mechanisms

A number of theoretical mechanisms may be offered for why immigrants, despite being disproportionately situated in economically disadvantaged status positions, have better than expected outcomes on violent victimization. The migration selection process itself sorts individuals who are more likely to be law-abiding, which would also reduce their exposure to violent victimization (Rivera et al. 1995).[2] This is similar to the "healthy immigrant" selection hypothesis. If selection is the main driver of better than expected violent victimization outcomes, second-generation immigrants may be more apt to be offenders and victims compared to their parents, because they have lost the set of incentives to be law-abiding—as they have no memory or experience of living in a foreign country and have citizenship status. While this pattern has been suggested in the sociological literature (Thrasher 1927), it is difficult to verify given that age is highly correlated with offending and victimization, such that adolescents are more likely than parents to experience these outcomes. Establishing exactly how immigrant status influences the etiology of offending and victimization is complicated, but there are a variety of mechanisms by which immigrant households may provide buffers from the potential negative effects that conditions of socioeconomic disadvantage place on youth.

Social scientists have studied a variety of social and psychological factors related to the risk of serious delinquency and youth violence. The common variables include social processes related to household poverty, school, peer groups, individual beliefs and attitudes, family, neighborhood poverty, and other community structural disadvantages (Hawkins et al. 1999). Immigrant status may assert a different influence on any of these attributes and explain the results of lower than expected exposure to violent victimization. Individual-level features associated with crime and violence include poor cognitive development, emotional and temperamental problems, deviant attitudes and beliefs, and exposure to delinquent peers (Loeber and Farrington 2001). And while Latino youth have higher rates of depression, suicide attempts, and anxiety disorders, they make only one-third to one-half as many visits to outpatient mental health services (Centers for Disease Control and Prevention [CDC] 2006), suggesting that mental health differences are not a particularly salient candidate explanation.

Additionally, research on assimilation is replete with studies describing the increasing difficulties that immigrant children face during assimilation and acculturation that can result in behavioral problems associated with delinquency and violent victimization (e.g., Sullivan et al. 2007). Peers have a tremendous effect on one another's academic and employment futures, as well as providing emotional support, companionship, and informal social control (Berndt and Keefe 1995). If living in an immigrant household places youth in association with fewer delinquent peers, this could explain some of the reasons why immigrants self-report lower levels of violent victimization. After all, it is well known that the association with delinquent peers and one's own criminal behavior are the strongest predictors of violent victimization (Hawkins et al. 1999). Research has found that peer groups differ by immigrant status, such that Asian American immigrant youth on average have more achievement-oriented peers than other groups (Steinberg, Dornbusch, and Brown 1992), and African American youth appear to experience more peer delinquency and victimization. Social control aspects of life are also salient for explaining the variance in both crime and victimization outcomes among youth and potential differences with immigrants. Some research has identified a strong cultural and familial identity in the children of immigrants to be associated with positive outcomes because their families reinforce values such as hard work and education (Rambaut 1997; Portes 1995). Immigrant families may also have an advantage because they are more likely to bond together and establish social ties and cooperative kin-based economic and childrearing practices (Zhou 1997). And it appears that family cohesion deteriorates with longer duration of residence in the United States (Gil and Vega 1996).

Education is another important factor for criminal involvement and victimization. Some families immigrate to the United States specifically for the educational opportunities for their children (Caplan, Choy, and Whitmore 1991). Immigrant parents influence their children's academic aspirations and achievement through a variety of mechanisms, including having higher educational aspirations for their children (Fuligni and Fuligni 2007) and valuing the educational system (Suarez-Orozco 1989). Studies that look at immigrants and children of foreign-born parents find that students do not have as much difficulty in

American schools as would be expected, and that immigrants and children of immigrants value education and have relatively high aspirations (Caplan, Choy, and Whitmore 1991; Suarez-Orozco 1989).[3]

Neighborhood poverty and related structural disadvantages accompanied by a greater relative concentration of delinquent peer groups may place immigrants within different social environments. This is the age-old "Chicago School" explanation that links spatial patterns of crime and delinquency and immigrant settlement. A few studies have explored resilient communities, pointing to neighborhood factors that mediate the relationship between neighborhood disadvantage and child outcomes, as well as to community efficacy and social capital as important buffers (Sampson, Raudenbush, and Earls 1997). Immigrant communities have been found to have stronger informal social networks and to be more oriented toward family and community, despite their higher levels of poverty (Wilson 1998). While recent immigrants may be more likely reside in more economically disadvantaged neighborhoods, there is evidence that they are not affected as severely by the risk factors as U.S.-born residents. The mediating factors of social capital and collective efficacy in neighborhoods may be related to the cultural norms of the immigrant groups, thus acting as a protective buffer for youth from immigrant households.

Additionally, the settlement patterns of new immigrants vary greatly by group and geographic location such that many move into "immigrant enclaves" where they are relatively segregated from the U.S.-born population (Logan, Zhang, and Alba 2002; Portes and Zhou 1993). Whether the increasing segregation of immigrants into ethnic enclaves translates into greater protection for youth from violent victimization has not been demonstrated in any convincing set of empirical studies. But the finding that increasing concentrations of immigrants in high-poverty neighborhoods lower levels of homicide (Martinez, Stowell, and Lee 2010) and violent crime in city neighborhoods (MacDonald, Hipp, and Gill 2009) provides some basis for speculating that ethnic enclaves may provide partial buffers from violent victimization among youth living in immigrant households.

Important Questions

Social science research has demonstrated that immigrant status is associated with a number of social outcomes, but there has been less attention to how immigrant households are linked to violent victimization among adolescents. We examine the extent to which social interactions with peers and informal social controls exercised by neighbors and families can account for the apparent paradox that adolescents in immigrant households, who are more likely to live in positions of social disadvantage, have better than expected violent victimization outcomes. We explore how immigrant household status is associated with social processes linked to violent victimization and the extent to which immigrant status is linked to these outcomes through the mediating effects of social control, social learning, and neighborhood dynamics.

There are two principal theoretical frameworks under which we can understand the link between immigrant households and violent victimization among youth. The immigrant selection argument would expect a direct reduced likelihood of violent victimization through the sorting effect that produces a social context more amenable to healthy outcomes for youth, even when placed in social environments of considerable disadvantage. This perspective is consistent with the "Hispanic paradox" literature, and we would expect that youth in immigrant households would have reduced risk for victimization compared to similarly situated nonimmigrant youth. The second theoretical model is based on sociological theories of assimilation that argue that youth from immigrant families are at reduced risk of violent victimization because they have stronger family social bonds and cultural expectations that act as buffers when living in social disadvantage. Based on sociological theories of immigrant assimilation and cultural adaption, one would expect that a reduced risk for experiencing violent victimization would occur through the mediating effects of social control and social learning, whereby immigrant households would place greater emphasis on school and family obligations and buffer youth from the adoption of deviant attitudes and beliefs common in disadvantaged neighborhoods.

Study Setting and Design

In this article, we rely on household survey data collected as part of a study examining individual and neighborhood features of youth violence in Los Angeles (L.A.), California. The data were originally collected as part of a study examining whether business improvement districts (BIDs) were associated with community-level processes linked to youth violence. Data from a household survey of parents and youth living in L.A. neighborhoods exposed to BIDs were compared to a matched group of neighborhoods not exposed to BIDs. The primary purpose of the household survey was to assess the dynamics of youth violence at both the individual and neighborhood levels and to examine whether BIDs have any effect on incidence of youth violence in neighborhoods. A quota sample of 810 family households (one adult and one 14- to 17-year-old youth) was chosen via list-assisted sampling methods in census tracts that contained BIDs (n = 147) and a matched sample of census tracts without BIDs (n = 85).[4] A final total sample of 737 eligible households agreed to participate in the survey. The overall effective response rate was 40.2 percent. Of these 737 interviews, 85 percent (n = 626) completed a complete parent/youth dyad in 188 neighborhood census tracts (see MacDonald et al. 2009).[5] The sampling plan yielded a probability sample of residents with a large enough sample allocated to neighborhoods to estimate between-neighborhood differences. The household survey involved assessments of parent and youth perceptions of neighborhood incivility and social cohesion, family relationships, bonds to school and family, and exposure to youth violence. We defined households as "immigrant households" if the primary caregiver (parent) indicated he or she was non-U.S. born.[6]

Under a guarantee of confidentiality, all youth subjects were asked about youth violence victimization during the prior year. The main dependent variable was computed using five individual survey questions about whether the youth responding to the survey had experienced (1) another youth trying to steal something from her or him by force, (2) another youth threatening him or her with a gun, knife, or club, (3) another youth hitting him or her so badly that he or she needed bandages or a doctor, (4) a physical attack by a group of two or more youth, and (5) seeing someone in the neighborhood being assaulted by a group of two or more youth. The prevalence of each of the individual violence exposure variables for youth ranged from a low of 3 percent for serious injury to 16 percent for witnessing an assault. The exposure to violence scale was calculated hierarchically using a multilevel model (see, e.g., Sampson, Raudenbush, and Earls [1997] and Sampson, Morenoff, and Raudenbush [2005] for a similar approach). To measure theoretically useful individual-level risk factors of violent victimization, we incorporated measures of social control and social learning. In terms of social learning factors, we included a measure of deviant attributes/beliefs that is a combination of six items that asked youth how strongly they agreed with the following: if someone disrespects another youth, it is important to act tough; youths have to threaten people; give thugs/gang members a lot of respect; youth don't respect other youth; and youth don't think much about the future. The scale ranges from 1 (*strongly disagree*) to 4 (*strongly agree*). Higher scores reflect more deviant attitudes and beliefs (Cronbach's alpha = .65).[7]

Research also suggests that offending and victimization are associated with the extent to which youth are bonded to institutions of family and school. Bonds to family and school were assessed based on eight 5-point scaled items that gauged how much—with responses ranging from *not at all* to *very much*—the youth agreed with the following statements about school and family: (1) You are close to people at school, (2) You are part of your school, (3) You are happy to be at school, (4) The teachers treat you fairly, (5) Your parents care about you, (6) People in your family understand you, (7) You and your family have fun together, and (8) Your family pays attention to you. These items were combined into an average summed scale (Cronbach's alpha = .76). Higher scores on this scale reflect greater levels of bonding to family and school.

In addition to individual measures of social learning and social control, we also included an adapted version of the collective efficacy measure created by Sampson, Raudenbush, and Earls (1997). Research indicates that the level of neighborhood social cohesion and willingness of residents to engage in informal social control activities is linked to crime and violence (see Sampson et al. [2002] for a review). Respondents were asked about fifteen items related to this concept, now commonly referred to as *collective efficacy*. The level of neighborhood social cohesion was assessed from nine items that asked parents their level of agreement—with responses ranging from *strongly agree* to *strongly disagree*—the following statements about their neighborhood: (1) People around here are willing to help their neighbors, (2) This is a close-knit neighborhood, (3) People in this neighborhood can be trusted, (4) People in this neighborhood generally don't get along with each other, (5) People in this neighborhood do not share the same values, (6) Parents in this neighborhood know their children's friends, (7) Adults in this neighborhood know who the local children are, (8) Parents in this neighborhood generally know each other, and (9) People in this neighborhood are willing to do favors for each other, such as watching each other's children, helping with shopping, or watching each other's houses when someone is out of town. The level of perceived informal social control in the neighborhood was assessed from six items that asked residents how likely—with responses ranging from *very likely* to *very unlikely*—it was that neighbors would do something if (1) children were skipping school and hanging out on a street corner, (2) children were spray-painting graffiti on a sidewalk or building, (3) children were showing disrespect to an adult, (4) a fight broke out in public, (5) a youth gang was hanging out on the street corner selling drugs and intimidating people, or (6) a local school near home was threatened with closure due to budget cuts. Consistent with previous work (Sampson, Morenoff, and Raudenbush 2005), these two scales were closely associated ($r = .60$; $p < .01$) and were combined into a single average summed scale, with higher scores representing higher levels of perceived neighborhood collective efficacy (Cronbach's alpha = .86). We also included a measure of *neighborhood disorder* that was a combination of ten questions about the parents' perceptions of how large a problem—with responses ranging from *big problem* to *not a problem*—were ten signs of physical and social disorder in their neighborhoods: (1) litter or trash in the streets, (2) graffiti, (3) vacant housing or vacant storefronts, (4) poorly maintained property, (5) abandoned cars, (6) drinking in public, (7) selling or using drugs, (8) homeless people or street panhandlers causing disturbances, (9) groups of teenagers hanging out on street corners without adult supervision, and (10) people fighting or arguing in public. The ten items were combined into an average summed scale (Cronbach's alpha = .93).[8] Higher scores indicated that respondents perceived more social and physical disorder in their neighborhood.

A few variables were added into the models as statistical controls, including the youth's gender, age, whether or not the youth is non-Latino (non-Hispanic white, black, or Asian), and household socioeconomic status (SES). To assess SES, we included an average summed index of the parental respondent's reported level of education, household mortgage or rent, and household income. Education was measured on a 6-point scale from less than a high school diploma to a graduate or professional degree. Household mortgage or rent was measured on a 6-point scale from $500 or less to more than $2,500 per month. Household income was measured on a 6-point scale from $20,000 or less to $100,000 or more.[9]

Analytic Approach

To investigate the theoretical mechanisms through which residing in an immigrant household is associated with exposure to youth violence, we estimate a series of multilevel variance components models that take into account the hierarchical structure of youth violent victimization outcomes and respondent households being nested within neighborhoods.[10]

In the first set of descriptive models we estimate the effect of immigrant status on violent victimization, controlling for gender, ethnicity (non-Latino vs. Latino), and family SES. We then add additional covariates to this model that measure social control and social learning attributes to see how much of the effect of immigrant household status remains once these variables are included.

In the second set of models, we estimate the direct and indirect correlations between immigrant status and violent victimization. We test whether classic sociological variables of social control and social learning mediate the link between immigrant households and the risk for violent victimization for youth through a series of two-stage regression models. In the first-stage estimation (path a), our measures of family and school bonds, cultural deviance, collective efficacy, and neighborhood disorder are modeled as endogenous variables— meaning that their values are a function of immigrant household, gender of youth, age of youth, ethnicity (Latino vs. non-Latino), and family SES. Five separate models are estimated. In the second-stage estimation (path b), the predicted values from path a are used to estimate the effect of deviant attitudes, family and school bonds, and community-level attributes of collective efficacy and disorder on violent victimization. Finally, to estimate the *partial correlation* of immigrant household status and other endogenous variables on violent victimization, we estimate the effect of these variables controlled for the predicted level of exogenous risk/protective factors estimated from path a. To capture the total correlation of immigrant status across paths, we multiply the conditions of paths a and b and add the conditional relationship of path c ([path a x path b] + path c). A visual depiction of this modeling is depicted in Figure 1.

Finally, to directly compare the effects of immigrant status on youth violence, removing the correlation with all other observed variables, we estimate a doubly robust selection model. Here we estimate the probability (p) that a respondent lives in an immigrant household conditional on all observed variables, commonly referred to as a propensity score. Following the work of Robins, Rotnitzky, and Zhao (1995) and Lunceford and Davidian (2004), we use a doubly robust estimator, where both immigrant household status and control variables are modeled on the probability of experiencing violent victimization and by weighting observations according to the inverse of their probability of having features similar to those of immigrant households. Subjects from immigrant households receive an inverse probability weight (IPW) equal to $1/p$, and subjects in nonimmigrant households receive a weight of $1/1 - p$, according to their propensity score. These IPWs down-weight cases in the analysis for immigrant households that have observed features characteristic of immigrants and up-weight cases for nonimmigrant households that have features characteristic of immigrants and in effect realign immigrant and nonimmigrant households to be comparable on all observed confounders. The potential confounding effect of differences between immigrants and nonimmigrants on attributes correlated with youth violent victimization is adjusted for by modeling the effect of both immigrant status and control

FIGURE 1
Structural Equation of Immigrant Status on Exposure to Youth Violence

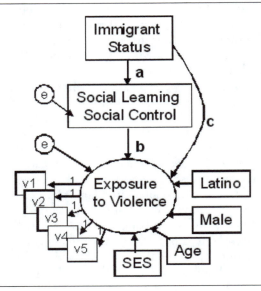

variables on victimization (outcome model), and by weighting observations by their IPWs. If either model is correct, the doubly robust estimate is an unbiased test of the effect of immigrant status on violent victimization.

Results

Table 1 shows that youth from immigrant households were no different from nonimmigrants on each measure of violent victimization as well as the overall exposure to violence, without taking account of the different individual household and environmental characteristics between groups. Immigrant and nonimmigrant households did differ on a number of domains. Youths from immigrant households had on average more deviant attitudes and beliefs and were less bonded to school and family. Youths from immigrant households were from communities with higher environmental risk for violent victimization, including living in neighborhoods with higher rates of disorder and lower levels of collective efficacy. Youths from immigrant households were also more likely to be Latino and come from families with lower socioeconomic statuses, and were more likely to be female respondents. These differences underscore the importance of comparing immigrants to similarly situated nonimmigrants on likelihood of violent victimization. One can easily imagine that living in lower-SES families and being exposed to higher levels of community disorder and lower collective efficacy alone would place immigrant youth at greater risk for violent victimization.

TABLE 1
Sample Descriptive Statistics of Key Measures

	Nonimmigrant Household (n = 301)	Immigrant Household (n = 422)	Difference
Dependent variables			
Youth violent victimization (Y) (η)	6.3%	7.5%	
Steal something by force	8.0%	4.9%	
Threatened with a gun, knife, or club	3.8%	5.4%	
Hit so badly that he/she needed bandages or a doctor	1.5%	2.5%	
Attacked by a group of youth	5.7%	8.2%	
Witnessed group assault	12.6%	16.9%	
Independent variables			
Deviant attitudes and beliefs (Y)	1.91 (.47)	2.11 (.50)	°
School and family bonds (Y)	8.38 (1.01)	8.24 (1.12)	°
Collective efficacy (P)	2.96 (.48)	2.71 (.44)	°
Neighborhood disorder (P)	1.45 (.41)	2.03 (.65)	°
Control variables			
Male (Y)	57.3%	51.9%	°
Age (Y)	15.35 (1.45)	15.36 (1.42)	
Non-Latino (Y)	16.5%	85.3%	°
Household SES (P)	3.96 (1.40)	2.41 (1.25)	°

NOTE: P = parent survey; Y = youth survey.
$°p < .001$.

Table 2 starts with a simple set of iterative models. The coefficients from these models are displayed in terms of odds ratios—values larger than 1.0 suggest increased odds of youth violence, and values less than 1.0 suggest reduced odds. The results displayed in Table 2 show that in model 1 when immigrant households are compared to nonimmigrants, there is a slightly increased risk of violent victimization when one takes into account only age and gender. However, when one includes a covariate for SES in model 2, the direction of the effect switches, suggesting that youth from immigrant households are at significantly reduced odds of violent victimization compared to nonimmigrant youth. Model 3 includes a random effect parameter for neighborhood location (k), which allows for unmeasured correlation across neighborhood locations and shows a similar reduction in the likelihood of violent victimization for youth from immigrant households. Model 4 includes additional covariates for deviant attitudes, school and family bonds, and neighborhood disorder and collective efficacy. Across all specifications residing in an immigrant household substantially reduces one's risk of violent victimization, all within a range of 43 to 58 percentage reduction in the relative odds.

TABLE 2
Effects of Immigrant Household Status on Youth Violent Victimization, Controlling for
Individual- and Neighborhood-Related Attributes

	1	2	3	4
Immigrant household	1.28°	0.57°°	0.53°	0.42°°
Non-Latino		0.40°°	0.36°	0.31°°
Age	0.95	0.93	0.95°	0.95
Gender	1.80°°	1.76°°	1.74°°	1.50°°
SES		0.88°	0.92	1.10
Deviant attitudes				2.15°°
School and family bonds				0.69°°
Disorder				1.32°
Collective efficacy				0.82
N	i = 3,105	i = 3,105	i = 3,100 j = 620 k = 178	i = 3,035 j = 607 k = 178

NOTE: Coefficients are displayed as odds ratios. All models control for the five-item matrix of
violent victimization items. i = items; j = households; k = neighborhoods.
°$p < .10$. °°$p < .05$.

TABLE 3
Effects of Immigrant Household Status, Individual, and Community Effects on Youth
Violent Victimization

	Non-Latino	Age	Gender	SES	First a	Second b	Direct c	Indirect $a \times b$	Total $a \times b + c$
Deviant attitudes	−.03	.02	.13	−.05	−.01	3.60°	−.56°	−.03	−.59°
School and family bonds	−.16°	.02°	−.23°	.06°	−.16°	−1.65°	−.56°	.26°	−.29°
Disorder	−.24°	−.009	.03°	−.08°	.18°	1.13°	−.56°	.20°	−.35°
Efficacy	.001	−.02°	−.005	.06	.007	−2.74°	−.56°	−.01	−.57°

NOTE: Coefficients are in linear form for column A and log-odds for columns B and C. N =
621 households.
°$p < .05$ (two-tailed test).

Table 3 shows the results from the structural equations models. After controlling for gender, age, non-Latino ethnicity, and family SES, the path a models
show that immigrant household status is related to *lower* social bonds and higher
neighborhood disorder. The findings from path a models suggest that there is a
strong selection effect in that immigrant households are exposed to features

TABLE 4
Doubly Robust (DR) Comparison of Immigrant and Nonimmigrant Household Status on
Youth Violence

	Immigrant Weighted	Nonimmigrant Weighted	Effect Size	DR Estimate (z-Value)
Immigrant	—	—	—	−.03 (−2.09)
Non-Latino	.48	.52	−.04	
Age	4.37	4.39	−.005	
Gender	.54	.59	−.05	
SES	3.15	3.28	−.04	
Deviant attitudes	2.00	1.96	.03	
School and family bonds	8.29	8.43	−.06	
Disorder	1.75	1.65	.08	
Collective efficacy	2.81	2.87	−.06	
Immigrant	—	—		

NOTE: n = 3,040 items, 608 individuals.

(lower social bonds and higher neighborhood disorder) that heighten the likelihood of violent victimization. The *direct correlation* of immigrant status (path *c*) is negative when controlling for the structural equation predicted by path *a*. This demonstrates that immigrant status has a negative association with violent victimization over and above family/school, deviant attitudes, and community-level attributes of disorder and collective efficacy. Across all five models, the *total effect* of immigration household status on violent victimization ($a \times b + c$) is significant and negative.

The findings in Table 3, however, should be interpreted only as descriptive models as the direction of the pathways was imposed and the correlations in errors between models were assumed to be independent, which are strong assumptions for this set of structural equation models.

The results presented thus far suggest a strong selection effect of being an immigrant, underscoring the fact that immigrant households live in comparably different neighborhood environments and that immigrant youth have different peer and family socialization. We attempted to control for these differences in our structural equation models, but these models make strong assumptions about the process generating the data. Rather than relying on structural equation models, we next compare the effects of immigrant household status on violent victimization after fully removing all other observed variables through a doubly robust propensity score model that weights observations by their inverse probability weight (IPW) of having features characteristic of immigrant households prior to estimating differences in the probability of victimization.[11] Table 4 shows that assigning subjects their IPW equalizes the average differences between immigrants and nonimmigrants on observed variables prior to estimating the standardized differences in victimization outcomes. The results from the doubly robust estimate show that immigrant households have a reduced probability of violent victimization ($p = .025$). To put these results into more concrete terms, 7.5 percent of immigrant youth report violent victimization, compared to 6.3 percent of nonimmigrant youth. However, applying the IPW adjustment drops the expected percentage of violent victimization for immigrant youth to 6.3 percent and raises the expected percentage of violent victimization for nonimmigrant youth to 9.4 percent, again suggesting that immigrants have lower marginal probabilities of violent victimization.

Conclusions

In this article, we presented evidence contrary to popular culture and media depictions of immigrant youth and showed that youth living in immigrant households are at substantially reduced risk of experiencing violent victimization. Importantly, our analysis was based on a predominately Hispanic group of immigrant households, comparing them to others living in similar neighborhoods and social contexts in Los Angeles. These findings are consistent with the Hispanic paradox literature from public health but are contrary to the age-old wisdom of sociologists (Taft 1933; Sellin 1938; Shaw and McKay 1942), who would have expected that social control and social learning mechanisms would explain much of the difference in youth violence outcomes between immigrant and nonimmigrant households.

Importantly, we also controlled for neighborhood-related processes of collective efficacy and disorder and yet still find that immigrant households have significantly lower youth violence exposure. What might account for the apparent discrepancy between sociological theory of assimilation and adaptation from the 1930s and the lack of uncovering these processes in explaining the differences in youth violence outcomes between immigrant and nonimmigrant households? Why is it that youth in immigrant households living in disadvantaged areas, who have similar risk profiles with respect to individual-, family-, school-, and community-level processes, have lowered exposure to violence? Conversely, what puts older immigrant generations at heightened risk?

The age-old explanation for differences between immigrant and nonimmigrant households and outcomes for youth should be viewed within its historical context. During the early part of the twentieth century, American inner-city slums in manufacturing towns were inhabited disproportionately by immigrants. The quality of infrastructure and housing in inner-city immigrant enclaves during this period of time was comparable to present-day developing world standards. Put simply, squalor and poverty were part and parcel of the story for many immigrant families in the United States, and opportunities for economic prosperity were limited. But this process is not static. In fact, Shaw and McKay (1942) note in their work that the influx of immigrants had a dynamic effect on Chicago neighborhoods. They emphasized that there is nothing unique about the immigrants themselves, just that the social context of migration and assimilation produces a consistent connection between immigrants, youth crime, infant mortality, and other negative outcomes. This pattern was also true for African Americans who were also relatively new migrants to Chicago neighborhoods.

What was missing from this work was a comparison of immigrant to nonimmigrant households living below the poverty line for generations and in neighborhoods of considerable social disadvantage. Immigrants in gateway cities such as Los Angeles come with a belief in America as the "land of opportunity" and settle into neighborhoods already populated with their fellow coethnics, seeking financial and social support networks to assist in the process of acculturating into life in the United States (Charles 2006). For immigrants, then, the classical assimilation model appears operable, in which the ability to move into any neighborhood in the future can occur through improvement in work earnings (cf. Portes and Zhou 1993). Could it be that something happens to youth living in households who have gone through generations of living in poverty and disadvantage in American cities that puts them at higher risk than those who are new arrivals and plan to move out of these transitional neighborhoods?

There is a stark contrast in the experiences of immigrant households and nonimmigrant underclass residents who have limited mobility options and have experienced significant place stratification for generations (Massey and Denton 1993). Morenoff and Astor (2006), for example, note that first-generation immigrant youth are at reduced risk of criminal behavior compared to second- and third-generation youth living in neighborhoods of comparable disadvantage. One could reasonably expect by the third generation that behavioral outcomes for those still living in relative social disadvantage will look very similar to youth whose families have an immigrant lineage further generations back.

It is also important to emphasize that many neighborhoods in Los Angeles and other large U.S. cities have transitioned into Latino immigrant enclaves. Once a neighborhood transitions to majority immigrant Latino enclave, restaurants, grocery stores, and other businesses transition to serving this new clientele, which also may be accompanied by a social cohesion characteristic of ethnic enclaves (Portes 1995) and the greater potential for improved socioeconomic outcomes (Zhou 1997). In such an environment, the enforcement of norms becomes more realistic and does not present the culture of conflict that American sociologists (Taft 1933; Sellin 1938) noted in their earlier explanations of the connection between immigration and crime. To the extent that these immigrants are more inclined toward prosocial norms consonant with mainstream society, this can bring about the informal social control that theorists posit will reduce the amount of crime and violence in such neighborhoods.

In this article, the informal social controls exerted by family and neighborhoods do not account for all of the observed differences in violent victimization outcomes between immigrant and nonimmigrant households. It is quite possible that a more extensive list of variables could capture the differences. On the other hand, the process of migration to the United States in search of work and opportunity may itself create a relative buffer from negative life outcomes for youth living in areas of disadvantage that is not easily captured in quantitative varia-bles. Rather, the process of extensive social support from family and coethnic networks, basic expectations about life outcomes, and a perspective about how good things are in the United States relative to country of origin life experiences may instill in children of immigrant parents a need to stay out of trouble. This explanation is at its roots sociological and a story of assimilation, but it is the dif-ferent side of the same coin presented by sociologists in the 1930s.

This is a story of how immigrant youth fare better than nonimmigrant youth in comparable social circumstances. And the theory that develops from this per-spective is one of how stable underclass poverty, failing schools, and the break-down of family and neighborhood informal social controls lead American youth to experience considerable disadvantage. Importantly, this is a story of sustained generational disadvantage, which is consistent with the empirical literature show-ing a link between the level of concentrated poverty in neighborhoods and vio-lence (Sampson et al. 2002).

The question we need to ask ourselves is how to prevent the grandchildren of immigrants from experiencing the underclass fate and how to restore informal social controls to neighborhoods where it has eroded. Maybe part of this question can be answered by examining the shared hope and expectations that recent immigrants have for their children and finding ways to restore this same sense for nonimmigrant families living in disadvantaged neighborhoods. The immigrant paradox should then be viewed through the lens of nonimmigrant experiences and the need for more egalitarian social and economic policy to bring about change to the inner city.

Notes

1. These findings are consistent with what others have termed "downward" assimilation (Rumbaut et al. 2006).

2. Sampson (2008) provides a similar commentary for why cities with higher populations of immi-grants have lower rates of crime.

3. However, research has identified an "oppositional culture" of immigrant children who reject intel-lectual pursuits and other so-called "American values" due to feelings of oppression and exclusion (Zhou 1997).

4. The sampling was designed to match respondent households in intersecting BID areas and a com-parison group of households living in non-BID neighborhoods that were statistically comparable in their exposure to ten social and economic features as measured by the 2000 census (see MacDonald et al. 2009).

5. Ninety-six households provided a parent interview but not a complete youth interview, and fifteen households provided a youth interview but not a complete parent interview. Human subject protection committees (HSPCs) from RAND, Research Triangle International (RTI), and the Centers for Disease Control and Prevention (CDC) approved the procedures for the survey.

6. Our definition of immigrant households is necessarily broad because the survey did not ask caregivers to indicate the birth location of other parents in the household.

7. We also included a measure of association with delinquent peers, which is composed of nine dichotomous questions about whether the youth's friends or people he or she regularly "socializes with or hangs out with" engaged in destruction of property, stolen property, burglary, motor vehicle theft, assault, aggravated assault, or assault with a deadly weapon; drank alcohol at least once a week; or smoked mari-juana at least once a month (Cronbach's alpha = .75). However, because we are concerned with modeling risk factors for violent victimization that are independent and not determined by the outcome, we chose

to exclude this measure from our models presented here. Socializing or hanging out with youth who engage in crimes, such as drug use and stealing motor vehicles, may expose one to more violent victimization, or violent victimization may lead certain youth to associate with delinquent peers for protection. This makes interpretation of direct effects of this variable ambiguous, and it may parse out some of what we want to explain. Supplemental analyses were conducted with this measure of delinquent peer association included in the models, and the direction of the immigrant household effect on youth violent victimization was substantively similar to those presented in this article.

8. "Don't know" items were recoded into the middle of the range.

9. The average inter-item covariance for this summed index was 1.41 (alpha = .75), with an average correlation coefficient of .50.

10. Here, the outcome represents the odds ratio of experiencing a violent victimization, $P(Yikjt = 1)/P(Yikjt = 0)$, for respondent household j residing in neighborhood census tract k (see Sampson, Morenoff, and Raudenbush [2005] for a similar specification).

11. This approach is referred to in epidemiology as a marginal structural model (Snowden, Rose, and Mortimer 2011).

References

Abraido-Lanza, Anna F., Bruce P. Dohrenwend, Daisy S. Ng-Mak, and J. Blake Turner. 1999. The Latino mortality paradox? A test of the salmon bias and health migrant hypothesis. *American Journal of Public Health* 89 (10): 1543–48.

Alba, Richard, and Victor Nee. 2003. *Remaking the American mainstream: Assimilation and contemporary immigration.* Cambridge, MA: Harvard University Press.

Bennet, William S. 1909. Immigrants and crime. *The Annals of the American Academy of Political and Social Science* 34:117–24.

Berndt, Thomas J., and Keunho Keefe. 1995. Friends' influence on adolescents' adjustment to school. *Child Development* 66:1312–29.

Butcher, Kristin F., and Anne Morrison Piehl. 1998. Cross-city evidence on the relationship between immigration and crime. *Journal of Policy Analysis and Management* 17 (3): 457–93.

Caplan, Nathan, Marcella H. Choy, and John K. Whitmore. 1991. *Children of the boat people: A study of educational success.* Ann Arbor: University of Michigan Press.

Centers for Disease Control and Prevention. 2006. Youth risk behavior surveillance—United States, 2005. *Surveillance Summaries* 55(SS-5).

Charles, Camilla Z. 2006. *Won't you be my neighbor? Race, class, and residence in Los Angeles.* New York, NY: Russell Sage Foundation.

Davis, Robert C., and Edna Erez. 1998. *Immigrant populations as victims: Toward a multicultural criminal justice system.* National Institute of Justice, Research in Brief. Washington, DC: U.S. Department of Justice.

Desmond, Scott, and Charis E. Kubrin. 2009. The power of place: Immigrant communities and adolescent violence. *Sociological Quarterly* 50:581–607.

Finch, Brian K., and William A. Vega. 2003. Acculturation stress, social support, and self-rated health among Latinos in California. *Journal of Immigrant Health* 5 (3): 109–17.

Fuligni, Andrew J., and Allison S. Fuligni. 2007. Immigrant families and the educational development of the children. In *Immigrant families in contemporary society*, eds. Jennifer E. Lansford, Kirby Deater-Deckard, and Marc H. Bornstein, 231–50. New York, NY: Guilford.

Gil, A. G., and W. A. Vega. 1996. Two different worlds: Acculturation stress and adaptation among Cuban and Nicaraguan families in Miami. *Journal of Social and Personal Relations* 13:437–58.

Hagan, John, and Alberto Palloni. 1999. Sociological criminology and the mythology of Hispanic immigration and crime. *Social Problems* 46 (4): 617–32.

Hart, Hastings H. 1896. Immigration and crime. *American Journal of Sociology* 2 (3): 369–77.

Hawkins, J. David, Richard F. Catalano, Rick Kosterman, Robert Abbott, and Karl G. Hill. 1999. Preventing adolescent health-risk behaviors by strengthening protection during childhood. *Journal of Pediatric and Adolescent Medicine* 153:226–34.

Kirk, David, and John Laub. 2010. Neighborhood change and crime in the modern metropolis. *Crime and Justice: A Review of Research* 39:441–502.

LeClere, Felicia B., Richard G. Rodgers, and Kimberley D. Peters. 1997. Ethnicity and mortality in the United States: Individual and community correlates. *Social Forces* 76 (1): 169–98.

Lee, Matthew T., Ramiro Martinez Jr., and Richard Rosenfeld. 2001. Does immigration increase homicide? Negative evidence from three border cities. *Sociological Quarterly* 42 (4): 559–80.

Loeber, Rolf, and David P. Farrington. 2001. *Child delinquents: Development, intervention, and service needs.* Thousand Oaks, CA: Sage.

Logan, John R., Wenquan Zhang, and Richard D. Alba. 2002. Immigrant enclaves and ethnic communities in New York and Los Angeles. *American Sociological Review* 67 (2): 299–322.

Lunceford, Jared K., and Marie Davidian. 2004. Stratification and weighting via the propensity score in estimation of causal treatment effects: A comparative study. *Statistics in Medicine* 23: 2937–60.

MacDonald, John M., Ricky N. Bluthenthal, Daniela Golinelli, Aaron Kofner, Robert J. Stokes, Amber Sehgal, and Terry Fain. 2009. *Neighborhood effects of crime and youth violence: The role of business improvement districts in Los Angeles.* Santa Monica, CA: RAND Corporation.

MacDonald, John M., John R. Hipp, and Charlotte Gill. 2009. Neighborhood effects of immigrant concentration on crime: Do immigrants make communities safer? Working Paper, University of Pennsylvania, Department of Criminology, Philadelphia.

Martinez, Ramiro, Jr., Jacob I. Stowell, and Matthew T. Lee. 2010. Immigration and crime in era of transformation: A longitudinal analysis of homicides in San Diego neighborhoods, 1980–2000. *Criminology* 48:797–830.

Massey, Douglas S. and Nancy A. Denton. 1993. *American apartheid: Segregation and the making of the underclass.* Cambridge, MA: Harvard University Press.

Morales, Leo S., Marielena Lara, Raynard S. Kington, Robert O. Valdez, and Jose J. Escarce. 2002. Socioeconomic, cultural, and behavioral factors affecting Hispanic health outcomes. *Journal of Health Care for the Poor and Underserved* 13 (4): 477–503.

Morenoff, Jeffrey D., and Avi Astor. 2006. Immigrant assimilation and crime: Generational differences in youth violence in Chicago. In *Immigration and crime: Race, ethnicity, and violence*, eds. Ramiro Martinez Jr. and Abel Valenzuela Jr., 36–63. New York, NY: New York University Press.

Palloni, Alberto, and Elizabeth Arias. 2004. Paradox lost: Explaining the Hispanic adult mortality advantage. *Demography* 41 (3): 385–415.

Portes, Alejandro. 1995. Economic sociology and the sociology of immigration: A conceptual overview. In *The economic sociology of immigration: Essays on networks, ethnicity, and entrepreneurship*, ed. Alejandro Portes, 1–41. New York, NY: Russell Sage Foundation.

Portes, Alejandro, and Min Zhou. 1993. The new second generation: Segmented assimilation and its variants among post-1965 immigrant youth. *The Annals of the American Academy of Political and Social Science* 530 (1): 74–96.

Rivera, Frederick P., Jonathan P. Shepherd, David P. Farrington, P. W. Richmond, and Paul Cannon. 1995. Victim as offender in youth violence. *Annals of Emergency Medicine* 26 (5): 609–14.

Robins, James M., Andrea Rotnitzky, and Lue Ping Zhao. 1995. Analysis of semiparametric regression models for repeated outcomes in the presence of missing data. *Journal of the American Statistical Association* 90:106–21.

Rumbaut, Ruben G. 1997. Ties that bind: Immigration and immigrant families in the United States. In *Immigration and the family: Research and policy on U.S. immigrants*, eds. Alan Booth, Ann C. Crouter, and Nancy Landale, 3–45. Mahwah, NJ: Lawrence Erlbaum.

Rumbaut, Rubén G., Douglas S. Massey, and Frank Bean. 2006. Linguistic life expectancies: Immigrant language retention in Southern California. Population and Development Review 32 (3): 447–60.

Sampson, Robert J. 2008. Rethinking crime and immigration. *Contexts* 7 (1): 28–33.

Sampson, Robert J., Jeffrey D. Morenoff, and Thomas Gannon-Rowley. 2002. Assessing "neighborhood effects": Social processes and new directions in research. *Annual Review of Sociology* 28:443–73.

Sampson, Robert J., Jeffrey D. Morenoff, and Stephen W. Raudenbush. 2005. Social anatomy of racial and ethnic disparities in violence. *American Journal of Public Health* 95 (2): 224–32.

Sampson, Robert J., Stephen W. Raudenbush, and Felton Earls. 1997. Neighborhoods and violent crime: A multilevel study of collective efficacy. *Science* 277:918–24.

Schmidley, Dianne A. 2001. *Profile of the foreign-born population in the United States: 2000.* U.S. Census Bureau, Current Population Reports, 23-206. Washington, DC: Government Printing Office.

Schreck, Christopher J., Jean Marie McGloin, and David S. Kirk. 2009. On the origins of the violent neighborhood: A study of the nature and predictors of crime-type differentiation across Chicago neighborhoods. *Justice Quarterly* 26 (4): 771–94.

Scribner, Richard 1996. Paradox as paradigm—The health outcomes of Mexican-Americans. *American Journal of Public Health* 86 (3): 303–5.

Sellin, Thorsten. 1938. Culture conflict and crime. *American Journal of Sociology* 44 (1): 97–103.

Shaw, Clifford R., and Henry D. McKay. 1931. *Social factors in juvenile delinquency.* Report No. I 3, vol. II. Washington, DC: National Commission on Law Observance and Enforcement.

Shaw, Clifford R., and Henry D. McKay. 1942. *Juvenile delinquency and urban areas.* Chicago, IL: University of Chicago Press.

Silverman, Jay G., Michele R. Decker, and Anita Raj. 2007. Immigration-based disparities in adolescent girls' vulnerability to dating violence. *Journal of Maternal and Child Health* 11:37–43.

Singh, Gopal K., and Mohammad Siahpush. 2002. Ethnic-immigrant differentials in health behaviors, morbidity, and cause-specific mortality in the United States: An analysis of two national data bases. *Human Biology* 74 (1): 83–109.

Snowden, Jonathan M., Sherri Rose, and Kathleen M. Mortimer. 2011. Implementation of G-computation on a simulated data set: Demonstration of a causal inference technique. *American Journal of Epidemiology* 173 (7): 731–8.

Steinberg, Laurence, Sanford M. Dornbusch, and Bradford B. Brown. 1992. Ethnic differences in adolescent achievement: An ecological perspective. *American Psychologist* 47 (6): 723–29.

Suarez-Orozco, Marcelo M. 1989. *Central American refugees and U.S. high schools: A psychosocial study of motivation and achievement.* Stanford, CA: Stanford University Press.

Sullivan, Summer, Seth J. Schwartz, Guillermo Prado, Shi Huang, Hilda Pantin, and Jose Szapocznik. 2007. A bidimensional model of acculturation for examining differences in family functioning and behavior problems in Hispanic immigrant adolescents. *Journal of Early Adolescence* 27 (4): 405–30.

Taft, Donald R. 1933. Does immigration increase crime? *Social Forces* 12 (1): 69–77

Thrasher, Frederick M. 1927. *The gang: A study of 1313 gangs in Chicago.* Chicago, IL: University of Chicago Press.

Tonry, Michael. 1997. Ethnicity, crime, and immigration. *Crime and Justice* 21:1–29.

Wilson, Tamar D. 1998. Weak ties, strong ties: Network principles in Mexican migration. *Human Organization* 57 (4): 394–403.

Zhou, Min. 1997. Growing up American: The challenge confronting immigrant children and children of immigrants. *Annual Review of Sociology* 23:63–95.

Zhou, Min, and Carl L. Bankston. 2006. Delinquency and acculturation in the twenty-first century: A decade's change in a Vietnamese American community. In *Immigration and crime: Race, ethnicity, and violence*, eds. Ramiro Martinez Jr. and Abel Valenzuela Jr., 117–39. New York, NY: New York University Press.

Why Some Immigrant Neighborhoods Are Safer than Others: Divergent Findings from Los Angeles and Chicago

By
CHARIS E. KUBRIN
and
HIROMI ISHIZAWA

Contrary to popular opinion, scholarly research has documented that immigrant communities are some of the safest places around. Studies repeatedly find that immigrant concentration is either negatively associated with neighborhood crime rates or not related to crime at all. But are immigrant neighborhoods always safer places? How does the larger community context within which immigrant neighborhoods are situated condition the immigration-crime relationship? Building on the existing literature, this study examines the relationship between immigrant concentration and violent crime across neighborhoods in Los Angeles and Chicago—two cities with significant and diverse immigrant populations. Of particular interest is whether neighborhoods with high levels of immigrant concentration that are situated within larger immigrant communities are especially likely to enjoy reduced crime rates. This was found to be the case in Chicago but not in Los Angeles, where neighborhoods with greater levels of immigrant concentration experienced higher, not lower, violent crime rates when located within larger immigrant communities. We speculate on the various factors that may account for the divergent findings.

Keywords: immigration, crime, neighborhoods, spatial analysis

Charis E. Kubrin is an associate professor of criminology, law, and society at the University of California, Irvine. Her research examines neighborhood correlates of crime. She is coeditor of Crime and Society: Crime (3rd ed.; Sage 2007) and coauthor of Researching Theories of Crime and Deviance (Oxford 2008) and Privileged Places: Race, Residence, and the Structure of Opportunity (Lynne Rienner 2006).

Hiromi Ishizawa is an assistant professor of sociology at George Washington University. Her research interests are in social demography, immigration, and urban sociology. A current research project examines the effect of political context on various measures of immigrant integration.

NOTE: We thank John McDonald and Robert Sampson for comments on an earlier draft of the article. We are especially grateful to Ruth Peterson and Lauren Krivo for providing us with the data, which were prepared with funds from the National Science Foundation (SES-0080091).

DOI: 10.1177/0002716211431688

One of the most consistent findings to emerge from the criminological litera-ture is that immigrants are less crime-prone than the native-born. Nearly a century of research documents this. In the early 1930s, the National Commission on Law Observance and Enforcement, also known as the Wickersham Commission, devoted an entire report to the topic of "Crime and the Foreign-Born," analyzing the extent of their criminal involvement, their relations with the criminal justice system, and public attitudes toward the immigrant population and crime. The Commission reached the conclusion that, when controlling for age and gender, foreign-born persons committed proportionally fewer crimes than their native-born counterparts (National Commission on Law Observance and Enforcement 1931). Fast forward 70 years; this conclusion has not changed. In a 2000 review essay for the National Institute of Justice, Martinez and Lee (2000, 496) note, "[T]he major finding of a century of research on immigration and crime is that immigrants . . . nearly always exhibit lower crime rates than native groups."

Although studies on the individual-level association between immigrant status and criminal offending are plentiful, there is a comparative shortage of research on the macro-level relationship between immigration and crime, including studies published at the neighborhood, city, and metropolitan levels (Ousey and Kubrin 2009). This is problematic because as Reid et al. (2005, 764) point out, "Although micro-level research may indicate that immigrants have a lower level of offending than native-born persons, such findings do not take into account the ecological impacts of immigration processes that may influence aggregate rates of criminal offending." In other words, immigration is an aggregate-level phenomenon whose effects may extend far beyond the argument that immigrants are more (or less) crime-prone than nonimmigrants. Immigration affects demographic, economic, and social structures in ways that may impact overall crime rates, net of any dif-ferences in the individual-level offending of immigrants (Ousey and Kubrin 2009). It is entirely possible, therefore, that immigrants are less criminal than nonimmi-grants but that immigration could create crime by disrupting social conditions in areas (thereby increasing crime among the foreign-born and native-born alike). These considerations underscore the necessity of differentiating between an immigrant-crime and immigration-crime nexus and of distinguishing between two key questions: (1) Are immigrants more likely than the native-born to commit crime? and (2) Do immigrants adversely affect the crime rate? They also suggest caution in generalizing from one unit of analysis (e.g., individual immigrants) to another (e.g., groups of immigrants) (Mears 2002, 285).

Recently, to fill the void in the literature, there has been a proliferation of aggregate-level studies on the immigration-crime link. Most are conducted at the neighborhood level (Desmond and Kubrin 2009; M. Lee and Martinez 2002; M. Lee, Martinez, and Rosenfeld 2001; Martinez, Lee, and Nielsen 2004; Martinez, Stowell, and Cancino 2008; Nielsen, Lee, and Martinez 2005; Sampson, Morenoff, and Raudenbush 2005; Stowell and Martinez 2007). These studies assess whether, and to what extent, levels of immigrant concentration are associated with neigh-borhood crime rates, controlling on a range of factors known to be linked to crime.

The basic conclusion to emerge from this research parallels what is found at the individual level: immigrant concentration is negatively associated with crime rates or not associated with crime at all.

In the current study, we build on the existing neighborhood literature by incorporating the larger community context into an assessment of the immigration-crime relationship. We ask, How does the larger community context within which immigrant neighborhoods are situated condition the relationship between immigration and crime? More specifically, our goal is to determine whether neighborhoods with high levels of immigrant concentration that are situated within larger immigrant communities are especially likely to enjoy reduced crime rates. We examine these issues in neighborhoods in Chicago and Los Angeles—two cities with significant and diverse immigrant populations. Below we elaborate on the hypothesized immigrant concentration–neighborhood crime relationship and discuss why there might be added benefit for those neighborhoods situated within larger immigrant communities.

Conceptual Framework

Despite popular perception that immigration and crime go hand in hand, there are sound reasons to believe that immigration impacts social life in ways that decrease crime rates. Here we review perspectives that suggest that more immigration leads to less neighborhood crime. Included are arguments on immigrant selection effects, formal social control, immigration revitalization, employment and ethnic entrepreneurship, and family structure. The perspectives vary both in terms of whether the behavior of immigrants, natives, or both groups is in question and in terms of the implications regarding added benefits to those neighborhoods embedded within larger immigrant communities, as opposed to those more spatially isolated.

Immigrant selection effects

Immigrants do not represent a cross-section of the sending population but instead are a self-selected group. Typically, immigrants who decide to come to the United States do so for the opportunity to improve their life chances. According to selectivity theory, then, they are more likely to have low criminal propensities (Stowell et al. 2009). That is, the self-selection of migrants into the United States in search of work and economic advancement suggests they may have strong incentives to remain law-abiding and to avoid interactions with the criminal justice system. According to Tonry (1997, 21), "Many immigrants come to the U.S. to pursue economic and educational opportunities not available in their home countries and to build better lives for themselves and their families. Most are hard-working, ready to defer gratification in the interest of longer-term advancement, and therefore likely to be conformist and to behave." Because a criminal conviction can result in deportation for immigrants, including lawful permanent residents, it is argued that those who wish to stay in the country have a greater stake in conformity. It is also argued that the deterrent effect of the threat of deportation can make immigrants less likely to commit crimes (Butcher and Piehl 1998, 672). Such arguments offer reasons to anticipate an inverse relationship between immigrant concentration and neighborhood crime rates.

Formal social control

A formal social control argument considers the public response to immigration, particularly increasing immigration, and the effect this response may have on crime in the community via enhanced formal social control efforts (Ousey and Kubrin 2009). Moral panic theory is instructive here. A moral panic occurs when "a condition, episode, person or group of persons emerges to become defined as a threat to societal values and interest; its nature is presented in a stylized and stereotypical fashion by the mass media and politicians" (Cohen 1972, 9). Moral panic theory has made significant inroads into immigration research, especially in light of exaggerated and turbulent reactions to "outsiders" (Welch 2002). Consistent with this line of reasoning, it is argued that increased immigration is often accompanied by rising fear among local residents that crime is worsening in the community, even when it is not. Rising fear and concern may prompt residents to urge public officials to "do something" about the worsening crime problem. The most frequent response is a crackdown on crime through the deployment of more police officers to apprehend criminals. According to deterrence theory, this should result in less crime as residents—the foreign-born and native-born alike—adjust to the perception they are more likely to get caught and punished for committing a crime. Indeed, studies on the deterrent effect of police size find support for this argument (see Kubrin et al. [2010] for a review). In short, immigration may be negatively associated with crime rates across neighborhoods due to deterrence resulting from enhanced formal regulation by institutions such as the police.

Immigration revitalization

Social disorganization theory, as originally conceived, theorized a positive association between immigrant concentration and neighborhood crime rates. This was due to several reasons. First, it was argued that immigration to an area causes residential turnover, or the frequent movement of populations in and out of a community. Residential turnover weakens social ties, as residents are unable to create dense friendship networks and friendships are short-lived. This leads to decreases in informal social control, or the capacity of a group to regulate its members according to mutually desired goals—such as the desire to live in a safe and crime-free environment. Examples of informal social control include the monitoring of spontaneous play groups among children, a willingness to intervene to prevent acts such as truancy and street-corner "hanging" by teenage peer groups, and the confrontation of persons who are disturbing public space (Sampson, Raudenbush, and Earls 1997). Weak ties and decreased informal social control, in turn, lead to heightened crime rates.

Immigration is also associated with crime according to social disorganization theory because it generates racial and ethnic heterogeneity, which, like residential mobility, can undermine the strength and salience of informal social control in communities. Here it is argued that in areas with diverse racial and ethnic groups living in close proximity, interaction between members will be lower than in racially and ethnically homogeneous communities. Reasons point to cultural differences between the groups, language incompatibility, and the fact that individuals prefer members of their own race or ethnicity to members of different races or ethnicities. As a result, residents will be less likely to look out for one another and will not take as great an interest in their neighbors' activities, resulting in less informal social control and, ultimately, more crime.

Recently, scholars have challenged these claims, arguing instead that immigration can revitalize communities and actually strengthen informal social control. Martinez (2006, 10) notes, "Contemporary scholars are now more open to the possibility that an influx of immigrants into disadvantaged and high-crime communities may encourage new forms of social organization and adaptive social structures. Such adaptations may mediate the negative effects of economic deprivation and various forms of demographic heterogeneity (ethnic, cultural, social) on formal and informal social control, thereby decreasing crime." Referred to as the immigration revitalization thesis, the argument is that far from being a criminogenic force, immigration contributes to the viability of urban areas, especially those that have experienced significant population decline (M. Lee et al. 2001, 564; see also Portes and Stepick 1993). This revitalization is due to several factors, including strong familial and neighborhood institutions and enhanced job opportunities associated with ethnic enclave economies (Reid et al. 2005, 762).

Employment and ethnic entrepreneurship

Immigrant communities may have less crime because they can provide residents with employment opportunities that might otherwise not be available to them. A substantial literature on ethnic enclaves finds that in such communities, immigrants are able to secure employment that yields better returns to their human capital than would be found in the secondary labor market outside of the area (Waters and Eschbach 1995, 438). Although the jobs may be low-wage, they help offset poverty, a strong correlate of crime.

In some immigrant communities, there is a high degree of institutional completeness, where out-group contact is minimized and the community is largely self-sufficient. Often in these neighborhoods, a thriving business district not only keeps shop owners and their family members employed, but it constitutes an ethnic economy that can serve the entire community (Aguilar-San Juan 2005, 46).

These ethnic economies have become increasingly critical over the past several decades of deindustrialization, when the loss of blue-collar/manufacturing jobs has served to increase employment difficulties for racial and ethnic minorities. One result has been that some immigrants fare better in the labor force compared to native minorities, what Portes and Zhou (1992, 498) describe as the "peculiar American paradox of rising labor market marginalization of native-born blacks and Puerto Ricans, along with growing numbers and employment of third world immigrants."

This is certainly the case among Latinos, who have relatively low levels of joblessness. Scholars note that Latinos have a strong attachment to the economy through low-paying but fairly stable jobs. As Martinez (2002, 133) explains, "Attachments to the world of work even through subsistence-paying jobs are part of the bond that fortifies Latino communities and helps them absorb the shock of widespread poverty." Such integration into the labor force may help explain the relatively lower crime rates among immigrants in general and Latino immigrants in particular.

Family structure

A final perspective that posits a negative immigration-crime relationship suggests that immigration alters aggregate family and household structures in ways that strengthen informal social control and impede crime (Ousey and Kubrin 2009). This is because immigrants, on the whole, are more likely to have traditional intact, or two-parent, family structures. Lower divorce rates and more two-parent households reduce family disruption—a strong correlate of crime. To the extent that immigrants have greater intact family structures and corresponding pro-family cultural orientations, it is likely that neighborhoods with more immigrants will have less crime.

Findings from a recent study by Ousey and Kubrin (2009) support this argument, at least at the city level. In their study, they investigated the longitudinal relationship between immigration and violent crime across U.S. cities from 1980 to 2000. They first determined whether within-city, over-time change in immigration was associated with within-city change in violent crime. After finding that increases in immigration led to decreases in violent crime, they examined the efficacy of several alternative theories by assessing whether changes in demographic structure, economic deprivation, labor markets, illegal drug markets, police force capacity, and family structure could account for the observed longitudinal immigration-crime association. Their key finding is that the negative relationship between immigration and violent crime appears largely due to the fact that immigration is negatively associated with divorce and single-parent families, both of which are positively correlated with violent crime. In essence, this argument suggests that communities with high concentrations of immigrants will have lower crime rates due to less family disruption.

In sum, several perspectives offer sound reasons to anticipate that immigration impacts social life in ways that decrease crime rates in neighborhoods. From these arguments and the findings of a small but growing literature at the neighborhood level, it logically follows that one would anticipate further benefits to those immigrant neighborhoods that are situated within larger immigrant communities, compared to those that are more spatially isolated. Although further crime reductions in such communities seem intuitively plausible, no research has actually tested this assumption. Here we build on the existing neighborhood literature by incorporating the larger community context into an assessment of the immigration-crime relationship.

Data and Methodology

We perform a series of regression analyses using census data on characteristics of neighborhoods in conjunction with violent crime data for census tracts in Chicago and Los Angeles. Census tracts approximate neighborhoods and are the smallest geographic level for which the data are available.

Data

We use data collected by Ruth Peterson and Lauren Krivo as part of the National Neighborhood Crime Study (NNCS). The NNCS comprises a sample of 9,593 census tracts that are wholly or partly inside the boundaries of large U.S. cities. Relevant to our purposes, the NNCS includes tract-level crime data and information on social disorganization, structural disadvantage, and socioeconomic inequality collected from the 2000 U.S. Census of Population and Housing Summary File (SF3).[1]

From the larger NNCS data set, we selected census tracts located in Chicago ($n = 876$) and Los Angeles ($n = 865$). In both cities, tracts that have small populations (i.e., fewer than 300 residents) and/or are dominated by institutionalized populations (i.e., greater than 50 percent of the population resides in group quarters) were excluded from the analyses, in line with existing research (Krivo and Peterson 1996, 623). This resulted in a final sample size of 817 tracts in Chicago and 827 tracts in Los Angeles.

Dependent variable

Our dependent variable captures violent crime levels in Chicago and Los Angeles neighborhoods. Violent crime includes homicide and robbery. As explained in Peterson and Krivo (2010, 130), rapes and aggravated assaults are not included because of missing data problems. For rape, this is mainly due to the refusal of police departments to provide data as a matter of law or policy. Aggravated assaults are missing largely because of the poor quality of the data provided. In addition to minimizing missing data problems, including only homicide and robbery in our violent crime measure indirectly addresses the potential effect that underreporting of crime may have on neighborhood crime rates, as homicide and robbery are less susceptible to underreporting (Fajnzylber, Lederman, and Loayza 2002, 1326). Following common practice, our dependent variable represents the three-year (1999–2001) average count of homicides and robberies within a tract.

Independent variables

Our key independent variable is *immigrant concentration*, which is composed of two measures: percentage foreign-born and percentage Latino in a tract. Although we originally intended our immigrant concentration measure to consist of only percentage foreign-born, in both cities the two measures are highly correlated, primarily because Latinos have constituted the largest immigrant group entering the United States in recent decades (Martinez 2006, 9; Rumbaut and Ewing 2007, 3). In our Los Angeles sample, percentage foreign-born and percentage Latino are correlated at $r = .72$. In Chicago, they are correlated at $r = .76$. Such high levels of covariance between these measures suggest that estimating their unique effects on crime would be difficult. For this reason, in each city we combine the measures into an index using factor analysis. In Los Angeles, factor loadings for both measures are high at .926, and nearly 86 percent of the variance in foreign-born and Latino is accounted for by the first principal component (eigenvalue = 1.71). In Chicago, factor loadings for both measures are also high at .938, and over 88 percent of the variance in foreign-born and Latino is accounted for by the first principal component (eigenvalue = 1.76). This measure of immigrant concentration has been used extensively in previous research (Morenoff and Sampson 1997; Ousey and Kubrin 2009; Sampson and Morenoff 2004; Sampson, Raudenbush, and Earls 1997; Stowell et al. 2009).

In addition to immigrant concentration, we include another measure that considers the greater spatial concentration of the foreign-born population in both cities, or the clustering of tracts with a high percentage immigrant population. This measure, which we call *immigrant neighborhoods*, takes into account the clustering of immigrants in neighboring tracts. It allows us to distinguish between neighborhoods that are situated within areas of greater immigrant presence compared to those that may be more spatially isolated.

To capture the presence of immigrant neighborhoods, we conduct exploratory spatial data analysis (ESDA) using GeoDa (Anselin 2003). Exploratory spatial data analysis is a tool to examine broader spatial patterns of interest across geographic areas of different sizes. In our case, we are interested in determining the spatial distribution of immigrants across neighborhoods in Chicago and Los Angeles. In line with prior research (Logan, Alba, and Zhang 2002), we use a measure of spatial autocorrelation, local indicators of spatial association (LISA) (Anselin 1995), to capture the clustering of tracts with a high percentage of foreign-born residents in each city. LISA is a location-specific statistic that identifies the location of immigrant neighborhoods by taking into account unusually high or low percentages of foreign-born residents in a focal census tract as well as the percentages in neighboring tracts.[2] Our definition of neighbor is less restrictive than alternative options since our aim is to examine whether the broader community context within which immigrant neighborhoods are situated conditions the relationship between immigration and crime. In the analysis, we define "neighbor" as any tract that shares a common boundary with a focal tract (first-order neighbor) and any tract that shares a common boundary with first-order neighbors (second-order neighbor). Thus, we use a contiguity-based spatial weight, the cumulative first- and second-order rook weight, to identify immigrant neighborhoods. We consider a high-high spatial cluster identified by LISA (that is, a census tract with a high value of percentage foreign-born that also has neighboring census tracts with high values of percentage foreign-born) as an immigrant neighborhood. If a census tract is part of an immigrant neighborhood, it is coded as 1 in the dataset (nonimmigrant neighborhoods are coded as 0). All spatial clusters identified in this study are significant at the $p < .05$ level.

Additional variables were constructed from the 2000 Census to reflect critical neighborhood differences in poverty, race, unemployment, age composition, family structure, and residential instability. These include the *percentage jobless* (percentage of civilian labor force age 16 to 64 who are unemployed or not in the labor force), *percentage female-headed households* (percentage of households that are female-headed with no husband), *percentage high school graduates* (percentage of adults age 25 and over who are at least high school graduates), *percentage in poverty* (percentage of the population for whom poverty status is determined whose income in 1999 was below the poverty level), *percentage black* (percentage of the total population that is non-Hispanic black), *residential instability index* (index comprised of percentage renters, or percentage of occupied housing units that are renter occupied, and percentage movers, or percentage of population ages 5 and over who lived in a different house in 1995[3]), *percentage young males* (percentage of the total population who are males between the ages of 15 and 24), and *population* (tract population). The neighborhoods and crime literature has demonstrated that these characteristics are related to community crime rates in a variety of cities throughout the United States (see Peterson and Krivo 2010, 33–37).

Previous community-level studies have found it necessary to address problems of collinearity among the disadvantage-related independent variables. To diagnose potential collinearity, we examined variance inflation factor (VIF) scores, which confirmed a high degree of collinearity among many of these measures. Using these diagnostics and previous research as a guide (Sampson, Morenoff, and Raudenbush 2005, 226), we performed exploratory factor analysis with varimax rotation for both Chicago and Los Angeles. Not surprisingly, the results suggest the disadvantage-related variables load on a single component, which we label *neighborhood disadvantage*. For Chicago, neighborhood disadvantage explains 71 percent of the variance and is composed of the following variables (factor loadings in parenthesis): percentage jobless (.94), percentage female-headed households (.91), percentage high school graduates (−.65), percentage in poverty (.89), and percentage black (.78). For Los Angeles, neighborhood disadvantage explains 81 percent of the variance and is composed of the following variables: percentage jobless (.94), percentage female-headed households (.83), percentage high school graduates (−.92), and percentage in poverty (.91). Percentage black did not load on this index and, for this reason, is treated as a separate covariate in the Los Angeles regression models.[4]

Analytic strategy

An examination of the univariate distributions revealed skewness in the violent crime rate, not surprising given that urban spatial data such as these are frequently nonnormal in their distribution. Because we are analyzing relatively rare events within small units, we use violent crime counts instead of rates and run negative binomial regression (see also Peterson and Krivo 2010, 131), the most widely recognized Poisson-based model that allows for overdispersion in the data. As recommended by Osgood (2000, 33), we include tract population as an exposure variable (population at risk) and constrain this coefficient to equal 1. Controlling for population size in this way is comparable to analyzing rates.

After providing descriptive statistics, we present findings from a series of negative binomial regression analyses. In the first model, we examine whether immigrant concentration is negatively associated with neighborhood violent crime levels using a baseline model where only immigrant concentration is included. In the second model, we introduce into the analysis the standard neighborhood crime correlates to determine whether any immigrant concentration effect withstands these controls. In the third model, we incorporate a measure of immigrant neighborhoods to assess if neighboring immigrant concentration levels additionally matter for crime. Finally, we conduct a series of robustness checks to determine whether the findings are sensitive to how immigrant neighborhoods are defined. We run models separately for Chicago and Los Angeles to determine whether, and how, the findings may vary across differing social contexts.

Results

Table 1 reports descriptive statistics for all variables in the analyses. The three-year average violent crime rates differ greatly between the two cities, with Chicago's (8.7) being roughly twice that of Los Angeles (4.3). Measures that comprise the immigrant concentration index also vary. Overall, Los Angeles has a greater immigrant presence; the average percentage foreign-born in L.A. tracts is 40.9 percent, compared to 17.7 percent in Chicago. Latinos comprise a much larger share of immigrants in Los Angeles, as the average percentage Latino across L.A. tracts (46.9 percent) is twice that of Chicago tracts (22.7 percent). Not surprisingly, then, as indicated in Table 1, the average percentage black is significantly higher in Chicago (42.4 percent) than Los Angeles (10.4 percent). A final difference is the

TABLE 1
Descriptive Statistics for Chicago and Los Angeles

	Chicago		Los Angeles	
	Mean	SD	Mean	SD
Dependent variable				
Three-year (1999–2001) average homicide and robbery rate per 1,000	8.68	8.05	4.26	5.36
Independent variables				
Immigrant concentration				
Percentage foreign-born	17.72	17.48	40.90	15.68
Percentage Latino	22.68	28.59	46.93	29.33
Neighborhood disadvantage				
Percentage jobless	40.44	15.34	39.54	11.08
Percentage female-headed households	22.84	16.40	15.52	8.01
Percentage high school graduates	69.14	16.87	63.21	23.64
Percentage in poverty	22.28	16.10	22.11	13.70
Percentage black[a]	42.40	43.63	10.39	16.52
Residential instability				
Percentage renters	57.84	22.52	59.88	26.54
Percentage movers	45.46	14.61	49.61	10.89
Percentage young males	7.29	2.53	7.39	3.53
Immigrant neighborhood (number of tracts)	244		249	
Exposure variable				
Total population	3,514	2,556	4,421	1,348
N	817		827	

a. Percentage black did not load on the neighborhood disadvantage index in Los Angeles.

average percentage female-headed households, which is greater in Chicago (22.8 percent) than in Los Angeles (15.5 percent).

Other neighborhood characteristics, however, are generally comparable across the two cities. For example, both have similar average jobless levels (40 percent), poverty levels (22 percent), and percentage high school graduates (69 percent in Chicago and 63 percent in Los Angeles). Levels of residential instability are also remarkably similar, with both cities averaging around 59 percent renters and 48 percent movers across tracts. Finally, the average percentage young males is nearly identical at 7 percent.

Also comparable across the two cities is the number of census tracts that comprise immigrant neighborhoods. Table 1 reveals that, as identified through local indicators of spatial association (LISA), 244 census tracts are classified as part of a larger immigrant community in Chicago. Likewise, 249 census tracts are classified as a part of larger immigrant community in Los Angeles. In both contexts, these tracts have higher levels of percentage foreign-born *and* are surrounded by neighboring tracts with high immigrant concentration levels.

TABLE 2
Characteristics of Immigrant Neighborhoods in Chicago and Los Angeles

	Chicago		Los Angeles	
	Immigrant Neighborhood	Other	Immigrant Neighborhood	Other
Three-year (1999–2001) average homicide and robbery rate per 1,000 Immigrant concentration	4.83	10.32	5.43	3.76
Percentage foreign-born	39.01	8.65	58.26	33.42
Percentage Latino	49.81	11.13	70.60	36.73
Neighborhood disadvantage				
Percentage jobless	36.89	41.95	46.68	36.46
Percentage female-headed households	13.97	26.61	17.51	14.67
Percentage high school graduates	61.40	72.43	43.89	71.54
Percentage in poverty	16.82	24.60	32.06	17.82
Percentage black	4.99	58.33	4.57	12.89
Residential instability				
Percentage renters	54.53	59.25	78.46	51.87
Percentage movers	46.91	44.84	52.93	48.18
Percentage young males	8.04	6.96	8.82	6.78
N	244	573	249	578

NOTE: Values in table represent means.

Although both cities have roughly the same number of immigrant neighborhoods, the composition of these neighborhoods, it turns out, is quite different. Moreover, for both Chicago and Los Angeles, there are considerable differences in levels of crime, immigrant concentration, and disadvantage between immigrant neighborhoods and their counterparts. Table 2 presents the characteristics of tracts located within immigrant neighborhoods and compares them to their counterparts in each city.

Looking at Table 2, it is evident that average violence levels differ greatly in immigrant neighborhoods when compared to their counterparts in both Chicago and Los Angeles. The average percentage foreign-born and percentage Latino also differ. Even greater differences, however, are noted with respect to average levels of percentage black across the two neighborhood types. Finally, disadvantage levels vary significantly in immigrant neighborhoods compared to other neighborhoods, both in Chicago and Los Angeles. Only levels of residential instability are similar in immigrant and other neighborhoods in Chicago, and in both cities, the average percentage young male is nearly identical across the two neighborhood types.

Perhaps of greater interest is the fact that immigrant neighborhoods *themselves* are quite distinct in Chicago and Los Angeles. As Table 2 shows, Chicago immigrant neighborhoods have, on average, roughly half the violent crime rates of other neighborhoods in that city (4.8 compared to 10.3), yet just the opposite is true in Los Angeles, where immigrant neighborhoods have greater violent crime rates compared to their counterparts (5.4 versus 3.8). Also quite different is the distribution of immigrants. The average level of immigrant concentration in Los Angeles immigrant neighborhoods (58.3) is higher than in Chicago (39.0), as is the average percentage Latino (70.6 percent in Los Angeles compared to 49.8 percent in Chicago).

But the main difference between the two cities is evident from the indicators of neighborhood disadvantage. While Los Angeles's immigrant neighborhoods are more disadvantaged than their counterparts in that city, the opposite pattern is found for Chicago, where immigrant neighborhoods are less disadvantaged than their counterparts. That is, levels of joblessness, family disruption, and poverty are greater in Los Angeles immigrant neighborhoods (relative to their counterparts), while levels of joblessness, family disruption, and poverty are lower in Chicago immigrant neighborhoods (relative to their counterparts). In essence, the very character of immigrant communities is context dependent.

An important question then is: How might these compositional differences affect the immigration-crime relationship in Chicago and Los Angeles? Are immigrant concentration and spatial embeddedness within a larger immigrant community likely to affect violence in a similar manner across the two contexts? Moving beyond descriptive statistics, we turn to multivariate analyses to address these questions.

Tables 3 and 4 present the results of negative binomial regression models for Chicago and Los Angeles, respectively. Turning first to results for Chicago, model 1 includes only the immigrant concentration measure. As shown, the coefficient is significant and negative, indicating that areas with higher levels of immigrant concentration experienced lower violent crime levels in Chicago, a finding consistent with prior research and our expectations.

Following the baseline model, in model 2 we add several control variables including neighborhood disadvantage, residential instability, and percentage young males. Also consistent with prior research, we find that both disadvantage and instability are significantly positively associated with violent crime levels, in line with social disorganization theory. But of greater interest is the fact that immigrant concentration remains significant after including these measures in the model. Although the coefficient is reduced somewhat (from −.32 in model 1 to −.18 in model 2), it remains significant, suggesting that neighborhoods with higher levels of immigrant concentration have lower violent crime levels, even after controlling for a variety of neighborhood crime correlates. In fact, in model 2, the exponentiated coefficient reveals that a unit increase in immigrant concentration would decrease the expected number of violent crimes by 16.5 percent (percentage change = $[\exp(-.18) - 1] \times 100$), holding all else constant.

The central focus of this study is to determine whether neighborhoods with high levels of immigrant concentration experience even greater reductions in

TABLE 3
Negative Binomial Regression Results for Neighborhood
Characteristics on Violent Crime Count: Chicago

	Model 1	Model 2	Model 3
Immigrant concentration	−.32***	−.18***	−.10**
	(.02)	(.03)	(.04)
Neighborhood disadvantage		.50***	.50***
		(.03)	(.03)
Residential instability		.25***	.24***
		(.03)	(.03)
Percentage young males		−.00	−.00
		(.01)	(.01)
Immigrant neighborhood			−.22**
			(.08)
Constant	−4.83***	−4.94***	−4.86***
	(.03)	(.08)	(.08)
Total population	(Exposure)	(Exposure)	(Exposure)
χ^2	6,694.17***	3,027.60***	3,006.14***
−2 log likelihood	−3,294.10	−3,110.31	−3,106.46

NOTE: Entries are unstandardized coefficients followed by standard errors in parentheses.
**$p < 0.01$. ***$p < .001$.

violent crime if they are spatially embedded within larger immigrant communities. Thus, in model 3, we introduce our immigrant neighborhood measure. Results from the full model indicate that beyond the level of immigrant concentration, being part of a larger immigrant community decreases violent crime in Chicago tracts (the coefficient for the immigrant neighborhood measure is significant and negative). That is, while tracts with high immigrant concentration have less violent crime, those tracts that are spatially embedded within larger immigrant communities have even less violent crime. The exponentiated coefficient indicates that neighborhoods that are part of a larger immigrant community have 19.8 percent less violent crime compared to those outside of immigrant communities, holding all else constant.

To what extent can the findings in Chicago be replicated in Los Angeles? Turning to model 1 of Table 4, we see the results begin to diverge. Contrary to what was found in Chicago, the baseline model shows that immigrant concentration has a significant, positive effect on violent crime in Los Angeles. Once the control variables are introduced to the analysis, however, the effect becomes negative (see model 2). The exponentiated coefficient indicates that, holding all else constant, a unit increase in immigrant concentration would decrease the expected number of violent crimes by 10.4 percent. Overall, findings in model 2 are generally consistent with the results for Chicago, with the exception that

TABLE 4
Negative Binomial Regression Results for Neighborhood
Characteristics on Violent Crime Count: Los Angeles

	Model 1	Model 2	Model 3
Immigrant concentration	.17***	−.11*	−.23***
	(.03)	(.05)	(.06)
Neighborhood disadvantage		.42***	.43***
		(.05)	(.05)
Residential instability		.33***	.30***
		(.04)	(.04)
Percentage young males		−.25**	−.21*
		(.09)	(.09)
Percentage black		.12***	.14***
		(.02)	(.02)
Immigrant neighborhood			.37***
			(.07)
Constant	−5.48***	−5.36***	−5.58***
	(.03)	(.17)	(.17)
Total population	(Exposure)	(Exposure)	(Exposure)
χ^2	7,909.93***	4,618.76***	4,452.57***
−2 log likelihood	−3,196.67	−3,019.19	−3,006.97

NOTE: Entries are unstandardized coefficients followed by standard errors in parentheses.
*$p < .05$. **$p < 0.01$. ***$p < .001$.

percentage young male is negatively associated with violent crime levels in Los Angeles. Moreover, recall that percentage black is included as a separate covariate in the Los Angeles analysis; as indicated in model 2, percentage black is significantly, positively associated with violent crime levels.

The main divergent finding is apparent in the full model (model 3), where the immigrant neighborhood variable is significant and positive. Contrary to our expectations and in contrast to results for Chicago, census tracts that are part of larger immigrant neighborhoods are likely to have more violent crime compared to census tracts outside of immigrant neighborhoods in Los Angeles. The exponentiated coefficient indicates that neighborhoods within larger immigrant communities have a 44.8 percent higher violent crime level, holding all else constant.

Supplemental Analyses

We conducted supplemental analyses to ensure the robustness of the findings reported above. In particular, we investigated whether the results may be influenced by the definition of "neighbor" used to measure immigrant neighborhoods. In our main analyses, we defined "neighbor" as any tract that shares a common boundary with a focal tract (first-order neighbor) and any tract that shares a common boundary with first-order neighbors (second-order neighbor), using the cumulative first- and second-order rook weight. However, in the supplemental analyses, we identified immigrant neighborhoods using two additional methods to define "neighboring tracts." First, neighbor is defined as any tract that shares a common boundary or vertex, referred to as a first-order queen weight. Second, we restricted the cumulative first- and second-order rook weight by using only the first-order neighbors. We reestimated the models using these new immigrant neighborhood measures. The results did not differ from what we presented in the main analyses for Los Angeles. However, for Chicago, the immigrant neighborhood variable was no longer significant in the results using the more restrictive definition of neighboring tract, first-order neighbor.

We also examined whether the results may be sensitive to the significance level used to identify immigrant neighborhoods. To assess this, we reduced the significance level from .05 to .01 and .001, and we created new immigrant neighborhood variables for each significance level. Not surprisingly, the number of tracts identified as "immigrant neighborhoods" declined as the significance level was reduced. We reestimated the models using these new measures. The results for Los Angeles did not differ from what we presented using a significance level of .05. However, the immigrant neighborhood variable lost its significance in the results for Chicago using .001 significance levels. Thus, while immigrant concentration is still negatively associated with violent crime levels in Chicago, there is no longer an added benefit to being situated within a larger immigrant neighborhood.

Understanding Divergent Patterns

Collectively, the findings from the analyses indicate that immigrant neighborhoods are some of the safest neighborhoods in Los Angeles and Chicago. In both cities, we found that immigrant concentration was significantly negatively associated with violent crime levels, even after controlling for standard neighborhood covariates. This finding is in line with our expectations and consistent with the studies discussed above.

What the findings also indicate, however, is that immigrant neighborhoods embedded within larger immigrant communities have lower than average violent crime levels in Chicago yet higher than average levels in Los Angeles. What accounts for this divergent finding? Why are violent crime levels higher in Los Angeles immigrant neighborhoods that are spatially concentrated within larger immigrant communities?

To begin to understand these divergent patterns, we examined the spatial distribution of violent crime across immigrant neighborhoods in Chicago and Los

FIGURE 1
Violent Crime and Immigrant Neighborhoods: Chicago

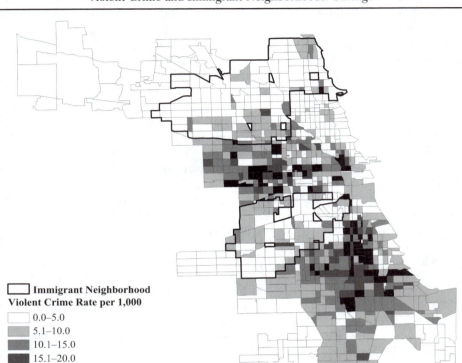

Angeles, respectively, as demonstrated in Figures 1 and 2. As shown in Figure 1, two clusters of census tracts form two larger immigrant neighborhoods in Chicago based upon our LISA measure. The immigrant neighborhood located to the north end of the city covers several areas, including Albany Park, Avondale, Belmont Cragin, Dunning, Edgewater, Hermosa, Irvine Park, Lincoln Square, Logan Square, Montclare, North Park, Portage Park, Rogers Park, Uptown, and West Ridge. The other immigrant neighborhood is in the center of Chicago and comprises Archer Heights, Armour Square, Bridgeport, Brighton Park, Gage Park, Lower West Side, McKinley Park, New City, South Lawndale, and West Elsdon.

Also evident in Figure 1 is that these immigrant neighborhoods overlap significantly with areas of less crime. In fact, the average violent crime rates of both neighborhoods are low and remarkably similar. The neighborhood in the north of Chicago has an average crime rate of 4.64 across the tracts; likewise, the

FIGURE 2
Violent Crime and Immigrant Neighborhoods: Los Angeles

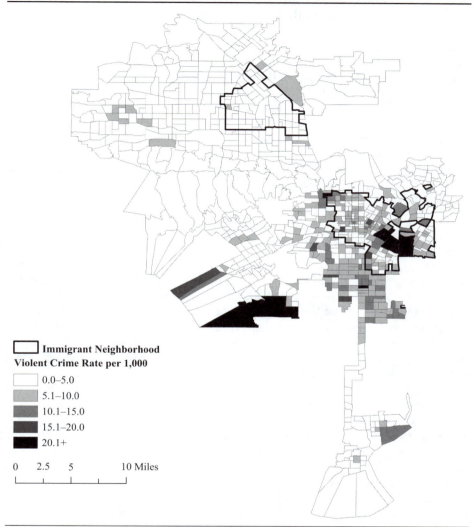

neighborhood in the center of Chicago has an average rate of 5.13. Moreover, both have lower average rates compared to Chicago as a whole (8.68). Thus, the dynamics that lead to lower crime levels appear to operate similarly in both Chicago immigrant neighborhoods.

Similar to Chicago, two immigrant neighborhoods are identified in Los Angeles using our LISA measure. One neighborhood is located north of downtown and comprises Arleta, North Hollywood, Valley Glen, Van Nuys, Panorama

City, and Sun Valley. The other is located in the south of the city and incorporates Koreatown, Pico Union, Westlake, and Wilshire Center and stretches to Hollywood to the north; South LA to the south; Mid-Wilshire to the west; and Chinatown, Boyle Heights, and Lincoln Heights to the east. As Figure 2 shows, unlike in Chicago, these two neighborhoods have vastly different crime patterns. The average violent crime rate is roughly three times greater in the immigrant neighborhood located to the south (6.30) compared to the one located to the north (2.74). In essence, then, the distribution of violent crime across immigrant neighborhoods is quite distinct in Chicago and Los Angeles. In Chicago, both neighborhoods, despite any differences in composition, enjoy relatively low crime levels. Alternatively, in Los Angeles, we find that one neighborhood parallels what we find in Chicago, with low violent crime levels, while the other has much higher levels. In the remainder of the article, we speculate about possible explanations for these divergent findings.

Conclusion

Prior studies have repeatedly shown that neighborhoods with higher immigrant concentration levels have lower crime rates, or that there is no association between the two. We have yet to understand, however, how the larger community context within which immigrant neighborhoods are situated conditions the relationship between immigration and crime. In our study, we examined whether neighborhoods with high levels of immigrant concentration that are located within larger immigrant communities are likely to enjoy even greater crime reductions. Our findings indicate that immigrant concentration is negatively associated with violent crime, in accordance with prior studies. Yet we also find that while immigrant neighborhoods embedded within larger immigrant communities have lower than average violent crime levels in Chicago, those in Los Angeles report just the opposite—higher violent crime levels.

The larger message is clear: context matters. But how does context matter and in what ways? To fully answer this question, one must compare the characteristics of the immigrant neighborhoods both within and across the cities. In addition, a more complete understanding of each neighborhood's historical development is necessary. Finally, one would do well to scour the ethnographic literature on Los Angeles and Chicago immigrant communities to get a feel for what is happening "on the ground," which also may provide insight into how and why context matters. Although it is beyond the scope of the present study to fully account for what may be creating the divergent patterns we observe, below we offer three explanations that, in our opinion, likely have some impact.

One possible explanation is consistent with social disorganization theory, which asserts that racial and ethnic diversity may be associated with high crime rates in communities. For starters, recall the earlier discussion about how such diversity can undermine ties between neighbors, reducing informal social control. Moreover, although neighborhoods with diverse immigrant populations can offer institutional support to their members, resources that are enjoyed by one ethnic group are not automatically transferable to members of other ethnic groups. As just one example, supplementary education institutions for children of Chinese immigrants, which have been growing in number since the late 1980s, not only promote educational achievement but also "serve as a locus of social support and control, network building, and social capital formation" (Zhou 2009, 161). While this type of ethnic institution helps children of Chinese immigrants succeed academically and build social ties regardless of socioeconomic background, access to such resources and opportunities is not necessarily available for members of other ethnic groups residing in the neighborhood. That is, social and economic cooperation among immigrants from diverse backgrounds is not axiomatic; as such, variation in racial and ethnic diversity levels across the immigrant communities in our study may be what is driving, in part, the divergent findings.

A quick glance at the data for Los Angeles reveals nonuniformity in racial and ethnic diversity levels across the immigrant neighborhoods. For example, while Hispanics constitute approximately two-thirds of the population in both neighborhoods, the one in the south has a higher proportion of Asians (15 percent compared to just 8 percent for the north), creating greater diversity. Unfortunately, due to limitations of census data, we are unable to disentangle immigrant status by race and ethnicity. Still, we believe further investigation of these issues may inform the divergent patterns noted in the data.

Another explanation consistent with social disorganization theory relates to residential turnover among immigrants. According to the model of spatial assimilation, immigrants first settle in older central city neighborhoods where there is a high concentration of coethnics (Massey 1985). This residential pattern is fed by chain migration, in which new immigrants rely on the social networks of their family members and friends when selecting destinations. As the number of new residents increases, more ethnic organizations are established to offer services for residents (Breton 1964). However, the immigrant neighborhood is a temporary residential location for many immigrants. As immigrants acculturate and achieve socioeconomic mobility, they move to areas that offer improved residential amenities, creating high rates of turnover. Residential turnover may lead to decreases in informal social control and higher crime levels in those immigrant neighborhoods, as social disorganization theory predicts. In line with this argument, then, it may be that the immigrant neighborhood in the south of Los Angeles is a more temporary area for immigrants than is its counterpart to the north. In sum, racial and ethnic diversity and the temporal nature of neighborhoods within which immigrants reside may help us understand the pattern of results found in the study.

Another explanation for the divergent findings may be related to immigrant generational status (i.e., first, second, third, etc. generation). Generational status is important because it has direct bearing on the cultural assimilation of immigrants. Assimilation refers to "the decline, and only at some ultimate end-point the disappearance, of an ethnic distinction and its allied differences" (Alba and Nee 1997, 7). The process of assimilation involves, among other things, the acquisition of English language proficiency, higher levels of education, valuable job skills, and other attributes that ease immigrants' entry into U.S. society and improve their chances of success in the U.S. economy (Rumbaut and Ewing 2007, 2).

As this definition implies, scholars have long argued that assimilation represents the most direct path toward upward mobility and later "success" in life for immigrants. Yet recent work challenges this notion, suggesting that assimilation may not be a wholly beneficial process. This has certainly been true with respect to assimilation and crime. A growing literature finds that assimilated immigrants have higher—not lower—rates of criminal involvement compared to unassimilated immigrants (Y. Lee 1998; Morenoff and Astor 2006, 47; Zhou and Bankston 2006, 124). A related literature shows that the children of immigrants (the second generation), who are typically more assimilated than their parents, have higher crime rates than their parents (Morenoff and Astor 2006, 36; Rumbaut et al. 2006, 72; Sampson, Morenoff, and Raudenbush 2005; Taft 1933; Zhou and Bankston 1998). Findings such as these have led scholars to describe an "assimilation paradox" (Rumbaut and Ewing 2007, 2), where the crime problem reflects "not the foreign born but their children" (Tonry 1997, 10).

What accounts for these patterns? One explanation relates to the consequences of the "Americanization" experience of immigrants. Because many immigrants settle in disadvantaged neighborhoods upon arrival into the United States, part of that experience involves navigating the "challenges confronting immigrant children in U.S. neighborhoods in a social context promoting dropping out of school, joining youth gangs, or participating in the drug subculture" (Portes and Rumbaut 2001, 59). This alternative path is referred to as downward assimilation or downward mobility (Morenoff and Astor 2006; Rumbaut et al. 2006, 73) because socialization for some immigrants does not encourage a path toward upward mobility but instead results in adopting a deviant lifestyle. In essence, "The children and grandchildren of many immigrants—as well as many immigrants themselves the longer they live in the United States—become subject to economic and social forces, such as higher rates of family disintegration and drug and alcohol addiction, that increase the likelihood of criminal behavior" (Rumbaut and Ewing 2007, 2).

Another explanation considers the challenges associated with navigating two, often conflicting, worlds, particularly for the second generation: "Born or raised in the United States, they inherit their immigrant parents' customs and circumstances but come of age with a distinctively American outlook and frame of reference and face the often-daunting task of fitting into the American mainstream while meeting their parents' expectations, learning the new language, doing well in school, and finding decent jobs" (Rumbaut et al. 2006, 65). A case study of Vietnamese youth in a Vietnamese enclave in New Orleans documents this tension. Zhou and Bankston (2006) find the youth in their study are subject to two opposing sets of contextual influences: on one hand, the ethnic community was tightly knit and encouraged normative behaviors such as respect for elders, diligence in work, and striving for upward social mobility into mainstream American society; on the other hand, the local American community was socially marginalized and economically impoverished. Interviews with the youth reveal they reacted to this situation by developing oppositional subcultures to reject normative means to social mobility (p. 119).

Regardless of which processes may be operating, what the findings in the literature imply is that generational status and assimilation likely play an important role in understanding the divergent patterns documented in our study. It may be the case that violence is more prevalent in the immigrant neighborhood located in the south of Los Angeles because the residents living in those census tracts, on average, are more assimilated compared to those residents living in the immigrant neighborhood located in northern Los Angeles. This is an empirical question. An important next step, then, is to compare generational status and assimilation levels across the two immigrant neighborhoods in Los Angeles. Measures of assimilation include language use and English proficiency, citizenship, spatial concentration of ethnic groups, and interethnic social relations. Some of these are available from the census and could be examined across the various immigrant neighborhoods.

A final explanation that may help account for the study's divergent findings addresses the issue of differentiation in structural conditions (beyond immigrant concentration) in surrounding neighborhoods. In our analysis, we control for disadvantage levels within immigrant neighborhoods. But such an approach may be limited, in part because it overlooks the embeddedness of neighborhoods within larger areas of disadvantage (or advantage). Inequality in the character of nearby neighborhoods, we argue, may account for why crime patterns vary.

This argument is not farfetched. Peterson and Krivo (2010) document the role of nearby neighborhoods for understanding why crime rates are higher in predominantly African American compared to predominantly white neighborhoods in their study of nearly nine thousand neighborhoods in over ninety U.S. cities. They find that notable gaps in violence remain unaccounted for across black and white communities, even after controlling for the "usual suspects," including racialized community conditions. They theorize this may result from "spatial inequality," or the uneven spatial distribution of black and white communities in terms of their proximity to resources. They argue, "A common feature of many African American neighborhoods, whatever their internal character, is proximity to communities with characteristics typically associated with higher crime rates, such as high levels of disadvantage and residential turnover. In contrast, white areas are often surrounded by neighborhoods where crime-promoting conditions are relatively absent and factors that discourage crime, such as external community investments, are prevalent" (p. 91). In fact, Peterson and Krivo (2010) document support for this argument. They find that even after controlling for internal neighborhood conditions, three characteristics of proximate areas—residential instability, disadvantage, and the prevalence of white residents—affect violent crime rates. In essence, being located near more highly disadvantaged neighborhoods tends to increase violence by intensifying violent crime in neighboring communities.

Following this line of reasoning, the divergent findings we document may be attributable, in part, to the fact that the Los Angeles immigrant communities are differentially situated in terms of their spatial proximity to areas with higher or lower levels of crime-producing social conditions. In particular, the high-crime immigrant neighborhood may be spatially proximate to areas with high levels of social deprivation and other detrimental conditions, such as the presence of gangs, which create unique risks for crime. Alternatively, the lower-crime immigrant neighborhood may be located close to areas of privilege, which provide access to social, political, and economic resources that keep violence low. Consider, for example, that there are significant differences in gang membership and activity in the northern and southern immigrant neighborhoods in Los Angeles. In particular, South Central L.A. immigrant neighborhoods are located in the middle of established gang turfs. One area in particular, Boyle Heights, is home to several violent gangs including Big Hazard and Krazy Ass Mexicans. By contrast, gangs are not nearly as prevalent in immigrant neighborhoods located to the north. Once again, the extent to which differentiation in structural conditions (beyond immigrant concentration) in surrounding neighborhoods accounts for the divergent findings is an empirical question that can and should be examined in future research.

By no means are these the only explanations worth considering. Yet as a starting point, we argue much can be gained by exploring in greater detail the immigrant communities themselves on many dimensions including racial and ethnic diversity, residential turnover, generational status/assimilation, and spatial proximity to areas with higher or lower levels of crime-producing social conditions.

We close with one additional recommendation for future researchers. In line with our maxim, "context matters," we encourage researchers to examine these issues in additional cities beyond Chicago and Los Angeles. In our selection of study sites, we opted to focus on established immigration gateway cities, or areas with long immigration histories and large and diverse immigrant populations. Of interest, however, is the extent to which the findings reported here apply in new or emerging immigrant destination contexts such as Atlanta, Phoenix, or Seattle. In all three cities, immigration levels have grown considerably over the past two decades, and not always without growing pains. Also of interest is potential variation in findings based upon whether cities are "immigrant-friendly," such as those designated "sanctuary cities," compared to those without such designation. Clearly, there are many directions one could explore. At a minimum, though, we hope the divergent findings spur researchers to continue examining the not-so-straightforward relationship between immigration and crime.

Notes

1. For an overview and additional information about NNCS data, see Peterson and Krivo (2009).

2. It is calculated as $I_i = \frac{z_i}{m_2} \sum_j w_{ij} z_j$, with $m_2 = \sum_j z_i^2$, where z_i and z_j are the deviation from the sample mean of the variable of interest (percentage foreign-born) and w_{ij} is an element of a row-standardized spatial weight matrix.

3. The index represents the average of the standardized scores of these two variables.

4. Examination of collinearity diagnostics revealed no multicollinearity in the parameter estimates presented below for Chicago (i.e., no VIF was greater than 4). In the analyses for Los Angeles, however, there is very slight collinearity between the immigrant concentration and neighborhood disadvantage measures, with VIFs of 4.14 and 3.78, respectively. This is consistent with findings from other research on Los Angeles neighborhoods (Kimbro 2009). Given the study's focus on immigrant concentration and the importance of controlling for disadvantage, we argue both must be included in the model despite their high correlation. We reran the analyses including only each measure, and the substantive conclusions remain unchanged.

References

Aguilar-San Juan, Karin. 2005. Staying Vietnamese: Community and place in Orange County and Boston. *City and Community* 4:37–65.

Alba, Richard D., and V. Nee 1997. Rethinking assimilation theory for a new era of immigration. *International Migration Review* 31:826–74.

Anselin, Luc. 1995. Local Indicators of Spatial Association—LISA. *Geographical Analysis* 27:93–115.

Anselin, Luc. 2003. *GeoDa™ 0.9 user's guide*. Urbana: University of Illinois.

Breton, Raymond. 1964. Institutional completeness of ethnic communities and the personal relations of immigrants. *American Journal of Sociology* 70:193–205.

Butcher, Kristin F., and Anne Morrison Piehl. 1998. Recent immigrants: Unexpected implications for crime and incarceration. *Industrial and Labor Relations Review* 51:654–79.

Cohen, Stanley. 1972. *Folk devils and moral panics: The creation of mods and rockers*. London: Macgibbon and Kee.

Desmond, Scott A., and Charis E. Kubrin. 2009. The power of place: Immigrant communities and adolescent violence. *Sociological Quarterly* 50:581–607.

Fajnzylber, Pablo, Daniel Lederman, and Norman Loayza. 2002. What causes violent crime? *European Economic Review* 46:1323–57.

Kimbro, Rachel Tolbert. 2009. Acculturation in context: Gender, age at migration, neighborhood ethnicity, and health behaviors. *Social Science Quarterly* 90:1145–66.

Krivo, Lauren J., and Ruth D. Peterson. 1996. Extremely disadvantaged neighborhoods and urban crime. *Social Forces* 75:619–50.

Kubrin, Charis E., Steven F. Messner, Glenn Deane, Kelly McGeever, and Thomas D. Stucky. 2010. Proactive policing and robbery rates across U.S. cities. *Criminology* 48:57–98.

Lee, Matthew T., and Ramiro Martinez Jr. 2002. Social disorganization revisited: Mapping the recent immigration and black homicide relationship in northern Miami. *Sociological Focus* 35:363–80.

Lee, Matthew T., Ramiro Martinez Jr., and Richard Rosenfeld. 2001. Does immigration increase homicide? Negative evidence from three border cities. *Sociological Quarterly* 42:559–80.

Lee, Yoon Ho. 1998. Acculturation and delinquent behavior: The case of Korean American youths. *International Journal of Comparative and Applied Criminal Justice* 22:273–92.

Logan, John R., Richard D. Alba, and Wenquan Zhang. 2002. Immigrant enclaves and ethnic communities in New York and Los Angeles. *American Sociological Review* 67:299–322.

Martinez, Ramiro, Jr. 2002. *Latino homicide: Immigration, violence, and community*. New York, NY: Routledge.

Martinez, Ramiro, Jr. 2006. Coming to America: The impact of the new immigration on crime. In *Immigration and crime: Race, ethnicity, and violence*, eds. Ramiro Martinez Jr. and Abel Valenzuela Jr., 1–19. New York, NY: New York University Press.

Martinez, Ramiro, Jr., and Matthew T. Lee. 2000. On immigration and crime. In *Criminal justice 2000: The nature of crime: Continuity and change*, vol. 1, 485–524. Washington, DC: National Institute of Justice.

Martinez, Ramiro, Jr., Matthew T. Lee, and Amie L. Nielsen. 2004. Segmented assimilation, local context and determinants of drug violence in Miami and San Diego: Does ethnicity and immigration matter? *International Migration Review* 38:131–57.

Martinez, Ramiro, Jr., Jacob I. Stowell, and Jeffrey M. Cancino. 2008. A tale of two border cities: Community context, ethnicity, and homicide. *Social Science Quarterly* 89:1–16.

Massey, Douglas S. 1985. Ethnic residential segregation: A theoretical synthesis and empirical review. *Sociology and Social Research* 69:315–50.

Mears, Daniel P. 2002. Immigration and crime: What's the connection? *Federal Sentencing Reporter* 14:284–88.

Morenoff, Jeffrey D., and Avraham Astor. 2006. Immigrant assimilation and crime: Generational differences in youth violence in Chicago. In *Immigration and crime: Race, ethnicity, and violence*, eds. Ramiro Martinez Jr. and Abel Valenzuela Jr., 36–63. New York, NY: New York University Press.

Morenoff, Jeffrey D., and Robert J. Sampson. 1997. Violent crime and the spatial dynamics of neighborhood transition: Chicago, 1970–1990. *Social Forces* 76:31–64.

National Commission on Law Observance and Enforcement. 1931. *Report on crime and the foreign born*. Washington, DC: Government Printing Office.

Nielsen, Amie L., Matthew T. Lee, and Ramiro Martinez Jr. 2005. Integrating race, place and motive in social disorganization theory: Lessons from a comparison of black and Latino homicide types in two immigrant destination cities. *Criminology* 43:837–72.

Osgood, D. Wayne. 2000. Poisson-based regression analysis of aggregate crime rates. *Journal of Quantitative Criminology* 16:21–43.

Ousey, Graham C., and Charis E. Kubrin. 2009. Exploring the connection between immigration and violent crime rates in U.S. cities, 1980–2000. *Social Problems* 56:447–73.

Peterson, Ruth D., and Lauren J. Krivo. 2009. *The National Neighborhood Crime Study*. Prepared with funds from the National Science Foundation (SES-0080091). Columbus: Ohio State University, Criminal Justice Research Center.

Peterson, Ruth D., and Lauren J. Krivo. 2010. *Divergent social worlds: Neighborhood crime and the racial-spatial divide*. New York, NY: Russell Sage Foundation.

Portes, Alejandro, and Ruben G. Rumbaut. 2001. *Legacies: The story of the immigrant second generation*. Berkeley: University of California Press.

Portes, Alejandro, and Alex Stepick. 1993. *City on the edge: The transformation of Miami*. Berkeley: University of California Press.

Portes, Alejandro, and Min Zhou. 1992. Gaining the upper hand: Economic mobility among immigrant and domestic minorities. *Ethnic and Racial Studies* 15:491–521.

Reid, Lesley Williams, Harold E. Weiss, Robert M. Adelman, and Charles Jarett. 2005. The immigration-crime relationship: Evidence across U.S. metropolitan areas. *Social Science Research* 34:757–80.

Rumbaut, Ruben G., and Walter A. Ewing. 2007. *The myth of immigrant criminality and the paradox of assimilation: Incarceration rates among native and foreign-born men*. Washington, DC: Immigration Policy Center, American Immigration Law Foundation.

Rumbaut, Ruben G., Robert G. Gonzales, Golnaz Komaie, Charlie V. Morgan, and Rosaura Tafoya-Estrada. 2006. Immigration and incarceration: Patterns and predictors of imprisonment among first- and second-generation young adults. In *Immigration and crime: Race, ethnicity, and violence*, eds. Ramiro Martinez Jr. and Abel Valenzuela Jr., 64–89. New York, NY: New York University Press.

Sampson, Robert J., and Jeffrey D. Morenoff. 2004. Spatial (dis)advantage and homicide in Chicago neighborhoods. In *Spatially integrated social science*, eds. Michael Goodchild and Donald Janelle. New York, NY: Oxford University Press.

Sampson, Robert J., Jeffrey D. Morenoff, and Stephen W. Raudenbush. 2005. Social anatomy of racial and ethnic disparities in violence. *American Journal of Public Health* 95:224–32.

Sampson, Robert J., Stephen W. Raudenbush, and Felton Earls. 1997. Neighborhoods and violent crime: Testing social disorganization theory. *Science* 277:918–24.

Stowell, Jacob I., and Ramiro Martinez Jr. 2007. Displaced, dispossessed, or lawless? Examining the link between ethnicity, immigration, and violence. *Journal of Aggression and Violent* Behavior 12:564–81.

Stowell, Jacob I., Steven F. Messner, Kelly F. McGeever, and Lawrence E. Raffalovich. 2009. Immigration and the recent violent crime drop in the United States: A pooled, cross-sectional time-series analysis of metropolitan areas. *Criminology* 47:889–928.

Taft, Donald R. 1933. Does immigration increase crime? *Social Forces* 12:69–77.

Tonry, Michael. 1997. Ethnicity, crime, and immigration. *Crime & Justice: A Review of Research* 21:1–29.

Waters, Mary C., and Karl Eschbach. 1995. Immigration and ethnic and racial inequality in the United States. *Annual Review of Sociology* 21:419–46.

Welch, Michael. 2002. *Detained: Immigration laws and the expanding I.N.S. jail complex*. Philadelphia, PA: Temple University Press.

Zhou, Min. 2009. *Contemporary Chinese America: Immigration, ethnicity, and community transformation*. Philadelphia, PA: Temple University Press.

Zhou, Min, and Carl L. Bankston. 2006. Delinquency and acculturation in the twenty-first century: A decade's change in a Vietnamese American community. In *Immigration and crime: Race, ethnicity, and violence*, eds. Ramiro Martinez Jr. and Abel Valenzuela Jr., 117–39. New York, NY: New York University Press.

Extending Immigration and Crime Studies: National Implications and Local Settings

By
RAMIRO MARTINEZ JR.
and
JACOB I. STOWELL

One of American society's enduring debates centers on the immigration and violent crime relationship. This classic debate is revisited using data for individual homicide incidents and census-tract-level homicides in Miami, Florida, and San Antonio, Texas, in the 1980s and 1990s, respectively. The article starts with these two comparative cases because they mirror the immigration influx, Latino growth, and homicide decline seen throughout the country since 1980. These findings are also replicated in an analysis of the immigration and crime influx across the nation using U.S. counties in 2000. In sum, results from comparative cases, different time points, homicide motivations, and individual/community/national levels—and even controlling for Latino regional concentration—are reported. The findings were clear and unequivocal: more immigrants did not mean more homicide, and that outcome held across time and place.

Keywords: Latino; violence; homicide; immigration; U.S.-Mexico border

National concern over immigrant crime patterns and the impact of immigration on crime reappeared in 1980, several decades after early linkages were examined by the founders of American sociology. That anxiety emerged after "Mariel" Cuban refugees landed in southern Florida, an event that eventually energized largely dormant anti-immigrant groups and commentators, who soon claimed "Hispanic immigrants" threatened "American" society by avoiding assimilation and created national secu-

Ramiro Martinez Jr. is a professor in the School of Criminology and Criminal Justice and the Department of Sociology and Anthropology at Northeastern University. He recently received the American Society of Criminology's Division on People of Color and Crime Lifetime Achievement Award.

Jacob I. Stowell is an associate professor in the School of Criminology and Criminal Justice at Northeastern University. His work has appeared in journals such as the American Journal of Sociology, Social Science Quarterly, *and* Aggression and Violent Behavior. *His current research focuses on the temporal influence of immigration on patterns of lethal and nonlethal violence.*

DOI: 10.1177/0002716212437363

ANNALS, *AAPSS*, 641, May, 2012

rity issues, among other problems (Portes and Stepick 1993; Huntington 2004). Immigrant opponents had long focused primarily on the consequences of Mexican border crossers on local economies and crime in the southwestern United States. But "Mariel" soon generated opposition to the Cuban exodus, galvanized nativists, and nationalized the immigration issue by drawing attention to large numbers of newcomers outside of the Rio Grande area (Huntington 2004). Unfortunately, the immigrant/crime connection was not seriously considered throughout most of the 1980s, and the relevance of studying the effects of immigration on crime was not apparent until recent demographic transformations sparked research in this area.

This article is a study of immigration and crime with national implications and local settings. The geographic range of this article starts locally, concentrating on Miami, Florida, and San Antonio, Texas, in the 1980s and 1990s, respectively, and concludes with a national focus. We start with these two comparative cases because they mirror the immigration influx, Latino growth, and homicide decline seen throughout the country since 1980. Of course, immigration flows and changes in other places occurred beyond these two Latino cities, yet these transformations varied across time and place (nationally and locally), and these cities reflect the continuum in these experiences. At one end, San Antonio is composed primarily of a Mexican-origin population with a moderate level of immigration by the U.S.-Mexico border, a region long considered dangerous. Miami, in contrast, is now a majority Latino and immigrant city but was an urban Southern city changed forever by the influx of Cubans from the Mariel Harbor, an event that arguably gave rise to the anti-immigrant forces now dominating the national landscape. Thus, while the immigration and crime experience in each city is unique, they also reflect those of most major urban areas. Local context matters, and the similarities and differences were harbingers of an ongoing national transformation.

In response to the notions that Spanish-speaking immigrants are more dangerous than native-born counterparts and that immigrant communities are more violence-prone than others, we ask two broad questions in this article. First, on average, are immigrants involved in violence more than the native-born? Studies based on racial/ethnic/immigrant variation in violent crime have largely avoided answering this question and rarely include "undocumented" in these studies. What happens when an influx of newcomers shows up in one city, as in the case of the 1980 Mariel boatlift in Miami? Did the Mariels engage in specific types of homicide motivation, especially drug homicides, more than native-born or older immigrants over the 1980s? Along these lines, political rhetoric suggested that the border was a dangerous place over the 1990s and that those of Mexican origin engaged in high levels of drug and gang homicides. What was the extent of homicides within San Antonio's Latino population, and how does it compare relative to others in the city? Examination of homicide incident patterns provides answers to important questions on immigrants and homicide propensity that form a foundation for the rest of the article.

Second, to what degree, if any, does the growth of immigration influence community-level violence? Macro-level studies based on the effect of immigration on violence might understate the effect of immigration on homicides because they do not include specifically investigations of killings associated with newcomers. Does the level of immigration impact drug killings in Miami or gang/drug homicides in San Antonio, Texas?

Last, what impact did immigration have on national-level homicides at the start of the current century? Did the level of foreign-born increase homicide? What about counties where Latinos are concentrated? Should those counties not have more Latino homicide? It stands to reason that more Latinos settling in a short period of time would mean more homicide. Moreover, does immigration similarly shape black, white, or Latino homicide across U.S. counties?

Recall that most immigrants and Latinos, the largest ethnic minority group in the United States and one long thought of as heavily immigrant, reside in forty urban counties (Fry 2008).[1] The study of immigrants, immigration influx, and crime requires examining places where immigrants reside and, of course, where violent crime data are available. We begin by focusing on two majority-Latino cities at different time points—the city of Miami, Florida, in the 1980s and the city of San Antonio, Texas in the 1990s. We end with a look at all U.S. counties in 2000 and examine the immigration and crime influx across the nation. Did the immigrant transformation of Miami have long-term implications for crime in San Antonio and later the nation? Certainly we can learn something different from each research setting and use that knowledge to round out our understanding of national patterns. Taken together, this provides a fuller and more complete picture of the immigrant status/immigration/crime linkages by looking at detailed micro-level homicide incidents and moving to incorporate those data into the macro-level context at the community and national level.

Miami and the Mariels

The Miami population has been primarily immigrant/Latino for 30 years (Miami-Dade County Facts 2009)[2]. Part of this composition is due to proximity given Miami's location on the Caribbean, making it a natural destination point for Cuban exiles fleeing a communist regime since 1959. This also made Miami a permanent destination for most of the 125,000 Cubans leaving through the Mariel Harbor from May to September 1980 (Portes and Stepick 1993). This group was more impoverished, was less educated, had fewer resources, was younger, and was more stigmatized than previous Cuban arrivals. In other words, "Mariel" provides a rare opportunity to observe the impact of "undocumented" immigrants on local crime and offers a "natural experiment" on immigration and crime (Card 1990).

Given the nature of the Mariel boatlift and the unique circumstances surrounding the influx, accurate population estimates are difficult to determine. Moreover, it was not a "legal" but rather an "unauthorized" movement of an undetermined number of migrants from abroad (Card 1990). Still, estimations place the total number of "Mariel" immigrants at around 125,000 refugees, and the vast majority settled in the city of Miami or the Miami-Dade County area (Portes and Stepick 1993).[3] Most commentators (Huntington 2004, 247–51) also assumed that the

TABLE 1
Miami Homicide Victim and Incident Characteristics, 1980–1989 ($N = 1,741$)

	White	Black	Latino	Haitian	Mariel Cuban	Jamaican	All
Individual							
% 18–24 yrs	12.3	27.4	15.8	5.6	12.9	27.3	18.8
% 25+ yrs	84.8	65.5	81.1	84.7	87.1	63.6	76.5
% male	76.6	83.1	81.3	84.7	93.4	97.0	83.9
% alcohol	13.4	11.2	13.8	8.2	30.8	18.2	22.2
Homicide incident							
% outdoor	37.4	57.4	39.6	54.2	49.6	18.2	47.9
% drug	13.5	16.7	13.2	16.7	16.0	54.5	17.5
% intimate	8.2	12.9	14.4	9.7	7.0	3.0	11.7
% escalation	14.0	36.7	35.0	23.6	44.1	27.3	33.0
% robbery	28.1	10.9	14.4	23.6	10.5	6.1	13.8
% multiple victim	18.1	7.1	13.9	4.1	14.7	18.2	11.7
% gun	44.4	70.9	77.2	72.2	82.4	84.8	72.4

SOURCE: City of Miami Police Department homicide reports and Miami-Dade Medical Examiner's Office homicide reports.

Mariel portion of homicides was more than those of other racial/ethnic/immigrant groups in the city and that their participation in gun-, robbery-, and drug-related homicides was excessive due to the "illegal" nature of the boatlift, their unique deficits in human/social capital, and the manner in which they were absorbed into disadvantaged communities (Portes and Stepick 1993).

Access to original homicide data in the Miami Police Department permits examination of detailed information on victim race/ethnicity/immigrant status and the circumstances surrounding a homicide incident (Martinez, Nielsen, and Lee 2003). Table 1 describes the individual homicide characteristics of six major racial/ethnic/immigrant groups in the city of Miami over the 1980s. Those are white (non-Hispanic), black (non-Hispanic), Latino (non-Mariel Hispanic), Haitians, Mariel Cubans, and Jamaicans. Comparing and contrasting Mariel homicide victimization to that of other racial/ethnic/immigrant groups also allows us to examine homicide motivations such as drug-related homicides, a type of violence not usually reported to national crime counting systems.

The descriptive statistics in Table 1 start by comparing the homicide-prone group or percentage of young adult homicide victims aged 18 to 24 years. The totals of young adult black and Jamaican homicide victims are 27.4 percent and 27.3 percent, respectively, compared to totals of white, Latino, and Mariel Cubans of 12.3 percent, 15.8 percent, and 12.9 percent, respectively. All groups are higher than the Haitian total of 5.6 percent. Overall, almost 19 percent of Miami homicide victims were in the young adult category, with Mariel immigrant percentage lower than the city average. The individual-level data also suggest that the Mariels were older and more likely to be male, and had been drinking alcohol at a higher level than the city average when they were killed.

Clearly, the Mariels were engaged in homicide events. A question of central importance, however, is whether there were important differences between them and others in terms of homicide incident characteristics. A simple comparison notes that Mariels were killed outdoors, over a drug-related circumstance, during a robbery, and in a multiple-victim killing at levels in line with the city of Miami average. The descriptive statistics are highlighted because the public imagination linked Mariels to wanton killings over outdoor drug markets with multiple gun victims (Portes and Stepick 1993). There was a gap between the Mariel immigrants and non-Mariels. The unauthorized newcomers were killed at *lower* levels of intimate homicides but *higher* levels of killings that started as an argument, escalated, and turned deadly in the course of a gun-related homicide. In other words, the Mariels were killed at slightly higher levels in routine homicides that escalated into lethal events, and usually by a fellow newcomer, not over violent street robbery or drug-related killings. Throughout the 1980s, Mariel Cubans were targeted by immigrant opponents, as well as by anti-immigrant legislation designed to prevent them from settling outside of Miami. Moreover, they were portrayed as hardened criminals in the popular media even though little data existed supporting the drug-crazed killer portrayed in movies such as *Scarface* (Martinez, Nielsen, and Lee 2003; Huntington 2004).

While not shown here, a more rigorous test using categorical data analysis indicated relatively few differences in the likelihood of the different types of homicide associated with victim or offender immigrant status[4] (Martinez, Nielsen, and Lee 2003). Similar to Table 1 and contrary to media images, escalation offenses comprised the largest categories for Mariel Cuban, African American, and (non-Mariel) Latino victims; for non-Latino white victims, robberies, followed by escalation offenses, were the two largest categories of motives. Among offenders, escalation offenses constituted the largest category of motives, particularly for Mariel Cubans, non-Latino whites, Latinos, and African Americans. Offender ethnicity had relatively few significant effects on homicide motives, with the most notable exception found for robbery incidents. The results indicate that the odds of being involved in robbery rather than escalation homicides are lower for Latino and Mariel Cuban offenders than for African American offenders. Overall, the Mariels were not overinvolved in the types of homicides (e.g., drugs, robberies) that might be consistent with the stigmatizing public perceptions that tend to generate the most public fear (Martinez, Nielsen, and Lee 2003).

San Antonio Drug/Gang Violence and the Border

Not surprisingly, the hysteria generated over Mariel led to a national backlash that foreshadowed the current rise of anti-immigrant angst and legislation targeting newcomers. The spark set off by the boatlift struck a chord among those concerned about the persistent Mexican immigration into the southwestern United States and the "Hispanization" of southern Florida propelled unsubstantiated claims that the "Cubanization of Miami" led to more drug-related crime, race riots, and political violence without empirical evidence to support these contentions (Huntington 2004). In post-Mariel Miami, immigration commentators expressed concern about the assimilation patterns in the "Cuban-led Hispanic city" and how the linguistic and ethnic makeup in the local population created a separate "cultural community and economy" that created a milieu in which assimilation and Americanization were both unnecessary and undesired. Some of these concerns were later expressed elsewhere when fear rose that the "Hispanization of the Southwest" would lead to a separate Quebec-style region (Huntington 2004). In short, contemporary anti-immigrant angst was energized by the 1980 Mariel boatlift, and events in Miami foreshadowed anxiety over the growing Mexican-origin (Latino) population across southwestern cities—Los Angeles, San Diego, and of course San Antonio in the 1990s.

The intensity of the boatlift contrasted with the longer, slower, and sustained crossing (legality aside) across the Rio Grande from Mexico into the southwestern United States. In absolute terms, the number of Mexican-origin individuals far exceeds the Cuban immigrant population, but until recently had yet to reach the proportions seen in Miami. That has changed. San Antonio has long been heavily Mexican-origin and is now a majority-Latino city. Unlike Miami, it is more than 300 years old and has a large native-born Latino population. As an old southwestern city, its ethnic makeup reflects border proximity and history of settlement.

As their numbers increased in San Antonio in the 1960s and 1970s, Mexican-origin Latinos in general and in the barrios specifically became more vocal about enduring social and economic problems such as segregation, poverty, and racism—issues that fueled the black civil rights movement in the 1950s (Montejano 2010). Unlike Cuban Miami, angst in the extremely poor urban barrios fueled concern about police brutality and annual gang wars. San Antonio has old public housing units anchoring the barrios or "courts" dating back to at least the days of the zoot-suit wearing "pachucos" of the 1930s and 1940s (Montejano 2010; Martinez, Stowell, and Cancino 2008). Places such as the Alazan-Apache and Villa Veramendi courts served as routine gang violence sites through the 1970s. To this day, many of these extremely poor areas have an enduring gang problem (Montejano 2010; Valdez 2007).

David Montejano (2010, 31) describes the competition for economic resources and status among youth cliques in the San Antonio barrios. Complementing our San Antonio Police Department (SAPD) homicide sources, Montejano writes how a clash would quickly turn frightening when a young male bumped into someone. Many would misinterpret an encounter, a shrug, or a chin, or assume a public slight, which potentially escalated a minor fight into a serious assault or worse. Of course, these were not encounters between unattached individuals. Barrio youths would turn to fellow group members to abet retaliation, feuds continued, cyclical violence persisted, and gang conflict reigned. Thus, economically disadvantaged barrio communities incubated varying degrees of gang warfare for decades (Montejano 2010; Valdez 2007).

Eventually urban renewal and political change transformed many of the urban corridor neighborhoods in the 1980s. The city population slowly abandoned downtown, moving outside the "Loop" and beyond the city limits. Even affirmative action in the SAPD changed police-community relations in the westside and southside barrios with the hiring of local Chicano Latinos (Montejano 2010). It is not surprising that when center-city residents left for the new suburbs, street gangs and accompanying violence eventually reemerged in the urban communities. Sociologist Avelardo Valdez (2007) argues that the resulting economic marginalization and social isolation of Latino barrios made San Antonio a nascent gang city throughout the 1980s. A decade later, San Antonio youth gangs avoided the "turf" warfare battles fought by an earlier generation and were engrossed in serious crimes and drug activity mimicking the youth violence/crack cocaine epidemic then spreading across the rest of urban America. Yet much as in other places across the Southwest, more Mexican immigrants crossed the Rio Grande in search of service-sector work, settled with coethnics around the old barrio areas, buffered the effects of violence, and even revitalized some isolated barrio communities (Montejano 2010; Nevins 2002). Although in a different way than in Miami, immigration also played a role in that transformation of San Antonio.

The renewed immigrant movement into border cities in the 1980s and 1990s drew attention, and much of it was not flattering or sympathetic (Huntington 2004). When commentators talk about immigration, immigrant Mexicans, and the border, they tend to characterize the border area as lawless, out of control, and hyperviolent (Huntington 2004). This dovetails with the claim by immigrant opponents that an influx of immigration not only increased homicides along the southwestern border but also heightened drug- or gang-related homicides in U.S.-Mexico border communities. Many border communities now advocate for stricter immigration policy as a mechanism for fighting local crime, and federal agencies encourage increased border security to thwart undocumented immigration, supposedly reducing local violent and property crimes (Nevins 2002).

Access to SAPD homicide data provides the opportunity to examine detailed information on victim race/ethnicity, homicide incident characteristics, and especially motivations drawn from case narratives (Martinez, Stowell, and Cancino 2008). Unlike Miami, the SAPD homicide unit did not regularly code nativity status. Undoubtedly, Mexican-origin Latinos are more likely to be first- or second-generation in San Antonio and were involved in homicide events. Clearly there were some differences between the largest ethnic group in San Antonio and others in terms of homicide incident characteristics. The issue is, again, whether the differences were significant in terms of border stereotypes or drug and gang killings.

In Table 2, the individual homicide characteristics in San Antonio over the 1990s are provided. The individual characteristics panel starts by comparing the homicide-prone group in the age 18 to 24 category. The total of young adult black homicide victims is highest (32.7 percent) and that of whites is lowest (23 percent), with Latinos in the middle (27.3 percent). Overall, 27 percent of San Antonio homicide victims were in the young adult category, with Latinos in line with the city average. The individual-level data also suggest that the Latino victims were more likely to be

TABLE 2
San Antonio Homicide Victim and Incident Characteristics, 1990–1999 ($N = 2,661$)

	White	Black	Latino	All
Individual				
% 18–24 yrs	23.5	32.7	27.3	27.1
% 25+ yrs	70.2	58.0	59.2	61.5
% male	68.9	79.7	83.4	79.5
% alcohol	24.8	19.9	27.1	25.1
Homicide incident				
% outdoor	38.1	43.3	42.7	41.4
% drug	9.9	20.3	10.5	12.0
% intimate	14.0	11.2	09.7	10.9
% gang	13.0	23.6	26.5	22.9
% escalation	26.4	25.3	29.3	27.7
% robbery	18.2	12.0	11.5	13.4
% gun	54.0	75.5	64.8	64.6

SOURCE: City of San Antonio Police Department homicide unit and Bexar County Medical Examiner's Office.

male and had been drinking alcohol at a slightly higher level than the city average when they were killed.

Another simple comparison reveals that Latinos were killed outdoors, over a drug-related circumstance, between intimates, during a robbery, and in gun-related killings at a level *in line with* or *lower than* city averages. If drug-motivated killings (e.g., fight over drug market, quality of drugs, etc.) were high among a group most likely to be influenced by immigration and if the border were out of control, it should be expected that Latino homicides would be higher than seen in the descriptive statistics. This serves as yet another reminder that while the public imagination linked border Latinos to killings over outdoor drug markets, and with gun victims, the levels are not as high as expected given border proximity and barrio concentration.

There was, however, a gap between the Latino and non-Latino gang homicides. The number of Latinos killed over a gang killing (e.g., retaliation) was slightly *higher* (27 percent) than the city average (23 percent). The same finding held for escalation homicides. In other words, Latinos were killed at a slightly higher level of gang-related retaliations and over the course of an argument than in the rest of the city. Throughout the 1990s, there was a great deal of concern over the crack cocaine epidemic, like now over border crime, but there is little evidence that those incidents were endemic in San Antonio. There was some evidence that Latino gang-related retaliation killings were higher than for whites and blacks. The issue is whether they were significantly higher in San Antonio, especially in immigrant areas. The answer to that question follows.

The Miami and San Antonio individual parallels are worth noting. Homicide victims are younger in San Antonio than in Miami (19 to 27 percent), which is probably a reflection of the older foreign-born population in the latter. Victims in both cities are heavily male, and almost a quarter had been drinking before they were killed. Most interesting are the findings reflected in the homicide incidents. Miami had a higher level of gun- and drug-related homicides than San Antonio but relatively similar levels of outdoor killings, intimate homicides, and killings in the course of a robbery. The most pronounced difference was in the percentage of gang-related homicides in each city—none in Miami and almost a quarter (23 percent) in San Antonio.

The following offers a detailed account of the Miami and San Antonio immigration/ homicide linkage. But it is guided by a series of questions raised in the previous section, requiring a disaggregation of the homicide data at the community/census tract level. Just exactly how does immigration impact Miami and San Antonio homicides over the 1980s and 1990s, respectively? What happens when we measure escalation, gang, and/or drug homicides? And what role did immigration play on drug/gang-related killings? A detailed examination of immigration (percentage foreign-born) on homicides across Miami and San Antonio neighborhoods at different time points reminds us that local settings matter and offers some answers to these questions.

Data and Methods

Data for our dependent variable, the number of *homicide victims*, was obtained from internal files stored in the city of Miami Police Department (MPD) and SAPD homicide investigation units. The MPD and SAPD data were also supplemented with records from the Miami-Dade County and Bexar County Medical Examiner's Offices. The reports were gathered by hand, copied directly from police department files written by the lead homicide investigators that provided detailed summaries of events preceding the killing, incident address, and other information not readily available in such sources as the FBI's Supplemental Homicide Reports (SHR). This included victim age, gender, and race or ethnic-specific (non-Latino white, non-Latino black, Hispanic, other) data.

The primary homicide motivation was constructed by the lead author and based on prior work (Martinez 2002).We start by directing attention to the most common homicide motivation: *escalation* homicide, a killing that typically starts as an argument over a routine matter and escalates into a lethal event. Given the concern over immigrants and gang violence and the stereotypes of immigrants and drug-related homicides, two other dependent variables were created. The number of *gang*-motivated homicides, usually gang retaliations, and the number of *drug-related* killings were also created after careful reading of the homicide narratives by the lead author. It is important to note again that access to original homicide data permitted the unique construction of these homicide measures and the consideration of local context in more detail. Given the 1980 Mariel boatlift, attention is directed to Miami homicide data over the 1980s. Because San Antonio drug/gang/ youth homicides peaked over the 1990s, homicide motivations over that decade are examined. The homicide incident was geocoded using the address of the killing and then aggregated using 1990 census data in Miami and 2000 census data in San Antonio at the tract level.

For the independent variables, we replicate the work of Sampson and Morenoff (2004) in Chicago. An index of *disadvantage* is created to represent economic disadvantage in urban neighborhoods. This composite indicator is composed of measures of the percentage of tract residents who live below the poverty line, the percentage of families that are headed by females and who have children under age 18, the percentage of households receiving public assistance, and the percentage of workers who are unemployed.

Other variables include *residential stability*, an index created by adding z-scores for percentage of housing units that are owner-occupied and percentage of persons who lived in the same house five years earlier. The *percentage of the population working in a professional occupation* is a proxy for affluence. Focusing on the pernicious effects of concentrated disadvantage is necessary, but it may obscure the potential protective effects of affluence. Scholars have noted that neighborhoods with relatively affluent residents, especially residents employed in professional or managerial jobs, increasingly buffer residents from violence (Morenoff and Sampson 1997; Sampson and Morenoff 2004). Also included is a proxy for informal social control, defined as the *relative presence of adults per child*. This indicator is created as the ratio of adults (aged 18 and older) to children (aged 17 and younger). Finally, the *percentage young male* variable represents the crime-prone age category by controlling for percentage of the population that is male and aged 18 to 34 years.

Finally, we employ an *immigration concentration index* that is consistent with prior research when analyzing structural characteristics and homicide (Sampson and Morenoff 2004). The index was created by adding z-scores for percentage of the population that is foreign-born and percentage of population that is Hispanic/Latino. According to common media stereotypes, we would expect areas with large concentrations of recent immigrants, particularly Mariels in the 1980s or border-crossers situated on or near the U.S.-Mexican border, to have higher levels of homicide because newcomers are thought to further disrupt already disorganized communities (Sampson and Bean 2006).

Results

How is the level of immigration related to violence? This question motivates the rest of this section. We start by examining the immigration index across Miami 1990 census tracts and begin with a discussion of the social and economic impacts shown in Table 3. However, it is important to make a few points. First, replicating the same set of control variables used by Sampson and Morenoff (2004) required some modification. The disadvantage index is highly correlated with the percentage professional (–.60). When both indicators are in the model, the variance inflation factor (VIF) value for disadvantage is just a bit over 3.0, which suggests issues of multicollinearity. So the measure of affluence was removed in the case of Miami.

TABLE 3
Negative Binomial Regressions for Homicides, Miami Census Tract, 1980–1989 ($N = 75$)

A. Homicide Types	Total (B)	Drug (B)	Escalation (B)
Intercept	−6.643°°°°	−7.378°°°°	−7.641°°°°
Disadvantage index	0.199°°°°	0.061	0.295°°°°
Residential stability	0.030	−0.158	0.061
% professional	N/A		
Immigrant concentration	−0.193°°°°	−0.385°°°°	−0.115
Adult/child ratio	0.071°°°°	0.056°°	0.073°°°
% young male	0.068°°	−0.017	0.051
B. Victim Ethnicity	Latino	White	Black
Intercept	−3.201°°°°	−6.854°°°°	−5.532°°°°
Disadvantage index	0.182°°	0.330°°°	0.088
Residential stability	−0.104	0.032	0.022
% professional	N/A		
Immigrant concentration	−0.495°°°°	−0.214°	−0.002
Adult/child ratio	0.045	0.050°°	0.110°°°°
% young male	−0.042	0.104	0.018

°$p < .10.$ °°$p < .05.$ °°°$p < .01.$ °°°°$p < .001.$

Also, unlike in San Antonio, the number of gang-related homicides was so low that we were unable to include that type of homicide motivation in the analysis. Throughout our discussion, we refer to the importance of local settings and the unique nature of these two Latino cities. These modifications demonstrate the importance of accessing original homicide data and exploring variations in community conditions, and how these influences are masked at the national level given that most macro-level studies are unable to examine detailed data.

We begin with a discussion of homicide and homicide motivations, as shown in Table 3, panel A. By definition, at least according to commentators and the popular media, we should expect more homicides in immigrant-heavy communities, and we should have more drug homicides in areas with high levels of immigration because that influence includes the much-maligned 1980 Mariel boatlift refugees. Contrary to stereotypes, however, immigration is negatively associated with total homicides and drug homicides. For example, the number of homicides and drug-related homicides were lower in Miami neighborhoods with increased levels of immigration.

A similar pattern is apparent in the examination of race/ethnic-specific homicides in panel B. The effect of the immigration concentration index was negative, meaning that higher levels of immigration predicted lower levels of Latino homicides in general and non-Latino white homicide victims to a lesser extent. Again, levels of Latino homicides (and white homicides) were significantly lower in communities with more

TABLE 4

Negative Binomial Regressions for Homicides, San Antonio Census Tract, 1990–1999
($N = 242$)

A. Homicide Types	Total (B)	Gang (B)	Drug (B)	Escalation (B)
Intercept	−5.990****	−8.981****	−7.358****	−7.223****
Disadvantage index	0.823****	0.011****	0.080****	0.517***
Residential stability	0.120**	0.027**	0.006*	0.035
% professional	−0.021**	−0.024***	−0.009	−0.040***
Immigrant concentration	0.074	−0.005**	−0.005	−0.006
Adult/child ratio	0.227****	−2.416**	−2.151	−0.021
% young male	−0.068****	0.008***	−0.004	−0.008

B. Victim Ethnicity	Latino	White	Black	
Intercept	−6.896****	−8.233****	−5.253****	
Disadvantage index	0.357***	0.252	0.453**	
Residential stability	0.145**	0.052	0.082	
% professional	−0.020**	−0.015	−0.025	
Immigrant concentration	0.004	−0.014**	−0.006	
Adult/child ratio	0.073**	0.101*	0.035	
% young male	−0.049**	−0.010	−0.069**	

*$p < .10$. **$p < .05$. ***$p < .01$. ****$p < .001$.

immigrants—including those in which the Mariel Cubans resided. These findings suggest that immigrant influx over the 1980s contributed to lower levels of Latino homicide, the group typically expected to display a homicide rise over the period.

Table 4 takes a close look at the factors that influence homicides in San Antonio's 242 census tracts. Four negative binomial regression models are presented for total, drug, gang and escalation homicide outcomes. Our results indicate that neighborhood disadvantage significantly influences all three types of homicide—total, gang, and drug. Neighborhoods with higher levels of disadvantage experience significantly more homicides, including those that are gang- and drug-related. Residential stability, percentage professional, adult to child ratio, and young male emerge (but the latter two in opposite directions) for total and gang homicides.

As for the main variable of interest—the immigration concentration index—an interesting pattern emerges by type of homicide in Table 4, panel A. The effect of immigration on homicides in the near-border city is negative or null and did not *increase* the overall number of San Antonio homicides or gang, drug, or escalation killings. In line with previous research showing that immigrant neighborhoods are inversely related to homicide, areas in San Antonio with more immigrants also have significantly *fewer* gang-related homicides (Martinez, Stowell, and Cancino 2008; Valdez 2007). This pattern suggests that heavily immigrant communities tend to buffer gang warfare and that areas with more immigrants have less lethal gang violence.

What about race/ethnic-specific homicides in a majority Latino city? This relationship also holds for race/ethnic-specific homicide counts in San Antonio. As demonstrated in panel B, controlling for a host of community-level structural and compositional characteristics, the immigration index has a null effect on total homicides but a negative effect on white, black, and Latino homicides. That is, race/ethnic-specific homicides were not significantly higher in immigrant-heavy areas. Overall, border proximity did matter, at least with respect to gang homicide and white homicide in San Antonio, but not in the anticipated direction. More immigrants meant fewer gang and non-Latino white homicides.

As noted in the beginning, this is a story of "local context with national pretensions" (Montejano 2010) that reflects the over-time growth of immigration. The geographical scope of the article started in Miami with the 1980 Mariel boatlift and moved to San Antonio neighborhoods in the 1990s. Miami was unique, reminding us that a large-scale exodus of undocumented "aliens" initially inundated the area, but the consequences of crime were not as alarming as portrayed in the media. The San Antonio reference is significant because a similar immigrant crime storyline played out in other border cities at the end of the last century across the southwestern United States. Both cities were offered because the local immigration and crime context was extreme in Miami but relatively moderate in San Antonio a decade later, prompting us to recall that immigration transformation does not necessarily unfold in a uniform manner. Still, the parallel cases did not produce evidence that more immigrants meant more homicide or that more neighborhood immigration meant more violence. These local immigration/crime stories were part of the national immigration transformation but also leave questions regarding how immigration may impact crime on a broader scale.

National-level studies

At the start of the new century, immigrants and Latinos moved in greater numbers across the country and established a presence across the nation (Crowley and Lichter 2009). Between 1980 and 2000, the percentage of the foreign-born U.S. population doubled, and while the immigrant population remained concentrated in traditional destinations in the southwestern United States, Chicago, New York City, and other East Coast cities, some of that group moved to areas outside of traditional regional settlement in search of work or fleeing turmoil (Crowley and Lichter 2009). By 2000, the United States had arguably become a more multiethnic, multicultural, multilingual society since the start of the previous century. Several factors contributed to the increase in the presence of Latinos in new destination areas—some tied to immigration and the search for employment, others linked to higher fertility rates among Latino families.

Fry (2008) notes that while the absolute numbers of immigrants were often small, states with large overall percentage increases were North Carolina, Arkansas, Georgia, Tennessee, South Carolina, Nevada, and Alabama. But again, the largest concentrations of Latinos and immigrants were still in the traditional Sunbelt states, especially California and Texas. California had the largest number of foreign-born residents (9.9 million), followed by New York (4.2 million), Texas (4.0 million), and Florida (3.5 million). When combined, 21.6 million foreign-born—or more than half (56 percent) of the total foreign-born population—lived in just these four states. California's foreign-born alone represented over one-fourth of all newcomers (Fry 2008). While immigrants moved across the country into new areas, they remained concentrated along the U.S.-Mexico border, along the Caribbean coastline, and of course in New York City and Chicago (Fry 2008).

To examine the national-level immigration and crime linkage, we chose to look at available public health homicide data because readily available crime data do not provide reliable group-specific outcomes (white, black, and Hispanic/Latino). Instead we employ county-level homicide data from the National Center for Health Statistics (NCHS) through the Centers for Disease Control and Prevention (CDC) to examine the relationship between immigration and race/ethnic-specific homicide victimization. A comment is necessary before proceeding. Unlike the data collected from the police departments, the NCHS data do not include detailed information on immigration status or information on the homicide motivations. Nor does the NCHS data allow census-tract-level exploration, thereby excluding community-level analysis. However, they provide homicide victim counts, in this case (1997 through 2001) including some victim demographic information (i.e., race, Hispanic/Latino origin, age, gender) gathered at the county level through local medical examiner's offices. Because homicides are extremely rare events, even at the county level, minimum county population and homicide count thresholds are placed to avoid skewed, unreliable, and unstable estimates. In keeping with the determinants used in the previous Miami and San Antonio analyses, the same set of control variables are included (Morenoff and Sampson 1997).

Recall the earlier discussion on large influxes of Latinos in new destination areas. Crowley and Lichter (2009) report places experiencing hyper-Latino growth had few negative economic consequences for local populations. Also, many of these new destinations experienced larger declines in crime than other nonmetropolitan areas, and comparatively low crime rates were found in destinations with large recent influxes of Latinos. If more Latinos meant more problems in new destinations areas, that should have been evident in this article. In the discussion to follow, we acknowledge the heightened growth in the Latino population since 1980, which has remained concentrated among traditional destination areas.

In the national-level analyses, we include *Latino concentration*, a variable controlling for the twenty-five largest U.S. counties by Latino population size (Fry 2008). We do so for several reasons. First, we create this dummy variable (1 = largest twenty-five Latino counties; else = 0), since about 60 percent of the nation's Latino population resides in these twenty-five counties. Second, this regional concentration corresponds with the national share of all Latino homicide victims in these areas (65 percent). Moreover, these counties also happen to be places with the largest Hispanic population increase and intensity since 2000. We expect this variable should control for the concentration of Latino in terms of both population and homicide.

TABLE 5
Negative Binomial Regressions for Homicides, U.S. Counties ($N = 311$)

	Total	White	Black	Latino
Intercept	−8.935°°°°	−9.163°°°°	−7.014°°°°	−8.771°°°°
Disadvantage index	0.148°°°°	0.014°	0.080°°°°	0.050°°°°
Residential stability	0.014	0.052	−0.023	0.016
% professional	0.000	−0.018°°°°	−0.012°°°	−0.014°°
Immigrant concentration	−0.005	−0.003°°	−0.006°°°	−0.008°°°°
Adult/child ratio	−1.873°°°°	−1.789°°°°	−2.362°°°°	−0.897
% young male	−0.010	−0.017	−0.018	0.027
Latino concentration	0.223 °	0.066	0.197°	0.291°°°°
N	311	311	311	311

NOTE: Latino population of five thousand and at least one Latino homicide over study period.
°$p < .10$. °°$p < .05$. °°°$p < .01$. °°°°$p < .001$.

The research of Crowley and Lichter (2009) focused on new hyper-Latino places highlighted in Fry's 2008 Pew Report. The Fry report lists the "25 largest counties with largest Hispanic growth," which are all in new destination counties. While these "new destination" counties are initially present in the full homicide data file, once any of the selection criteria are applied the total number of new destination counties in the sample drops to only *three or four* counties. Recall a minimum county population size of 100,000 residents and 5,000 Latinos or 5 percent of the county population is used to stabilize the results and avoid highly skewed rates. When the *sole* minimum population size cutoff is reduced to 1,000 Latinos only, we pick up 19 more of the new destination counties, but the total sample size grows from 311 to over 1,000 counties. This approach was not taken given the fact that most of these "new" counties did not experience *any* Latino homicides over the period under investigation, and many had only *one* Latino homicide over the *entire* five-year time period.

Turning to Table 5, a consistent picture emerges in the multivariate analysis regarding the association between social and economic indicators and levels of total homicide and race/ethnic-specific killings. First, the immigrant concentration index has a statistically significant and *negative* impact on white, black, and Latino homicide victimization. That is, even after holding constant an array of indicators associated with levels of homicide, including economic disadvantage, more immigration means lower levels of homicide victimization for all groups including Latinos. This finding resonates with others in this volume and with an emerging body of research literature that focuses on immigration and violence over time and identifies how increases in the foreign-born population contributed to the large reductions in violence observed (Stowell et al. 2009).

In Table 5, as expected, Latino regional concentration is positively associated with the total, black, and Latino homicide counts. Controlling for social and economic factors including the immigration index, counties where the Latino population is concentrated, relative to those where the population concentration is lower, have more homicides. Again, note that most of the so-called new destination counties were omitted once minimum population and homicide thresholds were imposed. It stands to reason that most Latino homicides are in counties where Latinos reside, not in new destination counties with a low Latino population base and no homicides. In sum, we find continued empirical support for the notion that greater economic disadvantage and fewer immigrants means more homicide, and that the negative immigration effect holds across the nation (Sampson and Bean 2006; Martinez, Stowell, and Cancino 2008).[5]

Conclusion

As their numbers increased in 2000 and Latinos became the largest ethnic minority group in the United States, concern rose about the Spanish-speaking newcomers. Some suggested that this group was different than others because they could not (or did not want to) assimilate and that they were different from earlier European immigrants in other important ways (Martinez 2002). Others were concerned that the latest newcomers were more violence-prone than previous immigrants (Huntington 2004). Undoubtedly the Mariel immigrants and the recent Mexican immigration waves were different from previous newcomers or traditional border crossers. They were singled out by many and blamed for a host of social and economic problems even in the absence of serious research studies substantiating that more immigrants meant more crime (Huntington 2004; Nevins 2002).

While it is important to acknowledge that this study supports the immigrant/immigration buffers violence literature, we sought to move beyond this finding by comparing San Antonio, as representative of emerging majority-Latino cities in the 1990s, and Miami, as an alternative immigrant, heavily Cuban-origin city in the 1980s. We reported results from comparative cases, different time points, types of homicide motivation, and individual/community/national levels, and even controlled for Latino regional concentration. The findings were clear and unequivocal—more immigrants did not necessarily mean more homicide, and that held across time and place.

We did find immigrant Mariels engaged in Miami escalation homicides more than other immigrant/racial/ethnic groups. And we did find that structural characteristics, especially economic disadvantage, are most important for understanding census-tract and county-level variations of violence. Yet we also found drug homicides were lower in Miami immigrant communities, and San Antonio Latino communities with a stronger professional group apparently thwarted gang homicides. The finding that more immigrants mean less violent crime also held at the national level across counties in 2000. These various contexts matter, as we see there is a high degree of consistency in the findings; they matter because immigration tends to have a robust negative or null effect—locally, nationally, and for many homicide types. The research settings for immigration histories are different, but we find no clear evidence that immigrant concentration is associated with higher levels of lethal violence. Taken together, this serves as another reminder that local conditions matter, are reflected in larger processes, and have national implications.

Although these findings hold across time and place, much remains the same. While conducting archival research and reading newspaper stories on the 1980 Mariel boatlift, we shook our heads at the familiarity of the settings that seem largely unchanged: linking immigrants to drug cartels, the need to connect to border gang warfare, "aliens" having "animal"-like qualities, and the "hordes" crossing the border and creating "national security" concerns—all of this still sounds familiar. More than familiar memories remain, however. For Miami and later San Antonio, the immigrant and Latino growth brought about social, economic, and political progress for local communities. In the first decade of the current century, crime in general and homicide specifically have dropped to historic lows, and those low homicide rates are evident in counties across the nation, even in places where immigrants landed in historic numbers in 1980, and even in places with a long history of gang warfare near the U.S.-Mexican border.

Just as important, from our perspective, has been that the national-level findings contradict public demand, and policy responses to reduce immigrant/immigration-related crime, which require large commitments of capital and resources, are out of step with the actual needs in many areas. These places might be directed to understand more completely the role of employment in professional occupations and how to encourage Latino movement into this specific sector of the economy. Nevertheless, it is clear that future research cannot ignore the patterns of immigrant and Latino movement into other communities; nor can it ignore the growth of the Latino "middle class" and its possible protective effect in other contexts.

National-level studies assume that local context matters little, while the limited number of comparative studies, including this one, suggest otherwise. Comparative approaches across places, including individual, city, and national-level studies, will yield more insight into the role of local context for understanding race/ethnicity, crime, and violence. Together, these efforts to understand immigration and crime can trace some part of their origins and findings to the story of the Mariels in Miami.

Notes

1. By 2000, 69 percent of the total Hispanic population resided in sixty-five counties, almost all of which were in the southwestern states, Chicago, Miami, and a handful of East Coast cities (Fry 2008).

2. See www.miamidade.gov/planzone/Library/research/MDC-Facts-2009.pdf.

3. Portes and Stepick (1993) estimated about 75 percent of the Mariel population settled in the greater Miami area after the 1980 census was taken. Most (61.1 percent) moved into the city of Miami. Thus, about 57,000 Mariels were in the city limits throughout the 1980s, or roughly 16 percent of the 1990 total city population (Portes and Stepick 1993).

4. Analyzing the Mariel data at the census tract level is not an option. Most were killed in or around coethnics, and it is almost impossible to retrieve Mariel-specific population estimates at the tract level.

5. We should note that including the Latino population concentration variable controls for population size. When it is omitted, the direction and significance of the other social and economic variables remain very similar.

References

Card, David. 1990. The impact of the Mariel boatlift on the Miami labor market. *Industrial and Labor Relations Review* 43:245–57.

Crowley, Martha, and Daniel T. Lichter. 2009. Social disorganization in new Latino destinations. *Rural Sociology* 74:573–604.

Fry, Richard. 2008. *Latino settlement in the new century*. Research Report. Washington, DC: Pew Hispanic Research Center.

Huntington, Samuel P. 2004. *Who are we? The challenges to America's national identity*. New York, NY: Simon & Schuster.

Martinez, Ramiro, Jr. 2002. *Latino Homicide: Immigration, community and violence*. New York, NY: Routledge.

Martinez, Ramiro, Jr., Amie L. Nielsen, and Matthew T. Lee. 2003. Reconsidering the Mariel legacy: Race/ethnicity, nativity and homicide motives. *Social Science Quarterly* 84:397–411.

Martinez, Ramiro, Jr., Jacob Stowell, and Jeff Cancino. 2008. A tale of two border cities: Community context, ethnicity, and homicide. *Social Science Quarterly* 89:1–16.

Montejano, David. 2010. *Quixote's soldiers: A local history of the Chicano movement, 1966–1981*. Austin: University of Texas Press.

Morenoff, Jeffrey, and Robert J. Sampson. 1997. Violent crime and the spatial dynamics of neighborhood. *Social Forces* 76:31–64.

Nevins, Joseph. 2002. *Operation gatekeeper: The rise of the "illegal alien" and the remaking of the U.S.-Mexico boundary*. New York, NY: Routledge.

Portes, Alejandro, and Alex Stepick. 1993. *City on the edge: The transformation of Miami*. Berkeley: University of California Press.

Sampson, Robert J., and Lydia Bean. 2006. Cultural mechanisms and killing fields: A revised theory of community-level racial inequality. In *The many colors of crime: Inequalities of race, ethnicity and crime in America*, eds. Ruth D. Peterson, Lauren Krivo, and John Hagan, 8–36. New York, NY: New York University Press.

Sampson, Robert J., and Jeffrey D. Morenoff. 2004. Spatial (dis)advantage and homicide in Chicago neighborhoods. In *Spatially integrated social science*, eds. Michael Goodchild and Donald Janelle, 145–70. New York, NY: Oxford University Press.

Stowell, Jacob I., Steven F. Messner, Kelly F. McGeever, and Lawrence E. Raffalovich. 2009. Immigration and the recent violent crime drop in the United States: A pooled, cross-sectional time series analysis of metropolitan areas. *Criminology* 47:889–928.

Valdez, Avelardo. 2007. *Mexican American girls and gang violence: Beyond risk*. New York, NY: Palgrave Macmillan.

Immigrants and Social Distance: Examining the Social Consequences of Immigration for Southern California Neighborhoods over Fifty Years

By
JOHN R. HIPP
and
ADAM BOESSEN

This project studied the effect of immigrant in-mobility on the trajectory of socioeconomic change in neighborhoods. The authors suggest that immigrant inflows may impact neighborhoods due to the consequences of residential mobility and the extent to which these new residents differ from the current residents. The authors use Southern California over a nearly 50-year period (1960 to 2007) as a case study to explore the short- and long- term impact of these changes. The authors find no evidence that immigrant inflow has negative consequences for home values, unemployment, or vacancies over this long period of time. Instead, the authors find that a novel measure they develop—a general measure of social distance—is much better at explaining the change in the economic conditions of these neighborhoods. Tracts with higher levels of social distance experienced a larger increase in the vacancy rate over the decade. The effect of social distance on home values changed over the study period: whereas social distance decreased home values during the 1960s, this completely reversed into a positive effect by the 2000s.

Keywords: immigrants; neighborhoods; social distance; home values; disorder; residential mobility

John R. Hipp is an associate professor in the Departments of Criminology, Law and Society and Sociology at the University of California, Irvine. His research interests focus on how neighborhoods change over time, how that change both affects and is affected by neighborhood crime, and the role networks and institutions play in that change. He approaches these questions using quantitative methods as well as social network analysis. He has published substantive work in such journals as American Sociological Review, Criminology, Social Forces, Social Problems, Mobilization, City & Community, Urban Studies, and Journal of Urban Affairs. He has published methodological work in such journals as Sociological Methodology, Psychological Methods, and Structural Equation Modeling.

Adam Boessen is a doctoral student in the Department of Criminology, Law and Society at the University of California, Irvine. His primary research interests include the community of context of crime, spatial analysis, social network analysis, and juvenile delinquency. His work uses quantitative methodologies to examine the relation between residential mobility and crime, the measurement and conceptualization of neighborhoods, and the impact of incarceration on juvenile offenders.

DOI: 10.1177/0002716211433180

Given the extensive influx of immigrants into the United States over the course of its history, it is natural to ask whether this influx has consequences for neighborhoods. Scholars have documented a clustering pattern in which immigrants tend to settle into particular neighborhoods, as well as the actual location of these clusters (Alba et al. 1995, 1999; Logan, Alba, and Zhang 2002; South, Crowder, and Chavez 2005a). However, the more general question is whether an immigrant influx has some deleterious consequences for a neighborhood over time, or actually has positive consequences. While assessing the quality of a neighborhood is not an easy task, scholars have suggested some features that make a neighborhood more desirable than others, including the physical characteristics, a lack of physical disorder, lower crime rates, and a robust economic environment (Adams 1992; Hipp 2009; Woldoff 2002). More desirable neighborhoods as a consequence of these features will usually also have higher land values (Gibbons and Machin 2003; Troy and Grove 2008), suggesting that higher land values are one potential proxy for the desirability of a neighborhood.

In what follows, we begin by discussing how immigrant inflow might matter for a neighborhood. Using the neighborhood literature as our lens, we argue that any residential inflow to a neighborhood potentially affects two dimensions: (1) general residential instability and (2) the demographic and cultural composition (what we will refer to as *social distance*) (Poole 1927). Immigrants, just as is the case with other migrants to a neighborhood, will affect a neighborhood through one of these two possible processes. Following that, we explore how the influx of immigrants and social distance within the neighborhood may have both short- and long-term consequences for neighborhoods. Whereas short-term effects can be considered those that occur over a few years, long-term effects are those that capture a less ephemeral change to the neighborhood, and thus extend 10 or 20 years. We then describe our study site of neighborhoods in Southern California over the 1960 to 2007 period and the data we use to explore these questions. After presenting the results, we close with a consideration of the implications of the findings.

The findings over this nearly 50-year period show minimal evidence that an immigrant influx has negative consequences for a neighborhood. There is little evidence that an increase in immigrants decreases home values, and such an influx actually *decreases* unemployment rates. There is some evidence that neighborhoods with more immigrants experience more vacancies over time, which may reflect preferences in response to such inflow. Importantly, we find that a novel measure of social distance is a much stronger predictor of the economic changes in these neighborhoods. It appears that general social distance among residents on several economic and demographic characteristics is more important for explaining neighborhood change than is immigrant inflow.

Considering Neighborhood Change: Residential Instability

The simple movement in and out of a neighborhood by households creates residential instability. This instability via residential mobility occurs regardless of whether the new household's residents moved within the same metropolitan region, moved from another metropolitan area within the same country, or immigrated from another country. Neighborhood scholars routinely focus on instability because it can have implications for the social ties among residents. For example, residents who have shared a longer period of time in the neighborhood have a greater likelihood of striking up a friendship (Caplow and Forman 1950; Festinger, Schachter, and Back 1950). In contrast, a person who has lived a long time in a neighborhood where the other housing units are experiencing constant turnover will be less likely to have established social ties with neighbors. Thus, network scholars refer to propinquity as the physical closeness of persons and how it increases the likelihood of interaction. And greater shared time in the neighborhood increases the chances of developing social ties (Hipp and Perrin 2009).

Social ties are important for numerous reasons. For example, such ties can increase residents' sense of attachment to and satisfaction with the neighborhood (Hipp and Perrin 2006; Kasarda and Janowitz 1974; Sampson 1988, 1991). These ties can also increase willingness to engage in activities that might improve the neighborhood (Freudenburg 1986; Sampson, Raudenbush, and Earls 1997) and reduce the desire to move out of the neighborhood at the first sign of trouble (Clark and Ledwith 2006; Parkes and Kearns 2003). In the criminology literature, this sense of cohesion and attachment is posited to reduce the level of crime in the neighborhood through residents' willingness to engage in informal social control (Sampson, Raudenbush, and Earls 1997; Silver and Miller 2004; Warner 2007). As a consequence, neighborhoods in which immigrants are entering may have higher levels of residential instability, or at least foster a perception that they have more residential instability.

On the other hand, residential mobility, at least in small doses, might also have positive implications for neighborhoods through its effect on social ties. That is, residential mobility does not necessarily extinguish the social ties that were formed through comembership in the neighborhood: in some instances, the ties will be maintained, and the consequence will be more spatially dispersed social networks for the residents of a neighborhood. Given that more dispersed social networks allow residents to gain resources from the larger community, what Albert Hunter (1995) termed public control, these ties may help in combating crime and disorder in the neighborhood. Thus, one mechanism through which immigration can affect neighborhoods is the extent to which it impacts the residential turnover of the neighborhood.

Who is moving in?

While residential mobility can increase the level of residential instability in a neighborhood, this mobility can also change the *composition* of the neighborhood if the new households moving in differ in some fashion from those already there. In such instances, the demographic composition of the neighborhood can change. To the extent that the new residents have *similar* demographic and compositional characteristics, mobility could potentially lead to increases in the ties among residents within the unit. On the other hand, there will be change if the new households differ from the existing ones. For example, if the new households moving in are of a different socioeconomic status—either higher or lower—this will change the level of economic resources in the neighborhood. If the new households moving in are at a different stage in the life course, this will change the demographic composition of the neighborhood. Or, if the new households moving in are young couples with children, and they are replacing elderly households with no children present, the characteristics of the neighborhood will be changed. Another important dimension in a number of societies is the skin color of the new residents moving in. To the extent that this differs between the new residents and those leaving, this will change the racial/ethnic composition of the neighborhood. Similarly, if the new residents are from a notably different culture compared to the residents currently living in the neighborhood, this will also change the culture of the neighborhood.

All of these differences between residents in various social categories create *social distance*, or what is sometimes referred to as "Blau-space" (McPherson and Ranger-Moore 1991; Mayhew et al. 1995). That is, the more social dimensions households within the neighborhood differ on, the more social distance between them (Hipp 2010a). One possible consequence of social distance is that it can affect the likelihood of social interaction among residents, which is important given the salience of networks to neighborhood research. Another possibility is that social distance can affect residents' *perceptions* about the neighborhood. As one example, Hipp (2010a) showed that social distance among the residents of micro-neighborhoods affected the level of perceived crime and disorder.

In instances in which the new residents differ from those leaving the neighborhood, there will be a change in the sociodemographic or cultural characteristics of the neighborhood. In the short term, the consequence will be a neighborhood with heterogeneity on whatever dimension is changing. For example, if the new residents have a considerably different socioeconomic status (SES), the level of economic inequality will increase in the neighborhood. As a second example, if the new residents differ on race/ethnicity, the level of racial/ethnic heterogeneity in the neighborhood will increase. These are short-term effects. If this pattern continues unabated, the result will be a transition of the neighborhood from one homogeneous state to another: in the first example, it might transition from a homogeneous neighborhood of low-income residents to one of all higher-income residents (as a consequence of gentrification). Or in the second example, it might transition from a homogeneous all-white neighborhood to one composed almost entirely of racial/ethnic minorities (as a consequence of white flight). During the period of change—whether this requires a few months or many years—there will be an increase in social distance. If this transition continues unabated, this will lead to a new equilibrium with low social distance.

The short-term state of the neighborhood of high heterogeneity is of much interest to neighborhood scholars. During this state, one might suspect that the neighborhood will become socially fractured. Social ties might be less likely to form, and thereby there will be few bridges across this social barrier. While these differences may create animosity between members of the different groups, this difference between the groups may in fact strengthen ties within the groups to further fissure the neighborhood. It is an open question whether such social distance could be bridged if the neighborhood were to remain at this level of heterogeneity rather than continuing to transition.

Social Distance and Immigration

Although immigrants moving into a neighborhood can affect the level of residential instability, arguably far more consequential is the fact that they will change the sociodemographic and cultural composition of the neighborhood. If immigrants differ on a number of dimensions from the current residents, immigrants will affect the level of social distance among residents, and social interaction across groups may be less likely. In some instances, the social distance can be quite notable. For example, social distance is created and maintained to the extent that immigrants come from a culture that has norms and values that differ from those of the dominant culture of the neighborhood. These cultural differences can lead to considerable social distance between the groups because they can limit social interaction and often bring about mistrust and misunderstandings. There can also be religious differences between the immigrants and the existing residents. Again, this can lead to social distance, especially to the extent that the differing religions lead to proscriptions that inhibit interaction for various reasons (Yang and Ebaugh 2001).

Language differences between immigrants and existing residents can also impact social distance. If the immigrants have limited ability to speak English (in the U.S. context), their ability to communicate with the existing population will be considerably reduced, leading to social distance between the groups. To the extent that immigrants communicate with one another in their native language, the existing population can also see this as an exclusionary tactic that further creates social distance and mistrust.

Social economic differences between immigrants and the existing residents may also be important if immigrants have limited access to neighborhoods and are forced to settle in a neighborhood whose residents have lower incomes than their own. Yet oftentimes this will not occur because households tend to move into neighborhoods that they can afford. Nonetheless, it is also possible that among the immigrants themselves there will be economic differences, which can lead to social distance (Beynon 1936). There may also be systematic differences in employment opportunities between the immigrating group and the established residents that lead to social distance (Aponte 1996; Light, Bernard, and Kim 1999).

Earlier we suggested that differences between residents might lead to social distance based on perceived differences due to skin color, and accordingly there can be differences in skin color between immigrants and the existing residents. Such racial/ethnic differences are important in many societies for restraining social interactions among residents and thereby lead to a sense of social distance on the part of immigrants (Portes 1984). While these differences might lead to outright racism and limitations on where immigrants can reside, they can also impact residents' perceptions of these new migrants and what effect they might have on neighborhood crime and disorder (Sampson and Raudenbush 2004).

Long-term consequences

Up to this point, we have been discussing the short-term consequences for a neighborhood when immigrants move in. Although in the short run this can lead to considerable social distance in the neighborhood, with further immigration a neighborhood will hit a point of maximum heterogeneity based on some particular dimension, at which point subsequent immigration will begin increasing homogeneity. In the long term, continued immigration would result in the neighborhood transitioning to a new equilibrium in which most of the residents are immigrants and therefore have little social distance among them.

As the immigrant presence in a neighborhood increases, the institutions that serve immigrants will also begin to emerge in the neighborhood. Thus, churches, restaurants, grocery stores, and other such amenities that cater particularly to the immigrant group will emerge. As these institutions proliferate, the neighborhood will transition into one with the sort of "institutional completeness" (Breton 1964) that allows immigrants to spend all of their time within the neighborhood. This allows immigrant residents to conduct all of their activities within the enclave (Wilson and Portes 1980).

Is there any reason to think that a high immigrant concentration would have negative consequences for the neighborhood in the long term? Although constructing such scenarios may seem somewhat farfetched, one argument is a compositional effect: immigrant residents are simply less committed to the neighborhood on average than the native population. This effect might occur if the immigrant group is unable to succeed economically within the U.S. economy. In this case, the economic resources in the neighborhood would dwindle, and this would affect the ability of the residents to maintain their residences through routine upkeep. Or this might occur if the immigrant members for some reason had a limited attachment to their neighborhood and therefore did not feel a commitment to maintaining it. Both of these scenarios seem rather unlikely, given that there is often a strong selection effect in which those migrating have particular skills that help them economically. Furthermore, immigrants often have a strong motivation to be successful and therefore will be just as, if not more, committed to fostering a desirable neighborhood as the native population. In some instances, certain immigrants might be quite economically *successful*, and the neighborhood would then be improved by such an influx.

Another possible scenario that might lead to negative consequences for the neighborhood would be if, in the name of institutional completeness, the immigrant neighborhood were successful in completely isolating itself from the larger community. This implies a neighborhood with a high degree of social interaction but very few social ties to the broader community. As we highlighted earlier, ties to the broader community may help to garner resources for the local area and are important for achieving what Albert Hunter (1995) referred to as public control. As such, isolation would have negative consequences for the neighborhood because its resources to address various neighborhood problems are contained only within the unit. Nonetheless, an important consequence of established immigrant communities is that such households have children, and those children grow up. These second-generation (or sometimes, 1.5-generation) members may then assimilate to varying degrees with the new country (Alba, Logan, and Stults 2000; Logan, Stults, and Farley 2004; South, Crowder, and Chavez 2005b). It is rarely the case that such later generations continue to live in the same neighborhoods and maintain the same level of isolation from the broader society as the first generation. As a consequence, in the long term we typically observe a transition of the neighborhood's degree of isolation. Accordingly, the mobility of the younger generation out of the neighborhood may be one mechanism that brings social ties from the broader community.

In fact, it is an open question of what happens to the neighborhood as the younger generation matures: one pattern commonly observed in immigrant neighborhoods of cities in the eastern United States was the exodus of the second generation to other locations. As a consequence, the neighborhood would eventually transition as the first generation aged out. Oftentimes that transition resulted in a new immigrant group moving into the neighborhood. In such instances, we might consider the relative constancy of the neighborhood in an abstract sense—it remains an immigrant neighborhood that is isolated from the larger community (and occasionally endures these transitions in which the demographic character of the neighborhood changes from one group as predominant to another group as predominant). Thus, the particulars of the change from one immigrant group to another are subsumed by the constancy of the immigrant nature of the population: indeed, this is precisely what was observed by the early Chicago School scholars (Shaw and McKay 1942).

In what follows, we first assess the effect of immigrant inflow on general residential instability. Following that, we explore immigrant influx by examining where immigrants are moving. We then view the relationship between immigrant influx and social distance in the neighborhood—using a general social distance measure, as well as assessing social distance along several dimensions separately. Finally, we ask what effect immigrant inflow has on the change in three measures of neighborhood quality and compare this effect with our more general measure of social distance.

Southern California as an Example Case

We focus on the Southern California region as an interesting case study because it is a major immigrant destination (Alba, Logan, and Stults 2000;

Logan, Alba, and Zhang 2002). It has experienced a large inflow of immigrants: in 1960, the average census tract in the region was 8.2 percent immigrant, and this increased slightly to 9.2 percent in 1970. However, a large burst has occurred since then, nearly doubling to 17.3 percent in 1980, rising to 25 percent in 1990, and reaching about 30 percent currently. We use census data for tracts over a nearly 50-year period (1960, 1970, 1980, 1990, 2000, 2007) from seven counties in Southern California (Imperial, Los Angeles, Orange, Riverside, San Bernardino, San Diego, and Ventura).[1] We use tracts given that their boundaries can be reconciled over this period of time. We placed all tract data into 2000 tract boundaries (there were 4,006 tracts with usable data in 2000). Given that we do not have information on one of our key measures in 1980 (new immigrants who arrived during that decade), we are limited to estimating models over four decades: (1) 1960–1970, (2) 1980–1990, (3) 1990–2000, and (4) 2000–2007.

Proxies for neighborhood desirability

Neighborhood quality is a difficult concept to measure, and therefore we constructed three different proxies. One measure that is sometimes used is the average home value in a neighborhood: to the extent that the desirability of neighborhoods is captured in land values, home values will be a reasonable proxy. Of course, home values represent both the quality of the housing as well as the land value. In principle, if one could control for the quality of the housing, then what remains is a measure of the value of the land (for examples, see Gibbons 2004; Gibbons and Machin 2003; Hipp, Tita, and Greenbaum 2009). Another way to account for the different types of housing across neighborhoods is to use longitudinal data: that is, by focusing on the *change* in the home values over a decade, one is implicitly controlling for the type of housing (since housing type typically does not change considerably over a decade), and therefore the observed changes are capturing changes in land values (and hence desirability of the neighborhood).[2] We adopt this latter approach here, as we constructed measures of the *average reported home value (logged)* at each decadal point. Studies have shown that although residents tend to overvalue their homes, there is little evidence of systematic overreporting or underreporting based on the characteristics of the neighborhood (Goodman and Ittner 1992; Kiel and Zabel 1999; Robins and West 1977).

Another characteristic of a desirable neighborhood is the ready presence of employment. Unemployment can cause economic hardship for residents and can increase the degree of loitering that occurs within a neighborhood (Gould, Weinberg, and Mustard 2002; Wang and Minor 2002). Unemployment can also foster an environment in which the adolescents in the neighborhood lack the role models who could inspire them to more vigorously pursue their own educational goals (Sampson and Wilson 1995). We therefore created a measure of the *unemployment rate* in the tract at each decade.

A measure that is sometimes used to capture the physical disorder of a neighborhood is the vacancy rate (Hipp 2010b; Taylor 1995). The presence of more vacant units itself can be a sign that the neighborhood is undesirable (given that in a desirable neighborhood the unit would be quickly filled). Neighborhoods with more vacant units also can be undesirable if these vacant units become blighted or are considered an eyesore. Such vacant units can also serve as breeding grounds for various criminal activities (Krivo and Peterson 1996; Stucky and Ottensmann 2009). We created a measure of the *percentage of vacant units* in the tract at each decadal point.

Other neighborhood measures

To capture short-term instability in the neighborhood, we created a measure of the *proportion of new households* during the decade. This is computed by using information on length of residence at the end of the decade: we sum the number of households that have lived in their unit 10 or fewer years, and divide this by the total number of households. We capture longer-term stability in the neighborhood with a measure of *residential stability* (the average length of residence of households in the tract).

To capture short-term change in the composition of the neighborhood, we created three measures. These measures focus on changes occurring for a neighborhood between two decades. The first measure captures *recent immigrant mobility* as the proportion of residents who are immigrants and moved in during the past 10 years. The second measure computes the degree of *racial/ethnic churning* over the decade (Pastor, Sadd, and Hipp 2001). We measured ethnic churning (EC) as

$$EC_k = \sqrt{\sum_i^J (G_{jt} - G_{jt-1})^2}, \tag{1}$$

where G represents the proportion of the population of ethnic group j out of J ethnic groups at time t (1990) and time $t-1$ (1980) in tract k. This gives a measure of the degree of racial/ethnic transformation that occurred in the tract during the decade: this is a sum of squares of differences, and we take the square root to return it approximately to the original metric (Hipp and Lakon 2010). If there is no change in the racial/ethnic composition, it will have a value of zero.

The third measure of change captures *general social distance* in the neighborhood. This novel measure builds on earlier work of Hipp (2010a) and takes into account social distance along seven dimensions: (1) elderly residents (aged 65 and above), (2) households with children, (3) young adults (aged 16 to 29), (4) education level (with at least a bachelor's degree), (5) owner/renter status, (6) language differences (those who speak English poorly), and (7) income inequality (Gini coefficient of household income). Although we would ideally account for the extent of social distance among all households in the tract, this would require household-level information on these characteristics (or at a minimum, cross-tabulations of all of these measures). We have only the marginal distributions for these seven measures. Therefore, we computed a Herfindahl index for each of the first six measures at a decadal point:

$$H_k = 1 - \sum_{j=1}^{J} G_j^2 \qquad (2)$$

where G_j is the proportion within dimension j and the proportion *not* within a dimension. This value is computed separately for each of the six dimensions (k) listed above. The exception is the Gini index, which already captures the degree of distance within a neighborhood (we divide this by 100 to place it in a similar metric). We then combine these K measures into a single measure of social distance:

$$SD = \frac{\sum_{k=1}^{K} H_k}{K} \qquad (3)$$

where K is the number of dimensions for the social distance measure (seven in this instance) and H_k is the Herfindahl value for the kth dimension of the K dimensions. Thus, this is computing the average Herfindahl value for each of the dimensions. We created this measure of social distance at each decadal point. To compute the degree of change in social distance during the decade, we simply subtracted the value at the beginning of the decade from the value at the end of the decade.[3]

To capture the demographic and racial/ethnic composition of the neighborhood, we created measures of the percentage *Asian*, percentage *Latino*, and percentage *African American* (with white and other races as the reference category). We measured *racial/ethnic heterogeneity* with a Herfindahl index (Gibbs and Martin 1962, 670) based on five racial/ethnic groupings (white, African American, Latino, Asian, and other races). To capture general social distance, we used our measures of *social distance* just described. We computed the *percentage immigrants* in the tract at each decadal point.

Spatial effects

Given that we are focusing on neighborhoods that are located in physical space, we accounted for this by creating spatially lagged variables of the outcome measures. That is, for each outcome variable, we also created a measure of the level of the variable in nearby tracts. We created this spatial lag measure by first creating a spatial weights matrix (W) based on a distance decay function capped at two miles. Thus, we assume that nearer tracts affect the focal tract more strongly, but tracts more than two miles away have no effect. We row-standardized this matrix. Therefore, we are capturing, for example, the average vacancy rate in tracts within two miles of the focal tract when accounting for the distance decay.

Analytic methods

We estimated a series of cross-lagged models. The general form of these models is

$$y_{t+1} = \beta_1 y_t + \beta_2 W y_t + \Gamma_2 \Delta X_2 + \Gamma_3 X_3 + \mu, \qquad (4)$$

where y is the outcome of interest (for example, logged home values) measured at the next time point $(t + 1)$, y_t is logged home values at the current time point, ΔX_{2t} is a matrix of the measures that change over the decade of interest (and their effects on the outcome are captured by the coefficients in the Γ_2 matrix), X_{3t} is a matrix of the remainder of the variables in the model measured at the current time point (and their effects on the outcome are captured by the coefficients in the Γ_3 matrix), and μ_t is a normally distributed error term. We estimated a separate equation for each decade to assess which model specification is robust over this period. Thus, we estimated models for (1) 1960–1970, (2) 1980–1990, (3) 1990–2000, and (4) 2000–2007.

Whereas we effectively measure our outcome variables as the change over the decade, several of our measures—percentage new residents, racial/ethnic churning, percentage new immigrants, and change in social distance—are also measured as change during the *same* decade. Thus, these measures capture relatively short-term change because the outcome and the predictors are within the same decade. On the other hand, average home values, percentage immigrants, racial composition, residential stability, vacant units, and the unemployment rate are measured at the *beginning* of the decade, and therefore are capturing midterm change, as they measure whether the level of a construct at the beginning of the decade is associated with the degree of change in the outcome during the following ten years. Finally, the variables of percentage immigrants and social distance measured at the beginning of the *previous* decade capture even longer-term change. Thus, these measures capture the effect at the beginning of a previous decade on the change in the outcome in the current decade, while also controlling for the short-term and midterm effects. The summary statistics for the variables are presented in Table 1.

Results

Neighborhood turnover

Our first question is whether an influx of immigrants directly increases the level of residential instability in a neighborhood. Thus, the outcome is the percentage of new residents in the tract during the current decade, and the results are presented in Table 2.[4] Our measure capturing the proportion of immigrants among the new residents is implicitly comparing the effect of new immigrants moving into the neighborhood to those moving from within the same country. We see weak, mixed evidence regarding the effect of an influx of immigrants on residential turnover. Whereas tracts experiencing an influx of immigrants during the 1980s experience less residential turnover, this effect is not significant in any of the other decades. We also assessed whether there is a bivariate relationship

TABLE 1
Summary Statistics for Variables in Models—Data for
Census Tracts in Seven Counties in Southern California

	1960		1970		1980		1990		2000		2007	
	Mean	SD	Mean	SD	Mean	SD	Mean	SD	Mean	SD	Mean	SD
Logged average home values	9.72	0.36	9.30	0.85	10.49	0.97	11.25	1.03	12.05	0.63	11.97	0.53
Spatial lag of logged average home values	9.75	0.29	9.35	0.72	10.59	0.70	11.35	0.82	12.10	0.46	11.38	0.62
Percentage immigrant	8.16	5.64	9.16	7.76	17.33	13.51	25.07	16.68	29.03	16.47	30.60	15.11
Social distance	0.34	0.03	0.37	0.03	0.37	0.03	0.38	0.03	0.37	0.04	0.33	0.04
Percentage African American	3.91	13.49	5.71	17.10	7.83	18.10	7.32	14.19	6.77	12.16	6.31	11.12
Percentage Latino	9.15	12.13	12.59	15.57	22.59	22.03	29.80	25.14	37.27	27.71	41.22	28.13
Percentage Asian					4.47	5.95	8.53	9.53	10.17	12.31	11.32	13.61
Racial/ethnic heterogeneity	19.01	16.03	23.69	16.28	35.12	16.17	42.98	16.34	47.22	16.87	47.24	16.98
Residential stability (average length of residence)	6.18	1.95	6.08	1.83	7.29	2.43	8.49	3.06	9.60	3.21	10.70	3.56
Percentage vacant units	6.29	4.55	7.76	11.37	6.53	7.53	6.56	7.21	5.17	7.03	6.74	7.68
Unemployment rate	5.83	3.02	6.11	2.64	6.30	3.31	6.96	4.30	7.65	5.24	7.71	4.13
Change measures												
Percentage new residents during decade			18.52	10.42	22.89	12.16	28.97	13.99	31.39	13.48	43.92	14.01
Racial/ethnic churning during decade			13.71	15.57	20.12	17.63	17.52	12.10	17.48	11.58	11.19	7.53
Percentage residents who immigrated in past 10 years			0.08	1.96			0.02	0.25	0.09	0.64	0.02	0.13
Change in social distance during decade			0.02	0.03	0.00	0.03	0.01	0.03	−0.01	0.02	−0.04	0.02

TABLE 2
Models Predicting the Percentage of New Residents in the Following Decade

	1960s	1980s	1990s	2000s
Average percentage new residents in past 10 years over study period	0.7403°°° (0.0122)	1.2642°°° (0.0120)	1.1320°°° (0.0135)	1.1055°°° (0.0160)
Percentage residents who immigrated in past 10 years	0.0219 (0.0600)	−3.1090°°° (0.5852)	0.1341 (0.2967)	−5.5965 (3.8156)
Change in average family income (absolute value change)	−14.9227°°° (0.6421)	−4.6045°°° (0.6851)	−1.2395 (0.7541)	−5.6177°°° (1.0552)
Racial/ethnic churning in past 10 years	−0.0092 (0.0115)	−0.1008°°° (0.0098)	−0.1182°°° (0.0132)	−0.0824°°° (0.0212)
Racial/ethnic churning squared in past 10 years	−0.0012°°° (0.0002)		0.0019°°° (0.0005)	
Change in social distance	68.03°°° (4.55)	37.38°°° (4.37)	60.02°°° (5.79)	15.74°° (7.33)
Change in social distance squared	−556.05°°° (58.16)	−175.81°° (81.57)		
Intercept	−15.11°°° (0.47)	−33.34°°° (0.58)	−32.09°°° (0.47)	−29.98°°° (0.59)
R-squared	.58	.77	.66	.57

NOTE: Standard errors in parentheses. N = 3,975 tracts. Units of analysis are census tracts in Southern California from 1960 to 2007.
°°$p < .05$. °°°$p < .01$.

between an influx of immigrants and the general level of residential turnover in a tract; even here, the correlation of these measures is quite low and always negative, with the values ranging from −.07 to just about 0. There is simply little evidence that an influx of immigrants increases the general level of instability in a neighborhood in Southern California over this 50-year period.

It is interesting to note that tracts undergoing a socioeconomic or racial/ethnic transformation actually experience *less* residential mobility than other tracts. Thus, a greater absolute value change in the average family income in the tract during the decade is actually associated with fewer new residents during that decade. This result is significant for three of the four decades. Likewise, a greater level of racial/ethnic churning is actually associated with fewer new residents in the tract during that decade (in the 1960s, this relationship was flat for low levels of ethnic churning, but negative at higher levels). Thus, racial/ethnic change in the composition of the neighborhood does not lead to higher levels of residential turnover. On the other hand, we do see that increases in our measure of overall social distance leads to increasing numbers of new residents: whereas it is a slowing positive effect in the two earlier decades, it is a linear positive effect in the two more recent decades.

Inflow of immigrants

We next ask where immigrants are *moving*. In these models, we predict which neighborhoods will experience an increase in immigrants. For these models, the outcome is the logit of the proportion of immigrants in the tract.[5] Unsurprisingly, immigrants are more likely to enter tracts that already had immigrants at the beginning of the decade, and those surrounded by tracts with more immigrants, as seen in Table 3. This spatial clustering conforms to prior research. There is a decelerating positive effect of the percentage immigrants at the beginning of the decade. The longer-term effect of the percentage immigrants in the tract at the beginning of the previous decade is quite mixed, suggesting that most of the effect is captured by the proportion of immigrants at the beginning of the decade. It is interesting to note that the spatial lagged effect of nearby tracts systematically weakens over the time period of the study, as the coefficients shrink from .0302 to .0107 to .0057 to .0026.

It is also the case that higher levels of general social distance and racial/ethnic distance increase immigrant inflow. Higher levels of racial/ethnic heterogeneity at the beginning of the decade increase the inflow of immigrants during the decade. Likewise, tracts with higher levels of general social distance at the beginning of the decade, and those experiencing an increase in general social distance during the decade, experience a larger inflow of immigrants. However, there is no long-term effect of social distance, as the effect of social distance at the beginning of the *previous* decade is actually negative.

Change in the components of neighborhood social distance

How is the influx of immigrants associated with the overall level of social distance in a neighborhood and social distance broken out by various dimensions? We assessed this by viewing the correlation between the measures of immigrant concentration and the various dimensions of social distance. In the top panel of Table 4, the first row shows that neighborhoods experiencing an increase in immigrants also experience a modest increase in general social distance in the neighborhood in four of the five decades (based on our unique measure). This correlation is about .13 during the 1960s and 2000s, about .07 in the 1970s and 1990s, and slightly negative during the 1980s. Viewing the separate dimensions, tracts that are experiencing an increase in immigrants also increase in social distance based on young adults (row 3), language (row 7), and modestly so for income inequality (row 8). However, such tracts simultaneously experience a decrease in social distance based on education (row 5) and elderly persons (row 2). Most notably, these tracts simultaneously experience more racial/ethnic change: although this correlation was just .07 during the 1960s, it was between .62 and .74 during the 1970s, 1980s, and 1990s.

Turning to a "snapshot" view, we see in the bottom panel of Table 4 that although neighborhoods with more immigrants had greater general social distance in the earlier years (row 10), this has reversed to a negative relationship in more

TABLE 3
Models Predicting Logit of Percentage Immigrants in the Following Decade

	1960s	1980s	1990s	2000s
Percentage immigrants at beginning of decade	0.0435°°° (0.0036)	0.0339°°° (0.0011)	0.0275°°° (0.0008)	0.0216°°° (0.0006)
Percentage immigrants at beginning of decade squared	−0.0007°°° (0.0001)	−0.0005°°° (0.0000)	−0.0004°°° (0.0000)	−0.0004°°° (0.0000)
Spatial lag of percentage immigrants at beginning of decade	0.0302°°° (0.0030)	0.0107°°° (0.0009)	0.0057°°° (0.0006)	0.0026°°° (0.0005)
Percentage immigrants at beginning of previous decade		−0.0108°°° (0.0012)	−0.0045°°° (0.0009)	0.0017°°° (0.0006)
Percentage immigrants at beginning of previous decade squared		0.0002°°° (0.0000)	0.0001°°° (0.0000)	−0.0001°°° (0.0000)
Change in social distance during decade	8.4°°° (2.3)	−2.0 (1.8)	−4.2°° (1.7)	−6.1°°° (1.2)
Social distance at beginning of decade	3.4°°° (0.4)	1.5°°° (0.2)	1.8°°° (0.2)	1.3°°° (0.2)
Social distance at beginning of previous decade		−0.5°°° (0.2)	−1.2°°° (0.2)	−1.0°°° (0.2)
Interaction: social distance at beginning of decade and change	−13.7°° (6.8)	17.3°°° (4.9)	19.2°°° (4.6)	21.1°°° (3.4)
Racial/ethnic heterogeneity	0.0019°° (0.0008)	0.0048°°° (0.0004)	0.0040°°° (0.0003)	0.0021°°° (0.0003)
R-squared	.49	.78	.83	.83

NOTE: Standard errors in parentheses. N = 3,434 tracts. Units of analysis are census tracts in Southern California from 1960 to 2007. All models control for the following variables at the beginning of the decade: percentage African American, percentage Latino, percentage Asian, residential stability (average length of residence), average home values (logged), spatial lag of average home values (logged), percentage vacant units, unemployment rate. They also include measures of percentage residents who are new in the past 10 years and its quadratic, and an intercept.
°°$p < .05$. °°°$p < .01$.

recent years. In breaking apart our social distance measure into various dimensions, we see that high-immigrant neighborhoods have higher levels of social distance for the presence of young adults, especially in more recent years (row 12), language (row 16), and income inequality (row 17). Interestingly, the association between immigrant neighborhoods and racial/ethnic heterogeneity (row 18) follows an expected pattern given the transition to ethnic enclaves as the strong positive relationship in earlier years vanished and became negative by the most recent time point. Given the large increase in the percentage immigrants in Southern California overall, this pattern is unsurprising, as immigrant

TABLE 4

Bivariate Correlations of Change in Immigrants with Various Measures of Social Distance for Various Years

	Bivariate correlation of change in percentage immigrants during decade with:					
	1960s	1970s	1980s	1990s	2000s	
1. Change in social distance (overall)	.13	.07	−.04	.06	.13	.07
2. Change in distance on aged 65 and up	.17	−.23	−.20	−.09	−.11	−.09
3. Change in distance on aged 16 to 29	.05	.13	.18	.11	.18	.13
4. Change in distance on presence of children	.17	−.06	−.02	−.02	.00	.02
5. Change in distance on education	−.18	−.18	−.18	−.14	−.07	−.15
6. Change in distance on owner/renter	.11	.03	−.02	.05	.03	.04
7. Change in distance on language		.34	.09	.22	.27	.23
8. Change in distance on income (inequality)	.27	.11	.01	.03	.08	.10
9. Ethnic churning	.07	.69	.74	.62	.30	.49

	Correlation of percent immigrants with:					
	1960	1970	1980	1990	2000	2007
10. Social distance (overall)	.18	.14	.07	−.16	−.16	−.23
11. Distance on aged 65 and up	.29	.30	−.02	−.28	−.34	−.28
12. Distance on aged 16 to 29	.03	.07	.24	.52	.53	.27
13. Distance on presence of children	.11	.07	−.03	.00	−.09	.07
14. Distance on education	−.05	−.13	−.32	−.46	−.45	−.41
15. Distance on owner/renter	.14	−.05	−.06	−.04	.06	.06
16. Distance on language		.33	.52	.31	.28	.00
17. Distance on income (inequality)	.36	.24	.29	.22	.26	.13
18. Distance on race/ethnicity (heterogeneity)	.33	.40	.40	.21	−.01	−.12

neighborhoods in recent years have become more homogeneous given the high proportion of immigrants. The explanation for the essentially zero correlation between language difference and percentage immigrants in the most recent year (row 16) is the same: this language distance effect is nonlinearly related to percentage immigrants. The pattern for social distance based on elderly persons has also changed over time (row 11): whereas high-immigrant neighborhoods had higher social distance based on elderly persons in 1960 and 1970, they had lower social distance for elderly persons since 1990. On the other hand, immigrant neighborhoods tend to have less social distance based on education, especially in more recent years (row 14). Thus, although immigrant enclaves tend to become racially homogeneous, we see here that such neighborhoods in Southern California nonetheless retain a high level of social distance when measured along certain other demographic dimensions.

Change in neighborhood home values

We next ask about the consequences of immigrants for the home values in the neighborhood—both in the short and long term. We see in Table 5 that a large influx of immigrants has quite weak effects on the simultaneous change in home

TABLE 5
Models Predicting Home Values in the Following Decade

	1960s	1980s	1990s	2000s
Percentage residents who immigrated in past 10 years	0.0030 (0.0058)	−1.1966°°° (0.4162)	0.0769 (0.1072)	−0.6622 (0.4522)
Percentage immigrants at beginning of decade	−0.0971°°° (0.0042)	0.0034°° (0.0015)	0.0120°°° (0.0013)	−0.0012 (0.0009)
Percentage immigrants at beginning of decade squared	0.0013°°° (0.0002)		−0.0002°°° (0.0000)	
Percentage immigrants at beginning of previous decade		−0.0103°°° (0.0017)	0.0040°° (0.0017)	0.0111°°° (0.0008)
Percentage immigrants at beginning of previous decade squared			0.0002°°° (0.0000)	
Change in social distance during decade	−29.54°°° (3.90)	9.03°° (3.69)	−11.44°°° (3.49)	14.91°°° (1.87)
Social distance at beginning of decade	−5.96°°° (0.63)	20.87°°° (3.83)	−19.11°°° (3.88)	0.70°° (0.33)
Social distance at beginning of decade squared		−28.07°°° (5.20)	23.77°°° (5.18)	
Social distance at beginning of previous decade		0.74°° (0.32)	21.52°°° (3.53)	0.23 (0.25)
Social distance at beginning of previous decade squared			−26.57°°° (4.86)	
Interaction: social distance at beginning of decade and change	77.31°°° (11.56)	−21.77°° (10.06)	28.06°°° (9.30)	−40.15°°° (5.08)
Racial/ethnic churning in past 10 years	−0.0112°°° (0.0014)	−0.0026°°° (0.0008)	−0.0101°°° (0.0008)	−0.0077°°° (0.0007)
Racial/ethnic churning in past 10 years squared	0.0002°°° (0.0000)			
R-squared	.75	.84	.67	.82

NOTE: Standard errors in parentheses. $N = 3,371$ tracts. Units of analysis are census tracts in Southern California from 1960 to 2007. All models control for the following variables at the beginning of the decade: percentage African American, percentage Latino, percentage Asian, racial/ethnic heterogeneity, residential stability (average length of residence), average home values (logged), spatial lag of average home values (logged), percentage vacant units. They also include measures of percentage residents who are new in the past 10 years and its quadratic, and an intercept.
°°$p < .05$. °°°$p < .01$.

values during the decade, as it reduced home values during the 1980s but was not significant in the other three decades. Likewise, the presence of more immigrants in the tract at the beginning of the decade showed mixed results, leading to lower home values during the 1960s, modestly higher home values during the 1980s and 1990s, and null effects during the 2000s. The long-term effects of immigrants is also mixed, as higher levels of immigrants at the beginning of the previous decade reduces home values during the 1980s, but increases them in the two more recent decades. Thus, there is little evidence that immigrants somehow reduce the desirability of the neighborhood, at least as measured by home values.

Turning to the other measures in these models predicting the change in home values, we see that social distance has important effects. We include measures of social distance at the beginning of the decade, the change during the decade, and their interaction. We also include measures of social distance at the beginning of the previous decade to capture more long-term effects. The findings for these social distance measures across these decades are quite strong, but they are also quite inconsistent. For example, the effects of concurrent change in social distance during the decade, as well as the effects of social distance at the beginning of the decade, flip signs over the four decades. Furthermore, the long-term effect of social distance is mixed over all waves.

Given the inconsistent findings for social distance over these decades, this may represent a structural change in this effect over our study period that is masked by our complicated model specification. Although we expect most of these processes we are testing here to have consistent effects, this need not necessarily always be the case. By estimating our equations separately over these four decades, we can assess the stability of the estimates over time. We assessed possible structural change for the social distance measure by simplifying the model in ancillary analyses: we excluded the simultaneous change in social distance measure and the measure from the prior decade. Indeed, these models tell a more consistent story, albeit one that illustrates a structural change over this period. We plot these results in Figures 1a through 1d for these four waves. For the 1960s, Figure 1a shows that a higher level of social distance at the beginning of the decade generally results in lower home values at the end of the decade. This is a nonlinear effect that becomes particularly pronounced at the highest levels of social distance. However, this effect has flattened considerably by the 1980s (Figure 1b), and now is clearly an inverted U shape. By the 1990s, the negative effect of social distance is gone, and now social distance shows a modest, though not significant, positive effect on home values at the end of the decade (Figure 1c). And in the most recent decade, the relationship has completely changed, and we now observe that higher levels of social distance at the beginning of the decade lead to *higher* home values at the end of the decade (Figure 1d). This effect is particularly pronounced at the highest levels of social distance. Thus, a structural change has occurred over this period in which social distance actually appears more desirable.

The effect of racial change is more consistent than is the effect of the more general measure of social distance. Higher levels of racial/ethnic churning are associated with home value decreases in all four decades. However, the effects of the racial/ethnic composition and racial/ethnic heterogeneity are mixed over the four decades.

Turning to the effect of residential stability, we see a longer-term effect. Neighborhoods with higher levels of residential stability at the beginning of the decade (average length of residence) experienced an increase in home values over the subsequent decade. It is interesting to note that this effect weakens over the study period and becomes nonsignificant by the most recent decade. On the other hand, short-term residential instability (percentage new residents in the

FIGURE 1A
Marginal Effect of Social Distance at Beginning of
Decade on Change in Home Values, 1960–1970

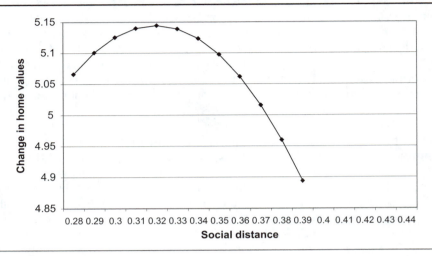

FIGURE 1B
Marginal Effect of Social Distance at Beginning of
Decade on Change in Home Values, 1980–1990

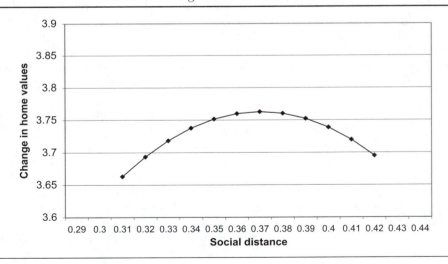

past 10 years) shows mixed effects on the change in home values—with a slowing positive effect in two decades, a slowing negative effect in another, and a U-shaped relationship in the other decade.

FIGURE 1C
Marginal Effect of Social Distance at Beginning of
Decade on Change in Home Values, 1990–2000

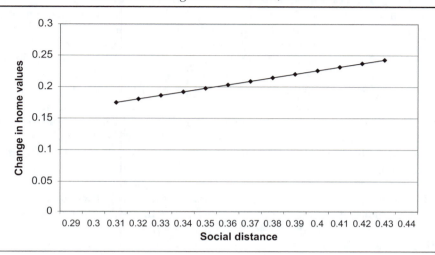

FIGURE 1D
Marginal Effect of Social Distance at Beginning of
Decade on Change in Home Values, 2000–2007

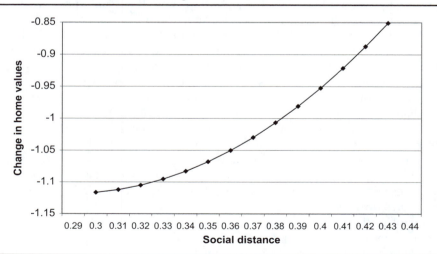

Change in neighborhood unemployment rates

We next view the effect of immigration on the unemployment rates of neighborhoods over time. In these models, displayed in Table 6, the short-term change in immigrants actually has a consistent *negative* effect on unemployment rates. A larger increase in immigrant inflow results in *lower* unemployment rates at the end of the decade. The longer-term effects of immigrants generally result in higher unemployment rates. In the two earlier decades, more immigrants at the beginning of the decade resulted in a higher unemployment rate by the end of the decade, and in the 1990s this positive effect only turned negative for tracts with very high concentrations of immigrants. In the most recent decade, although there is virtually no effect of the percentage immigrants at the beginning of the decade on the unemployment rate, there is a longer-term effect in which more immigrants in the prior decade reduce the unemployment rate at the most recent time point. To assess whether this lagged measure is capturing the effect of immigrants at the beginning of the decade, we estimated an ancillary model in which we excluded the previous decade measure, and we found that a higher percentage of immigrants at the beginning of the decade indeed reduces the unemployment rate by the end of the decade.

There was some evidence in these models that the level of social distance, and how it is changing, reduces unemployment rates. In the 1980s and 1990s it was tracts experiencing an *increase* in social distance that experienced falling unemployment rates. In addition, in those same two decades, tracts with higher levels of social distance at the beginning of the decade had lower unemployment rates by the end of the decade. Likewise, in the most recent decade, tracts with the highest levels of social distance at the beginning of the decade had the lowest levels of unemployment by the end of the decade. The long-term effect of social distance on the change in the unemployment rate in the subsequent decade is mixed: whereas this is a U-shaped relationship in the 1980s and a positive relationship in the 1990s, this appears to be a slowing negative relationship in the 2000s.

There is also evidence that racial/ethnic difference is positively related to the unemployment rate. Neighborhoods that experience more racial/ethnic churning during the decade generally experience increasing unemployment rates during the same decade. This effect was strongest in the 1980s, but has weakened in the two more recent decades. Whereas this concurrent racial/ethnic churning affects the change in unemployment during the decade, the evidence for the effect of racial/ethnic heterogeneity at the beginning of the decade is mixed. Thus, it is this racial/ethnic change, and not the level of heterogeneity, that appears important for the change in unemployment rates. There are racial composition effects, as neighborhoods with larger percentages of African Americans and Latinos have larger increases in unemployment rates, and neighborhoods with more Asians experience decreasing unemployment.

It appears that a turnover of residents in a neighborhood is associated with contemporaneous falling unemployment rates. Neighborhoods experiencing greater population turnover experienced a decrease in the unemployment rate in the three most recent decades (in the 1960s, this decrease was enjoyed only by neighborhoods with higher levels of population turnover given that this relationship had an inverted U shape). However, the level of residential stability at the beginning of the decade generally showed mixed effects on subsequent unemployment.

TABLE 6
Models Predicting the Unemployment Rate in the Following Decade

	1960s	1980s	1990s	2000s
Percentage residents who immigrated in past 10 years	-0.1°°° (0.0)	-0.6°° (0.2)	-0.5°°° (0.1)	-2.3°°° (0.5)
Percentage immigrants at beginning of decade	0.0267°°° (0.0072)	0.0297°°° (0.0080)	0.0125 (0.0107)	-0.0009 (0.0114)
Percentage immigrants at beginning of decade squared			-0.0010°°° (0.0003)	
Percentage immigrants at beginning of previous decade		-0.0005 (0.0094)	0.0188° (0.0103)	-0.0302°°° (0.0098)
Change in social distance during decade	8.6 (10.0)	-35.1°° (17.6)	-61.8°° (24.6)	25.6 (25.4)
Social distance at beginning of decade	-2.0 (1.8)	-13.8°°° (2.2)	-26.1°°° (3.5)	85.1°°° (31.4)
Social distance at beginning of decade squared				-132.3°°° (44.3)
Social distance at beginning of previous decade		-96.6°°° (19.2)	1.1 (2.7)	-73.8°° (33.0)
Social distance at beginning of previous decade squared		135.7°°° (26.8)		91.3°° (45.2)
Interaction: social distance at beginning of decade and change	-24.2 (29.4)	47.2 (48.4)	130.4°° (66.2)	-88.6 (70.5)
Racial/ethnic churning in past 10 years	0.0089°° (0.0041)	0.0718°°° (0.0057)	0.0245°°° (0.0068)	0.0402°°° (0.0115)
Racial/ethnic churning squared in past 10 years	0.0002°° (0.0001)	-0.0010°°° (0.0002)		-0.0018°°° (0.0007)
R-squared	.44	.68	.54	.31

NOTE: Standard errors in parentheses. $N = 3,425$ tracts. Units of analysis are census tracts in Southern California from 1960 to 2007. All models control for the following variables at the beginning of the decade: percentage African American, percentage Latino, percentage Asian, racial/ethnic heterogeneity, residential stability (average length of residence), percentage vacant units, unemployment rate, and the spatial lag of the unemployment rate. They also include measures of percentage residents who are new in the past 10 years and its quadratic, and an intercept.
°$p < .10$. °°$p < .05$. °°°$p < .01$.

Change in neighborhood vacancy rates

Finally, for the models with vacancy rates as an outcome, we see in Table 7 a short-term effect in which neighborhoods with influxes of immigrants experienced an increase in vacancy rates in three of the four decades. This is only a short-term effect, as the percentage of immigrants in a neighborhood at the beginning of a decade showed mixed effects (a positive effect on vacancies in the 1980s, but negative effects in the 1960s and 1990s). Likewise, there is no consistent long-term effect of immigrants at the beginning of one decade on the change in vacancy rates in the subsequent decade.

And whereas there is little evidence that racial/ethnic churning during the decade or heterogeneity at the beginning of the decade increases neighborhood vacancy rates (in fact, higher levels of racial/ethnic heterogeneity at the beginning of the decade actually appear to lead to decreases in the vacancy rate in the 1980s and 1990s), there are stronger effects for our general social distance measure. Neighborhoods with higher levels of general social distance at the beginning of the decade experience larger increases in vacancy rates over the subsequent decade during three of the decades (the exception is during the 1990s). At the same time, an increase in social distance led to the largest spike in vacancy rates for neighborhoods that began the decade with the *lowest* levels of social distance in these same three decades. Thus, increasing social distance seems to be particularly problematic for neighborhoods that previously were very homogeneous based on this general social distance measure. There is also evidence of a long-term effect, as neighborhoods with more social distance at the beginning of the *previous* decade experienced a larger increase in vacancy rates in the current decade.

General residential instability has only modest effects on the vacancy rate. During the two earlier decades, an increase in the general inflow of residents was accompanied by a decrease in the vacancy rate (though this effect weakened in the two most recent decades). However, there was no consistent effect of residential stability at the beginning of the decade on subsequent changes in vacancy rates.

Conclusion

This project has explored the consequences of immigrant influx into neighborhoods in the Southern California area over a 50-year period (1960–2007). Our findings indicate that there are few direct negative consequences of immigrant inflow on neighborhoods over time. There is no evidence that immigrant inflows reduce home values, or increase unemployment rates, over the long haul. We also found no evidence that the presence of more immigrants at the beginning of the decade leads to more vacancies by the end of the decade. The short-term influx of immigrants during the decade was actually associated with *lower* unemployment rates. We therefore have little evidence that immigrants somehow reduce the desirability of the neighborhood, at least as measured by home values or unemployment rates.

One important consequence of immigration for communities that we have suggested is the effect it has on social distance among residents. Taking into account the difference between residents based on such characteristics as age, the presence of children, educational attainment, ownership status, income, and language barriers proved to be an important measure of the differences that immigrant inflows bring to neighborhoods. General social distance appears to have consequences for neighborhoods. Higher levels of social distance appear to lead to more vacancies in neighborhoods over time. This was the case whether measuring simultaneous change in social distance during the decade, or the level of social distance at the beginning of the decade, or even when measuring it at the beginning of the previous decade. Our general measure of social distance, and not racial/ethnic difference, mattered for increasing vacancy levels, which

TABLE 7
Models Predicting the Percentage of Vacancies in the Following Decade

	1960s	1980s	1990s	2000s
Percentage residents who immigrated in past 10 years	1.1348°°° (0.0591)	−0.0709 (0.3038)	4.4345°°° (0.1749)	13.0863°°° (2.7734)
Percentage immigrants at beginning of decade	−0.0888°°° (0.0259)	0.0282°° (0.0111)	−0.0364°°° (0.0123)	0.0060 (0.0133)
Percentage immigrants at beginning of decade squared			−0.0008°°° (0.0003)	
Percentage immigrants at beginning of previous decade		0.0656°°° (0.0171)	−0.0109 (0.0122)	−0.0064 (0.0113)
Percentage immigrants at beginning of previous decade squared		−0.0018°°° (0.0006)		
Change in social distance during decade	150.6°°° (37.3)	36.1 (25.0)	−21.5 (31.8)	126.8°°° (27.2)
Social distance at beginning of decade	35.6°°° (6.0)	2.8 (3.1)	−15.0°°° (3.9)	−9.9°° (4.8)
Social distance at beginning of previous decade		10.0°°° (2.5)	7.5°° (3.1)	7.6°° (3.7)
Interaction: social distance at beginning of decade and change	−369.3°°° (109.0)	−74.9 (68.2)	36.6 (84.9)	−341.8°°° (75.1)
Racial/ethnic churning in past 10 years	−0.0066 (0.0084)	0.0035 (0.0061)	−0.0125 (0.0078)	−0.0152 (0.0112)
R-squared	.22	.64	.58	.52

NOTE: Standard errors in parentheses. N = 3,417 tracts. Units of analysis are census tracts in Southern California from 1960 to 2007. All models control for the following variables at the beginning of the decade: percentage African American, percentage Latino, percentage Asian, racial/ethnic heterogeneity, residential stability (average length of residence), percentage vacant units, spatial lag of percentage vacant units, average home values (logged), spatial lag of average home values (logged). They also include measures of percentage residents who are new in the past 10 years and an intercept.
°°$p < .05.$ °°°$p < .01.$

may represent short-term desirability of such neighborhoods. On the other hand, increasing levels of social distance actually led to lower unemployment rates. The effect of social distance on changes in home values was particularly striking, as it changed over the study period: whereas social distance decreased home values during the 1960s, this completely reversed into a positive effect by the 2000s. This suggests a structural change in the desirability of homes based on the presence of general social distance. This is an interesting finding and may reflect changes in housing preferences over recent decades that may accompany the move towards more New Urbanism ideals. Although we cannot be certain of this, this finding is certainly suggestive of such a possibility. It was notable that no such change over time was observed for the effect of social distance on unemployment or vacancy rates, consistent with a possible structural change in preferences.

Although immigrant inflow can create differences between residents based on race/ethnicity, we demonstrated that immigrant inflow created greater levels of social distance in neighborhoods based on other demographic dimensions. The effects of racial/ethnic difference in our models were generally weaker than the effects of the general measure of social distance. Racial/ethnic heterogeneity did not appear to have negative consequences in these models that controlled for the general level of social distance. Only short-term racial/ethnic churning had occasional consequences for neighborhoods: neighborhoods with more racial/ethnic churning during the decade simultaneously experienced increasing unemployment rates and falling home values. When we explored what aspects of social distance had the most salience for immigrant neighborhoods, language diversity, educational levels, and the proportion of young adults appeared to be the strongest drivers of social distance. And whereas inequality and race/ethnicity were also important for social distance, we did not see demographic shifts in regards to the presence of children. Taken as a whole, our results from a policy perspective might suggest that policies targeted at improving access to education may be particularly crucial for immigrants as one of the best ways to impact the consequences of social distance.

The importance of social distance highlights that it is not appropriate to treat "immigrants" as a unitary concept. The motivations for migration have consequences for the characteristics of immigrants, which can then lead to more or less social distance between them and those currently residing in the neighborhood of entry. For example, immigrants of high SES in the origination country who migrated in response to political upheaval (examples include Cubans and Iranians leaving those countries after political change) likely have a much different economic background than migrant farm workers who have immigrated from Central Mexico for economic reasons. Furthermore, there can be racial/ethnic differences between various immigrant groups, language differences in ability to speak English, gender differences of who is coming in, and even age and family structure. For all of these reasons, there is little reason to expect a unitary effect of "immigrants" on neighborhoods. Due to space constraints, we did not split immigrants into separate groups based on country of origin, but it may be important to take into account these characteristics in future research.

Although arguably an entirely separate project, another potential limitation to our study is that our models do not account for residents leaving the neighborhood. One important avenue for future research is to simultaneously examine how residents and immigrants leaving the neighborhood impact its social distance. For example, residential out-mobility may create less social distance between residents. Alternatively, neighborhood social distance can change simply as residents age in place (e.g., the aging of children of the area). Nonetheless, the reasons why new residents are moving into an area do not necessarily reflect the same reasons why residents might leave an area. Accordingly, the only potentially negative consequence of immigrants on neighborhoods was an increase in the vacancy rate. It seems likely that this reflects an exodus effect in response to immigrant influx, as in other models we found that a higher vacancy rate at the beginning of the decade actually reduced the likelihood of immigrant inflow. These results suggest that immigrants are moving into neighborhoods with few vacancies and therefore to areas that likely have higher population density.

Perhaps the most important conclusion for this study is that we found little evidence for immigration having deleterious consequences for neighborhoods in the Southern California region over a nearly 50-year period. Yet this seems reasonable given that immigration oftentimes represents a selection effect in which those who have more skills and more economic resources are more likely to immigrate. Nonetheless, it is worth emphasizing this finding given that it was robust over such a long period of time. We also found that an important determinant of change in neighborhood desirability is the level of *social distance*. Furthermore, we have emphasized that it is not enough to simply measure social distance based on race/ethnicity, or even income inequality. Our more general measure of social distance along a number of dimensions showed much stronger effects.

Notes

1. We refer to the last time point as 2007, as this is the midpoint of the five-year aggregated American Community Survey data that is used (aggregated over the 2005 to 2009 period). Also, we do not have tract data for Imperial and Ventura counties in 1960: given that these are both relatively small counties in population size in general, and were very small in 1960, this is of minimal consequence.

2. Of course, this will not be the case in a neighborhood undergoing gentrification, as a characteristic of such neighborhoods is that the residents who purchase such homes are typically improving them considerably. Nonetheless, such neighborhoods are the exception to the general pattern, and were not very common during the period our study covers.

3. For example, if a tract had 25 percent elderly residents (it would, by definition, have 75 percent nonelderly), H_1 would therefore have a value of .375 $[1-(.25^2 + .75^2)]$; if 50 percent of households had children, then H_2 would have a value of .5 $[1-(.5^2 + .5^2)]$; if 0 percent of residents were young adults (aged 16 to 29), then H_3 would have a value of 0 $[1-(.0^2 + 1^2)]$, and so forth. The Gini is computed on the binned income data using a software program developed by Francois Nielsen (http://www.unc.edu/~nielsen/data/data/htm), and is divided by 100 to place in the same metric. The mean of these seven individual H values provides the value of SD (total social distance). As an example for how social distance changes, this hypothetical tract might go from 25 percent elderly residents to 50 percent at the next time point, while the other six H values remained constant: given that H_1 increases from .375 to .5, the value of SD would increase .0179 (since this .125 increase would be divided by 7 to give the average increase across these seven dimensions). Note that, however, if the tract went from 25 percent elderly to 75 percent elderly, the level of social distance on this dimension would remain constant (since the percentage nonelderly has gone from 75 to 25 percent). Thus, a neighborhood with a high score on social distance will have residents who are more different based on our set of dimensions.

4. These equations include a measure of the average percentage new residents in the tract over the four decades. By doing so, we are capturing the amount of residential turnover in a decade relative to the *normal* amount of residential turnover in a tract. This averaged variable captures unobserved characteristics of the tract that are not in our model.

5. The logit is calculated as $\ln[P/(1 + P)]$, where P is the proportion of immigrants in the tract. This approach accounts for the ceiling effect as the proportion in the tract heads toward 1.

References

Adams, Richard E. 1992. Is happiness a home in the suburbs? The influence of urban versus suburban neighborhoods on psychological health. *Journal of Community Psychology* 20:353–71.

Alba, Richard D., Nancy A. Denton, Shu-yin J. Leung, and John R. Logan. 1995. Neighborhood change under conditions of mass immigration: The New York City region, 1970–1990. *International Migration Review* 29:625–56.

Alba, Richard D., John R. Logan, and Brian J. Stults. 2000. The changing neighborhood contexts of the immigrant metropolis. *Social Forces* 79:587–621.

Alba, Richard D., John R. Logan, Brian J. Stults, Gilbert Marzan, and Wenquan Zhang. 1999. Immigrant groups in the suburbs: A reexamination of suburbanization and spatial assimilation. *American Sociological Review* 64:446–60.

Aponte, Robert. 1996. Urban employment and the mismatch dilemma: Accounting for the immigration exception. *Social Problems* 43:268–83.

Beynon, Erdmann Doane. 1936. Social mobility and social distance among Hungarian immigrants in Detroit. *American Journal of Sociology* 41:423–34.

Breton, Raymond. 1964. Institutional completeness of ethnic communities and the personal relations of immigrants. *American Journal of Sociology* 70:193–205.

Caplow, Theodore, and Robert Forman. 1950. Neighborhood interaction in a homogeneous community. *American Sociological Review* 15:357–66.

Clark, William A. V., and Valerie Ledwith. 2006. Mobility, housing stress, and neighborhood contexts: Evidence from Los Angeles. *Environment and Planning A* 38:1077–93.

Festinger, Leon, Stanley Schachter, and Kurt Back. 1950. *Social pressures in informal groups*. Stanford, CA: Stanford University Press.

Freudenburg, William R. 1986. The density of acquaintanceship: An overlooked variable in community research? *American Journal of Sociology* 92:27–63.

Gibbons, Steve. 2004. The costs of urban property crime. *The Economic Journal* 114:F441–F463.

Gibbons, Steve, and Stephen Machin. 2003. Valuing English primary schools. *Journal of Urban Economics* 53:197–219.

Gibbs, Jack P., and Walter T. Martin. 1962. Urbanization, technology, and the division of labor: International patterns. *American Sociological Review* 27:667–77.

Goodman, John L., and John B. Ittner. 1992. The accuracy of home owners' estimates of house value. *Journal of Housing Economics* 2:339–57.

Gould, Eric D., Bruce A. Weinberg, and David B. Mustard. 2002. Crime rates and local labor market opportunities in the United States: 1979–1997. *Review of Economics and Statistics* 84:45–61.

Hipp, John R. 2009. Specifying the determinants of neighborhood satisfaction: A robust assessment in 24 metropolitan areas over four time points. *Social Forces* 88:395–424.

Hipp, John R. 2010a. Micro-structure in micro-neighborhoods: A new social distance measure, and its effect on individual and aggregated perceptions of crime and disorder. *Social Networks* 32:148–59.

Hipp, John R. 2010b. Violent crime, mobility decisions, and neighborhood racial/ethnic transition. *Social Problems* 58:410–32.

Hipp, John R., and Cynthia M. Lakon. 2010. Social disparities in health: Disproportionate toxicity proximity in minority communities over a decade. *Health & Place* 16:674–83.

Hipp, John R., and Andrew J. Perrin. 2006. Nested loyalties: Local networks' effects on neighborhood and community cohesion. *Urban Studies* 43:2503–23.

Hipp, John R., and Andrew J. Perrin. 2009. The simultaneous effect of social distance and physical distance on the formation of neighborhood ties. *City & Community* 8:5–25.

Hipp, John R., George E. Tita, and Robert T. Greenbaum. 2009. Drive-bys and trade-ups: The impact of crime on residential mobility patterns in Los Angeles. *Social Forces* 87:1777–1812.

Hunter, Albert. 1995. Private, parochial and public social orders: The problem of crime and incivility in urban communities. In *Metropolis: Center and symbol of our times*, ed. P. Kasinitz, 204-25. New York, NY: New York University.

Kasarda, John D., and Morris Janowitz. 1974. Community attachment in mass society. *American Sociological Review* 39:328–39.

Kiel, Katherine A., and Jeffrey E. Zabel. 1999. The accuracy of owner-provided house values: The 1978–1991 American Housing Survey. *Real Estate Economics* 27:263–98.

Krivo, Lauren J., and Ruth D. Peterson. 1996. Extremely disadvantaged neighborhoods and urban crime. *Social Forces* 75:619–48.

Light, Ivan, Richard B. Bernard, and Rebecca Kim. 1999. Immigrant incorporation in the garment industry of Los Angeles. *International Migration Review* 33:5–25.

Logan, John R., Richard D. Alba, and Wenquan Zhang. 2002. Immigrant enclaves and ethnic communities in New York and Los Angeles. *American Sociological Review* 67:299–322.

Logan, John R., Brian J. Stults, and Reynolds Farley. 2004. Segregation of minorities in the metropolis: Two decades of change. *Demography* 41:1–22.

Mayhew, Bruce H., J. Miller McPherson, Thomas Rotolo, and Lynn Smith-Lovin. 1995. Sex and race homogeneity in naturally occurring groups. *Social Forces* 74:15–52.

McPherson, J. Miller, and James R. Ranger-Moore. 1991. Evolution on a dancing landscape: Organizations and networks in dynamic Blau space. *Social Forces* 70:19–42.

Parkes, Alison, and Ade Kearns. 2003. Residential perceptions and housing mobility in Scotland: An analysis of the Longitudinal Scottish House Condition Survey 1991–96. *Housing Studies* 18:673–701.

Pastor, Manuel, Jr., Jim Sadd, and John Hipp. 2001. Which came first? Toxic facilities, minority move-in, and environmental justice. *Journal of Urban Affairs* 23:1–21.

Poole, Willard C., Jr. 1927. Distance in sociology. *American Journal of Sociology* 33:99–104.

Portes, Alejandro. 1984. The rise of ethnicity: Determinants of ethnic perceptions among Cuban exiles in Miami. *American Sociological Review* 49:383–97.

Robins, Philip K., and Richard W. West. 1977. Measurement errors in the estimation of home value. *Journal of the American Statistical Association* 72:290–94.

Sampson, Robert J. 1988. Local friendship ties and community attachment in mass society: A multilevel systemic model. *American Sociological Review* 53:766–79.

Sampson, Robert J. 1991. Linking the micro- and macrolevel dimensions of community social organization. *Social Forces* 70:43-64.

Sampson, Robert J., and Stephen W. Raudenbush. 2004. Seeing disorder: Neighborhood stigma and the social construction of broken windows. *Social Psychology Quarterly* 67:319–42.

Sampson, Robert J., Stephen W. Raudenbush, and Felton Earls. 1997. Neighborhoods and violent crime: A multilevel study of collective efficacy. *Science* 277:918–24.

Sampson, Robert J., and William Julius Wilson. 1995. Toward a theory of race, crime, and urban inequality. In *Crime and inequality*, eds. J. Hagan and R. D. Peterson, 37–54. Stanford, CA: Stanford University Press.

Shaw, Clifford, and Henry D. McKay. 1942. *Juvenile delinquency and urban areas*. Chicago, IL: University of Chicago Press.

Silver, Eric, and Lisa L. Miller. 2004. Sources of informal social control in Chicago neighborhoods. *Criminology* 42:551–84.

South, Scott J., Kyle D. Crowder, and Erick Chavez. 2005a. Geographic mobility and spatial assimilation among US Latino immigrants. *International Migration Review* 39:577–607.

South, Scott J., Kyle D. Crowder, and Erick Chavez. 2005b. Migration and spatial assimilation among US Latinos: Classical versus segmented trajectories. *Demography* 42:497–521.

Stucky, Thomas D., and John R. Ottensmann. 2009. Land use and violent crime. *Criminology* 47:1223–64.

Taylor, Ralph B. 1995. The impact of crime on communities. *The Annals of the American Academy of Political and Social Science* 539:28–45.

Troy, Austin, and J. Morgan Grove. 2008. Property values, parks, and crime: A hedonic analysis in Baltimore, MD. *Landscape and Urban Planning* 87:233–45.

Wang, Fahui, and W. William Minor. 2002. Where the jobs are: Employment access and crime patterns in Cleveland. *Annals of the Association of American Geographers* 92:435–50.

Warner, Barbara D. 2007. Directly intervene or call the authorities? A study of forms of neighborhood social control within a social disorganization framework. *Criminology* 45:99.

Wilson, Kenneth L., and Alejandro Portes. 1980. Immigrant enclaves: An analysis of the labor market experiences of Cubans in Miami. *American Journal of Sociology* 8 6:295–319.

Woldoff, Rachael A. 2002. The effects of local stressors on neighborhood attachment. *Social Forces* 81:87–116.

Yang, Fenggang, and Helen Rose Ebaugh. 2001. Transformations in new immigrant religions and their global implications. *American Sociological Review* 66:269–88.

The Limits of Spatial Assimilation for Immigrants' Full Integration: Emerging Evidence from African Immigrants in Boston and Dublin

By
ZOUA M. VANG

Residential integration with the dominant native-born population is believed to be a crucial stage in immigrants' overall assimilation process. It is argued that without residential integration it would be difficult, if not impossible, for immigrants to achieve full incorporation into the host society. This article compares the sociospatial experiences of African immigrants in the United States and Ireland. Results show that African immigrants in Ireland have achieved spatial integration with Irish nationals, while their counterparts in the United States remain spatially separated from white Americans. The extent to which African immigrants' integration in Ireland can produce other forms of assimilation is questionable, however. Likewise, despite being segregated from whites, African immigrants in the United States have made some modest spatial gains that may facilitate their integration. The cross-national comparison draws into question the generally accepted notion that residential integration is an important intermediary substage in the assimilation process.

Keywords: residential segregation; African immigrants; Ireland; race; inequality; assimilation; neighborhoods

Spatial assimilation, the process whereby immigrants come to share the same residential neighborhoods as members of the dominant native-born group, has been used extensively as a benchmark to gauge immigrant integration. In most traditional and new immigrant-receiving countries, the dominant native-born group is middle-class whites. Why is it important for immigrants to live in the same neighborhoods as dominant group members? The conventional wisdom is that segregation impedes immigrant integration. At a very basic

Zoua M. Vang is an assistant professor of sociology at McGill University. Her primary research interests involve immigration and immigrant adaptation in new (Ireland) and traditional (U.S., Canada) immigrant-receiving countries. Her current research focuses on neighborhoods and immigrant perinatal health, anti-immigrant attitudes in Europe, and the racialization of immigrants in Ireland.

DOI: 10.1177/0002716211432280

level, residence in disparate neighborhoods lowers the probability of physical and social contact between immigrants and nonimmigrants. To the extent that contact fosters meaningful social relations, segregation can derail intergroup relations by fueling mistrust and group stereotypes and by exacerbating perceptions of group difference.

At a structural level, the formation of immigrant enclaves often occurs in tandem with the institutionalization of ethnic businesses, churches, clubs, social services, and schools. This kind of institutional completeness can be advantageous for integration because it provides social support and employment opportunities for immigrants (Logan, Alba, and Stults 2003; Portes and Jensen 1989). For example, new arrivals who are shut out of the mainstream labor market because of insufficient knowledge of the host language can turn to ethnic businesses for employment. Nonetheless, when immigrants live apart in immigrant or ethnic enclaves—irrespective of whether it is voluntarily or involuntarily—this kind of physical separation is often regarded with suspicion by the dominant group and even labeled as dangerous because it supposedly discourages immigrants from assimilating the core values of the host society. Suspicions about immigrant enclaves and the parallel communities that they purportedly foster have circulated across many Western European countries in recent years (see Musterd and De Vos [2007] for a review of the debate in Europe).

Spatial assimilation is also firmly linked to immigrant integration from a theoretical standpoint (Alba and Nee 1997; Massey 1985). It is believed that a *perception* of sameness is important if not necessary for dominant group members to accept immigrants as suitable neighbors (Marston and Van Valey 1979). As immigrants become more culturally and economically similar to the dominant group, subjective and/or real differences in group status will be diminished, and as result, residential mixing will occur. Residential integration, in turn, is supposed to facilitate the formation of widespread primary group relations and, ultimately, help immigrants to achieve full integration into the host society.

The hypothesized association between residential integration and subsequent forms of assimilation has, for the most part, been borne out for each successive wave of international migrants in the United States. Residential integration facilitated the structural, marital, economic, and civic assimilation of pre-1924 European immigrants and post-1965 Asian and white Hispanic immigrants (Lieberson 1980; Iceland 2009). However, residential segregation has hampered the full incorporation of black immigrants and dark-skinned Hispanic immigrants (namely Hispanic subgroups with significant African ancestry such as Puerto Ricans and Dominicans) (Freeman 2002; Massey and Mullen 1984). The persistent pattern of black residential immobility in the United States is generally viewed as an impediment to black immigrants' full inclusion in American society. Furthermore, since place of residence is often associated with access to private and public amenities (e.g., quality schools, health facilities, etc.), employment opportunities, and less exposure to crime, a lack of residential integration may potentially threaten the life chances of black immigrants and their children (Charles 2003; Morenoff and Sampson 1997; Waters 1999).

FIGURE 1

Model of Spatial Assimilation: Predictors of Residential Integration and Links with
Structural and Subsequent Forms of Assimilation

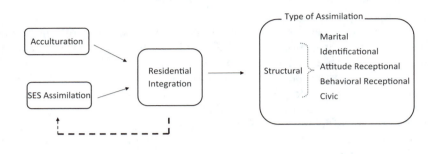

This article examines the sociospatial experiences of twenty-first-century African immigrants in Ireland and the United States—and locally, in Dublin and Boston. The cross-national comparison reveals important shortcomings with spatial assimilation theory and draws into question the generally accepted notion that residential integration is an important, intermediary substage in larger processes of immigrant assimilation. By juxtaposing Ireland with the United States, the study problematizes our reflexive assumptions about the relationships among socioeconomic status (SES), acculturation, race, residential segregation, and subsequent forms of assimilation.

Spatial assimilation as a way station

Spatial assimilation was not one of the original subprocesses or stages of assimilation that Gordon (1964) outlined in his influential treatise on immigrant adaptation. However, it has since been recognized as an important substage in immigrants' progression toward full incorporation in receiving societies (Alba and Nee 1997; Marston and Van Valey 1979). Spatial assimilation theory posits that upon arrival in a new country, immigrants will initially reside in immigrant enclaves, usually located in poor sections of the inner city where housing is cheap. As immigrants improve their economic position and adopt the host society's language, customs, norms, and values (a process known as acculturation), real and/ or subjective differences between themselves and dominant group members will disappear. Once social distance diminishes, the spatial gap between immigrants and nonimmigrants will also close.

Figure 1 summarizes the spatial assimilation model. SES and acculturation are the drivers of residential integration. The arrow flowing from residential integration back to socioeconomic assimilation in the figure reflects the idea that spatial assimilation can further improve immigrants' socioeconomic success (e.g., by enhancing their social networks or simply by placing immigrants in closer geographic proximity to where the good jobs are located). It is believed that meaningful interpersonal relations are likely to develop once immigrants and majority group members share the same residential spaces. The formation of primary group relations with dominant group members is the hallmark of structural assimilation, the stage or subprocess that paves the way for full integration—namely, marital, identificational, behavioral receptional, attitudinal receptional, and civic assimilation (Gordon 1964). In the absence of residential integration, immigrants may not be able to achieve structural assimilation or other assimilation outcomes (Massey and Mullen 1984).

Race and residential segregation

Spatial assimilation theory predicts that all immigrants, irrespective of race or ethnicity, will be able to achieve residential integration with the dominant group given sufficient acculturation and socioeconomic mobility. However, not all immigrants are able to follow the linear progression toward residential integration outlined by spatial assimilation theory. For black immigrants and Hispanic subgroups with significant African ancestry, race is a powerful master status that constrains subgroups' residential mobility (Darden and Kamel 2000).[1] Studies have shown that black immigrants tend to live in majority-minority inner-city neighborhoods where they are overrepresented (Freeman 2002) and have little opportunity for contact with white Americans (Crowder 1999). Moreover, black immigrants remain segregated from whites despite improvements in SES and acculturation (Iceland and Scopilliti 2008). The general consensus is that race is the defining factor in deciding the residential destinies of black immigrants in America. In fact, the persistent pattern of residential segregation for black immigrants has led some scholars to forecast a grim future in which all blacks, irrespective of nativity status, face unparallel forms of social exclusion in American society (Iceland 2009, 13).

It is not difficult to imagine a scenario in which black immigrants' limited residential gains lock them in the lowest position in American society alongside African Americans given the overwhelming empirical research on the negative effects of racial residential segregation on a variety of outcomes, such as poverty, crime, unemployment, and ill health. Such somber scenarios are based on the idea that residential integration with middle-class white Americans is the missing link in the assimilation process for immigrants. However, it is not clear that residential integration and structural assimilation (or other forms of assimilation) are as intimately connected in the current era for contemporary black immigrants as they were for pre-1924 European immigrants and post-1965 Asian and white Hispanic immigrants. Even among the latter two contemporary migrant populations, there is some evidence to suggest that successful integration is no longer solely tied to spatial proximity to whites.

In a critique of spatial assimilation theory and research, Wright, Ellis, and Parks (2005) questioned the use of whites as the reference group for assessing whether immigrants have successfully integrated into American society. The authors argued that the trajectory of initial inner-city residence among conationals and eventual dispersion into suburbs with white Americans is but one of many possible spatial outcomes. Furthermore, immigrants' continued residence among conationals or other minority groups within central-city neighborhoods or in multiethnic suburban neighborhoods should not be regarded as somehow reflecting a lack of integration or an inferior form of residential attainment. Wright and colleagues found evidence to support their claim that the locational attainments of immigrants can still be considered a "success" even if improvements in residential location do not entail proximity to whites. Using 1990 census data for the greater Los Angeles area, the authors found a pattern of dispersion away from initial immigrant settlements over time as immigrants remain longer in the country. The dispersion away from immigrant enclaves did not translate into coresidence with whites. Rather, immigrants were spatially integrating with native-born conationals or coethnics, and this dispersion process often represented an improvement in neighborhood quality for immigrants. Although the authors did not examine black immigrants in their study, the main concepts and implications of their research apply to black immigrants as well.

The current study

Will the residential patterns of black immigrants in the United States prevent them from fully integrating into American society? To answer this very important question, we must take a step back and reevaluate spatial assimilation theory. One useful approach for doing this is to compare and contrast the sociospatial experiences of black immigrants across different receiving contexts to assess how residential integration (or lack thereof) affects structural assimilation and other types of assimilation outcomes. The current study adopts this comparative framework and assesses the spatial assimilation of African immigrants in Ireland and the United States.

Ireland was selected as the comparison case because it represents a context in which residential integration is *possible* for black immigrants. The United States is a racially stratified society, meaning that race was and continues to be an important organizing principle for social life. Blacks and whites are segregated in many areas—in their residences; at school; in the workplace; and, during the Jim Crow era, on buses and in public restrooms. Even spiritual life has not escaped the ideology of racial separation. In contrast, Ireland has not had a history of being a racially stratified society. Social life in Ireland was organized around religious sect, class, settled versus itinerant status, and other social cleavages. Ideologies of racial group superiority/inferiority certainly exist in Ireland.[2] But race does not always dictate one's inclusion or exclusion in society. For example, membership in the dominant racial group does not necessarily translate into acceptance and group solidarity. This is evident from the experiences of Travellers, a white ethnic group that has had a long history of marginalization from the settled Irish community (Garner 2006). Patterson (2005) argues that in societies where race is not an organizing principle, racism can (and often does) exist, but race does not define intergroup relations, nor does it constrain people's life chances in the same manner as it does in racially stratified societies. Hence, it is possible that in Ireland, race is not a master status for blacks. As such, the spatial assimilation process should, in theory, unfold as predicted for African immigrants.

One question that naturally arises about cross-national comparisons is the comparability of the groups under investigation. In terms of relative size and national origin, the African immigrant populations in Ireland and the United States are similar. African immigrants make up less than 1 percent of the total U.S. population. But they are becoming a large proportion of the foreign-born black population; approximately one-third of the 2.8 million foreign-born blacks in the United States in 2005 were African-born (Kent 2007). The new, twenty-first-century African immigrants hail from a core group of sub-Saharan African countries, including Nigeria, Ethiopia, Ghana, Liberia, Kenya, Sierra Leone, Uganda, Cape Verde, and Sudan (Takyi 2002). Nigeria and Ethiopia are the two largest sending countries, accounting for one-third of all African-born blacks in the United States (Kent 2007). In Ireland, African immigrants constituted just a little over 1 percent of the country's 4.2 million people in 2006. However, African-born blacks, along with Asians, are among the country's largest racial minority groups. Nigerians are by far the largest nationality group represented among the African immigrants in Ireland. South Africa, Zimbabwe, and the Democratic Republic of Congo are the other major sending countries for the African immigrant population in Ireland (Central Statistics Office 2006).

One key difference between the African immigrant populations in the two countries is their immigration statuses. A majority of African immigrants in the United States are economic migrants, having entered the country on diversity visas or through family reunification. A sizable proportion—particularly those from war-torn countries such as Somalia and Sudan—also enter the United States as refugees (Kent 2007). Overall, however, economic migrants make up the bulk of the U.S. African immigrant population. In Ireland, refugee and asylum seeker are the immigration statuses of the majority of African immigrants. More than half of all asylum seekers in Direct Provision from 2003 to 2007 were from Africa (Reception and Integration Agency 2008). Far fewer African immigrants enter Ireland on student and work visas.

The difference in immigration statuses affects the initial settlement patterns of African immigrants in the United States and Ireland. For instance, refugees and asylum seekers in Ireland are initially housed in government reception centers, which are spread throughout the country. Thus, African immigrants in Ireland are more geographically dispersed than their counterparts in the United States. African immigrants in the United States tend to concentrate in urban centers such as Washington, D.C., New York, and Boston. However, secondary migration has resulted in large concentrations of African immigrants in cities such as Dublin and Galway, thus rendering the two groups comparable.

There may also be differences in the socioeconomic characteristics of the African immigrants in the two countries as a result of the different immigration statuses. Economic migrants tend to have greater human capital than refugees (Castles and Miller 2009). As such, African immigrants in the United States may be more educated and possess greater professional skills than their counterparts in Ireland. To the extent that SES differences exist, they would favor better integration outcomes for African immigrants in the United States, however. In other words, the higher SES of African immigrants in the United States should result in greater spatial proximity to white Americans, while the lower SES profiles of African immigrants in Ireland should translate into less residential integration with Irish nationals.

Methodology

Data

The comparative spatial assimilation analysis uses data from the U.S. and Irish censuses. Both the national and local analyses make use of population data at the census tract (CT) and enumeration district (ED) level for the United States and Ireland, respectively.[3] Population counts from the 2000 decennial census, Summary File 3 (SF3), were used to calculate segregation indexes for African immigrants in the United States (U.S. Census Bureau 2002). The SF3 contains sample data extracted from the census long form and includes information on race, ethnicity, ancestry, and place of birth. Segregation indexes for African immigrants in Ireland were derived from an unpublished file of the Small Area Population Statistics (SAPS) generated from the 2002 Irish Census of Population. Country/region of birth is the variable used to define the African immigrant population in each country. In the United States, foreign-born persons whose country of birth is in sub-Saharan Africa were categorized as African immigrants.[4] In Ireland, regional distinctions for Africa-born migrants are not available. Therefore, the African immigrant population in Ireland consists of migrants of both sub-Saharan and North African origin. This slight difference in definition, however, does not significantly compromise the comparability of the African immigrant populations in the two countries since the majority of black immigrants in Ireland also hail from sub-Saharan Africa.

The main reference group for African immigrants in each country is native-born whites. The native-born white population in the United States is defined as persons born in the country who marked white only on the race question and indicated that they are not Hispanic (hereafter, white Americans). The comparable reference group in Ireland is Irish nationals, defined as individuals born on the island (this includes a small percentage of both white and nonwhite Ireland-born children of immigrants; however, the majority of Irish nationals are whites with Irish ancestry). For analytical purposes, I also include native-born blacks (hereafter, black Americans) and non-EU15 European immigrants (the majority of whom are white) as additional comparison groups in the United States and Ireland, respectively. Persons born in the United States and self-identified as black alone were categorized as black American.[5] Non-EU15 migrants (hereafter, Eastern European immigrants) are persons from the Baltic and former Soviet bloc states in Eastern Europe, including nationals of one of the ten accession countries that joined the EU on May 1, 2004, or the additional member states that joined the EU on January 1, 2007) (Central Statistics Office 2010).

The inclusion of black Americans and Eastern European immigrants in the analysis provides additional insights into the relative importance of race in the spatial assimilation process for African immigrants. As a powerful master status in the United States for blacks, race ought to constrain the residential mobility of black Americans and African immigrants in similar ways, relegating both groups to similarly disadvantaged inner-city neighborhoods. In Ireland, race has not historically been an important organizing principle as noted above. However, some recent developments in the country—most notably, a 2004 referendum that denied automatic citizenship to the Ireland-born children of immigrants—have raised concerns that perhaps race is becoming an important social boundary in Irish society (Fanning and Mutwarasibo 2007). If race proves consequential for African immigrants' spatial assimilation in Ireland, then we ought to see greater disparity in the locational attainment of African and Eastern European immigrants.

Seven metropolitan areas in the United States meet the minimum population threshold recommended by Farley and Frey (1994). A metropolitan area was included in the analysis if it had twenty thousand or more African-born residents. In Ireland, six urban counties with five hundred or more African immigrants were included in the analysis. Restricting the analysis to these metro areas and urban counties ensures that calculations of segregation will be meaningful and reliable. For the local analysis, I focus on the Boston–New Hampshire primary metropolitan statistical area and the Dublin metropolitan area. The local analysis permits assessment of segregation patterns between central-city and suburban areal units.

Measures of segregation

A spatially modified version of the dissimilarity index, $D(s)$, is used to gauge segregation at the metropolitan area and county levels (Wong 1993).[6] Similar to the aspatial version, $D(s)$ provides information about the different distributions of two populations. Values range from 0 to 100, with 0 representing an even distribution of African immigrants and white Americans/Irish nationals across the study area, while 100 indicates complete segregation of the two groups.

Two indexes are used to assess local segregation patterns in Boston and Dublin. The first index, S_i, gauges the degree of exposure or interaction potential for African immigrants and white Americans/Irish nationals (Wong 2002).[7] The values range from 0 to 1, with higher scores reflecting more segregation and therefore less contact. The other local segregation index is the location quotient (LQ), which measures the relative concentration of a given population for a

TABLE 1

Shape-Adjusted Dissimilarity Index Scores Measuring African Immigrant Segregation
from Irish Nationals and U.S.-Born Non-Hispanic Whites

Urban County	African-Irish Segregation	Metropolitan Area	African-White American Segregation
Cork City	59	Atlanta	63
Dublin City	46	Boston–New Hampshire	63
South Dublin	32	Houston-Brazoria	62
Dun Laoghaire–Rathdown	33	L.A.–Long Beach	59
Fingal	33	Minneapolis–St. Paul	67
Galway City	23	New York–Northeast New Jersey	75
		Washington, D.C.– Maryland–Virginia	60
Average	38	Average	64

SOURCE: Author calculations based on the U.S. 2000 decennial census, Summary File 3 (SF3), and the 2002 Irish Census of Population (Small Area Population Statistics).

specific areal unit. Values greater than 1 mean that the group in question is more overrepresented in an areal unit than expected given its relative size in the study area. Underrepresented areas are those with scores of 0.67 or less (Chung and Brown 2007).[8]

Results

Aggregate segregation patterns on opposite sides of the pond

Table 1 shows the degree of residential integration with white Americans and Irish nationals for African immigrants in the United States and Ireland. Two patterns are noteworthy here. First, segregation levels vary substantially across the counties and metro areas in each country. In Ireland, African-Irish segregation is lowest in Galway City and approaches near-U.S. levels in Cork City. In the United States, African-white segregation is lowest in L.A.–Long Beach and highest in the New York–Northeast New Jersey metro area. However, there do not appear to be any systematic differences by region in the United States. The second pattern that stands out is the significantly lower level of segregation in Ireland compared to the United States. On average, only 38 percent of African immigrants in Ireland would have to relocate to a different neighborhood to achieve an even distribution of African and Irish residents. In contrast, 64 percent of African immigrants in the United State would have to move to achieve integration with white Americans.

The aggregate spatial patterns are reproduced at the local level as well, albeit with some important geographic variation. A map of the Dublin metropolitan area depicting African-Irish contact is displayed in Figure 2. Local segregation scores (S_i) were grouped into three categories reflecting high $(S_i < 0.90)$, moderate $(0.90 \leq S_i \leq 0.95)$, and low $(S_i > 0.95)$ contact. A similar map portraying African–white American contact in the Boston metro area is shown in Figure 3. In general, contact with the dominant group is much more prevalent and geographically widespread in Dublin than in Boston. Areas of high and moderate contact can be found in both central-city Dublin and its surrounding suburbs. In contrast, Boston not only contains fewer high-contact census tracts, but, where contact does occur, those areas tend to be limited to the inner-city and suburban areas adjacent to the city boundary. Interestingly, the areas of high and moderate African–white American contact are the same areas where African immigrants have a lot of exposure to black Americans (Figure 4). Thus, contact between African immigrants and whites is not restricted to the central city, but where contact does occur, it tends to take place in mixed-race census tracts where contact with native-born blacks is also likely to be high.

Spatial assimilation and neighborhood quality in Dublin and Boston

It is implied in spatial assimilation theory that residential integration will translate into equality of neighborhood characteristics for immigrants and nonimmigrants. Relatedly, place-based disadvantages are potential mechanisms through which segregation might derail immigrants' subsequent assimilation outcomes (e.g., structural, economic, civic, etc.). In this section, I compare the socioeconomic and demographic characteristics of the average African immigrant and Irish national or white American neighborhoods in Dublin and Boston, respectively. For comparison purposes, I also include Eastern European immigrant and black American neighborhoods. For this analysis, I first generated location quotient scores for each subgroup of interest in the two metro areas. Then, EDs and CTs with scores greater than 1.33 were coded as neighborhoods where the subgroup is overrepresented. This classification scheme resulted in nonoverlapping EDs and CTs for each subgroup. Next, I generated means and percentages for key SES and demographic characteristics for the nonoverlapping EDs and CTs and tested whether the characteristics meaningfully differ across the subgroup-specific neighborhoods. Note that in the case of Dublin, there is actually a substantial degree of overlap in the areas where African immigrants and other immigrant subgroups reside. In fact, local segregation patterns—based on a different segregation index—for African, Eastern European, and Asian immigrants are similar to one another; and because there is so much residential mixing among the different immigrant subgroups, no one group truly dominates an area (Vang 2010). Thus, the analysis presented here for Dublin exaggerates the small differences between the areas where African and Eastern European immigrants concentrate. Nonetheless, the analysis does reveal some interesting findings about the two groups' integration.

FIGURE 2
Contact between African Immigrants and Irish Nationals in Dublin, 2002

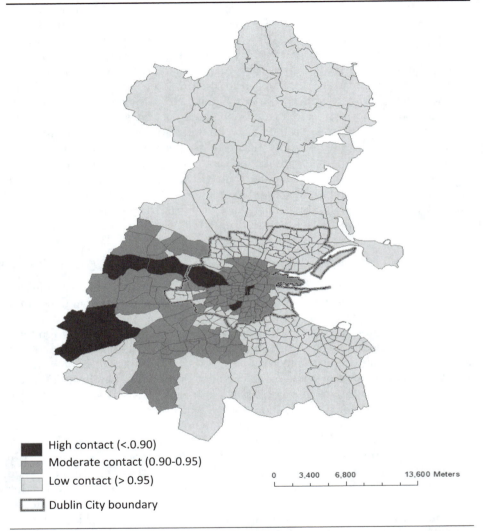

High contact (<.0.90)
Moderate contact (0.90-0.95)
Low contact (> 0.95)
Dublin City boundary

0   3,400   6,800   13,600 Meters

NOTE: Neighborhood is defined as the average Euclidean distance to the first nearest neighbor (988.15 meters or a little over half a mile radius). Counties shown: Dublin City, South Dublin, Fingal, and Dun Laoghaire-Rathdown.

 © Ordinance Survey Ireland/Government of Ireland
Copyright Permit No. MP005811

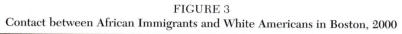

FIGURE 3
Contact between African Immigrants and White Americans in Boston, 2000

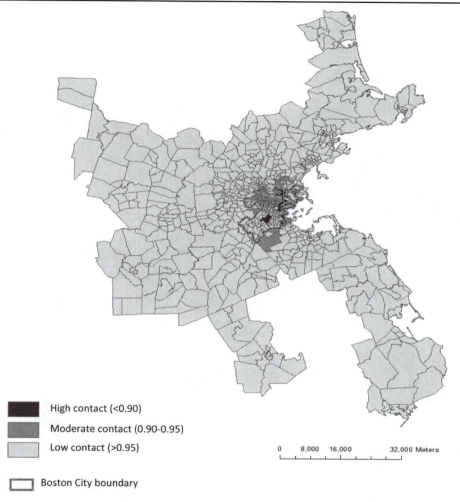

High contact (<0.90)

Moderate contact (0.90-0.95)

Low contact (>0.95)

Boston City boundary

0   8,000   16,000   32,000 Meters

NOTE: Neighborhood is defined as the average Euclidean distance to the first nearest neighbor (1,685.23 meters or roughly one-mile radius).

The distribution of the subgroup-specific neighborhoods in Dublin and Boston are shown in Figures 5 and 6, respectively. Consistent with the results for contact with Irish nationals, the neighborhoods where African immigrants tend to concentrate are located both in Dublin City and its southeastern and southwestern suburbs. In contrast, African immigrant concentrated neighborhoods in

FIGURE 4
Contact between African Immigrants and Black Americans in Boston, 2000

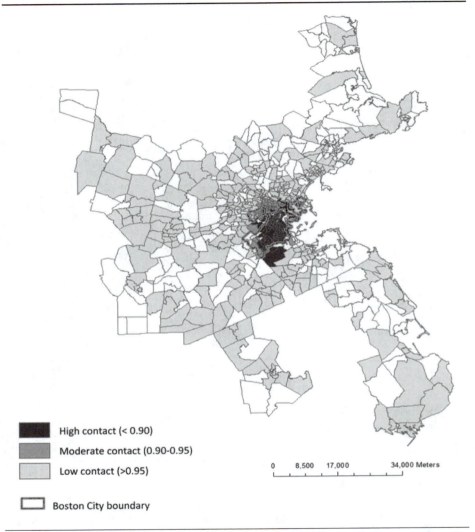

High contact (< 0.90)

Moderate contact (0.90-0.95)

Low contact (>0.95)

Boston City boundary

0   8,500   17,000   34,000 Meters

NOTE: Neighborhood is defined as the average Euclidean distance to the first nearest neighbor (1,685.23 meters or roughly one-mile radius).

Boston are more geographically dispersed across the metro area than is otherwise suggested by the above contact analysis. There are quite a number of suburban CTs that have 33 percent more African immigrants than would be expected, given the group's average metropolitan-wide representation. As will be discussed

FIGURE 5
African Immigrant, Eastern European Immigrant, and Irish Neighborhoods in Dublin, 2002

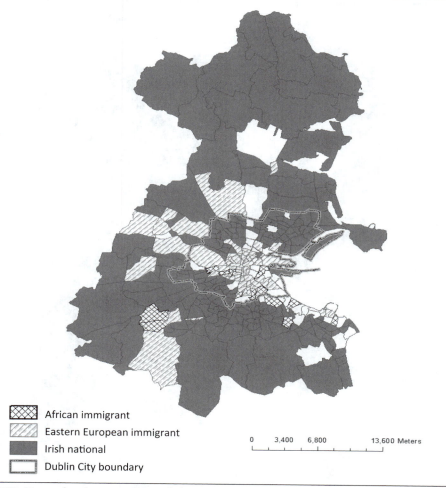

African immigrant
Eastern European immigrant
Irish national
Dublin City boundary

0   3,400   6,800   13,600 Meters

NOTE: For each subgroup, EDs with location quotient (LQ) scores greater than 1.33 were classified as a neighborhood where the group is overrepresented.

Ordnance Survey Ireland   © Ordinance Survey Ireland/Government of Ireland
Copyright Permit No. MP005811

in detail below, this geographic variation is what distinguishes African immigrant neighborhoods from black American neighborhoods.

The information in Table 2 shows that the neighborhoods where African immigrants and Irish nationals are overrepresented differ little in terms of their SES profiles. The only exception is that African neighborhoods tend to have a higher proportion of college-educated residents than Irish neighborhoods (18.99 vs.

FIGURE 6
African Immigrant, White American, and Black American Neighborhoods
in Boston, 2000

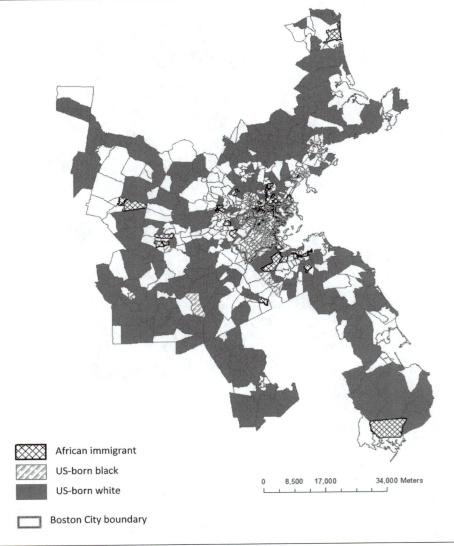

NOTE: For each subgroup, census tracts with location quotient (LQ) scores greater than 1.33 were classified as a neighborhood where the group is overrepresented.

8.72 percent, $p < .000$). The neighborhoods where the two groups are concentrated differ somewhat in terms of housing and demographic characteristics, however. Consistent with previous research (Vang 2010), African neighborhoods have

TABLE 2

Socioeconomic and Demographic Characteristics of Distinct African Immigrant, Irish National, and Eastern European Immigrant Neighborhoods / Enumeration Districts (EDs), Dublin Metropolitan Area

	(A) African Immigrant	(B) Irish National	p-Value (A vs. B)	(C) Eastern European Immigrant	p-Value (A vs. C)
SES characteristics					
% lowest SES group[a]	3.36	4.43	.244	4.38	.203
% lowest social class[b]	3.45	4.63	.210	4.50	.205
% unemployed	4.69	4.69	.526	6.53	.062
% female-headed household w/ children	10.89	11.89	.625	9.17	.382
% college educated (third-level degree or higher)	18.99	8.72	.000	15.33	.133
Housing characteristics					
% owner-occupied housing units (nonlocal authority)	51.26	75.31	.000	43.03	.209
% local authority housing	16.41	14.45	.705	14.24	.644
% residence in new housing[c]	9.83	5.92	.10	12.63	.530
Demographic characteristics					
% speaks Irish	38.24	36.92	.619	31.50	.012
% foreign-born	13.29	5.39	.000	21.10	.003
Number of enumeration districts	13	213		61	

SOURCE: Author calculations based on the 2002 Irish Census of Population (Small Area Population Statistics).

NOTE: SES characteristics for EDs are based on households, whereas demographic characteristics are from counts of individuals. P-values are from two-tailed t-tests.

[a]Lowest SES group = unskilled; SES group is an official Central Statistics Office (CSO) classification scheme created from occupation and employment status for persons 15 and older.

[b]Lowest social class = unskilled; social class is an official CSO classification scheme created from occupation.

[c]Units built since 1996 are considered new housing.

fewer owner-occupied housing units than Irish neighborhoods (51.26 vs. 75.31 percent, $p < .000$). Not surprisingly, areas where African immigrants concentrate have higher proportions of foreign-born residents compared to Irish neighborhoods (13.29 and 5.39 percent, respectively, $p < .000$). The similarity in neighborhood quality between African and Irish neighborhoods suggests a parity of life chances or, at the very least, the same access to place-based resources.

A comparison of the characteristics of African and Eastern European immigrant neighborhoods reveals that African immigrants tend to be slightly more integrated with Irish nationals. Areas where African immigrants concentrate tend to have higher proportions of residents who can speak Irish (the majority of whom are Irish nationals) and contain fewer foreign-born persons (38.24 vs. 31.50 percent, $p < .012$, and 13.29 vs. 21.10 percent, $p < .003$, respectively). There were no statistically significant differences between African and Eastern European immigrant neighborhoods in terms of SES characteristics, however. Despite growing reports of racial discrimination (McGinnity et al. 2006) and the racial undertones behind government efforts to limit immigrants' access to social resources and rights in Ireland (Lentin and McVeigh 2002), it seems that race has not prevented African immigrants and Irish nationals from becoming neighbors. Additionally, black racial group membership has not disadvantaged African immigrants relative to Eastern European immigrants in terms of neighborhood quality. Racism may be emerging as a prominent feature of intergroup relations and social life in contemporary Irish society, but it has yet to translate into structural exclusion to the same degree as it has for blacks in the United States.

Residential segregation has relegated African Americans to some of the most socioeconomically deprived inner-city neighborhoods in the United States (Massey and Denton 1993). Table 3 shows that this kind of neighborhood-based disadvantage is reproduced for African immigrants in Boston as well. Neighborhoods where African immigrants concentrate are more socioeconomically disadvantaged across every SES and housing indicator examined. For instance, residents in African neighborhoods earn about $23,000 less on average than those who live in white American neighborhoods ($45,159 vs. $68,374, $p < .000$). African immigrant neighborhoods are also less diverse than white American neighborhoods (0.49 vs. 0.18, $p < 0.000$). However, the picture of residential stagnation for African immigrants is complicated by the spatial *discordance* observed between the neighborhoods where African immigrants and black Americans tend to concentrate.

Unlike the situation in Dublin, where African and Eastern European immigrant neighborhoods differed little in neighborhood quality, there is greater inequality between African immigrants and black American neighborhoods in Boston. On average, African immigrant neighborhoods are less socioeconomically disadvantaged than black American neighborhoods. Residents in African neighborhoods earn about $9,000 more than residents in black American neighborhoods ($45,158 vs. $36,128, $p < .001$). Residents in the immigrant neighborhoods are less likely to be in poverty (14.95 vs. 20.79 percent, $p < .000$), more likely to be college educated (23.14 vs. 15.67 percent, $p < .000$), and less likely to be single mothers with children (6.8 vs. 15.84 percent, $p < .000$). Importantly, the neighborhoods where African immigrants are overrepresented are also more racially diverse than the neighborhoods where black Americans concentrate (0.494 vs. 0.638, $p < .000$). These differences in neighborhood diversity and socioeconomic characteristics are likely due to the greater geographic dispersion

TABLE 3

Socioeconomic and Demographic Characteristics of Distinct African Immigrant, White American, and Black American Neighborhoods / Census Tracts (CTs), Boston–New Hampshire (NH) Primary Metropolitan Statistical Area (PMSA)

	(A) African Immigrant	(B) White American	p-value (A vs. B)	(C) Black American	p-value (A vs. C)
SES characteristics					
Mean income ($)	45,158.61	68,374.09	.000	36,128.14	.001
(SD)	(18,082.55)	(20,308.57)		(12,693.61)	
% below poverty	14.95	4.42	.000	20.79	.001
% female-headed household w/ children	6.80	4.24	.000	15.84	.000
% unemployed	2.93	1.84	.001	3.62	.062
% college educated	23.14	27.25	.028	15.67	.001
Housing characteristics					
% owner-occupied housing units	37.53	73.22	.000	31.64	.087
Demographic characteristics					
Racial diversity	0.494	0.182	.000	0.638	.000
% foreign-born	26.52	7.87	.000	27.00	.781
Number of tracts	46	187		106	

SOURCE: Author calculations based on the U.S. 2000 decennial census, Summary File 3 (SF3).

NOTE: Census tracts with Location Quotient index values higher than 1.33 were considered areas where the group of interest was dominant. Racial diversity is measured with the Entropy Index (Iceland, Weinberg, and Steinmetz 2000), which calculates the degree of mixing for eight distinct racial groups: NH white alone, NH black alone, Hispanic, Asian, Hawaiian/ Pacific Islander, Alaskan/Native American, Mixed (2+ races), and Other. Higher scores reflect greater segregation (i.e., less diversity). *P*-values from two-tailed *t*-tests.

of African immigrant neighborhoods and their locational attainment in Boston's suburbs. In fact, research shows that nationwide African immigrants have made substantial gains in suburban residence: 40 percent of African immigrants in the United States reside outside of central cities, while one-third live in the urban core (Takyi and Boate 2006).

The results show that race undoubtedly limits the residential options of African immigrants in the United States. African immigrants face an uphill battle when it comes to residential integration with white Americans—as do African Americans and Afro-Caribbean immigrants. Nonetheless, exclusion from white suburban neighborhoods does not mean a complete absence of residential mobility. The better neighborhood profiles for African immigrants in Boston compared with black Americans suggest that meaningful spatial gains have been achieved, however modest.

Discussion

The centrality of residential integration in the larger assimilation process for immigrants is clearly laid out in spatial assimilation theory. Spatial separation from the native-born majority group is believed to impede immigrants' integration in receiving countries. In this article, I demonstrated that African immigrants in Ireland have achieved spatial integration with Irish nationals while their counterparts in the United States remain spatially separated from white Americans. I also showed that despite being segregated from whites, African immigrants in the United States have made some modest spatial gains compared with black Americans. What, if anything, can the spatial patterns of African immigrants in Ireland and the United States, and locally in Dublin and Boston, tell us about their long-term assimilation prospects? I address this question in this final section.

Integration without acculturation or socioeconomic assimilation

It is tempting to conclude from the results in this article that African immigrants in Ireland are well on their way toward full integration in Irish society. The extent to which the spatial gains of African immigrants in Ireland can produce structural and other forms of assimilation is questionable, however. This is because African-Irish residential integration occurred *without* widespread economic and cultural assimilation.[9] In other words, there is an uncoupling of spatial distance and social distance in the Irish case. Spatial integration is not the end result of Irish nationals' acceptance of African immigrants as economic and cultural equals. In fact, qualitative research shows that Irish nationals are just as averse to having black neighbors as are white Americans (Vang 2011). The remarkably high degree of residential integration observed for African immigrants in Ireland was facilitated not by diminished social distance, but rather by ecological factors—namely, the supply of new housing and private rental units. Demographic and institutional factors both played an important role in generating greater supplies of new housing and rental units in Ireland, which, in turn, opened up more housing opportunities for immigrants in mixed-income suburban neighborhoods (Vang 2010). Thus, processes of residential integration in Ireland do not adhere to the spatial assimilation model at all.

Research on the spatial patterns of high-SES immigrants in the United States and Canada reveal some holes in the spatial assimilation model as well. For example, highly educated immigrants often bypass residence in inner-city immigrant enclaves and attain residential propinquity with white Americans from the get-go. Alternatively, highly acculturated and socioeconomically mobile immigrant groups, such as Asians, may also remain segregated in immigrant and ethnic enclaves instead of coresiding with members of the dominant group (Fong and Wilkes 1999; Logan, Alba, and Zhang 2002). Interestingly, the spatial segregation of acculturated and socioeconomically mobile Asian immigrants has not prevented the widespread development of marital assimilation for members of this racial group (Lee and Boyd 2008).

The crucial difference between the Irish and American/Canadian situations, however, is the fact that in the former country, African immigrants have not reached economic parity with Irish nationals. Herein lies the crux of the problem. Residential integration without economic assimilation may take African immigrants only so far in Irish society. The inability of residential integration, absent economic assimilation, to produce full social inclusion is well illustrated in Telles's (2004) study of racial residential segregation in Brazil. Telles's research did not focus on immigrants per se. However, useful lessons can still be gleaned. Brazilian society is characterized by high levels of black-white residential integration and high rates of interracial marriage and friendships. Nonetheless, racial residential integration has not facilitated blacks' inclusion in the educational, economic, and political spheres of Brazilian society. Grave disparities in income, labor force participation, educational achievement, and political representation between blacks and whites, and to a lesser extent between mulattoes and whites, remain. Telles argues that the reason why residential integration did not help blacks to gain an equal footing in Brazilian society is that residential and social integration occurred only among poor and working/lower-class blacks and whites. Significant social and economic differences still existed between black Brazilians and middle-class white Brazilians. The study shows that parity in SES between subordinate group members (e.g., immigrants) and dominant group members is key to producing structural equality. Without economic assimilation, it is not clear that the spatial gains of African immigrants will necessarily lead to full incorporation in Irish society.

Parallel lives, unparallel outcomes?

In the United States, African immigrants have not been able to close the spatial gap between themselves and white Americans. But the lack of residential integration with whites does not necessarily mean complete residential immobility and place-based disadvantage, however. African immigrants seem to have made significant spatial gains when we compare their sociospatial experiences to those of black Americans. Not only are African immigrants more geographically dispersed throughout the Boston metro area's central-city and suburban neighborhoods, but the average neighborhood where African immigrants tend to concentrate is less socioeconomically deprived and more racially diverse than the average neighborhood where black Americans live.

If we view the sociospatial experiences of African immigrants solely in terms of their inability to penetrate majority-white suburban neighborhoods, the picture that emerges is indeed a grim one. Despite their high socioeconomic status and other group differences that make them stand apart from Afro-Caribbean immigrants and African Americans, African immigrants are not able to close the spatial gaps between themselves and white Americans. Compared to Asian and Hispanic immigrants, African-born blacks (and black immigrants in general) may be uniquely disadvantaged. However, if we view the residential attainment of African immigrants from the perspective proposed by Wright, Ellis, and Parks (2005), then the spatial distance observed between African immigrants and black Americans may take on greater significance. African immigrants may not be able to integrate into suburban white neighborhoods, but their moderate spatial separation from black Americans may expose them to fewer neighborhood-based disadvantages, thereby lessening the effects of neighborhood characteristics on individual life chances. In fact, research from the health field suggests that neighborhood characteristics have modest effects on African immigrants' health compared with individual-level risk factors (Grady and McLafferty 2007).

Importantly, African immigrants' modest spatial gains may produce subtle differences in group outcomes—differences that may affect African immigrants' long-term assimilation. This has already been borne out to some extent for Afro-Caribbean immigrants. Afro-Caribbean immigrants' segregation from white Americans raised earlier concerns that spatial proximity to African Americans in poor inner-city neighborhoods would undermine the integration of Afro-Caribbean immigrants and their children and lead to downward assimilation (Portes and Zhou 1993; Waters 1999). However, recent research shows that second-generation Afro-Caribbean immigrants in New York City have transitioned successfully into adulthood, especially when compared with black American peers (Kasinitz et al. 2008). Similar to African immigrants, Afro-Caribbean immigrants in New York City reside in more socioeconomically advantaged neighborhoods than black Americans (Crowder 1999; Kasinitz et al. 2008). The extent to which the differences in neighborhood characteristics contributed to second-generation Afro-Caribbean immigrants' success has not been empirically tested. Nonetheless, it is noteworthy that some forms of integration are taking place for second-generation Afro-Caribbean immigrants in spite of having grown up (and for many, continued residence) in segregated neighborhoods.

Of course, one may question the temporal nature of African immigrants' neighborhood attainment, especially given the history of neighborhood racial turnover in the United States. Perhaps what we are seeing is simply one snapshot in time, and the higher-quality, mixed-race neighborhoods where African immigrants are living now will eventually turn into socioeconomically deprived, predominantly black neighborhoods in the future. Indeed, research on mixed-race neighborhoods paints a gloomy picture of the viability of integrated communities. For instance, Friedman (2007) found that when observed longitudinally, mixed-race neighborhoods are not stable. Moreover, the greater presence of mixed-race neighborhoods is not due to the stability of these neighborhoods over time but is instead an artifact of their growth in absolute numbers over the past two decades. In light of this, African immigrants' residential gains may be tenuous and may not look very different from that of African Americans in the next 15 or 20 years. Yet the *inevitability* of the neighborhood racial turnover process is questionable. With continued migration and demographic shifts—particularly the growth in the Hispanic and Asian populations—it is possible that mixed-race, mixed-income neighborhoods will become a stable feature of the American urban landscape in the future. Thus, the higher-quality, racially diverse neighborhoods where African immigrants are currently living may not be just a temporary phenomenon.

Conclusion

Residential integration between immigrants and nonimmigrants is typically considered a desirable goal in most pluralistic, immigrant-receiving countries. Far from being merely an abstract liberal principle, residential integration is championed by members of the dominant group because its absence (i.e., segregation) is misconstrued as a sign of unwillingness on the part of immigrants to adopt the culture, norms, and values of the host society. As such, residential segregation is believed to be an impediment to immigrants' full integration and, therefore, a threat to social cohesion. The belief that residential segregation can stymie integration is so strongly held in some Western European countries that governments have even gone as far as to socially engineer integration through various housing policies (Musterd and De Vos 2007). However, it does not necessarily follow that spatial proximity between immigrants and dominant group members will result in structural, marital, economic, civic, and other forms of assimilation. Conversely, a lack of residential integration with dominant group members does not mean that immigrants are doomed to a life of social exclusion either, especially if immigrants are able to attain residence in majority-minority neighborhoods that are not socioeconomically disadvantaged.

Longitudinal data is needed to empirically test the association between residential integration and subsequent forms of assimilation for twenty-first-century African immigrants. However, the comparative analysis suggests that residential segregation from white Americans, while certainly undesirable, may not be the linchpin of social inequality for African immigrants in the United States. Relatedly, residential integration, however promising, may not be the key to social inclusion for African immigrants in Ireland.

The results in this article draw into question the centrality of residential integration in the assimilation process for African immigrants. In doing so, I am not advocating that governments cease efforts to facilitate residential integration; far from it. In societies where resources are tied to geography, residential segregation can have deleterious effects on residents' life chances. Moreover, segregation is often a sign of an unhealthy and unequal society. In pointing out the limitations of spatial assimilation for immigrants' full integration, I hope to engage both social scientists and policymakers in broader discussions of immigrant incorporation that emphasize socioeconomic (e.g., educational and employment opportunities for immigrants) as much as spatial pathways. Additionally, in racially stratified societies such as the United States, it may not be possible to bring about black-white residential integration through social engineering (i.e., forcing blacks and whites to live with one another). But it may be possible to weaken the association between segregation and adverse outcomes by strengthening the structural and social resources of the neighborhoods where black immigrants (and black Americans more generally) reside.

Notes

1. Three individual-level theories have been influential in explaining how race constrains residential mobility: (1) in-group preferences, (2) racial proxy, and (3) racial stereotyping (Charles 2003). The in-group preferences thesis attributes racial residential segregation to varying degrees of ethnocentrism among the races. In essence, it is argued that all groups exhibit ethnocentrism and preferences for same-race/same-ethnicity neighbors. Within this framework, segregation is the outcome of strong white preferences for living with other whites. In the racial proxy hypothesis, it is argued that since black neighborhoods are often associated with poorer amenities, inferior schools, high crime, and so forth, white avoidance of black neighborhoods is not due to race per se but rather the desire to avoid disadvantaged neighborhoods and low-socioeconomic-status neighbors. Finally, the racial stereotyping thesis attributes racial residential segregation to active out-group avoidance or domination. It is believed that white prejudicial attitudes and racial discrimination cause whites to avoid neighborhoods with blacks and other minorities. At the macro level, racism and institutional discrimination go hand in hand to further limit the spatial mobility of blacks and other racial and ethnic minorities. Institutional practices such as redlining by mortgage lending agencies, blockbusting by realtors, and restrictive covenants have been used in the past to shut blacks out of desirable neighborhoods.

2. Rolston and Shannon (2002) note that although the slave trade and slavery did not formally take root in Ireland, they were familiar features of Irish society during the eighteenth and nineteenth centuries: slave ships passed through the ports of Limerick and Dublin; Irish merchants provided goods to slave plantations in the Caribbean; and abolitionist movements cropped up in Belfast, Cork, and Dublin. The Irish in Ireland have also had a long history of encounters with black people through the slaves brought by the Vikings in the seventh century; servants and domestics of the English and Irish bourgeoisie in the eighteenth century; visiting abolitionists such as Charles Lenox Redmond, Olaudah Equiano, and Frederick Douglass during the eighteenth and nineteenth centuries; and black American soldiers stationed in Northern Ireland during the early twentieth century. The authors further note that more recently, peacekeeping and missionary activities of Irish soldiers and priests during the 1960s established international networks between Ireland and Africa. For example, the "black babies" humanitarian efforts of Irish Catholic missionaries to raise funds in Ireland for famine relief in Biafra during the late 1960s heightened awareness about Africa and its people (p. 84). Through these various encounters with blacks, Rolston and Shannon assert that the Irish have had "countless opportunities throughout history to be reminded of their relative superiority and while that lesson may have lain dormant at various times, it only needed the excuse of immigration to be awakened" (p. 88).

3. The range of the population size within enumeration districts (from fewer than 60 to roughly 24,000 people, with the largest EDs representing entire rural areas) differs from that of census tracts in the United States. Census tracts typically range between 1,500 and 8,000 people, with an average of 4,000 people (Iceland, Weinberg, and Steinmetz 2000). However, for the counties in the analysis, the *average* number of persons per ED ranges from a low of 639 to a high of 4,741.

4. Defining African immigrants based on country/region of birth is somewhat problematic because while most migrants from these sending countries/regions are black, not all African-born immigrants are

black. Indeed, some African-born immigrants may be white (e.g., those from South Africa) or Asian (e.g., those from East Africa). Nonetheless, the classification scheme used in the analysis is consistent with past research, which used country/region of birth as a proxy for black African immigrants (Freeman 2002; Logan 2007). Prior to the 2006 census, the Irish government did not collect information on race and ethnicity. Hence, country or region of birth is used as a proxy for race in the 2002 Irish Census of Populations.

5. Black Americans include African Americans as well as second-generation African and Afro-Caribbean immigrants. Thus, the black American population—a proxy for the African American population—overestimates the number of black persons of nonimmigrant stock. Likewise, the counts of African immigrants underestimate the true size of the African-born population since they exclude their U.S.-born children.

6. The global, spatial dissimilarity index is expressed as:

$$D(s) = D - \left[\frac{1}{2} \sum_i \sum_j w_{ij} |z_i - z_j| * \frac{\frac{1}{2}\left[(P_i / A_i) + (P_j / A_j)\right]}{MAX(P / A)} \right],$$

where z_i is the proportion of black residents in tract i, z_j is the proportion of black residents in neighboring tract j, w_{ij} is the length of the common boundary shared by tracts i and j, P_i/P_j and A_i/A_j are the perimeter and areas of tracts i and j, and Max(P/A) is the highest perimeter-to-area ratio found in the metropolitan area/county.

7. The local spatial segregation between two groups, a and b, in areal unit i is expressed as follows (Wong 2002):

$$S_{i_{B-W}} = 1 - \frac{a_i \sum_j c_{ij} b_j}{b_i \sum_j a_j},$$

where b_i is the proportion of group b in census tract i, and a_j is the proportion of group a in neighboring tract j. The term c_{ij} is a neighborhood connectivity matrix wherein, if $i = j$, then $c_{ij} = 0$; and if $i \neq j$, then $c_{ij} = 1$. That is, if i and j are neighbors (i.e., areal unit i shares a boundary with areal unit j), then the two groups can interact across their shared boundary. In the analysis, j is defined as a neighborhood of i if it is within 0.1021 mile of i. The value for the bandwidth was derived from calculating the average Euclidean distance of the first nearest neighbor in ArcGIS.

8. The location quotient is defined as

$$LQ_i = \frac{b_i / t_i}{B / T},$$

where b_i and t_i are the black population and total population counts for areal unit i, and B and T are the corresponding population counts for blacks and all residents in the entire study area.

9. African immigrants entered Ireland as temporary workers, students, and refugees or asylum-seekers (Mutwarasibo and Smith 2000; Quinn and O'Connell 2007). This last immigration status has had particularly negative effects on the SES of African immigrants because many spend their initial years in the country unemployed or with limited access to work. Once in the labor market, they face many barriers to gainful, full-time employment (Fanning, Loyal, and Staunton 2000). In fact, research shows that even when immigrants are able to obtain stable employment, their earnings are significantly lower than the earnings of comparable Irish nationals (Barrett and McCarthy 2006). Culturally, the historical ties between Africa and Ireland (Rolston and Shannon 2002) mean that many African immigrants in Ireland have some knowledge of the English language and Western institutions (e.g., schools and churches). Despite familiarity with Irish culture and institutions, however, qualitative research shows that full acculturation has yet to be achieved (Vang 2008). Indeed, perceptions of cultural difference (values, norms, dress, etc.) are held by members of both groups.

References

Alba, Richard D., and Victor Nee. 1997. Rethinking assimilation theory for a new era of immigration. *International Migration Review* 4:826–74.

Barrett, Alan, and Yvonne McCarthy. 2006. *Immigrants in a booming economy: Analysing their earnings and welfare dependence.* Discussion paper. Bonn, Germany: Institute for the Study of Labour.

Castles, Stephen, and Mark J. Miller. 2009. *The Age of migration: International population movements in the modern world,* 4th ed. New York, NY: Guilford Press.

Central Statistics Office. 2006. *Census 2006: Principal demographic results.* Dublin, Ireland: Government Publications Office.

Central Statistics Office. 2010. *Population and migration estimates, April 2010.* Dublin, Ireland: Government Publications Office.

Charles, Camille Z. 2003. The dynamics of racial residential segregation. *Annual Review of Sociology* 29:167–207.

Chung, Su-Yeul, and Lawrence A. Brown. 2007. Racial/ethnic residential sorting in spatial context: Testing the explanatory frameworks. *Urban Geography* 28 (4): 312–39.

Crowder, Kyle D. 1999. Residential segregation of West Indians in the New York/New Jersey metropolitan areas: The role of race and ethnicity. *International Migration Review* 33:79–113.

Darden, Joe T., and Sameh M. Kamel. 2000. Black residential segregation in the city and suburbs of Detroit: Does socioeconomic status matter? *Journal of Urban Affairs* 22 (1): 1–13.

Fanning, Bryan, Steven Loyal, and Ciaran Staunton. 2000. *Asylum seekers and the right to work in Ireland.* Dublin, Ireland: Irish Refugee Council.

Fanning, Bryan, and Fidele Mutwarasibo. 2007. Nationals/non-nationals: Immigration, citizenship and politics in the Republic of Ireland. *Ethnic and Racial Studies* 30 (3): 439–60.

Farley, Reynolds, and William H. Frey. 1994. Changes in the segregation of whites from blacks during the 1980s: Small steps toward a more integrated society. *American Sociological Review* 59 (1): 23–45.

Fong, Eric, and Rima Wilkes. 1999. The spatial assimilation model reexamined: An assessment by Canadian data. *International Migration Review* 33 (3): 594–620.

Freeman, Lance. 2002. Does spatial assimilation work for black immigrants in the US? *Urban Studies* 39 (11): 1983–2002.

Friedman, Samantha. 2007. Do declines in residential segregation mean stable neighborhood racial integration in metropolitan America? A research rote. *Social Science Research* 37:920–33.

Garner, Steve. 2006. The uses of whiteness: What sociologists working on Europe can draw from US research on whiteness. *Sociology* 40 (2): 257–75.

Gordon, Milton M. 1964. *Assimilation in American life: The role of race, religion, and national origins.* New York, NY: Oxford University Press.

Grady, Sue C., and Sarah McLafferty. 2007. Segregation, nativity, and health: Reproductive health inequalities for immigrant and native-born black women in New York City. *Urban Geography* 28 (4): 377–97.

Iceland, John. 2009. *Where we live now: Immigration and race in the United States.* Berkeley: University of California Press.

Iceland, John, and Melissa Scopilliti. 2008. Immigrant residential segregation in U.S. metropolitan areas, 1990–2000. *Demography* 45 (1): 79–94.

Iceland, John, Daniel H. Weinberg, and Erika Steinmetz. 2000. *Racial and ethnic residential segregation in the United States: 1980–2000.* Washington, DC: U.S. Census Bureau.

Kasinitz, Philip, John H. Mollenkopf, Mary C. Waters, and Jennifer Holdaway. 2008. *Inheriting the city: The children of immigrants come of age.* New York, NY: Russell Sage Foundation.

Kent, Mary M. 2007. Immigration and America's black population. *Population Bulletin* 62 (4): 1–16.

Lee, Sharon M., and Monica Boyd. 2008. Marrying out: Comparing the marital and social integration of Asians in the US and Canada. *Social Science Research* 37 (1): 311–29.

Lentin, Ronit, and Robbie McVeigh. 2002. *Racism and anti-racism in Ireland.* Belfast, Northern Ireland: Beyond the Pale Publications.

Lieberson, Stanley. 1980. *A piece of the pie: Blacks and white immigrants since 1880.* Berkeley: University of California Press.

Logan, John R. 2007. Who are the other African Americans? Contemporary African and Caribbean immigrants in the United States. In *The Other African Americans: Contemporary African and Caribbean immigrants in the United States*, eds. Y. Shaw-Taylor and Steven A. Tuch, 49–68. Lanham, MD: Rowman & Littlefield.

Logan, John R., Richard D. Alba, and Brian J. Stults. 2003. Enclaves and entrepreneurs: Assessing the payoffs for immigrants and minorities. *International Migration Review* 37 (2): 344–88.

Logan, John R., Richard D. Alba, and Wenquan Zhang. 2002. Immigrant enclaves and ethnic communities in New York and Los Angeles. *American Sociological Review* 67:299–322.

Marston, Wilfred G., and Thomas L. Van Valey. 1979. The role of residential segregation in the assimilation process. *The Annals of the American Academy of Political and Social Science* 441:13–25.

Massey, Douglas S. 1985. Ethnic residential segregation: A theoretical synthesis and empirical review. *Sociology and Social Research* 69:315–50.

Massey, Douglas S., and Nancy A. Denton. 1993. *American apartheid: Segregation and the making of the underclass*. Cambridge, MA: Harvard University Press.

Massey, Douglas S., and Brendan P. Mullen. 1984. Processes of Hispanic and black spatial assimilation. *American Journal of Sociology* 89 (4): 836–73.

McGinnity, Frances, Philip J. O'Connell, Emma Quinn, and James Williams. 2006. *Migrants' experience of racism and discrimination in Ireland*. Dublin, Ireland: Economic and Social Research Institute.

Morenoff, Jeffrey D., and Robert J. Sampson. 1997. Violent crime and the spatial dynamics of neighborhood transition: Chicago, 1970–1990. *Social Forces* 76:31–64.

Musterd, Sako, and Sjoerd De Vos. 2007. Residential dynamics in ethnic concentrations. *Housing Studies* 22 (3): 333–53.

Mutwarasibo, Fidele, and Suzanne Smith. 2000. *Africans in Ireland: Developing communities*. Dublin, Ireland: African Cultural Project.

Patterson, Orlando. 2005. Four modes of ethno-somatic stratification: The experience of blacks in Europe and the Americas. In *Ethnicity, social mobility, and public policy: Comparing the US and UK*, eds. Gary C. Loury, Tariq Modood, and S. M. Teles. Cambridge: Cambridge University Press.

Portes, Alejandro, and Leif Jensen. 1989. The enclave and the entrants: Patterns of ethnic enterprise in Miami before and after Mariel. *American Sociological Review* 54 (6): 929–49.

Portes, Alejandro, and Min Zhou. 1993. The new second generation: Segmented assimilation and its variants. *The Annals of the American Academy of Political and Social Sciences* 530:74–96.

Quinn, Emma, and Phillip J. O'Connell. 2007. *Conditions of entry and residence of third country highly-skilled workers in Ireland, 2006*. Dublin, Ireland: Economic and Social Research Institute.

Reception and Integration Agency. 2008. *Annual report 2008*. Dublin, Ireland: Government Publications Office. Available from www.ria.gov.ie.

Rolston, Bill, and Michael Shannon. 2002. *Encounters: How racism came to Ireland*. Belfast, Northern Ireland: Beyond the Pale Publications.

Takyi, Baffour K. 2002. The making of the second diaspora: On the recent African immigrant community in the United States of America. *Western Journal of Black Studies* 26 (1): 32–40.

Takyi, Baffour K., and K. S. Boate. 2006. Location and settlement patterns of African immigrants in the U.S.: Demographic and spatial context. In *The new African diaspora in North America: Trends, community building, and adaptation*, eds. K. Konadu-Agyemang, Baffour K. Takyi, and J. A. Arthur, 50–67. Lanham, MD: Lexington Books.

Telles, Edward. 2004. *Race in another America: The significance of skin color in Brazil*. Princeton, NJ: Princeton University Press.

U.S. Census Bureau. 2002. *Census 2000 Summary File 3: Technical documentation*. Washington, DC: U.S. Census Bureau.

Vang, Zoua M. 2008. Irish and American ghettos: Race and residential segregation in Ireland and the United States. PhD diss., Harvard University, Cambridge, MA.

Vang, Zoua M. 2010. Housing supply and residential segregation in Ireland. *Urban Studies* 47 (14): 2983–3012.

Vang, Zoua M. 2011. Micro-level processes of immigrant-native residential integration in Dublin. Paper presented at the annual meeting of the Population Association of America, 31 March–2 April, Washington, DC.

Waters, Mary C. 1999. *Black identities: West Indian immigrant dreams and American realities*. New York, NY: Russell Sage Foundation.

Wong, David W. S. 1993. Spatial indices of segregation. *Urban Studies* 30:559–72.

Wong, David W. S. 2002. Modeling local segregation: A spatial interaction approach. *Geographical and Environmental Modelling* 6 (1): 89–97.

Wright, Richard, Mark Ellis, and Virginia Parks. 2005. Replacing whiteness in spatial assimilation research. *City and Community* 4 (2): 111–35.

Studies of the New Immigration: The Dangers of Pan-Ethnic Classifications

By
STEPHANIE M. DiPIETRO
and
ROBERT J. BURSIK JR.

After a prolonged period during which studies of immigration and crime virtually disappeared from the literature, the topic has reemerged as a central theme of contemporary criminology. However, unlike the classic immigration studies that appeared in the first half of the twentieth century, most modern studies combine the various countries of origin into broad pan-ethnic groupings (such as Hispanic/Latino or Asian) that implicitly assume that criminological dynamics are relatively homogeneous within these aggregations despite the important social, cultural, and historical differences that are subsumed. This article utilizes data from the Children of Immigrants Longitudinal Study to illustrate the systematic within-category variation that such approaches can mask.

Keywords: ethnicity; immigration; delinquency

For more than a century, the criminological centrality of immigration research has ebbed and flowed as periods of rapid growth in the foreign-born population have given way to long stretches of stagnation. Although the early twentieth century was marked by a proliferation of work on immigration (see, for example, Wickersham Commission 1931), this emphasis eventually disappeared from all but the organized crime and gang-related research literature in the United States because of the steep decline in the number of émigrés following the passage of the National Origins (Oriental Exclusion)

Stephanie M. DiPietro is an assistant professor of criminology and criminal justice at the University of Missouri–St. Louis. Her research focuses primarily on the adaptation outcomes of immigrant youth, with a particular emphasis on violence and delinquency. She is the corecipient of the 2011 W. E. B. Du Bois Fellowship from the National Institute of Justice.

Robert J. Bursik Jr. is a curators' professor of criminology and criminal justice at the University of Missouri–St. Louis. In addition to immigration research, his work typically focuses on systemic models of neighborhood crime rates. He is a fellow and a past president of the American Society of Criminology.

DOI: 10.1177/0002716211431687

Act (1924) and the Immigration and Nationality (McCarran-Walker) Act of 1952, both of which greatly restricted the conditions under which foreign-born people could enter the United States.[1] Since the Immigration and Nationality Act of 1965 effectively abolished national-origins quotas, the United States has witnessed tremendous growth in the number of émigrés: the size of the foreign-born population increased by 57 percent between 1990 and 2000 alone, and its proportionate representation in the United States is at the highest level since 1930 (Schmidley 2001).[2] Not surprisingly, these dramatic demographic changes have ushered in a new era of criminological interest in immigration. However, unlike the classic studies in this tradition, and despite reservations that have been expressed in other disciplines, most current work examines differences among nonspecific, pan-ethnic categories such as "Asian" or "Hispanic/Latino." This article illustrates the problems that may arise when such global classifications mask significant country-of-origin variation in the criminological processes under consideration.

Background

In his foreword to Carpenter's (1927) analysis of the 1920 country-of-origin census data, Willcox notes that "our foreign-born population is a class the members of which have only one common characteristic . . . namely, that its members were not born in the United States. . . . [N]o conclusion stands out on the following pages more clearly than this, that little significant study of the foreign born can be made until they are divided into more homogenous groups by classifying them according to the country or district of birth" (p. xv). This observation clearly was engendered by the pronounced between-country variation Carpenter observed within such broad classifications as Northwestern European, Central/ Eastern European, Southern European, Asian, and American.

Carpenter's country-specific findings confirmed what already was becoming apparent in qualitative studies of that period. Park, Miller, and Thomas[3] (1921, 267), for example, concluded that "different races and nationalities, as wholes, represent different apperception masses and consequently different universes of discourse, and are not mutually intelligible." Their comparison of Polish immigrant communities in the early twentieth century, which were highly insular and attempted to reproduce the systems of relationships found in the old country, and Bohemian enclaves, which Park, Miller, and Thomas considered to be almost ideal for the purposes of assimilation, is especially illuminating in this regard (chapter VII). In particular, the roles of key community institutions, most notably Catholic churches and parishes, were extremely different for these two groups.

Although such striking differences were taken for granted by most scholars in the early twentieth century, some modern race/ethnicity-oriented social scientists have questioned the relevance of the specific country of origin in the contemporary United States, suggesting that a focus on global, pan-ethnic categories is now substantively warranted. Such aggregations are most meaningful, it is argued, because of the media's pervasive social construction of those categories (Davila 2001); the patterns of residential segregation found in many cities (Okamoto 2003); efforts to foster multiethnic solidarity (Lien, Conway, and Wong 2003); and, at least for Hispanics/Latinos, the social, ethnic, racial, and cultural homogeneity that would be expected in Mexico, Central and South America, and parts of the Caribbean after three centuries of Spanish rule (Oboler 1995, 17). Thus, it is not surprising that much has been made of the substantial increase observed between 1990 and 2000 in the proportion of Latino census respondents who categorized themselves in pan-ethnic terms (McConnell and Delgado-Romero 2004).

Nevertheless, the great majority of Latinos (85 percent) classified themselves in terms of specific countries. As Portes and Rumbaut (2001, 158) caution, while immigrant groups "are generally aware that they share common linguistic and cultural roots . . . [this] seldom suffices to produce a strong overarching solidarity." The persisting country-of-origin identification may in part reflect an appreciation of the profound racial, cultural, and structural variations in the postcolonial histories of the Hispanic/Latino countries that are at least as significant as the commonalities that do exist (Oboler 1995, 17; Kim and White 2010) or the "fundamentally different starting points, contexts of reception, and attendant definitions of the situation" that characterize the histories of racial and ethnic settlement in the United States (Rumbaut and Portes 2001, 4). In the context of those differences, studies of immigration and crime that rely solely on pan-ethnic classifications may be significantly constrained in their ability to capture many of the subtle complexities of that relationship (see Stowell and Martinez 2009, 316).

Unfortunately, for reasons outlined in the next section, almost all modern studies of immigration and crime have drawn their conclusions on the basis of nationally undifferentiated immigration statistics (such as Stowell et al. 2009) or pan-ethnic classifications (such as Martinez, Stowell, and Lee 2010; Table 1 in Ousey and Kubrin [2009] provides an excellent summary of this literature). The few studies that have disaggregated pan-ethnic patterns of immigrant crime clearly demonstrate the inferential dangers of such study designs. For example, Nagasawa, Zhenchao, and Wong (2001) observed significant differences among seven Asian and Pacific Islander ethnic groups not only in the prevalence of marijuana use and delinquency between the ages of 14 and 20, but also in the dynamics that led to such behavior. Likewise, Sampson, Morenoff, and Raudenbush (2005) show that young Puerto Ricans/other Latinos in Chicago are substantially more likely to engage in violent behavior than adolescents of Mexican descent; and Stowell's (2007) study of violence in three cities reveals substantial differences in the structural conditions of the neighborhoods into which members of various ethnic groups settle as well as differences in the social conditions associated with violence in these communities. Stowell and Martinez (2009) observed similar differences in Miami for Cubans, Hondurans, Nicaraguans, and Haitians. At the least, such findings indicate that the criminological utility of pan-ethnic categories cannot be taken for granted.

Criminological Data and the New Immigration

Although their reliability generally was questionable, richly detailed immigration and crime data were widely available in the first half of the twentieth century. For example, Van Vechten (1941, 140) observed that "most police departments record the nativity of the persons they arrest," and the Wickersham Commission was able to generate arrest rates for a detailed breakdown of the foreign-born population in thirty-one cities (1931, part II.II). Likewise, country-of-origin delinquency statistics were central components of such seminal primary data collection efforts as those of Shaw and McKay (Bursik 2006). These early works highlighted stark differences in the criminal behavior of immigrants across European countries. For example, in his 1922 testimony before the Congressional Committee on Immigration, Laughlin observed that rates of commitment to penal institutions were ten times greater among immigrants from Italy and the Balkans, compared with those from Great Britain, Ireland, and Scandinavia. Also variable were the so-called "typical" crimes committed by different immigrant groups. For example, whereas the Irish and Scottish were more often imprisoned for crimes related to drunkenness and public disorder, Italians were more often represented among the commitments for violent crimes.

However, detailed racial/ethnic classifications, immigrant-related or not, have become the exception rather than the rule in contemporary criminology, leading some researchers to express serious misgivings about the "grossly oversimplified" groupings found in standard data sources such as the Uniform Crime Reports (UCR) and the National Crime Victimization Survey (NCVS) (Marshall 1997, 2; see also Tonry 1997, 7–9, Sampson and Lauritsen 1997, 314–15). The situation is not especially problematic when analyses are restricted to geographic areas where pan-ethnic categories can safely be assumed to primarily reflect a single country of origin. For example, census statistics indicate that Bradshaw et al.'s (1998) claim that the homicides labeled "Hispanic" in the Bexar County, Texas (San Antonio), mortality files are "almost exclusively of Mexican origin" (p. 866) is warranted; Martinez (2002, 70) presents evidence that this also is the case in El Paso, Houston, and San Diego, as it is in Maricopa County, Arizona (Katz, Fox, and White 2011). However, Martinez also demonstrates that the assumption of homogeneity would be highly misleading in such popular Latin immigrant destinations as Chicago or Miami.

Although each has its weaknesses, three alternative sources of data provide partial resolutions of the problems highlighted by Marshall and others. The first is federal or state incarceration and arrest data (Scalia 1996; U.S. Department of Justice 1993). Hagan and Palloni (1999), for example, used the 1991 Survey of State Prisons to estimate age-adjusted rates of incarceration for persons from Mexico, Cuba, El Salvador, the Dominican Republic, Jamaica, Colombia, and

Guatemala. However, as Hagan and Palloni caution, these data preclude an identification of the factors that differentiate between incarcerated and nonincarcer-
ated immigrants, and the countries of origin of naturalized immigrants are not
identified. More recently, Rumbaut et al. (2006) used data from the 5 percent
Public Use Microdata Sample (PUMS) to assess racial, ethnic, and immigrant
group variation in rates of institutionalization. Although these data include information on nativity status and country of origin, the limited number of background variables makes it nearly impossible to engage in serious theory testing.
Nevertheless, these "official" data sources have been used to generate important
actuarial insights.

A second possibility is to exploit the classificatory detail provided by some
national and local surveys. For example, the National Longitudinal Study of
Adolescent Health differentiates among parental respondents born in Mexico,
Cuba, Puerto Rico, Central/South America, or some other Latin location; the
Asian categories are equally refined (China, Philippines, Japan, India, Korea,
Vietnam, or another Asian location; see Carolina Population Center 1999). The
Project on Human Development in Chicago Neighborhoods (PHDCN) provides similarly detailed information (Earls 1999). However, despite the post-
1965 surge in immigration, only 12.5 percent of the U.S. population is
foreign-born (Pew Hispanic Center 2010), and it is highly concentrated geographically.[4] Thus, even the most sophisticated survey designs will include relatively few foreign-born respondents, much less analytically sufficient numbers
of cases for most countries of origin. For this reason, despite the finely delineated racial/ethnic distinctions found in the PHDCN, Hispanic indicators in
Sampson, Morenoff, and Raudenbush's (2005) models can distinguish only
between Mexicans and all other Latin groups. Thus, as frustrating as it may be,
it often is impossible to simultaneously take advantage of country-specific classifications and maintain a minimally acceptable level of statistical power.

The third option is to use surveys that specifically target immigrant or ethnic
respondents. Surprisingly, unlike Canada, Australia, and New Zealand (Black et al.
2003), nationally representative surveys of immigrants and their children were
not conducted in the United States until the first wave of the New Immigrant
Survey went into the field in 2003 (Jasso et al. 2000). As such, the "targeted"
surveys usually have drawn their samples from a fairly restricted geographic area.
The Asian Student Drug Survey, for example, collected data from 13,374 ninth-
and twelfth-grade students in California (Nagasawa, Zhenchao, and Wong 2001).

The Present Study

In light of the aforementioned data limitations, it is not surprising that a relative
dearth of contemporary criminological research has distinguished among countries of origin, relying instead on pan-ethnic classifications such as "Latino"
or "Asian." The primary aim of this study is to illustrate how the diverse

backgrounds and experiences of immigrant groups usually amalgamated into these broad categories have resulted in differences in the levels of social capital, family structure and dynamics, and contexts of reception experienced by their children, and the subsequent impact of these factors on their success or failure in key areas of adaptation. We draw from a targeted survey, the Children of Immigrants Longitudinal Study (CILS), to answer three basic questions:

1. Do the children of immigrants from four nationalities (Cuban, Nicaraguan, Colombian, Dominican), usually combined into the single pan-ethnic category of Hispanic/Latino, differ significantly in levels of human capital, family structure and dynamics, and contexts of reception?
2. Do the distributions of aggressive behavior differ significantly among the four subgroups?
3. Do human capital, the context of reception, and family structure/dynamics have similar effects on aggressive behavior in these four subgroups?

Although these issues are similar in spirit to those posed in earlier examinations of the pan-ethnicity question, this study differs in several critical ways.

First, unlike studies that have analyzed data generated by law enforcement or judicial agencies, the self-reported nature of the CILS data eliminates the selection biases that characterize gate-keeping mechanisms such as arrest and conviction. In this respect, the study complements that of Nagasawa, Zhenchao, and Wong (2001) and Rumbaut et al. (2006) in its focus on Latino rather than Asian groups.

Second, with few exceptions (e.g., Nagasawa, Zhenchao, and Wong 2001), prior research has been restricted to the background information provided by arrest records, coroner reports, and/or census data. Although such data are invaluable in their own right and have provided important insights into the neighborhood or city factors associated with immigrant crime (such as Stowell and Martinez 2009), they cannot provide any information about more proximal factors.

Third, Portes and Rumbaut (2006, 92–93) have emphasized the importance of "contexts of reception" (i.e., the policies of the receiving government, the conditions of the local labor market, and the characteristics of and support received from conationals already residing in the host community) in shaping the adaptation outcomes of immigrants, particularly children. Unfortunately, although the aforementioned Nagasawa, Zhenchao, and Wong (2001) study analyzed the responses of a sample drawn from the highly diverse state of California, they did not control for the effects of this contextual variation, which is a critical omission. To avoid this problem, we have restricted our focus to a sample of adolescents living in the city of Miami, thereby holding many of these broad factors constant. However, since there also are more immediate contexts of reception that shape the lives of the children of immigrants, we incorporate measures of the respondents' school types and the perceived social climates of these environments.

Data and Methods

Sample and research setting

The CILS is a decade-long panel study of the characteristics and adaptation outcomes of first- and second-generation immigrant youth in two distinct areas of immigrant settlement: Southern California (San Diego) and Southern Florida (Miami and Ft. Lauderdale). Although data were gathered at three time points, we restrict our study to the first two waves of data collection when our measures of interest were collected. The initial survey was conducted in 1992 and 1993, when respondents were an average of 14 years old. Follow-up interviews were conducted three years later in 1995 and 1996, when respondents were approximately 17 years old. Of the original sample, 81.5 percent (n = 4,288) of the original sample was interviewed during the second wave of data collection.

The CILS data are particularly well suited to our needs for several reasons. First, it is one of the few data sources to include analytically sufficient numbers of youth from different countries of origin; the initial sample of 5,262 youth represents seventy-seven different nationalities. Second, unlike the cross-sectional design of other targeted surveys (e.g., Asian Student Drug Survey), the longitudinal design of the CILS enables us to establish temporal order between our key correlates and measure of aggressive behavior. Finally, architects of the CILS gathered detailed information about respondents' schools, enabling us to control for important contextual variation in factors such as school type and climate.

We restrict our sample to those respondents living in the city of Miami. Miami has long been a major hub of contemporary immigration and boasts one of the largest immigrant populations in the United States. Compared with the national average of 12.5 percent, immigrants compose nearly 50 percent of the total population of Miami-Dade County, which includes the city of Miami; roughly 93 percent of the foreign-born population comes from Latin America (U.S. Census Bureau 2010).

We limit our study to a subsample of 1,444 first- and second-generation immigrant youth who self-identified as one of four Latin ethnic groups: Cuban, Nicaraguan, Colombian, and Dominican. The resulting sample includes 943 Cubans, 274 Nicaraguans, 164 Colombians, and 63 Dominicans. We focus on these particular nationalities for three reasons. First, each of these groups represents a sizable proportion of the foreign-born population; in 2007, approximately 983,000 Cubans, 756,000 Dominicans, 555,000 Colombians, and 202,000 Nicaraguans were residing in the United States (U.S. Census Bureau 2010). Second, whereas substantial research has been conducted on Mexican immigrants—which is not surprising given their disproportionate representation among immigrant groups—less attention has been given to other Latin nationalities. Third, these four nationalities are emblematic of the variability in background characteristics and modes of incorporation that distinguish immigrant groups who have entered the United States under vastly different social and historical circumstances.

Compared to the other groups, Cubans occupy a relatively privileged position; composed predominantly of political asylees from Castro's revolution, the first major wave of Cuban émigrés, aptly designated the "golden exiles" (Martinez 2002, 35), possessed a level of affluence and education that was generally atypical among other "Hispanic" émigrés, and that helped shape what Portes and Rumbaut (2006) have coined a generally positive context of reception. Not only did they receive substantial assistance from the government to aid with resettlement, but their social status buffered them from the discriminatory treatment bestowed upon immigrants from Mexico and the Dominican Republic.

By contrast, Nicaraguan émigrés who fled the political and economic turmoil of the Sandinista regime two decades after the first Cuban migration were not afforded the same status. Although they shared a common history with Cuban immigrants as refugees from Communist regimes, the timing of the Nicaraguan exile had profound implications for their immigration experience. Having arrived in southern Florida in the wake of the 1980 Mariel boatlift, which had hardened public attitudes toward immigrants, Nicaraguan immigrants faced a hostile reception; "their avowals of political persecution and petitions of legal residence were consistently rejected at federal, state and local levels," leaving them with few resources with which to "forge a cohesive community" (Fernandez-Kelly and Curran 2001, 127–28).

Although the reasons for the Dominicans' migration to the United States are complex and varied, and include fear of political persecution and the desire for family reunification, since the 1970s their primary motivation has been economic (Portes, Guarnizo, and Haller 2002). Thus, while Dominican immigrants represent a diverse range of social capital—encompassing both professionals and rural laborers—a recent study of second-generation immigrants in New York showed that Dominicans were, on the whole, among the most disadvantaged in the sample (Kasinitz et al. 2008). Compounding their position of relative socioeconomic disadvantage, Dominicans have historically been the subject of racial discrimination, which is likely a reflection of their darker skin and their designation as phenotypically black upon arrival (Kasinitz et al. 2008). Take, for example, conservative pundit Heather MacDonald's unsubstantiated claim that Dominican communities in New York have "long shown elevated crime and welfare rates" (quoted in Martinez and Valenzuela 2006, 5).

Of the four groups in the sample, Colombian immigrants have perhaps been the most disadvantaged with respect to the social stigma associated with their nationality. Decades of political and drug-related violence, beginning with "La Violencia" in the late 1940s and persisting into the 1990s, have made Colombian immigrants less inclined to forge strong community ties with their fellow coethnics. Portes, Guarnizo, and Haller (2002, 285) attribute this resistance to "the stigma associated with the drug trade and the perennial suspicion that others may be involved . . . [which] leads Colombians to be distrustful of each other and less willing to engage in cooperative activities." Nevertheless, Colombian immigrants, on the whole, have enjoyed a relatively higher level of socioeconomic status than other Hispanic immigrant groups. Kasinitz et al. (2008) found, for example, that compared with Dominicans and Puerto Ricans, Colombian immigrants reported more two-parent households, a higher level of education, more workers in the household, and better residential locations in New York.

Measures

Dependent Variable. A dichotomous measure of aggressive behavior was derived from subjects' responses to an item that asked how many times in the course of the current school year they got into a physical fight at school (0 = never, 1 = one or more times). Fighting is one of the most prevalent forms of aggression and has been well established as an antecedent to more serious forms of violence. Sixteen percent of respondents reported engaging in at least one fight in the previous year.[5]

Independent Variables. We examine group variation in four key domains of immigrant adaptation: assimilation, human capital, family composition/dynamics, and school context of reception. Descriptive statistics for all study variables are shown in Table 1.

Assimilation. In line with prior research, which has shown marked generational differences in crime and violence (Morenoff and Astor 2006; Sampson, Morenoff, and Raudenbush 2005), we differentiate between those individuals born in the United States to immigrant parents and those who are foreign born. *Second generation* is a dichotomous variable indicating whether the respondent was born in the United States. Roughly 56 percent of the sample is second generation. We also include an index of *English language proficiency* as a proxy measure of assimilation. This measure is a four-item scale (α = .85) measuring how well respondents speak, understand, read, and write English. On average, respondents report a high level of English proficiency (3.8 out of 4).

Human capital. We include two measures of human capital in this study. *SES* is a composite index of parents' socioeconomic status. The index ranges from −1.66 to 1.85, with an average of 0.12 for the group. *GPA* is a measure of the respondent's grade point average; the average GPA for the sample is 2.38.

Family composition/dynamics. *Biological parents* is a dichotomous measure indicating whether respondents live with both biological parents as opposed to an alternative living arrangement (e.g., single-headed household). Approximately 64 percent of the sample resides with both biological parents. *Family cohesion* is a three-item scale (α = .84) that captures the level of closeness that respondents feel toward their families. Respondents were asked to indicate on a five-item Likert scale (*never* to *always*) how often the following statements are true:

TABLE 1
Demographic and Background Characteristics of Immigrant Youth by Country of Origin, Miami, Florida

	N	Demographics		Assimilation		Human Capital		Family Composition/ Dynamics		School Context of Reception		
		Percentage Male (n.s.)	Age°°°	Percentage Second Generation°°°	English Language Proficiency°°°	Parent SES Index°°°	GPA°	Percentage Living with Both Biological Parents (n.s.)	Family Cohesion°°	Percentage Attend Inner-City School°°°	Positive School Climate°°°	Percentage Perceive Discrimination°°°
Cuba	943	51	14.06 (0.82)	70.9	3.86 (0.29)	.18 (.68)	2.40 (0.86)	63.6	11.05 (2.97)	31.1	29.51 (4.70)	34.8
Nicaragua	274	47	14.40 (0.86)	6.9	3.72 (0.38)	.06 (.62)	2.41 (0.88)	65.7	11.56 (2.66)	25.5	30.30 (4.56)	51.1
Colombia	164	49	14.14 (0.84)	50.0	3.79 (0.36)	.05 (.66)	2.34 (0.80)	64.0	10.89 (3.06)	30.5	28.73 (4.44)	42.4
Dominican	63	35	14.27 (0.92)	66.7	3.77 (0.47)	-.18 (.70)	2.13 (0.93)	50.8	10.89 (3.16)	52.4	29.26 (3.49)	50.8
Total	1,444	49	14.14 (0.86)	56.2	3.82 (0.33)	.12 (.67)	2.38 (0.86)	63.5	11.12 (2.93)	32.3	29.56 (4.61)	39.4
F		2.283	12.470	158.741	13.146	7.898	2.159	1.662	2.76	5.828	4.24	9.670

°One-way ANOVA significant at $p < .10$. °°One-way ANOVA significant at $p < .05$. °°°One-way ANOVA significant at $p < .01$.

NOTES: N.s.=not significant. Standard deviations in parentheses.

"family likes to spend time together," "family members feel close," and "family togetherness is important." On average, respondents report a relatively high level of family cohesion (11.1 on a scale ranging from 3 to 15).

School context of reception. Next to the family, the school is arguably the most important institution for socializing youth. For immigrant adolescents, this particular context of reception takes on added salience, as schools are the primary environment in which they are exposed to "mainstream culture." We examine three dimensions of school context. *Inner-city school* is a dichotomous measure indicating whether youth are enrolled in an inner-city (1) versus suburban (0) school. Thirty-two percent of the sample attends an inner-city school. *Positive school climate* is a ten-item scale (α = .72) measuring the degree to which respondents regard their school climate as positive. Respondents were asked to rate their level of agreement (*disagree a lot* to *agree a lot*) with statements such as "there is real school spirit," "students make friends with students of other racial and ethnic groups," and "I don't feel safe at school" (reverse-coded). The average student regards his or her school climate as relatively positive (29.6 on a scale of 12 to 40). Finally, *discrimination* is a dichotomous measure indicating whether the respondent has felt discriminated against. Roughly 39 percent of the sample answered affirmatively to this question.

Analysis

To examine our first and second research questions, we conduct a series of one-way ANOVAs to assess group differences in assimilation, human capital, family characteristics, contexts of reception, and aggressive behavior. To examine our third research question, we conduct a series of logistic multiple regressions to assess whether the predictors of aggressive behavior differ across groups.

Results

Our primary aim in this study is to determine whether and to what extent the broad category of "Hispanic/Latino," under which these four nationalities have often been subsumed, masks important group variation in key domains of immigrant adaptation. Results of a series of one-way ANOVAs (shown in Table 1) indicate that these four groups are marked by significant variability in assimilation, human capital, family composition/dynamics, and school contexts of reception. First, we find significant group differences in the percentage of youth who are second generation (p < .01) as well as in the reported level of English language proficiency (p < .01). Whereas the majority of Cuban and Dominican youth (71 and 67 percent, respectively) and half the Colombian youth are second generation, less than 10 percent of Nicaraguan youth were born in the United States. Not surprisingly, given the differences in generational status, we find that

Cuban youth report the highest average level of English language proficiency, followed by Dominican and Colombian youth; Nicaraguans report the lowest.

Turning to the measures of human capital, we also find marked differences across groups. Cubans report the highest average levels of parental socioeconomic status; Dominicans, by contrast, report the lowest ($p < .01$). Given the varied migration history of these two groups, and the relative level of privilege with which Cuban immigrants settled in Miami, these differences are not surprising. A comparison of student GPAs reveals that Dominican youth also report the lowest achievement relative to the other youth, with an average GPA of 2.1, compared to an average of 2.3 to 2.4 for each of the other groups, although the ANOVA reaches only marginal significance ($p < .10$).

With respect to family composition and dynamics, we find no significant group variation in the percentage of youth living with both biological parents, but we do find that the groups differ with respect to the average levels of reported family cohesion ($p < .05$). Nicaraguan and Cuban youth report the highest level of family cohesion (11.6 and 11.1, respectively, on the cohesion scale), compared with an average of 10.9 for Dominican and Colombian youth. Given the prevailing stereotype of Hispanics as highly familistic and collectivistic, the significant group variation in the degree of family cohesion reported by youth is noteworthy.

Perhaps the starkest differences among the youth are evident in their respective school contexts of reception. First, whereas more than half of Dominican youth (52 percent) attend inner-city schools, fewer than a third of youth from each of the other groups attend inner-city schools ($p < .01$). We find significant variation in respondents' perception of their school climate as well. Nicaraguan youth report a more positive school climate than any of the other groups, while Colombian youth report the least positive climate ($p < .01$). Finally, we observe notable group differences in the percentage of youth reporting that they have experienced discrimination ($p < .01$). Whereas roughly half of Dominican and Nicaraguan youth report experiencing discriminatory treatment, this number is substantially lower for Colombian and Cuban youth (42 and 35 percent, respectively).

Our second research question assesses the extent to which these four groups differ in their levels of reported aggressive behavior (e.g., fighting). Figure 1 shows the percentage of youth who reported fighting at least once during the past school year. In light of recent research documenting higher rates of delinquency and violence among second-generation immigrants (Sampson, Morenoff, and Raudenbush 2005), we disaggregate the sample by generational status. Two findings are noteworthy. First, results of a one-way ANOVA indicate that group differences in fighting are significant among first-generation youth ($p < .05$), but not second. This finding resonates with the expectations of classic assimilation scholars (Gordon 1964) that the children of immigrants, particularly those who are born in the United States, will shed some of their distinctive ethnic traits and begin to resemble more closely their native-born counterparts.

Second, we find important differences by nationality in the prevalence of fighting across immigrant generations. Although the finding that second-generation

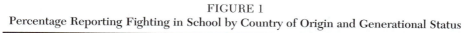

FIGURE 1

Percentage Reporting Fighting in School by Country of Origin and Generational Status

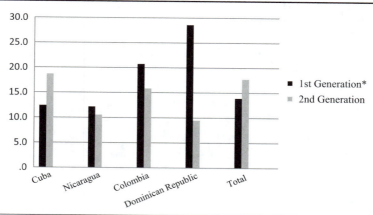

NOTE: One-way ANOVA significant at $°p < .05$.

immigrants report higher rates of crime and delinquency than their first-generation counterparts has been well substantiated by research spanning two distinct eras of immigration, our findings suggest that this pattern may be contingent on the particular group being studied. For only one group, Cubans, does the so-called pattern of "second-generation decline" (Rumbaut and Portes 2001) hold. For each of the other groups, we observe a greater frequency of reported fights among the first generation. Generational differences in aggressive behavior are most marked for Dominican youth; 29 percent of first-generation Dominican immigrants report fighting compared with less than 10 percent of second-generation youth.

We turn next to the results of our multiple logistic regressions of fighting on assimilation, human capital, family characteristics, and school context of reception by country of origin, shown in Table 2. Results of these analyses highlight important group differences in the criminological processes under consideration. First, with respect to the demographic correlates of fighting, we find that whereas males are significantly more likely to engage in fighting than females for three of the four groups, the strength and significance of this effect varies. For Cubans and Colombians, being male increases the odds of fighting by a factor of nearly 6, compared with about a 3.5 factor increase for Nicaraguans. Equality of coefficients tests indicate that the difference between Cubans and Nicaraguans is significant ($z = 7.68$). Notably, gender exerts no significant effect on fighting among Dominicans.

Turning next to the measures of human capital, we find that parental socioeconomic status is a significant risk factor for fighting for only one of the four groups; a unit increase in SES is associated with an 85 percent decrease in the odds of fighting among Dominicans ($p < .05$) but has no significant impact for any of the

TABLE 2

Logistic Regression of Fighting (Wave 2) on Demographics, Assimilation, Human Capital, Family Characteristics, and School Context of Reception (N = 1,444)

Independent Variables	Cuba		Nicaragua		Colombia		Dominican Republic		All Groups	
	Exp(B)	SE	Exp(B)	SE	Exp(B)	SE	Exp(B)	SE	Exp(B)	SE
Male	5.67	0.23°°°°	3.50	0.45°°°	5.83	0.53°°°°	5.91	1.06	4.84	0.18°°°°
Age	0.92	0.12	1.66	0.26	0.75	0.32	0.65	0.73	0.94	0.10
Second generation	1.53	0.24	0.84	0.97	0.54	0.48	0.12	1.20	1.21	0.17
English proficiency	0.76	0.31	1.13	0.53	1.02	0.71	2.91	1.26	0.48	0.94
SES	1.01	0.16	0.55	0.39	1.31	0.37	0.15	0.94°°	0.94	0.13
GPA	0.54	0.12°°°°	0.58	0.24°°	0.59	0.31	0.34	0.66	0.58	0.10°°°°
Living with biological parents	1.13	0.20	1.05	0.43	0.83	0.49	0.14	1.15	0.83	0.18
Family cohesion	0.93	0.03°°	1.07	0.08	0.96	0.08	1.02	0.19	0.96	0.03°
Inner-city school	0.75	0.24	0.57	0.52	0.95	0.51	0.64	1.11	0.75	0.19
Positive school climate	0.96	0.02°°	0.90	0.05°°	0.91	0.05	1.10	0.16	0.95	0.02°°°
Perceived discrimination	1.37	0.20	3.73	0.45°°°	1.85	0.47	2.10	0.98	1.57	0.16°°°
Number of cases	943		274		164		63		1,444	

°p < .10. °°p < .05. °°°p < .01. °°°°p < .001.

other groups. Also variable is the effect of GPA. Whereas a unit increase in GPA is associated with a more than 40 percent decrease in the odds of fighting among Cubans and Nicaraguans, we find no appreciable effect for Colombians or Dominicans. Notably, however, equality of coefficients tests indicate that the difference between Cubans and Nicaraguans is not statistically different from zero ($z = 1.41$).

Turning to the measures of family characteristics and dynamics, we find that for only one group, Cubans, is family cohesion a significant determinant of fighting ($p < .05$). A greater degree of perceived family cohesion is associated with lower odds of aggression for this group. Living with both biological parents has no significant effect on fighting behavior for any of the groups, net of other factors.

Finally, two measures relating to respondents' school context of reception, perceived school climate and experiences with discrimination, exert variable effects on fighting across groups. Whereas a more positive school climate is associated with a significant decrease in the odds of fighting among Cubans and Nicaraguans, it has no appreciable influence on fighting for Colombians or Dominicans. The difference in slopes for Cubans and Nicaraguans is significant ($z = 17.02$), suggesting that perceived school climate exerts a more potent influence on aggressive behavior for Cubans. Perceived discrimination exerts a powerful impact on fighting for Nicaraguans—having experienced discrimination increases the odds of fighting by a factor of nearly 4 ($p < .01$). Discrimination has no significant impact on fighting for any of the other groups.

Next, Figures 2 and 3 show the predicted probabilities of fighting by nationality and generational status, with all control variables held at their means. We examine these probabilities to determine what, if any, differences exist between the baseline levels of fighting observed across immigrant groups and what would be expected once all relevant background characteristics are controlled. Given the salience of social context in shaping immigrant youths' behavioral outcomes, we further disaggregate the sample by school type (inner-city versus suburban) to examine whether group differences in aggressive behavior may be conditioned by the broader school context in which immigrant youth are located. Results of a two-way ANOVA (not shown) suggest that group variation in the predicted probability of fighting is contingent on school context. Specifically, we find no significant variation by country of origin or generational status in the probability of fighting among the sample of respondents attending inner-city schools. However, we observe significant variation by country of origin ($F = 3.89$, $p < .01$) in the predicted probability of fighting among respondents attending suburban schools. Second, our findings suggest that generational differences in fighting may be conditional on the particular group being studied. With all background characteristics held at their means, Nicaraguan youth have the lowest probability of fighting (approximately 10 percent probability compared with 16 to 18 percent for the other groups). Notably, in contrast to the well-documented pattern of second-generation decline (i.e., higher offending among the second generation),

FIGURE 2
Mean Predicted Probability of Fighting by National Origin and Generation

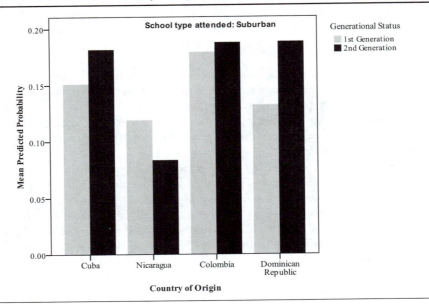

FIGURE 3
Mean Predicted Probability of Fighting by National Origin and Generation

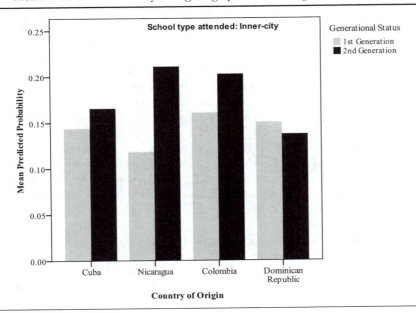

first-generation Nicaraguans are more likely than their second-generation counterparts to fight.

Discussion and Conclusion

Although criminological research has made considerable strides in moving
beyond the black-white racial dichotomy, studies of the new immigration have
been bedeviled by what Rumbaut et al. (2006, 85) argue is the "national bad habit
of lumping individuals into a handful of one-size-fits-all racialized categories
(black, white, Latino, Asian) that obliterate different migration and generational
histories, cultures, frames of reference, and contexts of reception and incorporation." Given immigration scholars' focus on nationality/ethnicity at the turn of the
century, the fact that contemporary scholarship has lagged so far behind the need
to understand the nature and extent of ethnic group variation in criminal behavior is surprising. The aim of this study was to illustrate the inferential dangers of
aggregating immigrants of different national origin into broad categories such as
"Asian" and "Latino" and to pave the way for more finely delineated studies of
the new immigration.

Our findings largely substantiate claims made by Willcox and others more than
80 years ago that a truly comprehensive understanding of the foreign-born and
their patterns of assimilation demands the disaggregation of groups by nativity
status and country of birth. Drawing from a sample of the children of immigrants
from four distinct countries of origin, we found significant group differences in
measures of human capital, family characteristics, and contexts of reception that
would have been obfuscated under the pan-ethnic classification of "Latino." For
example, the children of Cuban immigrants appear to fare better than most of
the other groups on several indicators, which is not surprising given their relatively privileged migration experience (Martinez 2002). Not only do they possess
relatively higher levels of human capital, they are also the least likely to have
experienced discriminatory treatment. By contrast, Dominican youth generally
fare worse than the other groups, reporting the lowest levels of human capital,
the highest attendance in inner-city schools, and the most perceived discrimination. Given that more than two-thirds of the Cuban and Dominican youth in the
sample were born in the United States, it seems clear that these differences cannot be explained by variation in nativity status alone.

Of paramount concern to the study of the new immigration is whether and to
what extent the factors associated with immigrants' variable backgrounds may
give rise to maladaptive behaviors such as crime and delinquency. Whereas a
burgeoning literature highlights the salience of human capital, family composition, and assimilatory status in explanations of immigrant criminality, it is unclear
whether such variables operate similarly across ethnic groups or whether differences in cultural repertoires, migration experiences, and contexts of reception
shape the criminological processes under consideration. In an effort to shed light

on this question, we analyzed group differences in the prevalence and predictors of one form of maladaptive behavior: fighting. Of course, it is worth noting that our measure of fighting represents a relatively benign form of criminality. Research on ethnic group differences in more serious forms of crime and delinquency is needed. Nevertheless, results of these analyses suggest that the criminological utility of pan-ethnic categories cannot be taken for granted.

First, in addition to finding significant group variation in the prevalence of fighting, our results suggest that the oft-cited finding that second-generation youth engage in more problem behaviors than their first-generation counterparts may hinge on the national origin of the group being studied. Looking first at the bivariate associations between country of origin and fighting, we found that whereas second-generation Cuban youth are more likely to engage in fighting than their first-generation counterparts, this pattern was reversed for each of the other groups. That is, contrary to what much contemporary immigration research suggests, we found a higher prevalence of fighting among the first generation than the second for most of the groups. These differences were obscured in estimates for the group as a whole, suggesting that the composition of "Hispanic" samples may obfuscate group differences in the association of nativity with crime and delinquency.

Second, we examined predictors of aggressive behavior by ethnic group to determine what, if any, differences exist in the criminological processes under consideration. An examination of the "Hispanic" group as a whole indicated that five variables were significant predictors of fighting: being male, having a low GPA, having a lower level of family cohesion, perceiving a less positive school climate, and experiencing discriminatory treatment. Notably, however, the disaggregated models revealed substantial variation across groups with respect to the strength and significance of these predictors. The only significant correlate of fighting among Dominican youth, for example, is parental socioeconomic status. Among Colombians, being male is the only significant predictor. Although the reduction in sample size and statistical power in the disaggregated models marks another limitation of this research, our findings nevertheless suggest that the common practice of lumping immigrants from distinct countries of origin into amorphous categories may not only disguise important differences in the prevalence of crime and other maladaptive behaviors but also in the explanatory processes used to explain these behaviors.

Finally, although our choice to restrict the sample to the city of Miami was made to control for variation in context that might be conflated with ethnic group differences, research that considers the intersection of individual and contextual determinants of offending across ethnic groups is certainly warranted. In an effort to shed some light on the role of social context in shaping the associations among generational status, national origin, and aggressive behavior, we disaggregated the sample by type of school (suburban versus inner-city) and examined the predicted probabilities of fighting across these two very different contexts. Two findings are noteworthy. First, results of a two-way ANOVA indicate that the only significant group differences in the predicted probability of fighting emerged in the sample of youth attending suburban schools. Notably, we found no significant group differences in our models of predicted behavior among inner-city youth. Our results suggest that the relative utility of pan-ethnic classifications may, to some extent, be contingent on the broader social context in which immigrant groups are studied. At the least, this finding raises the question of whether differences in nationality are less important in more disadvantaged contexts.

Second, holding all variables at their mean values, we found that Nicaraguan first-generation youth in suburban schools have higher predicted probabilities of fighting than their second-generation counterparts. Again, although our focus in this study is on a relatively minor form of criminal behavior, our findings nevertheless call into question the timeworn assumption that the first generation necessarily fares better than the second with respect to crime and delinquency. At the least, it warrants further consideration of how generational status intersects with ethnicity and social context to shape patterns of downward assimilation.

With the proliferation of research over the past decade, scholars have begun to reach a degree of consensus about the relationship between immigration and crime. Certain findings, such as the negative association between immigration and crime at the macro level and the pattern of generational decline observed in most contemporary studies of individual behavior, are fast approaching the status of an intellectual canon. Yet for reasons outlined above, most of this research has not endeavored to disentangle ethnic group differences, relying instead on broad amalgamations of ethnic groups. The findings of this study call such approaches into question. Although the focus of this research was on the individual-level associations among nativity, ethnicity, and aggressive behavior, our findings certainly speak to the inferential dangers inherent to macro-level research as well. As immigration continues to shape the landscape of this country, a better understanding of group differences in behavior and the criminological processes under consideration is of paramount concern.

Notes

1. Important exceptions are Finestone (1967) and Kitano (1967).

2. Despite the resurgence of interest, criminology has been much slower to consider the implications of the new immigration than many other social sciences. Four of the five review essays in the July 2004 issue of *Contemporary Sociology*, for example, focused on these dynamics.

3. Although this book usually is attributed to Park and Miller, it now is known that it primarily was the work of W. I. Thomas (Coser 1977). The Carnegie Corporation of New York, which had commissioned the study, refused to allow its publication unless Thomas's name was removed as author due to the scandal surrounding his forced resignation from the University of Chicago in 1918.

4. Over two-thirds of the foreign-born live in California, New York, Texas, Florida, New Jersey, and Illinois (Capps, Fix, and Passel 2002).

5. Although the comparison is far from exact, it is worth noting that this prevalence rate is about 26 percent higher than the 12.7 percent reported by the Centers for Disease Control (2011) for all Florida high school students during 2001, the closest year for which such data are available.

References

Black, Richard, Tony Fielding, Russell King, Ronald Skeldon, and Richmond Tiemoko. 2003. Longitudinal studies: An insight into current studies and the social and economic outcomes for migrants. Sussex Migration Working Paper No. 14, University of Sussex: Sussex Centre for Migration Research, Sussex, UK.

Bradshaw, Benjamin, David R. Johnson, Derral Cheatwood, and Steven Blanchard. 1998. A historical geographic study of lethal violence in San Antonio. *Social Science Quarterly* 79:863–78.

Bursik, Robert J., Jr. 2006. Rethinking the Chicago School of Criminology: A new era of immigration. In *Immigration and crime: Race, ethnicity, and violence*, eds. Ramiro Martinez Jr. and Abel Valenzuela Jr., 20–35. New York, NY: New York University Press.

Capps, Randolph, Michael E. Fix, and Jeffrey S. Passel. 2002. *The dispersal of immigrants in the 1990s. Brief #2: Immigrant families and workers: Facts and perspectives.* Washington, DC: Urban Institute.

Carolina Population Center. 1999. *National Longitudinal Study of Adolescent Health. Parental questionnaire code book.* Chapel Hill: University of North Carolina.

Carpenter, Niles. 1927. *Immigrants and their children 1920. Census Monographs VII.* Washington, DC: Government Printing Office.

Centers for Disease Control and Prevention. 2011. *Youth Risk Behavior Surveillance System.* Available from http://apps.nccd.cdc.gov/youthonline/App/Default.aspx.

Coser, Lewis. 1977. *Masters of sociological thought.* New York, NY: Harcourt, Brace, Jovanovich.

Davila, Arlene. 2001. *Latinos, Inc.: The marketing and making of a people.* Berkeley: University of California Press.

Earls, Felton. 1999. *Project on Human Development in Chicago Neighborhoods: Community survey, 1994–1995. Codebook.* Ann Arbor, MI: Inter-University Consortium for Political and Social Research.

Fernandez-Kelly, Patricia, and Sara Curran. 2001. Nicaraguans: Voices lost, voices found. In *Ethnicities: Children of immigrants in America*, eds. Ruben G. Rumbaut and Alejandro Portes. Berkeley: University of California Press.

Finestone, Harold. 1967. Reformation and recidivism among Italian and Polish criminal offenders. *American Journal of Sociology* 72:575–88.

Gordon, Milton M. 1964. *Assimilation in American life: The role of race, religion, and national origins.* Oxford: Oxford University Press.

Hagan, John, and Alberto Palloni. 1999. Sociological criminology and the mythology of Hispanic immigration and crime. *Social Problems* 46:617–32.

Jasso, Guillermina, Douglas S. Massey, Mark R. Rosenzweig, and James P. Smith. 2000. The New Immigrant Survey Pilot (NIS-P): Overview and new findings about U.S. legal immigrants at admission. *Demography* 37:127–38.

Kasinitz, Philip, John Mollenkopf, Mary Waters, and Jennifer Holdaway. 2008 *Inheriting the city: The children of immigrants come of age.* New York, NY: Russell Sage Foundation.

Katz, Charles M., Andrew M. Fox, and Michael D. White. 2011. Assessing the relationship between immigration status and drug use. *Justice Quarterly* 28:541–75.

Kim, Ann, and Michael J. White. 2010. Panethnicity, ethnic diversity, and residential segregation. *American Journal of Sociology* 115:1558–96.

Kitano, Harry H. L. 1967. Japanese-American crime and delinquency. *Journal of Social Psychology* 66:253–63.

Laughlin, Harry H. 1922. Analysis of America's modern melting pot. Testimony before the House Committee on Immigration and Naturalization. 67th Congress, 3rd session, 21 November 1922.

Lien, Pei-te, M. Margaret Conway, and Janelle Wong. 2003. The contours and sources of ethnic identity choices among Asian Americans. *Social Science Quarterly* 84:461–81.

Marshall, Ineke Haen. 1997. Minorities, crime, and criminal justice in the United States. In *Minorities, migrants, and crime: Diversity and similarity across Europe and the United States*, ed. Ineke Haen Marshall, 1–35. Thousand Oaks, CA: Sage.

Martinez, Ramiro, Jr. 2002. *Latino homicide: Immigration, violence, and community.* New York, NY: Routledge.

Martinez, Ramiro, Jr., Jacob I. Stowell, and Matthew T. Lee. 2010. Immigration and crime in an era of transformation: A longitudinal analysis of homicides in San Diego neighborhoods, 1980–2000. *Criminology* 48:797–829.

Martinez, Ramiro, Jr., and Abel Valenzuela Jr., eds. 2006. *Immigration and crime: Race, ethnicity, and violence.* New York, NY: New York University Press.

McConnell, Eileen Diaz, and Edward A. Delgado-Romero. 2004. Latino panethnicity: Reality or methodological construction? *Sociological Focus* 37:297–312.

Morenoff, Jeffrey D., and Avraham Astor. 2006. Immigrant assimilation and crime: Generational differences in youth violence in Chicago. In *Immigration and crime: Race, ethnicity and violence*, eds. Ramiro Martinez Jr. and Abel Valenzuela Jr. New York, NY: New York University Press.

Nagasawa, Richard, Qian Zhenchao, and Paul Wong. 2001. Theory of segmented assimilation and the adoption of marijuana use and delinquent behavior by Asian Pacific youth. *Sociological Quarterly* 42:351–72.

Oboler, Suzanne. 1995. *Ethnic labels, Latino lives*. Minneapolis: University of Minnesota Press.

Okamoto, Dina G. 2003. Toward a theory of panethnicity: Explaining Asian-American collective action. *American Sociological Review* 68:811–42.

Ousey, Graham C., and Charis E. Kubrin. 2009. Exploring the connection between immigration and violent crime rates: 1980–2000. *Social Problems* 56:447–73.

Park, Robert E., Herbert A. Miller, and William I. Thomas. 1921. *Old World traits transplanted*. New York, NY: Harper and Barnes.

Pew Hispanic Center. 2010. *Statistical portrait of the foreign-born population in the United States*. Washington, DC: Pew Research Center.

Portes, Alejandro, Luis Eduardo Guarnizo, and William J. Haller. 2002. Transnational entrepreneurs: An alternative form of immigrant economic adaptation. *American Sociological Review* 67:278–98.

Portes, Alejandro, and Ruben G. Rumbaut. 2001. *Legacies: The story of the immigrant second generation*. Berkeley: University of California Press.

Portes, Alejandro, and Ruben G. Rumbaut. 2006. *Immigrant America: A portrait*. 3rd ed. Berkeley: University of California Press.

Rumbaut, Ruben G., Roberto G. Gonzales, Golnaz Komaie, Charlie V. Morgan, and Rosaura Tafoya-Estrada. 2006. Immigration and incarceration: Patterns and predictors of imprisonment among first- and second-generation young adults. In *Immigration and crime: Race, ethnicity, and violence*, eds. Ramiro Martinez Jr. and Abel Valenzuela Jr. New York, NY: New York University Press.

Rumbaut, Ruben G., and Alejandro Portes. 2001. Ethnogenesis: Coming of age in immigrant America. In *Ethnicities: Children of immigrants in America*, eds. Ruben G. Rumbaut and Alejandro Portes, 1–20. Berkeley: University of California Press.

Sampson, Robert J., and Janet L. Lauritsen. 1997. Racial and ethnic disparities in crime and criminal justice in the United States. In *Ethnicity, crime and immigration: Comparative and cross-national perspectives*, ed. Michael H. Tonry, 311–74. Chicago, IL: University of Chicago Press.

Sampson, Robert J., Jeffrey Morenoff, and Stephen W. Raudenbush. 2005. Social anatomy of racial and ethnic disparities in violence. *American Journal of Public Health* 95:224–32.

Scalia, John. 1996. *Citizens in the federal criminal justice system, 1984–1994*. Special Report NCJ 160934. Washington, DC: U.S. Department of Justice, Bureau of Justice Statistics.

Schmidley, A. Dianne. 2001. *Profile of the foreign-born population in the United States: 2000*. U.S. Census Bureau, Current Population Reports, Series P23-206. Washington, DC: Government Printing Office.

Stowell, Jacob I. 2007. *Immigration and crime: The effects of immigration on criminal behavior*. New York, NY: LFB Scholarly Publishing.

Stowell, Jacob I., and Ramiro Martinez Jr. 2009. Incorporating ethnic-specific measures of immigration in the study of lethal violence. *Homicide Studies* 13:315–24.

Stowell, Jacob I., Steven F. Messner, Kelly F. McGeever, and Lawrence E. Raffalovich. 2009. Immigration and the recent violent crime drop in the United States: A pooled, cross-sectional time-series analysis of metropolitan areas. *Criminology* 47:889–928.

Tonry, Michael H. 1997. Ethnicity, crime and immigration. In *Ethnicity, crime and immigration: Comparative and cross-national perspectives*, ed. Michael H. Tonry, 1–30. Chicago, IL: University of Chicago Press.

U.S. Census Bureau. 2010. *Current Population Survey, annual social and economic supplement, 2010*. Washington, DC: U.S. Census Bureau.

U.S. Department of Justice. 1993. *Survey of inmates of state correctional facilities, 1991*. Washington, DC: U.S. Department of Justice, Bureau of Justice Statistics.

Van Vechten, Cortland C. 1941. The criminality of the foreign born. *Journal of Criminal Law, Criminology, and Police Science* 32:139–47.

Wickersham Commission. 1931. *Crime and the foreign born*. Report No. 10. Washington, DC: Government Printing Office.

Willcox, Walter F. 1927. Foreword. In *Immigrants and their children 1920. Census Monographs VII*, by Niles Carpenter. Washington, DC: Government Printing Office.

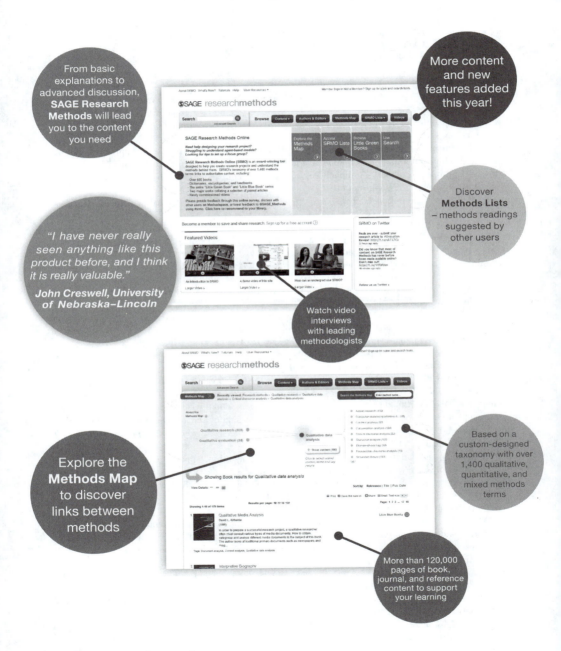